Human Behavior Theory and Applications

Human Behavior Theory and Applications

A Critical Thinking Approach

Elizabeth DePoy
Stephen French Gilson
University of Maine, Orono

Los Angeles | London | New Delhi
Singapore | Washington DC

Los Angeles | London | New Delhi
Singapore | Washington DC

FOR INFORMATION:

SAGE Publications, Inc.
2455 Teller Road
Thousand Oaks, California 91320
E-mail: order@sagepub.com

SAGE Publications Ltd.
1 Oliver's Yard
55 City Road
London EC1Y 1SP
United Kingdom

SAGE Publications India Pvt. Ltd.
B 1/I 1 Mohan Cooperative Industrial Area
Mathura Road, New Delhi 110 044
India

SAGE Publications Asia-Pacific Pte. Ltd.
33 Pekin Street #02-01
Far East Square
Singapore 048763

Acquisitions Editor: Kassie Graves
Editorial Assistant: Courtney Munz
Production Editor: Brittany Bauhaus
Typesetter: C&M Digitals (P) Ltd.
Copy Editor: Gretchen A. Treadwell
Proofreader: Eleni-Maria Georgiou
Indexer: Diggs Publication Services, Inc.
Cover Designer: Stephen French Gilson
Marketing Manager: Katie Winter
Permissions Editor: Adele Hutchinson

Printed in the United States of America

Library of Congress Cataloging-in-Publication Data

DePoy, Elizabeth.

Human Behavior Theory and Applications: a critical thinking approach/Elizabeth DePoy, Stephen French Gilson.

p. cm.
Includes bibliographical references and index.

ISBN 978-1-4129-9036-3 (pbk.)

1. Psychology. 2. Human behavior. I. Gilson, Stephen French. II. Title.

BF121.D439 2012
150—dc23   2011019178

This book is printed on acid-free paper.

11 12 13 14 15 10 9 8 7 6 5 4 3 2 1

Contents

Preface

While thinking and writing together in themselves are beloved to us, the process of creating this book has been unexpectedly enriching. We hope that its words, images, and ideas reflect our passion for theory as well as endow readers with a wealth of thinking and professional guidance.

We believe that whether or not one is aware of the role of theory, that it guides us in all areas of professional and personal life. So for us, theory is the foundation of all action, even if it remains tacit and submerged in the shadows of practice and skill. So our initial goal in writing the book was to develop and put an original organizational framework, explanatory legitimacy, to work to accomplish three purposes; highlighting and clarifying the essential role of theory in all aspects of social work practice, placing values that underpin and live in all theory in the spotlight, using this axiological framework as a thinking tool to align theories borrowed from other disciplines and professions with social work practice, ethics and values, and developing a critical tool for readers to use for exploration and analysis of theories not only for their content, but for their historical development, contextual relevance, evidentiary basis and purposive use in social work.

A second major goal for this book was to critically analyze and apply a range of theories to social work, from traditional developmental theory to the intellectual gems of the most contemporary theories that are rarely broached yet sorely needed to guide practice in the technological, global, diverse context of the 21st century.

And our third goal was to use this book to analyze how theory, knowledge, history, research, and practice are all integral parts of social work, none of which can be cast aside without losing the essence of social work.

The book contains three sections. In the first section, the chapters set the foundation for the remainder of the book. We discuss what theory is, what it is not and then introduce the reader to the five theory genres that they will encounter in the book: developmental, environmental, categorical, systems, and new and emerging. Developmental theories look at humans over time, some from birth to death, and others stretching beyond those classical boundaries. Attempting to respond to contemporary criticism of mind body separation while still discussing theories of the embodied and non-corporeal environments, the category of environmental theories is analyzed on a continuum from most proximal to most distal to the body. We then move to categorical theories, which parse human experience by population segment traditionally referred to as diversity. Systems theories, so central to social work are those which see humans as part of larger interactive entities. Finally, new and emerging theories move us into the late 20th and early 21st centuries through the lens of postmodern and post-postmodern imagery, words, and ideas.

Each of the five theory types is described, analyzed and illustrated through character studies. We discuss words and vocabulary as both reflecting and shaped by context, and then link theories to the evidence which is used to support their viability and application.

Section three puts all five theory types to work in social work. Each chapter links social work values to the values inherent in each theory type, illustrates uses of theory in practice and gives the reader the thinking tools, or what we refer to as thinking possessions, to critically analyze and make decisions about which theories to use to guide action.

Our collective skills coalesced over the two years that we have prepared this manuscript. The images and artwork that you see are original creations by Stephen, metaphors and language are by Liz, and the ideas come from our collective reading in diverse fields, debate between us, sometimes heated, and our discussions, all which energize our days. We hope that you engage the ideas, enjoy the words and imagery, and come to find theory both lovable and essential in your lives and practices.

Acknowledgments

We have many people to thank. First, our undergraduate and graduate students and friends not only read the manuscript in multiple versions, but provoked us through their questions and commentary to clarify, revise, revise, and revise. The reviewers provided precise and poignant feedback that joined the student provocation for even more revision. BJ Kitchin willingly gave us his talent, skill, and time assisting in technology that was essential for the imagery inside the book and on the cover. Finally, we thank the scholars and artists who penned, stroked and sculpted the work on which we built our ideas, whose work we critically approach and who spoke to us on their own pages, screens, objects, and visuals. Each of them is named in the bibliography and we hope that you meet them not only through our critical gaze but through direct engagement with their original productions.

SAGE Publications and the authors gratefully acknowledge the contributions of the following reviewers:

Bonita Hogue, *Virginia Commonwealth University*

Lynn Nybell, *Eastern Michigan University*

Heath B. Walters, *Lewis Clark State College*

Section I

Introduction to Theory

Introduction

And There Was Theory

Drawing 1.1 Theory Residence: A Good Place to Begin

Although common sense tells us that the study of theory about humans is central to professional human service practice, each year, our students come to class with trepidation about the nature of theory, about the difficulty in understanding theory, and with skepticism about the relationship between theory and practice.

This book aims to debunk the myth that theory is hard to master and instill enthusiasm about the wealth of theoretical ideas and their power in informing social work knowledge, research, and practice. This chapter introduces theory, explores its definitions, historical and current contexts, nonexamples, and applications. We hope not only to convince you that theory is the foundation of all professional activity, but also to excite you about the subject, and educate you in the breadth and depth of thinking about humans that is integral to informed practice.

Consider these exemplars just to whet your theoretical appetite. First, think about the notion of reputation. What is it and how is one's reputation established? Since Aristotle, theories of social propriety and social norms have told us what is desirable in diverse contexts and guided us to behave in a manner congruent with the nature of the reputation, or public persona and esteem, that we seek to establish (Friedman, 2007). These concepts, intertwined with theories of professionalism, frame social work ethics (National Association of Social Workers, 2010), which constrain and guide professional social work behavior and define who is a "good" social worker.

Now, think of appearance and beauty. Theories of what is beautiful not only influence how we adorn ourselves, but are foundational to views of health, nutrition, and appearance-based bias—topics of great concern to social work (Rhode, 2010). This important point is discussed later in the book, alongside an examination of visual culture and its contemporary hegemony in developed countries.

These examples highlight the complex issues and questions that social work encounters as we proceed into the 21st century. Yet, as Stoesz, Karger, and Carillo (2010) note, much of our theory is borrowed from other disciplines; we sit in the audience rather than on the stage of social work education and advancment of the scholarship necessary to keep social work alive, viable, and relevant to its mission. Thus, a second and major aim of this work is to meet the challenge Stoesz, Karger, and Carillo pose, and advance the intellectual work of social work, synthesizing and purposively using interdisciplinary thinking within theoretical frameworks that are custom fit to creative and productive social work thinking and action. Before introducing our theoretical framework, we first dissect theory in general and theories about humans in particular. Because of the vast theoretical landscape, much of the theory that we address in this book, at least until we reach the chapters on new and emerging theories, have been developed and engraved with Western world values and standards. We will travel to other parts of the intellectual globe, but highlight this bias as we inaugurate our first term with theory.

Theory Over Time

Theory of human nature and behavior has shifted and diversified over the centuries, from early views of humans and human phenomena as determined by gods, to contemporary advances that have allowed us to peer into the recesses of the human corpus and identify the human genome and its multiple miniscule—yet powerful—influences on human behavior. However, many ancient beliefs and theories remain at the roots, and even inhere in the substance, of contemporary ideas.

So, let us look back in Western history to identify the context in which theory of human behavior emerges, gains support, and becomes part of our intellectual tradition. Note that we emphasize Western theory, as it is the basis of social work thinking and action within the developed world. The text, however, also addresses non-Western theory, particularly in the global context of the 21st century, and then suggests resources and future inquiry that can round out this expansive picture.

Numerous references to the life span are found throughout the history of Western civilization. As far back as Aristotle, who advanced the notion of propriety (Yu, 2007), thinkers have examined and characterized how life unfolded and what individuals had to do or be to live successful lives. Aristotle conceptualized propriety as a hierarchy of virtue, function, and activity, setting the stage for the desirability of role and context specific functional expectations as the basis for theory development. However, because scientific method as we know it today was not established in ancient Greece, philosophy and religion—rather than contemporary disciplines supported by social science research—were central to inquiry about the nature of humans (Zima, 2007). Regardless of the way in which the ancients came to theorize about humans, many of the ideas currently rooted in scientific methodology can be recorded as far back as ancient civilization. For example, the Mayas, whose civilization flourished in Central America from 2600 BCE until 900 CE, characterized individuals with both human and animal characteristics. And today, although we do not identify humans as representing specific animals, we often use animal terms to describe personality types and behaviors (Cloninger, 2007). Or, consider the animal metaphors used to describe and fight cancer. Even the word *cancer* is derived from the word *crab* (Camus, n.d.).

Of particular importance to our focus on human behavior in context is the notion of psychophysical dualism, the existence of two entities: the physical and the psyche. The Mayas believed that the body was a vessel and that when it died, one's soul emerged, journeyed, and then retuned to earth in a new body (McKillop, 2006). Until the 17th century, the church addressed dualism as a distinction between the divine and the organismic. In the 17th century, dualism became an important debate in philosophy. However, Kant, in the 18th century, was the philosopher who gained acknowledgment for his treatment of and influence on thinking about dualism. He argued that humans cannot know the physical world, but rather can only ascertain mental images as their reality (Scruton, 2007). Interestingly, the neuroscience groundswell of the late 20th century found biologists reinterpreting Kant's work through neural networks, arguing that specialized nerves were actually responsible for what Kant referred to as phenomena of the mind of apperception (Smith, 2005).

It was not until the 18th century that science developed its methods of inquiry sufficiently to provide the foundation for contemporary systematic study of human behavior in context (Agamben, 2009). At this point in history, the contextual trends, such as increasing urbanization and industrial modes of production, were important in shaping emergent views of humans. Jansz and van Drunen (2004) noted that two major conceptual shifts, individualization and social management, were critical to the emergence of the field of psychology and related academic and professional arenas. Jansz and van Drunen define *individualization* as the intellectual, political, and social movements in which the focus on community and group was shifted to individuals, feelings, and internal life. The ideas of the French philosopher, Rousseau, among others (Jansz & van Drunen, 2004) exemplify this trend.

Individualization brought with it ideology in which the study of humanity turned its attention to the self and individual difference. For example, the fields of phrenology and physiognomy examined external features as indicators of skull size and internal characteristics, respectively, as representative of intelligence and character.

Social management refers to systematic efforts to control human behavior. As Jansz and van Drunen (2004) note, control previously exerted by military force moved inward and became the domain of professionals through theory and practice in fields such as social work, compulsory education, psychology, health, pharmacology, and medicine, among others that emerged over the centuries to follow.

In the 19th century, Quetelet (1835, 1969), who studied statistics among several other fields, conceptualized the "normal man." Through techniques of measurement, Quetelet characterized how typical humans changed over the life span. Quetelet's concept of average man was the foundation for determining the boundaries of "normal" and thus the realm of the abnormal (DePoy & Gilson, 2007; Quetelet, 1835, 1969). Quetelet therefore ensconced nomothetic thinking (characterizing humans as group members) over considering individuals (DePoy & Gilson, 2011). By the latter part of the 19th century, the cultural, social, political, economic, and intellectual contexts were ripe for a field of study to emerge that described and explained humans as internally driven. And thus, Wilhelm Wundt, who established the first psychological laboratory in Leipzig in 1879 (Jansz & van Drunen, 2004), formalized the field of psychology. However, the underlying theme of dualism remained, promoting questions and varied responses to describe and explain the role of diverse environments in influencing behavior, and in providing explanations for behavioral observations (Smith, 2005).

Although not the only thinkers to discuss the importance of human-context interaction, Dewey and Bentley (1976) in the early 20th century, were known for their seminal work in transactionalism, in which organism and environment were seen as interactive and interdependent (Dewey & Bentley; Smith, 2005).

The very brief discussion of history ends here as we move into the 20th century. The book proceeds to examine, analyze, and illustrate theories of human experience that have been advanced and built upon in the 20th and 21st centuries.

What Is Theory?

THINKING POINT

 Before you begin to read this section, define *theory*. Then, after reading our definitions, compare and contrast your before-and-after thinking.

Much of the discussion of theory that follows is informed by DePoy and Gitlin (2011), who have thought and written much about theory and its relationship to research and professional practice. We therefore have not reinvented the wheel, so to speak, but have applied their discussion of theory to our focus on historical and contemporary theory of human phenomena.

Theory Dissected

Numerous discussions can be found in books and other resources on the nature of theory, theory construction, and use of theory. Not surprisingly, there are many different "theories of theory" or maps that categorize theories according to their commonalities, differences, and levels of development. As an example, Seidman (2004) who focuses his work on social theory, has classified theory into three categories: (1) moral, (2) philosophical, and more contemporarily, (3) scientific. According to Seidman's theory of theories, moral theories are those that posit the nature of goodness and what is necessary to achieve it, while philosophical theories engage in conceptual thinking to unearth principles of knowledge. Although scientific theories have an aim similar to philosophical theories, only empirical evidence, or that generated by scientific methods, can be used to verify scientific idea systems as the basis for organizing, describing, and predicting observations. While the categories may differ according to the type of evidence that is acceptable to support theory (see subsequent discussion), Seidman then suggests that all theories aim to further the improvement of the human condition, whether through identifying what "should be" or predicting "what needs to be changed." As we discuss throughout the chapter, while we do not fully agree with Seidman's taxonomy, we do concur that *improvement,* an axiological construct that lays bare "what is desirable," is inherent in all theory. For example, some theories, such as those that address distributive justice (Rawls, 1971) and distribution of rights and privileges (Hohfeld, 1923) guide thinking and action with regard to whose behavior is worthy or unworthy for resources, group membership, and even citizenship. While these are not typically categorized as moral theories, we suggest that they are and thus we do not address a separate axiological theory category, because for us, all theories guide us to a differential "correct" set of thinking and action, depending on the theory, its view of humans, and its purpose. Rather, *explanatory legitimacy,* our social work conceptual framework presented next, looks explicitly at all theories as value based with moral principles inherent in each.

Our Theory of Theories

Given the ethical foundation of social work, we suggest that the most useful lens through which to view theory for social work analysis and use is multidimensional, synthesizing the four types of theory listed in Table 1.1 within an axiological scaffold, our theory of theories.

Table 1.1 Theory of Theories

Theory as function: descriptions, explanations, predictions
Theory as structure: parts of theories that comprise its elements
Theory as content: topical focus
Theory as evidence: credible support for a claim

Theory as Function

Theory as function refers to the purpose of a theory or the type of intellectual "work" it does. Looking through a purposive lens, theory can be parsed into three types: theories that describe, explain, and predict. Theories can achieve one, two, or all three purposes depending on their degree of development and structure.

The following scenario illustrates descriptive theory.

When you enter a new class on the first day of the semester, you most likely bring a pen or electronic device to record notes. This behavior does not occur spontaneously, but rather is informed by what has happened in previous classes. You have developed a descriptive theory of the commonalities of classroom objects.

Based on this description, you have expectations for courses in which one of the constants is your capacity to record what you and others have said, observed, or thought about. In this case, the descriptive ideas are organized as

Course = Information to be recorded = Device to record

Your evidence is your own and observed previous experience in school. Building on the descriptive theory example, to illustrate explanatory theory, consider the following idea.

Students bring recording devices to class because multiple forms of input (in this case hearing, seeing, and recording) aid learning.

Not only does this theory describe what students typically bring to class, but it also provides a reason for what is observed. Now consider another explanation.

Students bring recording devices to class because their memories are not good enough to remember what they hear.

Both explanations are equally as feasible. Both are interpretations of description. In examining theories of human behavior, many explanatory theories can be advanced for one descriptive phenomenon. How we theoretically describe, explain, and evaluate human experience in large part determines to whom and how we legitimately respond.

Provide an example, in your own experience of how multiple explanations have influenced responses.

Identify and distinguish a descriptive theory from an explanatory one.

Now, consider this exemplar of predictive theory.

If students do not come prepared to class with devices or methods to record what they have learned, they are likely to perform poorly throughout the semester.

This statement illustrates prediction, or the future view of what may happen based on what is known.

Attending to purpose is a critical element of analysis and comparison of theories. A discussion of structure thus helps illustrate how purpose is linked to level of development and abstraction.

Parts of Theory

According to DePoy and Gitlin (2011), there are four interrelated structural components subsumed under theory, which range in degree—or level of abstraction—and are linked to purpose. These are concepts, constructs, relationships, and propositions or principles.

Levels of Abstraction

First, it is important to examine the meaning of *abstraction*. Abstraction often conjures up a vision of the ethereal, the "not real." However, we borrow from DePoy and Gitlin (2011) and use the term as it relates to theory, to depict symbolic representation of shared experience.

Consider a group of people who all see a small handheld device with numbered buttons and a screen that reflects different images as the buttons are pushed.

The term *cell phone* is a concept, or first order abstraction, to describe the shared image. Intrinsically, the term does not have a meaning without its referent, the handheld device. Rather, words are abstractions because, by themselves, they have no meaning. But of course, not all words have referents that are directly observable or ascertainable through our senses. Some words are symbols for what cannot be sensed. Thus, different words represent different levels of abstraction, and a single word can represent multiple levels of abstraction.

The term love *can denote an observable such as "making love" or a more abstract construct such as "love thy neighbor."*

In Figure 1.1, levels of abstraction refer to the distance between a symbol and shared experience. Four levels of abstraction within theory, and the relationship of each to the other, illustrate how shared experience is the foundation on which abstraction is built.

Figure 1.1 Levels of Abstraction

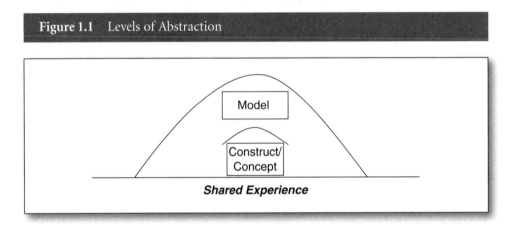

Again, we do not use the term *reality* as the foundation, because reality implies that there is only one viewpoint from which to build the basic elements of a theory. In contrast, we espouse *pluralism,* whereby human beings experience, and thus should acknowledge, the value of multiple realities and multiple perspectives about the nature of reality, cultures, and ethics (Dallmayr, 2010). As such, levels of abstraction must be built on *shared experience,* defined as the consensus of what we obtain through our senses.

Consider again the handheld device. Shared experience tells each of us that this is a cell phone, but the term cell phone *may also carry with it other meanings.*

Each type of experience, and thus the different descriptive meanings attributed to a single word or term, are equally as important to acknowledge.

As depicted in Figure 1.1, a *concept* is the first level of abstraction. A concept is merely a symbolic representation of an observable or experienced referent. Concepts are the basic building blocks of communication in that they provide the means to share our experiences and ideas with others. Without them, we would not have language and thus theory in any form.

In the case of the handheld device, the term cell phone *can function as a concept. At this basic level of abstraction, cell phone describes an observation many share. The words and terms such as* device, buttons, *and* screen *are also concepts because they are directly sensed.*

A *construct,* the next level of abstraction, does not have an observable or a directly experienced referent in shared experience. We refer to this rendering as *reportable* in that meaning has to be extracted from story or inference. It is thus at this level of abstraction that meanings become important to consider because two individuals who articulate the same construct may attribute disparate meanings to it.

As a construct, the term cell phone *may mean a communication mechanism to some and a bother to others.*

Although cell phone was identified as a concept previously, in this case, it functions as a construct because the observable is not the communicated meaning. Rather, the meaning of the term takes on the representation that cell phone evokes

Communication mechanism and bother are also constructs. What may be observed are the behaviors associated with these two phrases, such as talking and listening, or showing a facial expression of annoyance.

Categories are also examples of constructs. Each category is not directly observable; however, it is composed of a set of concepts or constructs that may or may not be observed. The category of ICT (information and communication technology) is a construct. Computers, MP3 players, and Internet devices all fit in this category. Further, categories can be broken into subcategories. The devices that connect to the Internet may be considered smart *while those that do not (cell phones with no data capabilities) are simply* telephones.

Abstraction, then, is complex and can be ordered in many ways. Consider now how else we might categorize ICT.

Rather than looking at ICT as divided by equipment, it may be split into the nature of information that is produced: voice, Internet data, video and so forth.

As these examples illustrate, no one category system is the correct one. Rather, these systems are abstractions that can be thought about in many ways.

So, what does ICT have to do with the study of theory about humans? Consider the following examples of constructs relevant to health and human service inquiry:

health, wellness, personality, religion, spirituality, culture, life roles, rehabilitation, poverty, illness, disability, functional status, and psychological well-being

Each construct may not be directly observable, but is made up of parts or components that can be observed or submitted to scrutiny in multiple configurations.

The complexity of this low level of abstraction shows why theories of human behavior are rich, diverse, and complicated.

Single-word symbols, or units of abstraction, discussed so far, are descriptive both in structure and purpose. At the next level of abstraction, single units are connected to form is relationship. A *relationship* may serve a descriptive or explanatory purpose and is defined as an association of two or more constructs or concepts.

Age may be associated with preference for a particular type of ICT.

This relationship has two constructs, age, and preference for ICT.

A *proposition* is the next level of abstraction. A proposition—or principle, which can also be descriptive or explanatory in purpose—is a statement that governs a set of relationships and gives them a structure.

More than their elders, younger generations prefer ICT for texting.

This explanatory proposition describes the structure of a relationship between age and preference for functionality of ICT. It also suggests the direction of the relationship and the influence of each construct on the other.

THINKING POINT

 Apply these levels of abstractions to another theory of your choice.

Now that we have examined levels of abstraction and suggested their link to purpose, two theories illustrate the distinction between descriptive and explanatory "work" of theories. A descriptive theory related to ICT may look like this:

Younger generations are more facile with texting that their elders and thus prefer it and use it more than elders do.

This theory merely works to depict what has been observed. It orders observation and can be verified or falsified within the context in which the theory emerged.

An explanatory theory might look like this:

Because younger generations have grown up with this technology, they are more facile with texting than their elders and thus prefer it and use it more than elders do.

This theory identifies the "why" by explaining the phenomena of ease of use and preference; both are verifiable and can lead to prediction.

A predictive statement would look like this:

Younger generations, who have grown up with this technology, will be more facile with texting than their elders and thus will prefer it and use it more than elders do.

Theory as Evidence

As noted previously, the role and nature of evidence in generating and verifying theory is equivocal. The trend in professional disciplines is to accept empirical evidence, or that which is generated through systematic research thinking and action (DePoy & Gitlin, 2011). So, we next look briefly at the logical foundations and related methods linked to the diverse levels of abstraction necessary to develop and test theory through systematic inquiry.

Figure 1.2 Logic Structures

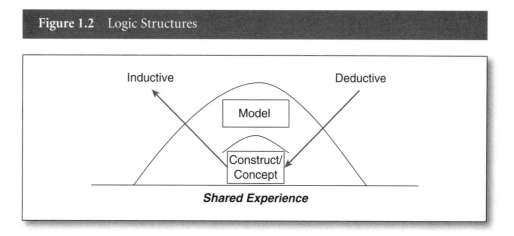

Figure 1.2 depicts the two primary logical reasoning approaches and directionality of thinking that are used in systematic inquiry. Each arrow represents a different way of reasoning and the specific logic of actions that distinguish naturalistic and experimental-type investigators in the conduct of their research. Experimental-type research, which is primarily used to verify or falsify existing theory, uses a deductive form of human reasoning. Deductive reasoning (also referred to as *logico-deductive* or *reductionist*) proceeds from a selected abstract to its reduction to parts, definition of the parts, and then measurement of magnitude of each part and relationship among parts.

A social worker proceeding from the theory that clinical depression is a mood state that manifests in flat affect, sleep disturbance, change in appetite, and dysphoria (APA, 2000) would measure the degree to which a client had these symptoms. If there were sufficient presence of each, the social worker would deduce, based on the general theory, that the client was clinically depressed. If the social worker started with a psychoanalytic theory of depression, which suggests that depression is anger turned toward the self, the social worker would measure internalized anger and verify depression on the basis of the assessment score.

Deduction seeks to uncover and document nomothetic understandings or those that examine commonalities within groups and differences between them. For this reason, the individual is not the focus of inquiry.

Consider depression again. We have all seen many clinical psychotherapeutic studies that seek to look at levels of anger in diverse groups with the intention of revealing group specific differences of magnitude as the basis for informing need and intervention.

Naturalistic inquiry, which is more typically used to develop and generate theory, proceeds inductively. Shared experience including but not limited to narrative, observations, interactions, and image is aggregated and scrutinized for the purpose of mining emergent themes. Thus, unlike experimental approaches that begin with the acceptance of a theory, naturalistic inquiry seeks to extract theoretical gems from observations.

Consider depression once more. Suppose the social worker did not agree with either of the theoretical approaches to explaining depression in the preceding example. To generate theory characterizing depression, the social worker might observe and interview individuals who report depression without preconceived ideas of the nature of depression.

Illustrating this approach is the work of DePoy and Butler (1996). In an effort to identify the unique nature of health and wellness of rural elder women, they conducted a series of open-ended, face-to-face interviews with elder women in a rural New England location. Their analytic strategy followed an inductive process in which they aggregated interview narratives and examined them for emergent themes and patterns. While DePoy and Butler were not looking for theory on depression, they were able to induce by nonexample, or what was not said about wellness and contentment, that the loss of nurturing roles was causative of great despondency in this group of women. Their findings did not support either of the previous theories of depression, but did reveal a clear theoretical abstract pathway to be further traversed.

Different from deductive inquiry, inductive strategies, called *idiographic,* aim to characterize uniqueness of individual phenomena. Those who suggest that group or nomothetic approaches result in essentialism and stereotype espouse inductive strategies.

As we proceed into the thicket of theories about human phenomena, knowing about these two logic structures may comfort us in understanding the absence of definitive monistic truth. Deductive inquiry begins with theory selection, an axiological and teleological process in itself. The social worker has an array of theories from which to select, as illuminated by the example of depression provided. Why one selects a particular theory over another as accurate is based on resonance of the theory with personal belief and value, as well as purpose. If you were working in a brief therapy context, for instance, you would not be well-advised to proceed with psychoanalytic theory as it begets elongated engagement with the client. Even at this early stage of your readings on theory, then, you now can understand why the nature of theory and inquiry is axiological and pluralistic. Inductive thinking and action are equally as equivocal. One can provide multiple interpretations, and thus explanations for observations as exemplified by the classic Mead-Freeman debate about what could best theorize observations of sexual behavior in Samoa (Cote, 1994). See Box 1.1.

BOX 1.1

In this debate, Margaret Mead proposed free sex as the descriptor for sexual activity in youth in Samoan culture. Rereading her work years later, Derek Freeman challenged her interpretation suggesting that the activity was nothing short of date rape.

A third reasoning strategy in systematic inquiry is abductive reasoning. Because this reasoning implies uncertainty, abduction was not fashionable in research thinking until recently. Abductive thinking involves selecting what is most plausible as explanatory. Rather than developing new theory in the absence of relevant frameworks, or testing existing theory, abduction requires some elements of "guessing," which is then followed by verification. What is valuable about abduction is that it allows selection from a wide array of knowledge rather than a single theory and, through its logical sequence, encourages and celebrates pluralism (DePoy & Gitlin, 2011).

But, remember the assertion that systematic inquiry was not the only support for theory, particularly in the 21st century when challenges to enlightenment thinking have resulted in the acceptance of diverse ways of knowing. Lyotard (1984) perhaps advanced one of the most vocal indictments of science, suggesting that it is a grand narrative, or a large set of symbols that concentrates power by obfuscating the absence of unbiased truth. Consider the work of Zima (2007) as an example. Foregrounding symbolism as the basis for understanding theory of humans and their interactions, Zima suggests that theory is purely discourse. That is to say, he defines theory as a set of linguistic symbols embedded within and influencing a cultural context. Note that there is no claim that theory emerges from, or is verified by, systematic inquiry. Building on Lyotard's thinking, the definition of theory as linguistic symbol topples the towering position of research thinking and action as the highest credible support for theory, and leaves a void to be filled by multiple ways of knowing.

Definitions of Theory

Definitions of theory span a large range, from abstracts (such as concepts about the nature of goodness or linguistic statements) to propositions, that only scientific methods can verify (Zima, 2007). From the multiple definitions of theory, four examples, presented in Table 1.2, represent the full range from structured to broadly conceptualized.

Table 1.2 Definitions of *Theory*

1. A well-substantiated explanation of some aspect of the natural world
2. An organized system of accepted knowledge that applies in a variety of circumstances to explain a specific set of phenomena
3. A concept that is not yet verified but that, if true, would explain certain facts or phenomena
4. A set of statements or principles devised to explain a group of observations or phenomena, especially one that has been repeatedly tested or is widely accepted and can be used to make predictions about natural phenomena

Source: Farlex, 2011

Among the multitude of definitions of theory, Kerlinger and Lee (2000) provide a simple but comprehensive definition, expanded here, and intended to be most useful to students of theory. Note that the term *useful* depicts purposive utility rather than monistic dogma. Kerlinger and Lee define *theory* as "a set of interrelated constructs, definitions, and propositions that present a systematic view of phenomena by specifying relations among variables, with the purpose of explaining or predicting phenomena" (p. 93). We add three dimensions to Kerlinger and Lee's definition. The first is description. As defined earlier, by *description,* we mean characterizing "what is" (DePoy & Gilson, 2004, 2011). Second, we concur with Zima (2007) and thus add the term *articulated ideas* to emphasize that theory is communicated through symbol, or if not, simply remains a set of personal ideas not considered to be theory. Third, we add *value-based* to highlight the axiological messages that are specified or embedded within theory. Thus, in this expanded definition, theory is a set of articulated, value-based, related ideas that has the potential to describe, explain, or predict human experience in an orderly fashion. The theorist develops and communicates a structural map of commonalities that the theorist expects to observe, has observed, or can predict.

What Theory Is Not

You might have already realized that none of the definitions of theory assert that theory is fact or truth. Thus, theory is not "reality." To the contrary, theory resides in the realm of the abstract and allows us to organize our thoughts, ideas, and observations into relationships. Theory can structure our thinking, can provide guidance for description, explanation, and action, and can provide a rationale for all aspects of our daily lives. Missing the important distinction between theory and shared experience can mislead us in interpreting descriptions and explanations for and responses to human behavior. Explanatory legitimacy, the conceptual framework used throughout the book to organize thinking about theory, provides the guidelines for distinguishing between description and explanation, and for determining which theories are relevant and useful, referred to as *legitimate* in our framework, for your professional decision making and action.

Explanatory Legitimacy: Application of Theory in Social Work Practice

Building upon the argument that theory is value based, explanatory legitimacy as a conceptual scaffold thus not only acknowledges value, but also suggests that value is the major reason for the purposive selection and use of theory to guide social work practice.

Explanatory legitimacy is embedded within and builds on the genre of legitimacy theories, which have a long, interdisciplinary history that is highly relevant and useful for social workers. According to Zeldich (2001), legitimacy theories can be traced as far back as the writings of Thucydides in 423 BCE, in which questions were posed and answered about the moral correctness of power and the way in which it was captured and retained. Although legitimacy theory was birthed by political theory, questions of legitimation have reared in numerous domains, including but not limited to social norms and rules, to distributive justice, and now, in our conceptualization, to who is a legitimate client or client group to capture social work attention and what social work responses should be legimated as sound professional practice. Thus, consistent with legitimacy approaches, explanatory legitimacy theory helps clarify the basis on which a phenomenon is seen as genuine, authentic, and worthy of social work response. As proposed earlier, explanatory legitimacy suggests that all theories are axiological regardless of their content. Each describes or explains desired human experience and how social work can help facilitate it.

Moreover, drawing on the work of Shilling (2008), explanatory legitimacy synthesizes pragmatism within its foundation in legitimacy, providing the analytic framework for clarifying theoretical purpose. Capitalizing on the clarity of seminal legitimacy thinkers such as Habermas (Finlayson, 2005) and Parsons (1951), the explanatory legitimacy framework clarifies theory types so that each can be compared to those similar in structure and subject. As discussed throughout the book, explanatory legitimacy lays bare the axiological context for each theory, critically and abductively evaluting each for use on its own or in concert with others.

Through explanatory legitimacy, three purposive elements of theory are therefore proposed: description, explanation, and legitimacy determination. *Legitimacy determination* is the value-based driver of social work action in that it identifies legitimate clients and guides credible social work response. The following example illustrates legitimacy determination.

Theory that describes typical and atypical cognitive development in children discusses commonalities in thinking and problem solving that are observed in most children and deviations from those commonalities. On the basis of descriptive cognitive development theory, then, infants are expected to first "think" through oral exploration. If they deviate by performing these skills too early or too late, they are considered to be atypical.

But, descriptive theory does not tell us why children do what they do.

THINKING POINT

How many explanations can you think of for why an infant might not follow a typical developmental pathway?

This question is left to be answered by explanatory theory. Explanatory theories tell why, and thus have the capacity to predict as well.

If theory explains developmental delays in cognitive activity caused by neurological impairment, we can explain and even predict the nature and length of the delay by knowing the nature and location of the neurological deficit.

THINKING POINT

Did you explain atypical development because of neurology or some other set of factors? What evidence supported your explanations?

Now, consider the legitimacy element.

If you work in a school in which advancement from one grade to the next is based on age-expected thinking skills, a child who has not acquired the "desired skills" captures social work attention. If the explanation is cognitive impairment, the student may become a legitimate client of social work within a rehabilitation framework. However, if the explanation is truancy, the legitimate response would be different.

Although this thinking may seem complex at this early point, as you read through the book and do your intellectual work, explanatory legitimacy will assist your reflection and understanding.

Generating and Validating Theory for Social Work Practice

In the field of social work, there are varying perspectives about what theories should guide social work activity and the "appropriate evidence" to support theory for use. Recently, many professions, including social work, have espoused evidence-based practice as most desirable. Relevant to discussion, analysis, and use of theory in social work practice, DePoy and Gitlin (2011) detail evidence-based practice as follows:

> It is a model of professional practice that draws heavily on research that uses particular methodologies to draw conclusions from research literature. Major aspects of evidence-based practice include which research methods and conclusions should underpin practice. (p. 317)

In disagreement with contemporary theorists such as Zima (2007) and DePoy and Gilson (2007), the "evidence" in evidence-based practice must emerge from research activity and most desirably from true experimental design, an experimental-type deductive strategy capable of supporting predictive relationships between intervention and outcome. However, within the explanatory legitimacy conceptual framework, the "legitimate" support for theory and its application are value-based and within the scope of individual professional judgment. Thus, throughout the book, the evidentiary basis of theory is discussed so that each reader can weigh the credibility of evidence supporting theory as one important analytic tool for purposive selection and use.

How to Use This Book

This book does not intend to, once again, reiterate a summary of the multiple theories of human behavior in the social environment. There are already many excellent books and sources that do so. Rather, the book's purposes are to

1. Provide the essential intellectual tools for organizing and critically thinking about the breadth, depth, and diversity of theories that inform our notions of humanity.

2. Ground theory in exemplar.

3. Advance a conceptual framework that provides the lens for readers to learn, discuss, analyze, and use theory to inform professional thinking and action.

This book aims not only to introduce theory, but does so in hopes that you will understand and celebrate the importance of theory in your professional thinking and action. We hope that you are as enamored as we are with theory, its generation, and its use for informing professional decision making and activity.

Section I of the book introduces theory and the conceptual framework through which to analyze theory, its derivation, strengths and limitations. Section II explores the breadth and depth of the theoretical genres introduced in Chapter 2. Section II is also devoted to putting the theories to intellectual and professional work. Section III illustrates how theories apply to identifying who is legitimate for social work attention and response, the fit of each genre with social work values, and how each guides legitimate social work professional action.

Each chapter concludes with a chapter summary. Throughout each chapter, illustrations provide opportunities for application, and thinking points allow contemplation. We encourage you to use these points for reflection and analysis, and gauge your learning as you proceed.

Summary

This chapter introduced theory, identifying two types, descriptive and explanatory, and then distinguished them from one another. Levels of abstraction and the four components of theory were next discussed and illustrated. A brief gaze backwards then set the contemporary context for an examination of theory of human behavior. Explanatory legitimacy, the conceptual framework that will guide analyzing and applying diverse theories to social work practice, was introduced. The discussion of theory concluded with a brief look at evidence and its contested nature.

References

Agamben, G. (2009). *The signature of all things: On method.* New York: Zone Books.

American Psychiatric Association. (2000). *Diagnostic and statistical manual of mental disorders* (4th ed.). Washington, DC: Author.

Camus, J. T. W. (n.d.). *Variation of cancer metaphors in scientific texts and press popularisations.* Retrieved from GoogleDocs: www.cs.bham.ac.uk/~amw/pdfVersions/Williams.pdf

Cloninger, S. (2007). *Theories of personality: Understanding persons* (5th ed.). Englewood, NJ: Prentice Hall.

Cote, J. (1994). *Adolescent storm and stress: An evaluation of the Mead-Freeman controversy.* Hillsdale, NJ: Lawrence Erlbaum.

Dallmayr, F. (2010). *Integral pluralism: Beyond culture wars.* Lexington: University Press of Kentucky.

DePoy, E., & Butler, S. (1996). Health: Elderly rural women's conceptions. *AFFILIA , 11*(2), 207–220.

DePoy, E., & Gilson, S. (2004). *Rethinking disability: Principles for professional and social change.* Pacific Grove, CA: Wadsworth.

DePoy, E., & Gilson, S. (2007). *The human experience.* Lanham, MD: Rowman & Littlefield.

DePoy, E., & Gilson, S. (2011). *Studying disability: Multiple theories and responses.* Thousand Oaks, CA: Sage.

DePoy, E., & Gitlin, L. (2011). *Introduction to research* (4th ed.). St Louis, MO: Elsevier.

Dewey, J., & Bentley, A. (1976). *Knowing and the known.* Santa Barbara, CA: Greenwood Press. Reprint.

Farlex. (2011). *Theory.* Retrieved from the Free Dictionary: http://www.thefreedictionary.com/theory

Finlayson, G. (2005). *Habermas: A very short introduction.* New York: Oxford University Press.

Friedman, L. (2007). *Guarding life's dark secrets: legal and social controls over reputation, propriety, and privacy.* Palo Alto, CA: Stanford University Press.

Hohfeld, W. N. (1923). *Fundamental legal conceptions as applied in juridical reasoning and other legal essays.* W. W. Cook, (Ed.) New Haven, CT: Yale University Press.

Jansz, J., & van Drunen, P. (2004). *A social history of psychology.* Malden, MA: Blackwell.

Kerlinger, F., & Lee, H. B. (2000). *Foundations of behavioral research.* New York: Harcourt.

Lyotard, J. F. (1984). *The postmodern condition: A report on knowledge.* Minneapolis: University of Minnesota Press.

McKillop, H. (2006). *The ancient Maya: New perspectives.* New York: W. W. Norton.

National Association of Social Workers. (2010). *Code of ethics.* Retrieved from www.socialworkers .org/pubs/code/default.asp

Parsons, T. (1951). *Toward a general theory of action.* Cambridge, MA: Harvard University Press.

Quetelet, L. A. (1835). *Essai de physique social.* Paris: Bachelier, Imprimeur-Libraire.

Quetelet, L. A. (1969). *A treatise on man and the development of his faculties: A facsimile reproduction of the English translation of 1842.* Gainsville, FL: Scholars' Facsimiles & Reprints.

Rawls, J. (1971). A theory of justice. Cambridge, MA: Belknap Press.

Rhode, D. (2010). *The beauty bias: The injustice of appearance in life and law.* New York: Oxford University Press.

Scruton, R. (2007). *Philosophy: Principles and problems.* New York: Continuum.

Seidman, S. (2004). *Contested knowledge.* Malden, MA: Blackwell.

Shilling, C. (2008). *Changing bodies: Habit, crisis, creativity.* Thousand Oaks, CA: Sage.

Smith, M. J. (2005). *Philosophy and methodology in the social sciences.* Thousand Oaks, CA: Sage.

Stoesz, D., Karger, H. J., & Carillo, T. E. (2010). *A dream deferred: How social work education lost its way and what can be done.* New Brunswick, NJ: Transaction Publishing.

Yu, J. (2007). *The ethics of Confucius and Aristotle: Mirrors of virtue.* New York: Routledge.

Zeldich, M. (2001). Theories of legitimacy. In J. Jost & B. Major (Eds.), *The psychology of legitimacy: Emerging perspective on ideology, justice and intergroup relations* (pp. 33–35). New York: Cambridge University Press.

Zima, P. V. (2007). *What is theory? Cultural theory as discourse and dialogue.* Indianapolis: Indiana University Press.

2

The Scope of Human Behavior and Experience in Diverse Environments

Overview of Theory Types

Drawing 2.1   Whole Theory: More Than the Sum of Its Parts

A Topical Taxonomy of Theories About Humans

Not surprisingly, just from the brief history provided in Chapter 1, there is a multitude of theories that seek to describe and explain human experience. In Chapter 1, we proposed explanatory legitimacy, a framework for analysis and valuation of theory for use in practice. But, you may have noted that this framework did not have any content. Rather, it provides thinking guidelines for all theories and their application. So, you may have been asking yourself, what about content? This chapter introduces the vast scope of theories and suggests a substantive taxonomy to easily organize theories into their content domains of concern. This allows examination of theories through the explanatory legitimacy microscope and builds a sound rationale to guide thinking and action.

Figure 2.1 depicts the thinking process through which theories are organized, examined, and selected as legitimate for the social work action and contextual situation.

Foundation Question: What Is Human?

Throughout the book, when we are unable to find answers to fundamental questions about the nature of a phenomenon, we often defer to what we refer to as *word soup,* denoted with the following gustatory symbol.

By word soup, we mean the host of definitions, synonyms, and etymology that detail the essential elements of a construct. As many theories within the new and emerging genre highlight (these theories are introduced next and discussed in more

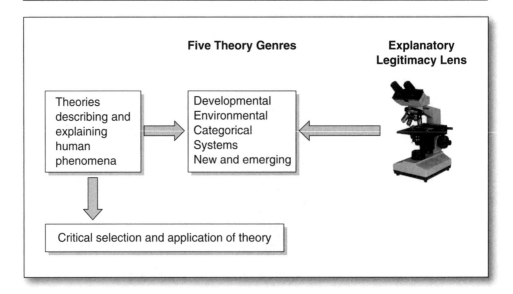

Figure 2.1 The Examining Lens of Explanatory Legitimacy: Making Sense of Theory

detail in Chapters 14 and 21) we often fall prey to assuming that we share common understandings of abstracts and symbols, the most basic of which are words and images. And, defaulting to a common definition for the word *human* is not exempt from this assumption. So, dipping briefly into word soup, Table 2.1 explores the diverse definitions.

Table 2.1   Definitions of *Human* on the Web

1. Characteristic of humanity; "human nature." (Farlex, 2011)

2. Relating to a person; "the experiment was conducted on 6 monkeys and 2 human subjects." (Hyperdictionary.com, 2001–2009)

3. Homo: any living or extinct member of the family Hominidae characterized by superior intelligence, articulate speech, and erect carriage. (Hyperdictionary.com, 2001–2009)

4. Having human form or attributes as opposed to those of animals or divine beings; "human beings"; "the human body"; "human kindness"; "human frailty" (WordNet, n.d.).

5. Humans commonly refers to the species Homo sapiens (Latin: "wise man" or "knowing man"), the only extant member of the Homo genus of bipedal primates in Hominidae, the great ape family. However, in some cases the term is used to refer to any member of the genus Homo (Wikipedia, n.d.).

6. S&M: an abbreviation of "Symphony and Metallica" as well as a play-on-words for sadomasochism, is a live album by the American heavy metal band Metallica, with the San Francisco Symphony Orchestra conducted by the late Michael Kamen, recorded on the 21st to 22nd of April, 1999 at Berkeley (Wikipedia, n.d.).

7. In the Star Trek science fiction universe, Humans/Terrans (Homo sapiens) are one of the races undertaking interstellar travel. Human beings were instrumental in the founding of the United Federation of Planets (Wikipedia, n.d.).

8. "Human" is a song by alternative rock band The Killers, and was released as the first single from the band's third studio album Day & Age. It premiered on Zane Lowe's evening show on BBC Radio 1 on September 22, 2008, with a digital release on September 30, 2008 (Wikipedia, n.d.).

9. Humans are a race available for player characters in the Dungeons & Dragons fantasy role-playing game. Although short-lived by comparison, humans are the most populous of all Dungeons & Dragons races (Wikipedia, n.d.).

These current definitions span a range from properties of people, to entertainers, to virtual symbols, and thus do not provide a single definition of the term—we therefore look backwards to historical word soup for elucidation.

According to Harper (2001–2010), the word *human* was identified first in the mid-13th century, denoting a property of "man" as distinguished from God by being tied to earth or *hummus*. According to Smith (2010), the question of what it means to be human, or what is a human, is not only a philosophical exercise but also forms the foundation for determining the essential elements of a good society. So, in concert with Smith, we look to diverse theories to define *human,* and throughout the book provide not one definition but multiple value-based definitions through the analytic portal of our theoretical frame of reference. Before we take on this herculean task, we consult those who have already traversed this path; some look at humans as what they do, others distinguish them by their structures, and still others define them by what they are not.

Current Topical Taxonomies

Remember that scholars have advanced many conceptual frameworks through which to organize and analyze this large literature.

THINKING POINT

Before reading further in this chapter, how many topical approaches to describing and explaining human phenomena can you list?

Before proposing our own topical taxonomy, we critically review a range of approaches relevant to social work for parsing theories by subject matter. Seifert, Hoffnung, and Hoffnung (2003) propose three basic categories of substantive viscera:

1. Theories that view behavior as a function of what lies within the boundaries of the human corpus or internal theories

2. Theories that suggest that human behavior results from the influence of factors external to the corpus

3. Theories that identify the interaction between the internal and the external as the basis for behavior

While this taxonomy provides an understandable and instructive structure, it does not do analytic justice to the breadth and complexity of human behavior theory. First, this taxonomy reifies the Cartesian dualist perspective not only for rhetorical and educational purposes, but is also taken to be "factual." As we revisit throughout the book, the boundaries of the corpus are not clear, nor is the distinction between body and the environment beyond it.

Consider a pacemaker. In what environmental context does it exist? When inserted into the organic body, does it become corporeal despite its nonorganic materials and mechanical control?

Questions about the separation of body mass from embodied perception continue to be posed with answers increasing in complexity as we move into the post-postmodern intellectual world where disciplinary boundaries shift and change.

THINKING POINT

 Can you think of any way to perceive your world other than through your own body?

A second objection to this taxonomy lies in its limited scope and precision. Because the conceptual framework only contains three chambers in which theories can reside, there is no place in this categorical home for theories that do not clearly conform to the entrance requirements for each room. As an example, where does spirituality fit? Is it external, internal, interactive, or something else?

Thomas (2001), building on Altman and Rogoff's (1987) work, identifies five overarching worldviews in which theory relevant to human phenomena can be organized:

1. Trait

2. Consequences

3. Interactional

4. Organismic

5. Transactional

A worldview of trait locates humanity within the boundaries of the corpus and holds elements such as personality, intelligence, and disposition responsible for defining identity and driving behavior. *Trait* refers to a constant and enduring feature not amenable to change. Thus, Thomas (2001) is suggesting that the theories within this division posit the "givens" of human commonality as well as difference among groups. Consequential views situate the explanations for and influences on human behavior in the environmental conditions external to the organic corpus, and suggest that behavior is a response to an actual or potential outcome of one's action. Thus, this classification, while still distinguishing "innies and outies" of Cartesian-based understandings of humans allows both on the same interactive playground.

The interactional category hosts and thus further synthesizes inside trait and outside elements. Through this set of theoretical lenses, human experience and behavior are explained as a function of complex relationships between one's corpus and the context surrounding it, to a greater or lesser degree depending on the theorist. Note, however, that the interactionist perspectives still view the corpus and surroundings as separate entities.

So, consistent with contemporary postmodern thought, Thomas (2001) suggests the organismic approaches that unite both domains in which the parts not only interact but cannot be parsed.

> *Let us visit with Simon to illustrate these five approaches. Simon is a 6-year-old, healthy male who is vivacious and very active. As he enters first grade, he is having increasing trouble being able to sit and attend to his lessons. If viewed through the trait lens, we might find him hyperactive. Because this trait is permanent unless unearthed by significant manipulation, a response would be to alter his interior physiology through medical intervention. However, from the consequential perspective, we look to his environment (e.g., the classroom) to explain his behavior. Through this theoretical pathway, enacting direct reinforcement of desired behaviors is expected to predict an orderly change in Simon.*

The interactionist view seeks to analyze the more complex and reciprocal effects of Simon's environment and his internal traits. We, therefore, might look at the type of environments that facilitate concentration for children who are inherently hyperactive and also then examine how the presence of hyperactivity colors environments themselves.

In these first three genres, environment and corpus are theorized as distinct from one another. Thus, each conceptual scope suggests that an exterior agent acts upon Simon's corpus until one produces the desired outcome for his interior body, his immediate environment, or both. However, moving to the organismic viewpoint, Simon and his exterior are not considered to be separate. Thus, multidisciplinary theory bears on thinking about and explaining Simon. Perhaps some change would be considered, but through a progressive diversity lens, as discussed later in the book, change may not be warranted at all. From this perspective, simply changing Simon's environment could not produce predictable changes in Simon's behavior, but rather, the changes would be complex and perhaps even unintended depending on the theoretical frame of reference chosen.

It is curious to note that Thomas (2001) does not consider chronology in his taxonomy, despite the host of developmental theories that have been advanced and used to organize thinking about human life and experience. Contributing this important dimension to the previous paradigms, Hutchison (2010) suggests complex categories of human behavior theory that locate the life course within a context of time and environment.

Johnson and Rhodes (2010), another social work duo, focus on the macroscope, so to speak, in proposing a classification scheme of theory. Still, using a Cartesian perspective, they segment environment theories by size, institution, and content. While, in part, Hutchison's as well as Johnson and Rhodes's approaches have merit and fit with current social work thinking, new intellectual space is needed to advance social work responses within the 21st century. Given post-postmodern interdisciplinary trends and new and emergent theories—in which disciplines such as engineering and spirituality are now being married and applied to an analysis of human behavior—previous taxonomies, such as those we previously sampled, can form the groundwork for new construction to solidly guide social work thinking and action. We therefore build on the excellent work of others to suggest that theories about humans fall into the five major substantive categories presented in Table 2.2.

Our Taxonomy

While topic areas may overlap and are not exclusive to a single category, each genre of theories emphasizes different axioms and values within a broad content arena.

> *Consider neurology. Within our topical taxonomy, neurology as a broad content area might be part of each category. Neurological maturation would be addressed by what we refer to as* developmental theories, *while neurological genetics might be located under* environmental theories *as they are concerned with neurological conditions produced by genetics.*

Table 2.2   Categories of Theory Describing and Explaining Human Phenomena
Developmental: descriptions and explanations of human experience that place value on conformity to "normal" longitudinal movement through time (e.g., biological aging, predeterministic and other developmental theories, life stages, life course, ontological, phylogenetic)
Environmental: descriptions and explanations of human experience that focus on conditions from proximal to distal from the human corpus and place value on influences from diverse environmental conditions (e.g. corpus, biology, cognition, social, virtual, physical)
Categorical: descriptions and explanations of individuals on the basis of membership in a population category (e.g., ethnicity, gender, nationality, sexual orientation, ability, etc.)
Classic and Contemporary Systems: descriptions and explanations of human experience that value interaction among system elements (e.g., closed and open system approaches, dynamics and connectivity [mind-brain], cultural systems, social systems, chaos, complexity)
New and Emerging: descriptions and explanations of human experience that value pluralism

Developmental Theories: Looking at Humans Over Time

The theoretical members of this group describe and explain human phenomena as a function of individual, group, and even phylogenetic passage and change through time. For that reason, these theories are longitudinal in that they are all anchored on chronological trajectory as the basis for describing, explaining, and determining the productivity of a life. This category includes the large range of theories that also have been referred to as *predeterministic, life stage, life span, life phase,* and related frameworks to theories which primarily focus on growth, maturation, and decline with time as its foundational organizer.

Environmental Theories: Looking at Humans as Sets of Conditions

Environmental theories address human phenomena through examining the influence of diverse environmental conditions on individuals. Different from developmental theories, which focus their gaze on chronological change, environmental theories are concerned with the presence of conditions and relationships among them. As discussed in Chapters 6–8, in this category, we propose a non-Cartesian approach to defining environment that ranges from proximal (embedded deep within human experience and the corpus) to distal (conditions considered to be distant). Because historical and many current theories claim a distinction between bodies and surrounding environments, for instructive purposes, we consider dualism in our discussion and analysis of environmental theories for those theories that are parsed into these two segments. Yet, we refer to the *proximal-distal continuum,* rather than demarcating a dividing line, allowing reflection upon an unclear and often absent border between body and not body.

Categorical Theories: Looking at Humans as Population Segments

The theories that belong within the classification of categorical theories propose that humans can be described and explained on the basis of their membership in specific groups. Under this theoretical banner, types of groups range from those created by one's individual characteristics such as race, sexual orientation, diagnostic category, genetic makeup, and gender to those conferred by membership in various sizes of observable or constructed groups such as families, social groups, professional groups, gendered groups, cultural groups, religious groups, and so forth. To a greater or lesser extent, depending on the theory, group membership and responses to it are therefore seen as the primary factors that elicit and shape one's life experience.

This class of theory is central to multicultural theories and cultural competence activity, in which group members are considered to be significantly influenced, oppressed, or afforded privilege on the basis of what we refer to as *bodies and backgrounds* groupings. Recent categorical theories, such as fuzzy set theory (Ragin, 2008), expand beyond binary membership (in or out), suggesting degrees of membership, and thus have great relevance for bringing population segmentation into the global advanced technological world of the 21st century.

Classic and Contemporary Systems Theories: Parts and Wholes

In system theories, human phenomena (primarily behavior and experience) are seen as the interaction of subelements of a whole. Systems theories have been applied to multiple human phenomena from individual corpuses in part or in total to large organizations and even more amorphous and abstract entities. What characterizes them all is the interaction between the subsystems, or elements, that comprise the larger system.

Among the traditional systems theories, systems are divided into two primary categories: open and closed. *Closed systems* are delimited by impermeable boundaries inside which the system elements interact and influence one another. Because of its finite limitations, studying the behavior of one or more elements should logically allow the prediction of behavior of the other elements.

Open systems are those with variations in the degree of permeability of their boundaries. All open systems can be influenced by systems outside of their primary elements and all have the potential to influence other systems. In this class of systems, behavior is not as readily predictable as that of closed systems since it is subject to influences beyond the system turf. Yet, logical links among internal and external sub-elements and influences are sought as explanatory of humans.

A contemporary extension of systems theory, chaos theory, addresses systemic behavior. From this theoretical stance, seemingly unrelated and nondeterministic behavior is a function of dynamic patterns that may not be directly ascertainable but can be posited. Thus, chaos in theoretical parlance does not mean random. Rather, it refers to a dynamic, nonlinear set of systemic processes. Social work has espoused systems theory in its various configurations to emphasize that humans and contexts are interactive.

New and Emerging Theories: Theory of the 21st Century

New and emerging theories include postmodernism, poststructuralism, postcolonialism, deconstruction, post-postmodernism, and related approaches. While many of the theoretical frames of reference that we have included in this group have been in existence for centuries, we refer to them as new and emerging because they have only recently been revised and applied to theorizing about human phenomena. As discussed in Chapter 11, correct this class of theory adheres to and values pluralism, interdisciplinarity, and multiple interpretations for human experience. Seminal to many of these musings is the significant role of language and image as symbol. For that reason, we locate explanatory legitimacy under this rubric. Finally, included in this category, are theories that note the importance of interdisciplinarity, virtual contexts, and technology.

Summary

This chapter presented an overview of topical taxonomies and then critically scrutinized several that have relevance for social work. A content-based taxonomy was then suggested to be subjected to the axiological scanner of explanatory legitimacy. Each of the five subcategories on the topical taxonomy depicts theoretical differences in views of the nature of human experience. Each category, with the exception of the last (new and emerging), contains traditional theories and the current theories that build on classical thought in that theoretical arena. New and emerging theories, although they build on and even contain previous work, are in large part reactive to it and thus challenge and even upend more traditional approaches to describing and explaining humans in light of our contemporary global, technologically advanced, economically based world.

References

Altman, I., & Rogoff, B. (1987). Worldviews in psychology: Trait, interactional, organismic, and transactional perspectives. In D. S. Altman (Ed.), *Handbook of environmental psychology* (pp. 1–32). New York: John Wiley & Sons.

Farlex. (2011). *Human.* Retrieved from the Free Dictionary: http://www.thefreedictionary.com/ human

Harper, D. (2001–2010). *On-Line etymology dictionary.* Retrieved from http://www.etymonline .com/index.php?search=ethnic&searchmode=none

Hutchison, E. (2010). *Dimensions of human behavior: The changing life course.* Thousand Oaks, CA: Sage.

Hyperdictionary.com. (2001–2009). *Human.* Retrieved from http://www.hyperdic.net/en/ human

Johnson, M. M., & Rhodes, R. (2010). *Human behavior in the larger social environment* (2nd ed.). Boston: Allyn & Bacon.

Ragin, C. (2008). Redesigning social inquiry: Fuzzy sets and beyond. Chicago: University of Chicago Press.

Seifert, K., Hoffnung, R., & Hoffnung, M. (2003). *Lifespan development.* Boston: Houghton Mifflin.

Smith, C. (2010). *What Is a person? Rethinking humanity, social life, and the moral good from the person up.* Chicago: University of Chicago Press.

Thomas, R. M. (2001). *Recent theories of human development.* Thousand Oaks, CA: Sage.

Wikipedia. (n.d.). *Human.* Retrieved from en.wikipedia.org/wiki/Human

WordNet. (n.d.). *Human.* Retrieved from http://wordnetweb.princeton.edu/perl/webwn?s=hu man&sub=Search+WordNet&o2=&o0=1&o7=&o5=&o1=1&o6=&o4=&o3=&h=

Section II

Theories That Describe and Explain

3

Overview of Developmental Theories

Looking at Humans Over Time

P erhaps the most widely used conceptual approaches to describing and explaining human activity, appearance, and experience are developmental.

From word soup, we ladle the following synonyms for the term *development*: expansion, elaboration, growth, evolution, unfolding, opening, maturing, maturation, maturity, ripeness (Dictionary.com, n.d.).

Drawing 3.1   Developmental Theories Word Soup

Inherent in each of these words is movement or growth on a hierarchy from diminutive to grand, from immature to mature, and so forth. Reflecting positive movement, developmental theories have typically been referred to as *stage, phase, life course theories,* and, more recently, *developmental science* (Damon & Lerner, 2006). Initial theories of human development were concerned with how individuals unfold in an orderly and sequential fashion. However, over the past several decades, human development has expanded beyond looking at the passage of the individual through time to positioning human function and capability within comparative hierarchical frameworks. We discuss all of these approaches within the genre of developmental theories, noting that they have different scopes and foci, but contain commonalities. What unites all of them is the role of "development" depicted as degree of maturation or directional movement as descriptive and explanatory of humans, their interactions, and their contexts. Some developmental theories posit specific stages through which individual humans or entities pass and must negotiate, while others see chronological maturation as a fluid process without discrete identifiable boundaries that delineate the boundaries of entrance and exit from one state into the next. Selected developmental theories focus on processes proximal to humans, while others look at the interaction of multiple factors to describe and explain maturation and functioning of humans. Still others look at human functioning within large distal contexts such as nation-states.

Of the many theorists who have suggested that passage through stages is an important factor in explaining human phenomena, Sigmund Freud (1856–1939) may be the most famous developmental theorist. In a sense, Freud may be viewed as an intellectual pioneer in that he departed from moral explanations for atypical human experience advanced by his contemporaries such as von Krafft Ebing (1840–1902). But, Freud is only one of many theorists who have looked at sequential, hierarchical unfolding as important to understanding human description, change, and comparison. Looking further back in the history of developmental theory (Mosher, Youngman, & Day, 2006), Adolphe Quetelet (1796–1874) has actually been hailed for his significant contribution to understanding human phenomena chronologically. Other important early theorists include Johann Heinrich Pestalozzi (1746–1827), William James (1842–1910), G. Stanley Hall (1844–1924), Alfred Binet (1857–1911), John Dewey (1859–1952), George Herbert Mead (1863–1931), and Charlotte Malachowski Buhler (1893–1974) (Mosher, Youngman, & Day, 2006). Unfortunately, these important theorists developed their work in isolation from one another and it was not until the early to mid-20th century that a seminal body of human developmental theory coalesced and then expanded to human flourishing in the late 20th century (Nussbaum & Sen, 1993).

According to Damon and Lerner (2006), early theories following human maturation over longitudinal time were primarily located in singular disciplines such as developmental psychology, motor development, and so forth. More recently, however, and in concert with postmodern and post-postmodern thinking, developmental theories have been renamed developmental science, capabilities, and so forth, indicating their interdisciplinarity with claims supported by systematic inquiry as well as institutional and even global evidence.

Given the breadth of developmental theories and the large scope of topical concern, and building on Thomas's (2001) taxonomy, we parse these theories into two categories, grand and specific, with important distinctions.

Distinguishing Between Grand and Specific Theories

Grand and specific theories are concerned with human movement and growth. Although not directly addressed in most theories, a hierarchy from least to most desirable—whether expressed as immature to mature, limited to fully developed, and so forth—is implicit in developmental theories.

Grand theories focus on and treat human phenomena holistically. That is to say, the unit of analysis is the whole person moving through time or context, and more recently, due to the erosion of dualism, contexts as elements of human functioning have been included in theories of human development. For example, Sigmund Freud and Erik H. Erikson (1902–1994), treated human growth and development as the total unfolding of an individual while Martha Nussbaum (2000) characterizes optimal human flourishing as an economic resource phenomenon linked to the degrees of freedom, so to speak, to access and actualize basic resources. These broad hierarchical theories, originating from roots in resource economics, concern themselves with the rank ordering of health and welfare on the basis of human functioning within entities including geographies such as nation-states (Klugman, 2009; Nussbaum & Sen, 2009). Although not typically discussed as theories of human development, we partially locate and discuss them in this category because of the moniker their own authors attribute to them, *human development and capabilities,* as well as their adherence to the axioms of this genre. Human development and capabilities theories are also discussed within new and emerging theories because they cross over into interdisciplinary postmodern thinking about humans in context.

Specific theories direct their focus to a narrow embodied domain, such as cognition, motor development, moral development, neurological development, genetics, psychological development, multisystemic development, and so forth.

Because of the enormity of literature, all of the theories and ideas cannot be critically examined in a single text. We have selected those that represent their categories and provide sufficient breadth and depth for illustration, analysis, use, and, of course, extrapolation.

Table 3.1 lists the theories and ideas discussed throughout the book and locates them within the categories of grand and specific approaches.

THINKING POINT

Think of other examples of grand and specific developmental theories. Compare them for scope and use in informing professional action.

Table 3.1 The Location of Developmental Theories

Grand Developmental Theories	Specific Developmental Theories
Psychoanalysis (Freud)	Cognitive development (Piaget, Case, Goldberg)
Ego psychology (Erikson)	Moral development (Kohlberg)
Analytical psychology (Jung)	Physical development (Gesell, Ashbaugh)
Adult development (Levinson, Gould, L'Abate, Strauch)	Spiritual development (Fowler)
Culture (Wexler)	Death and dying (Kübler-Ross)
Human development and capabilities (Sen, Nussbaum)	Neurobiology (Wexler)

Historically, the developmental approaches that address individual human unfolding over time have spanned the chronological domain from birth to death. However, currently, with elongated technological, spiritual, biological, and contextual gazes, "prebirth" and "postmortem" description and explanations have nudged their way into more traditional "womb to tomb" theories of individual human development. We defer our discussions of the prenatal and postmortem human, conditions that precede formal birth and succeed formal death, and definition of nations, governments, and contexts to other chapters, as they fit more comfortably under other genres in our taxonomy. Thus, Chapters 4 and 5 enter the world of developmental theory from infancy through old age. Chapter 4 begins the discussion of the hierarchical growth elements of human development and capability theory.

Developmental Theory Axioms

Before examining and illustrating the application of grand and specific approaches to human development, Table 3.2 identifies the axioms that delimit and guide our analysis.

As illustrated in the axioms, to a large extent, developmental theories advance the ideas that underpin many areas of our lives. They tell us what to expect as we reach certain ages, what not to expect, what our government is likely to afford us according to the level of development of a nation, what distinguishes one developmental group from another, and the nature of maturity. Moreover, these theories provide the explanatory basis for typical and atypical unfolding of an entity from its birth through death or origin through elimination. As such, we establish and evaluate individual lives, groups, governments, and even nations according to expectations of movement and change throughout their time spans; we compare single cases to theorized expectations, and determine the extent to which cases fit or do not fit within a

Table 3.2	Developmental Theory Axioms

1. Developmental approaches are based on how individual humans and human entities grow, mature, and compare to one another. Thus, these theories are explicitly or implicitly concerned with the hierarchical process of aging even if they do not identify that focus.

2. Developmental descriptions and explanations, to a greater or lesser degree, posit typical and desirable appearance, milestones, experiences, logical explanations, and qualities.

3. Developmental approaches are descriptive, explanatory, and prescriptive. These theories not only group phenomena according to a hierarchy of growth as well as what is assumed to be typical for a particular age or context and why, but also assert or imply what should be now and in the future. Thus, the typical is not only the most commonly observed for a cohort but becomes the standard for comparison and, often, for example or nonexample of desirability.

4. Developmental approaches propose the unidirectional longitudinal trajectory of growth. Related to corporeal experience and development as one ages, one grows and changes both quantitatively and qualitatively. A person, unless considered to be abnormal, cannot "ungrow" or grow backwards. Development of contextual entities is theorized to follow a similar trajectory from less to more desirable.

5. As individuals and entities develop, experiences are additive, in that past events impact the present and contemporary events influence future development, regardless of the longevity of the phenomenon.

6. Over time, humans and entities become increasingly mature and complex unless decline is theorized or observed.

7. Growth and development are not consistent throughout a single life or entity; that is, individual uniqueness emerges from the differential growth and development of some specific parts over others and rates of growth and development are not constant.

8. Developmental approaches provide the platform for contrasting individuals, groups and entities along specified standards. That is to say, these approaches identify the "typical and desirable," with varying correlates of maturation, and use these as metrics or benchmarks, so to speak, for comparison.

desirable range. We even use theories of development to create and market unique products to specific age and national groups.

Think of children's products. In children's books, websites, and other reading materials, we base the images, reading level, and even content on what is theorized to be of interest and relevance to children's ages.

Now, think of fashion. Certainly, we have all heard people say something like "that fashion is too old for you. It makes you look like your mother."

Nations even brand themselves to denote their maturation with regard to economic development, rights, and public good.

THINKING POINT

What other practices can you think of that developmental theories inform?

Of particular importance in this category of theory is the relevance of developmental descriptions to defining normalcy and average. Examined in greater detail in Chapters 4 and 5, developmental theorists, through observation of phenomena along a maturation trajectory, seek to find common characteristics, and thus uncommon characteristics, of people and entities grouped by age or maturity, and then, on the basis of these observations, of what is typical or average, propose what should be expected from each cohort or grouping. More recently, diversity variables have been introduced into developmental theories, segmenting populations and geographies and related expectations for subcategory norms. We address this important theoretical trend in Chapters 9 through 12, but bring it forward in this chapter to note the development of developmental theories in themselves and to foreground the contextual nature of these theories as well (Damon & Lerner, 2006). Consider the following examples to illustrate.

> *Jacqueline is a 26-year-old woman, who, shortly after birth, was diagnosed with Down syndrome and cognitive impairment. Let us think of those two constructs in terms of the axioms of developmental theory. White infants have typical appearances and behaviors that form the basis for developmental normalcy. Because Jacqueline's appearance differed from that of typical infants, she was suspect for "abnormality" caused by medical pathology, which was confirmed on the basis of examining her descriptive bodily appearances as compared to most other infants. Comparison against the typical standards of appearance for her ethnicity and age-group provided the rationale for further classifying her within a category of "abnormal." Unlike white infants, Jacqueline had almond shaped eyes. She also had atypical creases on the palms of her hands. Further observation and testing against a set of standards provided the evidence to support the deductive accuracy of her diagnosis. For example, Jacqueline's test results for intellectual function were below the standard for her age-group, her movements and muscle tone were different from her age cohorts, and so forth.*

> *Now consider Wanda and Melissa, Jacqueline's two sisters. They both illustrate the axioms of developmental theory from the normative perspective. As a young adult, Wanda was in the range for embarking upon marriage, and thus, her plans for intimacy and marriage are considered to be typical as well as desirable. As for Melissa, while she was considered normative throughout her childhood, because she conformed to what was typical of children within her age cohort, as she entered adolescence, she found that she was not sexually attracted to anyone, and thus decided to remain single. The acceptability of her absence of perceived sexuality is not as clear if examined through a developmental theoretical lens as that of her sister, Wanda.*

Now consider the Human Development Index, a measure of the level of development of a nation. This index parses nations into four major hierarchical categories, very high (the most desirable ranking), high (the top middle ranking), medium (second to lowest ranking) and low (lowest and least desirable ranking). Implicit in the scoring is that the highest ranked countries are "baked" and most desirable, while the lowest ranked countries are substandard or as labeled in previous iterations of this index, "underdeveloped" (United Nations Development Programme, 2009).

In contemporary and emerging theories, and even in some of the more contemporary developmental approaches, conceptualizations of what is typical, and thus desirable, have changed in response to increasingly diverse and global communities. However, within the rubric of classical and even many current developmental theories, Melissa and Jacqueline and countries such as Ethiopia would still be considered non-normative, substandard, or undesirable even though their differences may be accepted within new and emerging theories. The axioms of developmental theories identify what is common to all of the theories located in Chapters 4 and 5.

The Normal Curve: Mathematical Foundation of Developmental Theories

The normal curve is one of the most important constructs that provided the scholarly rationale for developmental lenses. Examining the logical foundation of developmental descriptions and explanations reveals Quetelet's (1835, 1969) mathematical shape of the normal or bell-shaped curve as the conceptual basis.

Looking in more detail at the mathematical construct, the lines at Points A and B represent the limits of normal or average. Thus, any score that falls between A and B would be considered normal, acceptable, or typical, while those falling outside of either A or B would be abnormal, substandard or suprastandard. What is above average (in some but

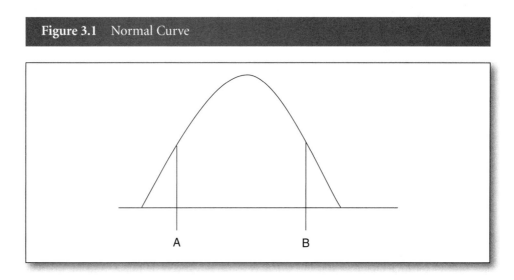

Figure 3.1 Normal Curve

not all instances) or average becomes prescriptive of what "should be" and specifies the ways in which phenomena are—and by implication, are not—expected to look and function. These norms change as one travels through chronological time, and abstract or geographic context.

At an early age, Jacqueline's behavior deviated from that of her peers in the same cohort. Falling outside of the "typical" performance of activity, she tested at slow cognitive development and below average cognitive function, or what is referred to as cognitive impairment. Because her IQ score fell below Point A on the normal curve for her age-group, she was considered subnormal, so to speak, and thus the deviance in her behavior was identified as an impairment diagnosed as a "developmental disability." Children who score within the typical range (between Points A and B) would be considered of normal intelligence and those scoring above would be considered superior.

Illustrating the undesirability of "above average" is hyperkinesis or excessive activity. Despite residing within the supranormal range of the bell-shaped curve, this level of activity begets the diagnostic label of attention deficit and hyperactivity disorder (Greene, 2010) and is served up for pharmacological manipulation.

Now, think of the term, midlife crisis. *This term usually refers to someone who is embarking on middle age, and "acts" like an individual who is of adolescent age.*

Now, illustrating the application of Quetelet's work to nations, consider the comparison between Norway and Togo. Norway is rated above average on all three indicators of development: life expectancy at birth, per capita income, and gross domestic product (United Nations Development Programme, 2009). Norway is therefore considered highly developed. Togo scored way below the mean or average, remanding it to an underdeveloped status.

THINKING POINT

 Think of examples of behavioral phenomena that are normal at some ages and not at others.

Inherent in the concept of midlife crisis is that the individual proceeding through midlife is acting in a manner that is typical of a teenager, and thus not expected and suitable for an older age cohort.

Or, think of the terms *immature* or *decent standard of living*. Implicit in both are desirables and undesirables.

Evidentiary Basis of Developmental Theories

Referring to the *development of developmental theories*, the legitimacy of evidence for supporting these theories has changed over time. As detailed in subsequent chapters, seminal classical theories, such as those advanced by Piaget and Freud, were anchored on the observations by the theorists themselves, without support from what is considered today as "science" or systematic inquiry. Piaget barely looked beyond the walls of his own domicile, creating his theory of cognitive development from observations of his own children. It is curious to think that Piagetian theory, which forms the basis of age expectations for capacity to learn, emerged from and inscribes Piaget's offspring as the "norm" of desirable thinking. Interestingly, Freud looked inward, and to his own patients—whom he himself defined as pathological—as subjects for theorizing about normal psychosexual development.

Moving forward in the 20th century, traditional developmental theorists posited and tested their ideas through contemporary measurement strategies (DePoy & Gitlin, 2011). This approach to asserting developmental "truth" is intriguing as well, given the deductive methods used to develop and validate measurement. Recall the discussion in Chapter 1 about logical methods of theory support. The sequence of measurement begins with the selection of a theory, proceeds to the isolation and lexical (dictionary) definition (word soup, anyone?) of particular concepts to be measured, parsing the concepts into measurable items, and then selecting a numeric plan for scoring. Validating the measure involves statistical testing that one can read about in any research methods text. Why, then, bother to discuss measurement here?

We suggest that the measurement process for validating a theory can be tautological. Tautological, in this case, is the circular thinking process of defining a phenomenon by its measurement and then measuring it by its definition. For example, in his book, titled *Brown,* Rodriguez (2003) seeks to debunk the truth value of the category of Hispanic. He suggests that people from diverse Spanish speaking nations are defined as *Hispanic* and then counted in large part because they speak Spanish as a first language and they originate from the delineated geography, reifying the category by counting its definitional elements. Measurement is discussed more fully as supportive of theory as the book proceeds. While nomothetic (statistical methods of inquiry that seek to reveal group commonalities and differences) form the investigatory foundation for many developmental theories, contemporary developmental theorists and researchers have begun to turn to multiple methods and varieties of evidence for creating and validating theory. Be on the lookout, then, for evidentiary support for developmental theory as you select legitimate frameworks for social work practice.

Summary

This chapter introduced two divisions of developmental theory: grand and specific. Axioms were then advanced that are common to developmental theories, followed by a discussion of the mathematical basis for the normal-not normal, average-not average binaries inherent in developmental descriptions and explanations. This chapter concluded with a discussion and commentary on evidence supporting theory, highlighting the need to be cognizant of the evidentiary foundation and validation methods for each theory.

References

Damon, W., & Lerner, R. M. (2006). *Handbook of child psychology* (6th ed.). Hoboken, NJ: John Wiley & Sons.

DePoy, E., & Gitlin, L. (2011). *Introduction to research* (4th ed.). St Louis, MO: Elsevier.

Dictionary.com (n.d.). *Development.* Retreived from http://dictionary.reference.com/browse/development

Greene, A. (2010). *Attention deficit hyperactivity disorder (ADHD).* Retrieved from Google Health: https://health.google.com/health/ref/Attention+deficit+hyperactivity+disorder+%28ADHD%29

Klugman, J. (2009). *2010 Human development report consultation.* Retrieved from hdr.undp .org/.../JENI-Busan_Presentation_2010_with_NHDR_teams.ppt

Mosher, R., Youngman, D., & Day, J. (Eds.). (2006). *Human development across the lifespan: Educational and psychological applications* (2nd ed.). Westport, CT: Praeger.

Nussbaum, M. (2000). *Women and human development: The capabilities approach.* Cambridge, MA: Cambridge University Press.

Nussbaum, M., & Sen, A. (1993). *The quality of life.* Oxford, UK: Clarendon.

Quetelet, L. A. (1835). *Essai de physique social.* Paris: Bachelier, Imprimeur-Libraire.

Quetelet, L. A. (1969). *A treatise on man and the development of his faculties: A facsimile reproduction of the English translation of 1842.* Gainsville, FL: Scholars' Facsimiles & Reprints.

Rodriguez, R. (2003). *Brown: The last discovery of America.* New York: Penguin.

Sen, A. (2009). *The idea justice.* Cambridge, MA: Belknap Press.

Thomas, R. M. (2001). *Recent theories of human development.* Thousand Oaks, CA: Sage.

United Nations Development Programme. (2009). *Human development reports.* Retrieved from http://hdr.undp.org/en/statistics/

4

Grand Developmental Theories

Looking at Individuals Developing as a Whole

This chapter turns our attention to what we have referred to as grand developmental theories. In Chapter 3, grand developmental theories were defined as those that treat individual human phenomena holistically, where the unit of analysis is the whole person and beyond proceeding through chronological movement, orderly change, maturation, or growth. Thus, while grand theories may address specifics such as sexual development, psychological development, national development, and so forth, they are different from specific developmental theories, which primarily delimit their attention to those areas. Grand developmental theories locate specific human phenomena within the scope of total personhood or context. As such, many people have said that these theories do not do as much "work" as specific developmental theories. What is meant by "work" is that they do not give sufficient detail to predict and are open to broad interpretation. Because we cannot discuss every grand developmental theory within the page limits of this book, we have selected theories that are seminal, such as Freud's theory of psychosexual development, and others which we believe represent the grand developmental genre up through contemporary times. These provide axiomatic exemplars for extrapolation to theories that are not discussed.

Traditional Grand Developmental Approaches and Their Successors

Now, let us begin our discussion of traditional grand developmental theories and their successors. Traditional grand developmental theories are those theories that have formed the foundation for description and explanation and upon which contemporary developmental theories have built. There are many excellent primary and secondary sources that detail developmental theories. The intent here is not to provide a summary, but rather to present information sufficient for analysis and application.

Foundational Thinkers:
Sigmund Freud and Erik Erikson

Of course, discussion of grand developmental theories must begin with Sigmund Freud and Erik Erikson. Both of these theorists are important not only for their own thoughts, but for the platforms that they provided to subsequent thinkers for theoretical development and application.

Even though greatly influenced by other thinkers of his era, Sigmund Freud (1856–1939) remains the most prominent of his time, for his origination of psychoanalysis, a practice of remediating pathology based on unknown, internal, or what Freud called unconscious explanations for human behavior. Freud was an Austrian thinker whose career spanned the late 19th and early 20th centuries. To a small extent, Freud's explanations of human development were based on individual case studies. That is to say, he observed and interviewed individuals, principally in his clinical practice, and then through induction, as discussed in Chapter 3, proposed hypotheses on the basis of what he saw as common to the aggregate of his clients. Freud's work is often criticized for its evidentiary foundation, as he anchored much of his theory on cases of those whom he himself labeled as "pathological" (Sigelman & Rider, 2009). We are not asserting that Freud was an inductive thinker, however, as discussed next.

Wilhelm Wundt, who was concerned with conscious psychological processes, initially influenced Freud. While in his 20s, Freud studied the work Josef Breuer (1842–1925) a well-known and respected Viennese physician who had developed the *talking cure* with his patients. One particular patient, Anna O., was treated using hypnosis for "hysteria" and "double personality." Later, Freud worked with French neurologist Jean Charcot (1825–1893), who used hypnosis to work with "hysterical" patients. These experiences were influential for Freud's ideas about the unconscious mind and memories, and his practice involved several women with "hysterical symptoms" with no known organic or corporeal cause. His analysis of Hans, a 5-year-old boy with a fear of horses, illuminated and informed some of his psychosexual explanations including the Oedipus complex. Hans's analysis was based on extensive mail correspondence with Hans's father and on one face-to-face session with Hans. Finally, Freud's explanations were largely derived from extensive self-analysis (Phares & Chaplin, 1997).

THINKING POINT

Can you see why Freud might have been criticized for using the evidence from these "cases" as the basis for his theory development?

Yet, to a great extent, despite his frequent use of case study methodology, Freud is credited with applying scientific reasoning to human development within the delimiting perimeter of biological and intrinsic explanations for human behavior. So, even though Freud used induction to search for commonalities in his patients, he contained these commonalities within a biological frame of reference—a deductive approach to reasoning. That is, Freud believed that the causes of all human behavior were biologically influenced psychological processes interior to the corpus, which were not within the awareness of each actor (Freud, 1949, 1964). He therefore located the commonalities among his cases within that theoretical rubric.

Freud observed that in infancy, babies are concerned with activities that focus on their mouths. This inductive observation led him to the conclusion that babies are oral. *To explain this observed phenomenon, he looked deductively to existing biological theory and thus explained orality as infantile sexuality, or a biological drive for satisfaction achieved through sucking and other activity related to and centered about the infantile mouth (Freud, 1938).*

Freud also used other existing theories deductively to explain how descriptive commonalities within his case studies could be understood by current constructs. In order to explain human behavior, he applied his knowledge of physics to the construct of personality. Two primary concepts based on human physics, so to speak, are important to understanding Freud's behavioral explanations: (1) psychic energy or libido, and (2) intrapsychic drives or instincts (Freud, 1938). Borrowing from Ernst von Brücke (1866), a physiologist at the Vienna Medical School and clearly reflecting Kantian dualism, Freud characterized human personality as an energy system—libido or psychic energy—in which instincts, or drives emerging from biological energy, were translated through mental processes, or the mind, into behavior. Although Freud suggested numerous instincts, he categorized them into two divisions, Eros, the drive towards life and pleasure, and Thanatos, the drive toward death and destruction. In the presence of tension between these two overarching instinctual categories, the normative individual seeks Eros. Of course, all of this intrapsychic activity occurs at a deep internal level, called the unconscious, that cannot be directly known by the actors. And thus, Freud's basic premises bring into question the degree to which humans exercise free will, since his theories posit unknown and uncontrolled intrapsychic drives as the basis for explaining all human action (Sigelman & Rider, 2009).

David, a 17-year-old high school senior, is about to graduate. However, about 3 months prior to his graduation, he decides that he wants to spread his wings, so to speak, take a

leave from school, and travel around the country. Is David exercising free will? Not neces-
sarily, if we apply Freudian theory as explanatory. While on the surface, David seems to be
making a choice, Freud might argue that he is exhibiting Thanatos, through destroying his
orderly passage through his final psychosexual stage of maturation. As we will see later in
the chapter, David's alleged decision could be a function of unresolved issues at earlier
stages of development.

One becomes familiar with the explanations for behavior by undergoing psycho-analysis, a process of bringing forth to the conscious or uncovering the content of the unconscious. If David wanted to uncover the unconscious reasons for his desire to leave, he would go regularly for psychoanalysis, which might involve numerous techniques including hypnosis and analysis of his dreams.

We used the term *mind* previously, and while there are many definitions of this construct (Calvin, 2004), Freud has a distinct deterministic, structural conceptualization that is critical to our understanding of how he viewed individual human development. According to Freud, the mind is comprised of three structural components: id, ego, and superego. The *id,* the unconscious part of the mind, is the locus in which instincts, impulses, and drives reside. The id, the seat of unregulated intrapsychic energy, is in constant conflict with the *ego,* the conscious component of the mind that is responsible for rational thought and controlled emotion and the element of ourselves which we can come to know (Kahn, 2002). Freud believed the ego holds instincts in check and is the moderator between the id and the *superego* component of the mind responsible for moral judgments. Freud explained that the superego resides in the conscious ego, but has components in the id that screen which thoughts will be filtered to inhabit the consciousness (Freud, 1949, 1964; Kahn, 2002).

Not unexpectedly, the three structures of the mind, each with different functions, interact through four primary functions: repression, sublimation, fixation, and regression. These processes, called *defense mechanisms,* are important explanations for human behavior. By repression, Freud meant that the id's unacceptable impulses were remanded to the unconscious. Consistent with physics, repressed energy does not disappear, so it must have an outlet. Sublimation, or the transference of energy to acceptable descriptive behaviors, is the desirable outlet; fixation—and its cousin, regression—are the undesirable consequences. Fixation refers to the inability to move on from age inappropriate, stage-related conflicts, whereas regression is the exhibition of immature, age, and stage inappropriate behaviors and concerns (Kahn, 2002).

Let us visit with David again. At the age of 17, according to Freudian theory, David is sup-
posed to be ready for mature love with a woman. However, he has not yet had any such
relationship, and prefers to be with his male friends. Because of trepidation about his recent
desire to engage in sex with his best friend, Kevin, David has decided to drop out of school,
and travel. Through the psychoanalytic lens, we might explain David's desire as fixation on
an earlier stage caused by an overdomineering mother and an absent father. This fixation
holds David back in his maturation, and thereby produces age inappropriate desires and
related behavior.

THINKING POINT

Apply the concept of id, ego, and superego to yourself. How does each concept describe you and your experience?

Now, let us turn to the next part of Freud's thinking, developmental-longitudinal conceptualizations, which focus that on his phases of psychosexual development from infancy to adulthood. Departing from those who viewed children as mini-adults, Freud characterized chronological growth from birth through genital maturation (Hoare, 2002) and proposed qualitatively different stages of the human passage through time. Recall the three structural elements of the mind: id, ego, and superego. According to Freud, maturation is predetermined and, for people considered "normal," follows the sequence of increasingly socializing and thus harnessing the id and its sexual energy, under the watchful eyes of the ego and superego. Each of the five stages occurs in a predetermined sequence that applies to all people, with some variation due to an individual's sex.

Each stage has a series of challenges or conflicts that must be resolved. Freud postulated that the failure to negotiate each stage in the desired manner resulted in psychopathology. In essence, inability to successfully resolve the central conflict and emerge from each stage in a predetermined fashion resulted in *fixation,* as introduced earlier, meaning the inability to leave behind the intrapsychic tasks that are to be completed at each stage, thereby seeing unhealthy remnants of earlier stages where they do not chronologically belong. Table 4.1 overviews the central descriptive tasks, the primary conflict, and explanations for both in each stage.

Table 4.1 Freud's Stages of Psychosexual Development

Stage	Oral Birth–1 Year	Anal 1–3 Years	Phallic 3–5 Years	Latent 6 Years– Adolescence	Genital Puberty +
Description	Feeding, sucking, differentiating the self from the mother, learning how to get one's pleasure needs met	Learning to control one's body and environment, pleasure through fecal expulsion	Genital locus of pleasure, desire for opposite sex parent	Sublimation of sexual energy to asexual accomplishments	Renewed sexual interest; development of mature, heterosexual relationships; sex specific genital primacy

(Continued)

Table 4.1 (Continued)

Stage	Oral Birth–1 Year	Anal 1–3 Years	Phallic 3–5 Years	Latent 6 Years– Adolescence	Genital Puberty +
Conflict	Weaning	Toileting and bowel control	Oedipus and Electra complex; penis envy for girls, castration anxiety for boys	Sublimation of overt sexuality	Renegotiation of Oedipus and Electra complexes to completion, supplanting of homosexual by heterosexual activities
Explanation	Libido located in oral region	Libido moves to anal region, tension between id and ego development	Libido moves from anal to genital region	Dormancy of libido	Successful transference of libidinal focus away from parent to opposite sex peers

As Table 4.1 illustrates, just the brief overview of stages of psychosexual development is not only descriptive and explanatory, but prescriptive as well.

THINKING POINT

 Provide examples from your own experience to illustrate how Freud's stages are prescriptive, and thus create the binary of normal and not normal.

Deviation from what Freud proposes as predetermined maturation has negative results in producing psychopathology that he referred to as *neurosis* or *psychosis*. These two classes of psychopathology were used as the basis for diagnostic categories through 1968 (Committee on Nomenclature and Statistics of the American Psychiatric Association, 1968), and still inhere in the current diagnostic taxonomy of psychopathology (American Psychiatric Association, 2010). Table 4.2 provides examples of unsuccessful negotiation of each stage (Freud, 1964, 1966; Giovacchini, 1977).

Enter David once again. If we were to explain his recent behavior through Freud's eyes, we might identify two stages that he could have failed to negotiate successfully, the phallic stage and the genital stages, both which could result in what Freud referred to as gender confusion.

Table 4.2 Examples of Consequences of Failing to Successfully Negotiate Stages

Oral	Anal	Phallic	Latent	Genital
Severe thought disorders such as schizophrenia, eating disorders, speech inhibitions	Stubbornness, the excessive need to control one's environment, or heightened aggressiveness; obsessive-compulsive neurosis or sadomasochistic tendencies	Pride, promiscuity, self-hatred, sexual orientation and gender identity disorders	Shame, disgust, intensified repression	Rebelliousness, lack of conformity or overconformity to rules, sexual and gender confusion

Freud's theories were as controversial when they were developed as they are today, albeit for different reasons. While contemporary theorists have challenged his predeterminism and essentialism particularly related to his characterization of women and of diverse sexual orientation (Blasius, 2001; Talburt, 2004), his contemporaries argued about the credibility of his theories on the basis of their epistemology. To some extent, he was credited with applying scientific reasoning to human development within the delimiting perimeter of biological and intrinsic explanations for human behavior. However, there are those who argue that because his theoretical tenets do not meet Popper's (1959) criteria for true science of verifiability and falsifiability through systematic investigation, Freud is more of a pseudoscientist than a scientist (Thornton, 2001). Others have contended that no contemporary psychological theory meets Popper's criteria (O'Neil, 1998).

As noted, Freud's theories were developed through his life experiences and case studies of clinical work with patients, not experiments or controlled studies. His analyses were based on his interpretations and, to some scholars (Kramer, 2006), misinterpretations of patients' experiences. For example, Freud's description of the Oedipal complex arose, in part, based on recollections from his own childhood and from therapy with numerous women who reported sexual abuse in their childhoods (Kramer, 2006; Thornton, 2001). Over time, he came to believe that many of these memories were false and a result of unresolved Oedipal conflicts from childhood. Yet, despite skepticism about his methods of inquiry, Freudian psychoanalysis has also been the basis for techniques such as hypnosis, in which repressed memories occurring as young as infancy are brought to light through therapeutic intervention (Kramer, 2006). Deciding the accuracy of these reports is left to the therapist based on interpretation and inference. With no systematic or empirical evaluation to validate assumptions, critics assert that psychoanalysis has led to legitimate cases of sexual abuse being written off as fantasy, while, concomitantly, therapists have been instrumental in the recalling of false repressed memories (Loftus, 1993; O'Neil, 1998; Tallis, 2001).

Erik Erikson (1902–1994), one of Freud's protégées and critics, built on Freud's developmental work and expanded it beyond young adulthood from birth to death. He underwent psychoanalytic training under Freud's daughter, Anna Freud, from 1927 to 1933, and then immigrated to the United States where he worked the remainder of his career. After arriving in the United States, Erikson studied a variety of people in contexts as he developed his descriptions and explanations of humans over chronological time. Among the groups that he observed and upon which he generated theory were World War II soldiers, American Indians, and "normal" and "troubled" children, including adolescents, experiencing what he referred to as *identity crises* (Pennington, 2002; Sharkey, 1997). Similar to Freud, Erikson (1958) engaged in psychoanalysis, but unlike his predecessor, Erikson applied "psychoanalysis as a historical tool" (p. 16). Erikson used psychoanalytic techniques to explain the behavior of historical figures such as Martin Luther and Mahatma Gandhi (Erikson, 1958, 1993). Erikson's interest in Gandhi was heightened when Erikson was in India lecturing and studying social behavior. It is interesting to note that, while Erikson focused on Luther's youth, his historical psychoanalysis concentrated on Gandhi's adult life, suggesting his maturing interest in expanding his developmental gaze beyond his teacher's, to the full chronology of the human life span.

From his observations, Erikson departed from Freud's view of adulthood. Thus, unlike Freud, who treated adulthood as a primarily static period where vestiges of infantile drives fought with the mature ego and superego, Erikson breathed theoretical life and growth into adulthood (Calvin, 2004). We see this expansion as Erikson's major contribution to developmental approaches in that he attributed dynamic life to later years.

> *Consider Lila, an 82-year-old woman, who has three grandchildren and seven great grandchildren. According to Freud, Lila's primary development would have peaked once she engaged in a mature intimate relationship. Since Lila's husband died when she was 60, Freud would have little to explain about Lila's life. Yet, Erikson provides attention to life after age 30, and thus sees Lila as a developing individual, not just a woman who has lived at the same level of maturity for 50 years (Erikson, 1982).*

Further, Erikson rendered Freud's theory of development more acceptable by clothing it, so to speak, in psychosocial rather than psychosexual fashions. By donning a more desirable and palatable covering on Freud's assertions of Eros as the driving causative factors of human behavior, Erikson continued in the theoretical tradition that described maturation as predetermined and fixed. Three forces—biological, inner psychological, and external social influences—explained descriptions of how people develop through Erikson's metaphoric stages.

In concert with our developmental axioms, according to Erikson, psychological and social stages were epigenetic in nature; that is, each stage is sequential and builds on previous stages with the successful resolution of each stage laying a foundation for each subsequent stage (Kail & Cavanaugh, 2010). Using Freud's concept of the ego, Erikson described development as ego-psychological or psychosocial in nature. Yet, different from Freud, whom Erikson saw as painting a negative description of development as psychosexual struggle, Erikson characterized growth as the acquisition of ego strengths throughout one's lifetime. Bringing the social world into the description of psychological maturation (Calvin, 2004), Erikson described the ego as autonomous from the Freudian id and emphasized the explanatory importance of parental, sibling, and social forces in personality development.

Building on Freudian predetermined stage theory, Erikson described psychological development as eight metaphoric stages, explaining the navigation and emergence from each by the degree to which one successfully resolved the developmental crisis presented therein. By *metaphoric,* we mean that the crises Erikson named were not the same for all individuals, but took on diverse meanings in context (Bloch & Singh, 2007).

> *If we look at two young boys, Denzel and Schmuel, through Erikson's eyes, we might see them at 8-years-old struggling to become "good" at something. Denzel has chosen music as his domain of achievement, while Schmuel has turned to his religion, Judaism, to begin his studies toward the rabbinical clergy. According to Erikson, what the boys have in common is not their interests, but rather their engagement in productivity, looking toward the future, and hoping to advance in their chosen domains.*

Bloch and Singh (2007) remind us that the metaphoric nature of Erikson's theory mediates against its essentialist application to explaining the nature of development. Thus, despite the predeterminism of Erikson's approach, his theories do not necessarily eschew diverse paths through the chronology of crisis resolution and growth. Metaphors have multiple interpretations and thus are more flexible than absolute assertions about what is normative and what is not.

Table 4.3 presents a summary of the eight stages and the metaphoric crisis to be solved (Erikson, 1980, 1982).

Table 4.3 Erik Erikson's Stages of Ego Development

Age	Stage	Positive vs. Negative Outcome	Consequences	Physical Activities	Social Sphere
Birth–1 year, infancy	Basic trust vs. mistrust	Secure attachments vs. mistrust of people, self, environment	Hope, fear	Feeding, eating	Mother, primary caregiver
1–4 years, toddlerhood	Autonomy vs. shame and doubt	Self-confidence and control vs. doubt of abilities and shame	Self-control, self-doubt	Urination and defecation, bowel and bladder control	Parents, relatives
3–6 years, early childhood	Initiative vs. guilt	Imagination and responsibility vs. fear of independence	Responsibility and purpose, unworthiness and inhibition	Mobility	Peers, family of origin

(Continued)

Table 4.3 (Continued)

Age	Stage	Positive vs. Negative Outcome	Consequences	Physical Activities	Social Sphere
5–13 years, middle childhood	Industry vs. inferiority	Sense of intellectual and physical competence vs. self image of inferiority	Competence, incompetence	School	Schoolmates, teachers
12–25 years, adolescence	Identity vs. role confusion	Strong identity and optimism for future vs. self-uncertainty in life roles, including sexual orientation or identity	Loyalty to others and sense of self, uncertainty about self	Expanded peer and social relationships	Peers, teachers, or mentors; associates independent of childhood and family of origin
20–40 years, early adulthood	Intimacy vs. isolation	Mutuality and intimacy in relationships vs. isolation and/or promiscuity	Mutual relationships, promiscuity, isolation from others	Expanded social spheres, work, educational world	Love relationships, partners, spouses
25–65 years, middle adulthood	Generativity vs. stagnation	Child rearing, mentoring vs. isolation, self-centeredness.	Caring, selfishness	Caring for children or mentoring future generation	Family of choice, work relationships
60 + years, later adulthood	Ego integrity vs. despair	Sense of fulfillment with life vs. despair and fear of death	Acceptance, meaninglessness, anomie	Self-care, diminishing physical abilities	Children and descendents, caregivers, social relationships

THINKING POINT

Compare and contrast Freud's and Erikson's stages. How are they similar, and different?

Looking at Erikson's stages of development from birth through the early adulthood years, Freud's hand in this work is recognizable. However, his last two stages of middle and later adulthood move beyond Freud's delimitation of development, which extends only until adulthood is reached.

Consider Lila again to compare how Freud and Erikson would characterize and explain her life. Lila was born in Buffalo, New York in 1923. She was the first of two siblings, both girls, who were the daughters of Henry, a steel worker, and his wife, Barbara. Lila had an uneventful early childhood, and thus, according to Freud she negotiated psychosexual oral, anal, and phallic stages successfully. According to Erikson, Lila achieved trust, autonomy, and initiative—having navigated well through the morass of her first three life crises.

In middle school, Lila was described as a quiet child who loved to play the piano. She had essentially no friends and her parents were concerned that she was not developing socially. Freud, at this point, might explain her behavior as potentially problematic, in that she has not developed associations with same sex peers. However, because she engaged in productive activity, and was not described as a girl who was ashamed of herself, she still might fit within the normal latency trajectory posited by Freud. Certainly, in Erikson's age appropriate crisis, Lila emerged as industrious rather than inferior, in that she was accomplished in her music.

It was not until Lila turned 14 that she presented a serious concern to her parents. She fell in love with a man who was 20 years older than she, and ran away with him to get married. At this juncture, did she have time to renegotiate her Electra complex or did she marry her father, so to speak? Was she able to successfully transfer her libidinal energy away from her father? Or, could Freud have explained her behavior as an unresolved Electra complex? Within Erikson's identity role confusion stage, Lila's behavior at least at 14 could well be explained by role confusion. That is, she looked to a father figure to address her uncertainty about herself. Freud would stop his explanations of Lila's development at this stage and might suggest pathology as an explanation for which psychoanalysis would be indicated. However, Erikson provides a scaffold for further examination and growth, and as we see, Lila was ultimately successful in her marriage, thus achieving intimacy over isolation.

As Lila raised her own children, she was generative and also continued to develop her talent in piano. When Lila's children left home to pursue their own adulthood, Lila, who had her talent and began to play in public concerts in her local area, remained generative. As she looks back on her life at 82, she has achieved ego integrity, as she is satisfied that she had a good life.

Note that Erikson (1982) explained old age as a time of reflection on one's history, rather than a time of active growth and development. Aging in contemporary literature is explained as much more active and forward moving in its trajectory than aging through Erikson's explanatory framework.

Successors to Traditional Approaches

There have been many theorists who have built on and expanded the work of Freud and Erikson. Of particular note is Carl Jung (1875–1961), who added the notion of collective unconscious as an explanation for the development of personality. By *collective unconscious*, Jung referred to the aggregate body of thoughts and experiences of one's ancestors. This important, but controversial, construct allowed Jung to explain phenomena such as cultural and national differences among groups of people. Jung was also one of the first theorists to concern himself with development during adulthood.

He coined the term *noon of life* to refer to the process of individual identity development at midlife and beyond (Jung Center, 2010).

> *Through Jung's lens, Lila's piano talent and love of music could be explained as an individuation process and perhaps as part of her collective unconscious as well.*

Alfred Adler and Karen Horney (Bloch & Singh, 2007) were also well known neo-Freudians. Similar to Erikson, who is also described as a neo-Freudian, Adler and Horney added dimensions beyond those that existed in an individual's proximal world, such as distal social factors, to the explanatory set of variables for personality development. L'Abate (1994) is a recent theorist who has built on life span theories of personality development to posit human development as the descriptive unfolding of competencies in home, work, and leisure. Although he credits culture as explanatory, L'Abate identifies the family as the major explanation for typical and acceptable development in all three contexts (Thomas, 2001).

> *Through L'Abate's eyes, Lila's family interaction and the norms of her culture could be viewed to obtain explanatory clues about her early marriage.*

Some theorists focus their grand gaze on a single age cohort. Given the view from classical developmental theories that an individual unfolds from birth, and thus needs a solid foundation early in life in order to mature into a valued adult, it is not surprising that significant effort has been devoted to child and youth development theorizing. Sigelman and Rider (2009) clearly illustrate this developmental principle in the following statements, "Infants' temperaments and their parents' parenting behaviors reciprocally influence one another and reciprocally influence one another over time to steer the direction of later personality development (p. 316). . . . Perhaps no period of life is more important in the development of self than adolescence" (p. 319).

Curiously, adolescence as a stage of the life span was not conceptualized until the late 1800s, by Stanley Hall, and even with Freud's attention to it as a stage of psychosexual development, he did not pay much attention to this age range beyond that part of his theorizing (Henig, 2010; Konstam, 2007). The acceptance of adolesence as a discrete stage and the debates about its nature as stormy or productive illuminate the social construction and reification, through action and praxis, of stages and milestones (King, 2004). Therefore, it is not surprising that despite its nascence, a new stage—*emerging adulthood*—is now being constructed as a stage unto itself (Arnett & Tanner, 2006; Konstam, 2007). Although not the first to posit emerging adulthood as a discrete developmental stage, Arnett (Arnett & Tanner, 2006) was perhaps one of the most influential theorists in characterizing the five common characteristics that comprise this theroetical construction and distinguish it from its neighbors, adolescence and adulthood: (1) identity, (2) instability, (3) narcissism, (4) ill-fit with adolescence or adulthood, and (5) options for future. By identity, Arnett suggested that exploration of diverse identities is inherent in this age range. Instability refers to the fluidity of moving in and out of varied identities and future visions. Narcissism depicts self-focus. Ill-fit with adolesence or adulthood defines the in-between uncertainty of identity and belonging, while options for future characterizes the forward gaze of individuals who are aging out of adolescence, but who have not yet selected an adulthood pathway to pursue.

Thus, emerging adults tend to focus on the self and display a sense of reluctance to achieve the classical adulthood markers of stable work, intimacy, and more recently, they delay procreation (Arnett & Tanner, 2006). Films such as *Failure to Launch* (Aversano, 2006) have reified emerging adolescence as a "truth," but have not posited nature or nurture as explanatory. So, while we locate emerging adulthood and even adolescence in this chapter because of their coherence with the axioms of developmental theories, the extent to which they belong in other theoretical categories such as environmental theories, is increasingly reasonable to ask.

Over the past several decades, there has been an increasing focus on aging. As noted earlier, while Erikson first addressed aging as a stage of reflection rather than active growth and development, numerous theorists and researchers have examined and characterized the elder years as a time of active engagement in growth and development. For example, Levinson (1978) posed a grand theory of the life cycle, characterizing adults as evolving through change in life structures. According to Levinson, adulthood is a period that synthesizes both stability and transition throughout three sequential stages: early, middle, and late adulthood. An important tenet of Levinson's theory is the recognition that each stage is not homogenous, but rather is characterized by uncertainty at entry that settles and becomes stable as the chronological stage advances. How each stage unfolds is explained by one's childhood foundation, within the context of social, economic, and cultural factors in one's environment. Levinson used the metaphor of seasons to explain the qualitative differences among life cycle stages.

Roger Gould (1979) posed a chronological theory in which passage of time and adulthood maturity was marked by an individual's relinquishment of the concept of safety and protection from parental figures. By the age of 35, Gould prescribes the desirability of complexity and mortality.

Recent theories of aging have increased in their complexity. As the population has aged, developmental theories have lengthened their gaze, moving from the notion that completion of adolescence was the end of growth and development to the identification of adulthood and elder years as vital and worthy. This is in large part because the graying of America theory, which explains elders as in decline and in a period of life review, is no longer relevant to the descriptive experience of many people who have surpassed the life spans that were typical in Freud's chronological time.

Initially, grand theories characterized aging as a time of disengagement from life roles and activities (Cumming & Henry, 1961).

> *If we would see Lila through this lens, we might explain her recent quiescence as a time of withdrawal from roles in preparation for death.*

However, in response, theorists such as Neugarten and her contemporaries (1968) advanced a more optimistic perspective in which they viewed aging as a continuation of one's life and lifestyle.

> *From this perspective, Lila's quiescence would be explained as an extension of her typical behavior and personality style.*

Building on the amalgamation of cohort and network perspectives, Antonucci, Birditt, and Akiyama (2009) have focused their grand gaze on aging with the *convoy model* of aging. Through this framework, development is facilitated by the quality of the collaboration, so to speak, between one's intrinsic features and the individual's social network. Although diverse in configuration and magnitude, convoy theory holds three types of social support as essential for development in aging: (1) aid, (2) affect, and (3) affirmation. These terms are broad interpretations of assistance, emotional support, and valuation afforded to each individual. Each must therefore be present, positive, and perceived as such in order for aging to engender health and wellness. Empirical support for this theory has been generated through numerous studies that employ multiple methods of inquiry.

Also portraying aging as integrative of corpus and conditions, Weiner (2010) journalistically detailed views of aging that locate it within a genetic perimeter but then indict organic decline and mortality as pathological conditions in need of cure. Logically linked to this current viewpoint and consistent with developmental theory, Axiom 1, which posits all human development as a process of aging, Weiner notes that contrary to the popular notion that gerontology focuses exclusively on the later years of life, gerontologists are becoming increasingly concerned with aging as an undesirable condition beginning at birth or even prior to that event.

From this perspective, Lila's "undesirable" condition would be diagnosed as pathology and treated in order to be cured.

Goldsmith (2004) and Konner (2010) expanded developmental theory beyond the limits of the human life span to the chronology of evolution. Goldsmith (2004) divided grand evolutionary theories of aging into two categories, adaptive and nonadaptive. Adaptive theories suggest that aging is an evolutionary process, not as characterized by Darwin, but rather explained as evolvability. According to Darwin, aging was antithetical to natural selection. In other words, the characteristics that caused aging decreased survival, and thus were not adaptive. However, genetic research has suggested that longevity of the life span is an important evolutionary characteristic in advancing the genetic strength of humans as a species, and thus the evolvability explanation has emerged. Nonadaptive theories explain aging as a decline process in which aging is an innate limitation of any life form.

Evolvability theorists would explain Lila's old age as advancing survival of humans, while nonadaptive theorists would explain her nonreproductive years beyond menopause as wasted within the scheme of survival of the fittest.

Konner (2010) queries the roles of genetics and evolutionary theory in explaining the passage of the fetus and young child through developmental milestones. "Mind is bathed in culture because biology makes it so" (p. 8). This eloquent quotation refers to Konner's claim that the contemporary confluence of genetic, neuroimaging and anthropological methods of inquiry foregrounds the role of evolution in skill acquisition in the developing child.

The grand theories presented in this chapter are just several among many. Chapter 5 illustrates that theories of motor development do not necessarily support contemporary grand theories of growth in aging, as there is no way to deny the changes in bodies, at least in this decade, as we pass through time (Basseches, 1984). As we proceed to the next chapters, keep in mind how these two views of human aging can be both complementary and conflictual.

Development as Nations

Before leaving grand theories, it is helpful to briefly address the theories of human development and capabilities posited by Nussbaum and Sen. According to the classical perspectives of Nussbaum and Sen (1993) and other scholars who developed the human development and capabilities framework, governments, policies, and economic systems are arranged in a hierarchy of maturity. The most mature not only provide rights and freedoms, but also enable citizens to reach their fully functional capacity and mature as well, as they so choose (Nussbaum, 2007; Sen, 2007, 2009). As noted, we introduced these frameworks in the chapter on development as they move beyond dualism in theorizing about maturity and development as the amalgamation of policy, regulation, resources, and people. Chapter 13 takes on the human rights slant of this broad approach to the development of human potential as a right of mature societies.

Evidence

Considering the iconic status of developmental theory in directing social expectations as well as professional and praxis decisions (even to the point of institutionalizing grade levels in public school), it is curious to note the absence of systematic inquiry as the basis for classical theory development and verification. Looking at the purpose and application of developmental theory, we note that these theories identify the commonalities within groups and the differences between varied groups. Thus, methodology to support these claims should befit the intellectual work. However, as briefly mentioned in the discussion of psychoanalysis, and as the diverse developmental theories that have emerged since these seminal theories have been advanced will reveal, many developmental theories are supported by case studies or sampling methods with limited nomothetic application. For example, a major criticism of Freud's thinking is that his case study and internally reflective methods do not meet basic epistemic standards to be called science (Popper, 1959). Moreover, inference of the three divisions of the mind—id, ego, and superego—from analysis of dream content and hypnotic-induced evidence is suspect in its support for Freud's claims.

Equally as methodologically culpable is Erik Erickson, who relied in large part on case studies of famous men to develop his theory (Cramer, Flynn, & LaFave, n.d.). More recent theories such as Levinson's (1978; Levinson & Darrow, 1973) have been criticized for methodological shortcomings, including the introduction of sampling bias into theory development, rendering broad generalization unsupported by empirical evidence (Levinson & Darrow, 1973).

We concur with the methodological criticisms of major developmental theory. However, these theories are works of literature and art in their own right and perhaps can be appreciated as such. While we can ask for evidence to guide our use of theory, reconceptualizing theory as metaphor and image allows us to detemine the resonance of theory with our professional hearts and judgements, ergo abduction. We are not suggesting that systematic evidence be eschewed as the basis for use of theory. However, as discussed in detail in subsequent chapters, theory as "map" opens the door for alternative evidentiary structures and material.

More recent theory, such as evolutionary and convoy theory, do meet Popper's requirments for science, in that they test constructs using nomothetic systematic inquiry strategies. What may be diminished through these nomothetic methods, however, is the uniqueness of individual maturation within theoretical parameters.

Summary

This chapter examined exemplars of grand developmental theories, of those which describe and explain the whole human passing through segments of a lifetime of growth and maturation. The discussion began with Freud, whose theories are not only relevant today in their own right, but have provided the platform for much debate, and a host of theoretical responses from acceptance to outright rejection. The chapter then moved forward in our own chronology of grand theories to visit with Erikson, who expanded previous growth beyond early adulthood to one's change in older years. Moving into the 20th century, Levinson and Gould were identified as seminal thinkers, followed by a broad methodological critique of grand developmental theory. Finally, the chapter located theories that move beyond development as individual movement through predetermined scripts; these look at the maturation of people in environment and then at people as environment.

References

American Psychiatric Association. (2010). *DSM-5: The future of psychiatric diagnosis*. Retrieved from Future of the DSM5: http://www.dsm5.0rg/Pages/Default.aspx

Antonucci, T., Birditt, K., & Akiyama, H. (2009). The convoy model. In E. L. Bengtson, M. Silverstein, & N. Putney (Eds.), *Handbook of theories of aging* (pp. 248–251). New York: Springer.

Arnett, J. J., & Tanner, J. L. (2006). *Emerging adults in America: Coming of age in the 21st century.* Washington, DC: American Psychological Association.

Aversano, S. (Producer), Astle, T., Ember, M. (Writers), & Dey, T. (Director). (2006). *Failure to Launch* [Motion Picture]. United States: Paramount.

Basseches, M. (1984). *Dialectical thinking and adult development.* Norwood, NJ: Ablex.

Blasius, M. (2001). *Sexual identities, queer politics.* Princeton, NJ: Princeton University Press.

Bloch, S., & Singh, B. (2007). *Foundations of clinical psychiatry* (3rd ed.). Melbourne, Australia: Melbourne University Press.

Calvin, W. H. (2004). *A brief history of the mind: From apes to intellect and beyond.* New York: Oxford University Press.

Committee on Nomenclature and Statistics of the American Psychiatric Association. (1968). *DSM-II diagnostic and statistical manual of mental disorders* (2nd ed.). Washington, DC: American Psychiatric Association.

Cramer, C., Flynn, B., & LaFave, A. (n.d.). *Critiques & controversies of Erikson.* Retrieved from Erik Erikson's 8 Stages of Psychosocial Development: http://web.cortland.edu/andersmd/ERIK/crit.HTML

Cumming, E., & Henry, W. (1961). *Growing old: The process of disengagement.* New York: Basic Books.

Erikson, E. H. (1958). *Young man Luther: A study in psychoanalysis and history.* New York: W. W. Norton.

Erikson, E. H. (1980). *Identity and the life cycle.* New York: W. W. Norton.

Erikson, E. H. (1982). *The life cycle completed: .* New York: W. W. Norton.

Erikson, E. H. (1993). *Gandhi's truth.* New York: W. W. Norton.

Freud, S. (1938). *The basic writings of Sigmund Freud.* (A. A. Brill, Trans.). New York: Modern Library.

Freud, S. (1949). *An outline of psychoanalysis.* New York: W. W. Norton.

Freud, S. (1964). New introductory lectures on psychoanalysis. In J. Strachey (Ed.), *The standard edition of the complete psychological works of Sigmund Freud* (Vol. 22, pp. 11–12). London: Hogarth.

Freud S. (1966). *Standard edition of the complete psychological works of Sigmund Freud.* (J. Strachey, Trans.). London: Hogarth Press and the Institute of Psycho-Analysis.

Giovacchini, P. (1977). Psychoanalysis. In R. Corsini (Ed.), *Current personality theories* (pp. 15–43). Ithasca, IL: F. E. Peacock.

Goldsmith, T. C. (2004). Aging as an evolved characteristic: Weismann's theory reconsidered. *Medical Hypotheses, 62*(2), 304–308.

Gould, R. L. (1979). *Transformations: Growth and change in adult life.* New York: Simon & Schuster.

Henig, R. M. (2010, August 22). What is it about 20-somethings? *New York Times Magazine,* 28–37.

Hoare, C. H. (2002). *Erikson on development in adulthood: New insights from the unpublished papers.* New York: Oxford University Press.

Jung Center. (2010). *The Jung page.* Retrieved from http://www.cgjungpage.org/

Kahn, M. (2002). *Basic Freud: Psychoanalytic thought for the 21st century.* New York: Basic Books.

Kail, R., & Cavanaugh, J. (2009). *Human development: A life-span view* (5th ed.). Belmont, CA: Wadsworth.

King, R. (2004, February). *Adolescence.* Retrieved from King's psychology Network: http://www.psyking.net/id183.htm

Konner, M. (2010). *The evolution of childhood: Relationships, emotion, mind.* Cambridge, MA: Harvard University Press.

Konstam, V. (2007). *Emerging and young adulthood: Coming of age in the 21st century.* New York: Springer Science.

Kramer, P. (2006). *Freud: Inventor of the modern mind.* New York: HarperCollins.

L'Abate, L. (1994). *A theory of personality development.* New York: Wiley.

Levinson, D. J., & Darrow, C. N. (1973). *The seasons of a man's life.* New York: Random House.

Levinson, D. J., with Darrow, C. N, Klein, E. B. & Levinson, M. (1978). *Seasons of a man's life.* New York: Random House.

Loftus, E. F. (1993). The reality of repressed memories. *American Psychologist, 48,* 518–537.

Neugarten, B. L. (1968). *Middle age and aging: A reader in social psychology.* Chicago: University of Chicago Press.

Nussbaum, M. C. (2007). *Frontiers of justice: Disability, nationality, species membership.* Cambridge, MA: Belknap Press.

Nussbaum, M., & Sen, A. (1993). *The quality of life.* Oxford, UK: Clarendon.

O'Neil, J. A. (1998). *Tallis on Freud.* Retrieved from Online Dictionary of Mental Health: http://human nature.com/freud/oneil.html

Pennington, B. (2002). *The development of psychopathology: Nature and nurture.* New York: Guilford Press.

Phares, E. J., & Chaplin, W. F. (1997). *Introduction to personality* (4th ed.). New York: Longman.

Popper, K. (1959). *The logic of scientific discovery.* New York: Basic Books.

Sen, A. (2007). *Identity and violence: The illusion of destiny.* New York: Penguin.

Sen, A. (2009). *The idea of justice.* Cambridge, MA: Belknap Press of Harvard University Press.

Sharkey, W. (1997). *Erik Erikson.* Retrieved from http://www.muskingum.edu/Npsych/psycweb/history/erikson.htm

Sigelman, C. K., & Rider, E. A. (2009). *Life-span human development.* Belmont, CA: Cengage.

Talburt, S. (2004). Constructions of LGBT youth: Opening up subject positions. *Theory Into Practice, 43*(2), 116–121.

Tallis, R. C. (2001). *Burying Freud.* Retrieved from Online Dictionary of Mental Health: http://human-nature.com/ freud/tallis.html

Thomas, M. (2001). *Recent theories of human development.* Thousand Oaks, CA: Sage.

Thornton, S. P. (2001). *Sigmund Freud.* Retrieved from Internet Encyclopedia of Philosophy: http://www.iep.utm .edu/f/freud.htm

von Brücke, E. W. (1866). *Diep Physiologie der Farben für die Zwecke der Kunstgewerbe* [Psychology of colors for the purpose of arts and crafts]. Leipzig, Germany: S. Huzel.

Weiner, J. (2010). *Long for this world.* New York: HarperCollins.

5

Specific Developmental Theories

Looking at Individuals Developing as Parts

This chapter discusses how developmental theorists have parsed the passage, and thus the development, of humans over time into specific descriptive and functional arenas, such as cognitive, moral, motor, and social behavior. Different from grand theories which describe human journeys as the movement of a total person through a full or part of a chronological life span, the theories in this chapter seek to describe and explain specific domains of behavior, appearance, and experience as individuals unfold, mature, and in some cases, decline over the longitude of a human life. All of the theories discussed in this chapter conform to the axioms advanced in Chapter 3. Again, because of its vast subject area, we cannot discuss the universe of theories that are concerned with specifics of human development in this chapter, and instead refer to the excellent reviews of theory that have been written. We have selected areas that we believe to be central to professional practice because of their substance and analytic potency. To us, no single domain of concern is any more important than another, so we urge you to critically read further and explore areas of human description and explanation to which are not attended here. So, let us now proceed to examine parts of humans in development.

Predeterministic Theories of Cognitive Development

Predeterministic cognitive developmental theorists seek to describe and explain human thought and learning as predetermined to develop and change over chronological time. Scholars such as Jean-Jacques Rosseau and William James (Bloom, 2010) wrote about infant cognition as disorganized and even "idiocy," which only could mature and develop with age. The most prominent, credible, and perhaps most influential classical theorist who described cognitive development as a series of longitudinal steps is Jean Piaget. His work has been seminal as the foundation for much of the age related educational and social policy and practice in the United States, and other countries as well. Let us visit with his ideas now.

Jean Piaget

Although most people know Jean Piaget (1896–1980) as foremost among developmental psychologists, he considered himself a genetic epistemologist. Piaget's early work focused on invertebrates, particularly mollusks. After obtaining his zoology degree in 1918, his interests and studies turned to psychology, to which he applied his early experiences in genetic epistemology. A close examination of his work will reveal the genetic influence on his explanatory biological perspective for human thinking. Of particular note and central to this thinking was the acceptance of the validity of knowledge on the basis of how it was constructed. For example, knowledge can be created by personal experience or through belief with no discernable object.

Piaget suggested that through acting on their environments and reasoning about them, individuals create their own knowledge from their experience of their *exterior* environments or what he referred to as the *process of constructivism* (Moseley, 2005). Inherent in this approach was the preference for higher-level thinking based on typical capacity to act, rendered credible through specific logico-deductive processes. Thus, to Piaget, one proceeded through sequential stages of cognition until the most desirable process, the ability to abstract through logical internal processes, was reached. This capacity, according to Piaget, distinguished humans from the animal world. The acquisition of abstract reasoning proceeded through an orderly, sequential, developmental process over longitudinal time that Piaget explained as genetically predetermined, unfolding with some influences from the exterior environment (Huitt & Hummel, 2003; Perry, 2005). Yet, the role of dialectic conflict in producing knowledge is also included in Piaget's theories through processes of accommodation, discussed later in this chapter (Morra, Gobbo, Marini, & Sheese, 2009).

It is interesting to note the influence of thinkers who were contemporaries of Piaget. An early influential theorist was Carl Jung, who also brought a biological explanatory lens to his description of human ontogeny (development of individual humans over time), as well as human phylogeny (development of human species over time). Piaget was also influenced, but from a negative perspective, by Alfred Binet, who was known for the development of standardized intelligence testing. Because Piaget was concerned with cognitive processes, he departed from Binet, who evaluated children's intelligence on the basis of content (Bringuier & Piaget, 1989). Counter to Binet's testing approach that scored children's intelligence on correct and incorrect responses to questions, Piaget sought to describe cognitive development through several processes, including observing his own children and conducting interviews to ascertain the process of their reasoning. Piaget developed and validated his theories using laboratory observation and interviews of his subjects. Observations of children playing and open-ended interviews with children of diverse ages created the data for his inferences about how children learned, reasoned, and developed. Through this early data collection, Piaget developed his notion of *egocentric thinking* in children. That is, different from Freud, who described egocentricity as a moral and immature personality trait, Piaget suggested that egocentrism, or idiosyncratic viewpoints, distinguished the child's reasoning from more mature reasoning. In essence, egocentric thinking is defined as the inability to see the world from others' points of view.

> *Consider Samantha. At age 4, Samantha's father took her for her first ride in his small Cessna airplane. Samantha and her mother were sitting in the back seat together, and as the plane left the runway, Samantha's quizzical expression turned to one of distress. Noticing her discomfort, Samantha's mother asked her what was wrong. In a tiny voice, Samantha said, "When are we going to get small and will it hurt?"*

From Samantha's viewpoint, and her limited experience of seeing airplanes at a distance, where they looked tiny to her, Piaget conceptualized her conclusion that the planes shrank in size as they proceeded to fly away from her as egocentric reasoning. At this young stage of cognitive development, Piaget posited that children can only reason on the basis of how they have been able to influence and perceive their environment, and thus, egocentric reasoning is descriptive of that phenomenon.

THINKING POINT

List other examples that illustrate egocentric thinking as described by Piaget.

Piaget's methods of data collection evolved after the first decade or two so that his preferred strategy of information gathering consisted of observing subjects' performances on predetermined concrete tasks, and then interviewing them about the cognitive processes they used in performance. Of all the research on children that Piaget completed, perhaps none was more influential on his own thinking than his observations of his own children. This prolonged longitudinal observation provided the primary data on which he developed his theories of cognitive development (Boeree, 1999; Campbell, 2006). However, his methods have been criticized for their narrow focus and underestimation of children's cognitive capacity (Moseley, 2005).

With an intellectual foundation in the biological sciences, as noted, Piaget compared and contrasted humans and animals and identified the capacity to engage in abstract symbolic reasoning (Piaget, 1970) as the descriptor that distinguished humans from all other animals. From an ontological perspective, Piaget drew parallels between the cognition of infants and youth and animals. He concluded that the earliest form of human reasoning was shared with animals in the form of primitive reflexes that protect organisms and drive action.

Consider an infant. Neonates have an innate sucking response.

Piaget explained this behavior as early cognition, but why? According to Piaget, even reflexive behaviors are explained as purposive. In other words, acting on one's environment, whether reflexively or voluntarily, elicits a response that produces learning. Thus, as a child moves and senses his or her world, the child learns through that behavior.

Over chronological time, Piaget observed the replacement of primitive reflexes with increasingly complex interior cognitive structures. He labeled these structures *schemata*. More specifically, schemata are knowledge structures that both form the scaffold for new knowledge and change as new learning takes place.

Piaget brought his biological background to bear on his understanding of human thought. From an interior biologic perspective, he explained chronological change as an internally driven balancing act of cognitive structures with environmental demands (Huitt & Hummel, 2003; Mahoney, 2003).

Piaget suggested four explanatory variables for cognitive maturation: "heredity, physical experience, social transmission, and equilibrium" (as cited in Thomas, 2001, p. 17). By heredity, Piaget referred to the inherited traits that shape cognitive strengths and the speed with which one passes through cognitive stages of development (see Table 5.1). Interaction with the physical world through manipulating objects and acting on one's environment through motor activity explain basic early learning, after which social transformation (being taught by others) shapes cognitive performance. Equilibrium balances each of the three explanations. It is important to emphasize here that motor activity, even after infancy is completed, is considered essential to cognitive development, rendering those with atypical motor skills at risk for cognitive abnormality within Piaget's framework.

Consider Zach, a 2-year-old boy who was born without arms. Because he has been unable to manipulate objects in his hands, turn them over to see all sides, and even put them in his mouth, he has not been able to explore his environment in a typical fashion. According to Piaget, Zach's physical limitations would impede his ability to form schemata about objects and their dimensions and thus might place Zach at risk for delayed cognitive development.

Moreover, Piaget's prescription of the critical nature of social transformation in producing cognitive competence raises questions about the degree to which children in environments with limited structures, teaching, and other opportunities can attain cognitive maturation.

Now think of Ory, a 4-year-old boy who lives with his parents in a remote rural area. Most of Ory's time is spent playing with his dog, since his parents are busy working in the blueberry fields. Because of their rural location, the family does not have a television and can receive only one radio station. Without the social transformation opportunity, Piaget would be skeptical about Ory's potential to cognitively develop at a pace similar to children who have social interaction with a host of people representing a range of ages.

THINKING POINT

Can you think of other examples that illustrate how Piaget's theory is limiting to the concept of human diversity?

Piaget further explained the changes in human thinking as the function of the two interacting dialectical processes: assimilation and accommodation. Using *assimilation,* humans view the world through their existing cognitive structures or schemata.

Consider Samantha again. She applied her previous observations of airplanes to reason about her imminent danger of being inside of a shrinking object.

Accommodation, on the other hand, through conflict and ultimate stage appropriate resolution, is the process in which we change our cognitive schemes to adapt to information presented in the environment (Morra, Gobbo, Marini, & Sheese, 2009).

Once Samantha learned that the plane did not shrink as it took off, she learned something new and accommodated her thinking to it. Think also of the infant who cries reflexively at birth. That child may learn that crying precipitates environmental changes such as the immediate appearance of his mother, thus his cries become increasingly intentional over time as he accommodates to new information.

More recently, theorists have built on accommodation and assimilation processes to propose the process of scaffolding. Similar to assimilation, scaffolding begins with the acquisition of a new concept or information; this is then associated with an existing foundational concept. Through relating old and new concepts, learning occurs and incrementally builds on previous knowledge (Williams, Huang, & Bargh, 2009).

We have located Piaget in the developmental specific category of theorists because of his sequential and cumulative taxonomy of cognitive development over chronology. He described four periods of development, each with substages. Through the dialectical interaction of assimilation and accommodation, humans move through the four overarching stages of chronological cognitive development presented in Table 5.1. Each stage is qualitatively different from, more complex than, and builds on previous stages. Moreover, one does not lose the schemata from previous stages over time, but rather retains and invokes them when appropriate.

Table 5.1 presents the descriptive elements of each stage of cognitive development, as theorized by Piaget (Child Development Institute, 2000–2010; Gruber & Voneche, 1995; Huitt & Hummel, 2003; Inhelder & Piaget; 1958; Piaget, 1954, 1985).

Table 5.1 Piaget's Stages of Cognitive Development

Cognitive Stage	Approximate Age*	Behavioral Explanation of Learning	Description of Behaviors	Examples
Sensorimotor period (birth–2 years)	Birth–2 months	Primitive reflexes to internal and external stimuli	Sucking reflex, startle reflex	Infant's coordination and strength of reflexes increases.
	1–5 months	Reflexes beginning to modify in response to experience	Finding that thumb sucking is pleasurable	Infant's inadvertent responses to experiences produce pleasure, which the infant attempts to reproduce.
	4–10 months	Increased curiosity about experiencing and manipulating the environment	Grasping, shaking, sucking objects, vocalization	Infant begins to learn about the world through intentionally exploring objects.
	7–14 months	Intentional behavior to produce results	Crying for attention, banging an object to produce noise	Child learns that specific behaviors produce specific ends.
	11–20 months	Experimentation by repeating actions with different objects or in different contexts for the purpose of ascertaining what will happen	Shaking different objects to see what will happen	Child learns the effects of behaviors with different objects or situations.
	16–26 months	Beginning use of symbolism in environmental interactions	Waving and saying "bye bye" to convey the same thing	Child learns to anticipate the effects of behaviors and act accordingly.
Preoperational phase	2–5 years	Egocentric and idiosyncratic thinking	Taking another child's toy without thought for consequences for the other child	Child learns and values ideas, beliefs, and emotions.

Cognitive Stage	Approximate Age*	Behavioral Explanation of Learning	Description of Behaviors	Examples
Preoperational phase (contd.)	4–8 years	Intuitive thinking, understanding rules, and acquisition of logical thought	Asking another child for a toy because grabbing it will cause the other child to cry and result in punishment	Child learns about rules and applies them to problem solving.
Concrete operational	6–13 years	Diminishing egocentric thinking, emerging problem solving using concrete data, actions yielding consistent results	Taking a ball of clay, shaping it into a snake, then reshaping it into a ball again; using reasoning tools such as simple addition and subtraction	Child learns that there are perspectives and interests different from one's own; logical cognitive operations using concrete data are applied.
Formal operational	11 years–adulthood	Developing mental operational skills such as abstract and hypothetical reasoning	Successfully completing math problems using concepts such as if $a + b = c$, then $c - b = a$	Individual learns to apply inductive and deductive logic to abstract situations and problems.

*Ages overlap to signify a range of typical acquisition of cognitive abilities.

As Table 5.1 illustrates, Piaget named and described the typical qualities and processes in each stage of cognitive development. Moreover, he prescribed the qualitative nature of cognition at each stage and any deviations therefrom were considered not normal. Piaget's work has been particularly influential in the education field because of his explanatory association between children's chronological age and their expected learning abilities (Smith, 1997).

Think of typical public education in elementary, junior high, and high school. Grades are arranged according to age, and age cohorts proceed through classes together to a greater or lesser extent. Some children are considered "gifted" and are often pulled out of classes for average students and placed in accelerated learning environments.

The children who are considered "slow learners" are also frequently pulled out of classes for average children and are placed in remedial or special education environments. However, for the most part, children who are considered to be of average intelligence proceed to advance in their education in a similar fashion, with each grade providing increasingly complex learning opportunities and expectations. If a child falls behind, the child can be "left back" to repeat a grade, but this action is socially undesirable because of the longitudinal theoretical assumption that social development follows a similar chronological trajectory to cognitive development.

Maria Montessori

While not considered to be a Piagetian thinker per se, we warrant discussion of Maria Montessori (1870–1952) here, given that she shares the influential spotlight with Piaget in educational theory. While the methods that she suggested to foster learning development differed from Piaget's, she too was a predeterminist. Learning capacity, according to Montessori, is innate and natural and can be best nurtured through an exterior environment that structures learning activity, exploration, and manipulation in the "correct" manner. Moreover, Montessori's age ranges were broader than Piaget's, perhaps because she developed her theory on atypical students who were considered cognitively impaired (Badrova, 2003).

> *Consider Kaitlin, a 6-year-old female, who was falling behind the other students in her first-grade public school. Her mother decided, then, to send her to a Montessori-based school. The class was not limited by age, but rather environments were structured with objects and learning materials that had to be mastered in a specific fashion before a student could move on to more complex tasks. Students could choose their activity, as Montessori based her methods on the tenet of innate curiosity as a motivator and catalyst for learning.*

Neo-Piagetian Thinkers

As noted before the detour to Montessori's theoretical home, Piaget, building on the work before him, identified predetermined genetic maturation as a central explanation for cognitive development. Neo-Piagetians, to a greater or lesser degree, view both description and explanation in the same light that Piaget proposed. However, as might be expected, each builds on Piaget's initial framework through the addition or revision of descriptive or explanatory variables. Using Piaget's framework of content-free structural development, Basseches (1984) added a fifth stage, postformal operations, to Piaget's theory, asserting that formal operational thinkers use their abstract skills to obtain the single best answer to a problem, whereas postformal thinkers use dialectical reasoning within a multicausal context (Baltes, 1984). Thus, according to Basseches (1984), being able to understand that there are multiple explanations for phenomena, each of equal viability, and then using that understanding as the basis for reasoning about relativity rather than absolutes, is a more advanced cognitive structure than simply being able to reason about ideas themselves. Looking back to abduction links this thinking style with logic and inquiry.

> *Daniel shattered his hip, and over three years, had six operations, after which his physicians told him that in order to walk, he would have to have his hip fused. This option was frightening for Daniel, since he was a competitive distance runner. In hopes that he would find other options to continue to run, Daniel sought counseling from a social worker. Using formal operational thinking, the first social worker followed evidence-based practice and provided empathy and suggestions for Daniel's future that involved finding an alternative sport to occupy the time that he would have devoted to running. Daniel then consulted a second*

social worker. As a postformal thinker, the social worker put herself in Daniel's place to try to see his perspective and then sought options not to supplant Daniel's beloved sport, but to help him run adaptively.

THINKING POINT

In thinking about Basseches's theory, it is surprising, given the aging population in the U.S., we are not more sensitive to and accepting of pluralism. How do you think that looking at differences between countries with diverse life spans could be an important agenda in examining and verifying the construct of postformal thinking?

Case (as cited in Thomas, 2001; Morra, Gobbo, Marini, & Sheese, 2009) also revised and detailed the descriptive elements of Piaget's sensorimotor, preoperational, concrete, and formal operational divisions, but rather than adding a stage, did so by specifying descriptive substages to differentiate thinking processes within Piaget's original descriptive taxonomy. By further breaking down each of the four major stages into smaller descriptive units, Case was able to account for differences in thinking among the same age cohort without violating the explanatory tenets of Piaget's seminal work. Reflecting contemporary genetics in his theory, Case added genetic factors to Piaget's predeterministic explanation as well (as cited in Thomas, 2001, p. 110).

Mary observed two sisters in her dance class. Katie was a 7-year-old, thin child and her sister, Jannah, was an 8-year-old girl who was somewhat overweight. In dance class, Katie was agile but not as quick as Jannah in learning new ballet positions and moves. Given their similar ages and diverse body shapes, Mary was surprised that their learning styles and demonstration of their learning were so different and opposite of what Mary expected respectively. But after both sisters were in Mary's class for a few months, Mary became familiar with their backgrounds and school performance. She learned that Katie preferred reading to movement-oriented activities and thus excelled, like her mother, in academics. Jannah, on the other hand, was just like her father, who loved to dance, engage in sports, and enjoy his mealtimes.

In addition to the scholars mentioned previously, several other trends have been important in neo-Piagetian thought. First, scholars have criticized and expanded Piaget's narrow definition of cognition as primarily logico-deductive to more domains of thinking, so to speak. Morra, Gobbo, Marini, and Sheese (2009) identify the inclusion of information processing theory within neo-Piagetian theories of the late 20th century. To us, an important and useful addition to Piaget's descriptive viewpoint suggested by neo-Piagetian researchers is the assertion of thought as a system of cognitive meaning making in which stages are not universal, discrete, or merely comprised of task-specific skills (Morra, Gobbo, Marini, & Sheese, 2009).

The example of Jannah and Mary illustrates this concept and its application to finding and understanding diversity within cognitive development. Understanding diversity is the variation and uniqueness of individual thought, even within posited stages of cognitive development. Thus, an individual can excel in one or more domains of cognition without being age appropriate in all (Moseley, 2005).

Moral Development

Closely tied to cognitive development is moral reasoning. Moral development refers to the increasingly complex descriptions and explanations over time for value acquisition, use, and judgments about right or wrong, good and bad, desirable and undesirable. Concern with morality has been a major theme in history, documented in the early writings of the Greek thinkers. And of course, Quetelet, the mathematician in the 19th century who developed the bell-shaped curve, and applied this statistical thinking to the definition of moral man was a founding father of moral developmental theory (DePoy & Gilson, 2007). We place moral development adjacent to the domain of cognition, because within developmental theories, many theorists view moral decision making as a series of cognitive operations that are delimited by their content, that of deliberating on what is correct, right, just, and ethical.

As an individual passes through time, developmental moral theorists, including Piaget, tie the complexity and worth of moral reasoning to cognitive maturation. What is implied is that those who mature typically and navigate cognitive growth as prescribed also can attain desirable levels of moral reasoning. However, consider the converse scenario. As noted in the discussion of Piaget's theory of cognitive maturation, the centrality of typical physical skill and richness of one's social transformative environment are critical in attaining cognitive competence, without which moral competence cannot be attained either.

Consider Ory again. Without playmates in his rural environment, will he know about the acceptable values of sharing and respect for other children?

Jean Piaget

Piaget posited a two-stage theory of moral development, closely linked to his stages of cognitive growth. According to Piaget, until age 7, children are described as residing in an amoral stage. It is not until concrete operations that children are described as moral reasoners, making decisions on the basis of absolutes. That is to say, behavior is right or wrong with no shades of deviation. Bad behaviors beget punishment despite the intentionality of an act (Morra, Gobbo, Marini, & Sheese, 2009). In the next stage, autonomous morality, children move from absolute thinking to relativistic reasoning. Moral rules are understood within a social context, and can be changed. According to Piaget, two interactive factors are important in explaining moral development, cognitive structures and social variables.

Both Katie and Jannah were raised in the same family with the same parents, and same behavioral expectations. One day, after dance class, Jannah and Katie were walking home. Instructed by their parents not to stop anywhere, they proceeded to walk and chat until Katie saw a woman a few yards ahead of them drop a five-dollar bill on the ground. Katie, who was the youngest, reasoned that they should just go home and leave the money on the ground. She feared that if they disobeyed their parents, they would and should be punished. But Jannah picked up the money and ran ahead to return it to the woman. She reasoned that if her intentions were "good," then her parents would not punish the sisters for coming home a bit late.

Lawrence Kohlberg

Lawrence Kohlberg (1927–1987) was a developmental psychologist who was heavily influenced by Piaget and J. M. Baldwin (Kohlberg, 1984). In the 1970s, he became well-known for his focus on describing and explaining moral development as three sequentially acquired grand levels of reasoning about right and wrong, each with substages (Kohlberg, 1984, 1986; Rich & DeVitis, 1994). A former student of Piaget, Kohlberg posited two interactive factors, genetically predetermined maturation and social experiences, as the explanatory basis for moral development.

As depicted in Table 5.2, Kohlberg described three sequential levels of cognitive development, each with discrete stages. He explained that individuals do not necessarily advance through stages; in essence postulating that few reach Stages 5 or 6.

The preconventional level consisting of three stages is characterized by the primacy of one's individual interests. The conventional level consists of two stages and is the level at which most adults typically operate. Moral judgments are based on norms and rules that exist in social contexts, such as family, in-group, community, and country. Loyalty to others and maintaining social order are valued on their own merits. Kohlberg describes the postconventional level as the highest level of moral attainment, and he suggests this type of reasoning is achieved by only a select few. At this level, moral reasoning is founded on a set of interior values and beliefs about right and wrong, despite the popularity of those beliefs and related consequences (Kail & Cavanaugh, 2010; Kohlberg, 1984, 1986). Table 5.2 allows further exploration of Kohlberg's descriptions of discrete stages within these three levels.

Table 5.2 Kohlberg's Levels and Stages of Moral Development

Level 1: Preconventional **Punishment and Reward Orientation**	Infants and children, adolescents, adults	Stage 0	Egocentric judgment	Decisions are based on what one likes and does not like or what helps or hurts, with no concept of rules.
		Stage 1	Heteronomous morality and obedience to authority	Obedience to authority and rules, right and wrong are determined by authority figures who also apply consequences.

(Continued)

Table 5.2 (Continued)

		Stage 2	Individualistic and instrumental relativistic thinking	Right and wrong are based on one's own interests but there is awareness of others' interests and exchange rewards. Punishment is to be avoided but is no longer an absolute indicator of right and wrong.
Level 2: Conventional **Social Norm Orientation**	Adolescents and adults	Stage 3	Interpersonally normative morality and concordance with social expectations	Good person-bad person orientation occurs in which people's motives, not necessarily actions, determine approval.
		Stage 4	Social system morality, law and order	Morality is based on laws and rules that maintain order and promote societal good. Compliance with laws, even those with which one disagrees, is moral.
Level 3: Postconventional **Internal Morals Orientation**	Some adults	Stage 5	Valuing human rights and social welfare	Adherence to rules promotes societal cohesion and benefits its members; however, laws become invalid when they fail to benefit individuals in society.
		Stage 6	Internal moral rules based on one's conscience and distributive justice	Internalized values such as social justice and individual rights may trump society's laws and rules.

Returning to Katie and Jannah, if we look at their behaviors, the reasoning of both girls can be explained in Kohlberg's taxonomy at the preconventional stage, with Katie situated at Stage 2 and Jannah at Stage 3.

Now consider Alan, a 36-year-old man who was just released from prison, where he served 9 months for larceny. He has just found out that his friend stole $156 from a locally owned gas station, and a plasma TV from Wal-Mart for his elderly, housebound mother valued at $1,500. Alan turned in his friend for the theft of $156, but did not say anything about the plasma TV. His reasoning would be explained by Kohlberg's highest postconventional level, in that Alan looked at his friend's altruistic act of giving to his mother as socially just and above the law.

Kohlberg developed and verified his initial theoretical propositions on a sample of 72 urban middle- and working-class boys in three age cohorts, 10, 13, and 16. In order to describe the reasoning process, not the final decision and action, Kohlberg's method involved posing an ethical dilemma to his subjects and recording both the factors that were important in an individual's cognitive deliberations, and how factors were used to derive a moral conclusion. This point provides a major area of criticism, in that Dehart, Sroufe, and Copper (2003) suggest that the behavioral consequences of moral judgment cannot be separated from the judgment process itself. Later in his career, Kohlberg diversified his sample to include girls and children who were incarcerated for delinquency, but his theory had been primarily developed and verified on a sample of boys. This gender bias was an important consideration for those who built on or challenged Kohlberg's notions of morality, such as Gilligan (1993). Gilligan's theories are examined in Chapter 8, and while she theorizes morality in girls and women, she is not included in this chapter because her thinking does not fall within the rubric of development and thus does not adhere to developmental axioms.

An important finding in recent research on moral development has countered the notion of infants and young children as amoral. As noted by Bloom (2010), classical developmental theories have portrayed infants as amoral at birth, thereby defining a major task of parenting as instilling a sense of right and wrong and fairness into their children. Studies being conducted at the Infant Cognition Center at Yale University (n.d.) have revealed that as children move out of neonate status and can enact intention, they have displayed not only self-focused moral thinking, but have applied this thinking to others as well. Although not communicated through words, infants participating in an experiment to hit a puppet who was determined to be acting unfairly towards another puppet (Bloom, 2010). This new knowledge raises many questions and challenges for parents, teachers, and others who have conceptualized their child-rearing jobs on the basis of morals as acquired over the longitude of development, linked to higher-level cognitive development, and in need of the mentorship and guidance of a watchful adult.

THINKING POINT

 What are the ethical dilemmas that emerge from applying predeterministic theories of moral reasoning to diverse populations and individuals?

Before leaving Piaget and Kohlberg, we want to bring your attention to the importance of these frameworks in another issue beyond academic promotion and parenting. As noted, in the United States, and other countries where public education is anchored on developmental principles, grades and curricula are organized according to age cohorts, with expected typical competencies universally distributed within each cohort. Thinking refracted through developmental theories places all neonates, except for those who are "abnormal" at birth, on an even plane with a common set of cognitive skills and to a large extent, theorizes an age cohort as an entity comprised of individuals who grow and mature at relatively the same rate or within a standard perimeter. Those who deviate from expectations are considered of substandard or superstandard intelligence and its cousin morality. However, given the emphasis on social input and the unequal access to transformative resources inherent in this educational system, the structure of schools in advancing only those who are typical to a higher grade is tautological to some extent. That is to say, without increasingly complex transformative opportunity, cognitive development as well as moral maturation in its wake may be limited or curtailed, yet unless one develops prescriptively, the individual does not have access to growth-producing opportunity.

Beyond Piaget and Kohlberg

There are numerous theorists who have approached morality as developmental. Contemporary theories not only are more complex in their definition and treatment of stages of moral development, but also bring other areas of human experience to bear on theorizing about morality. As an example, Hoffmann (2000) discusses moral development as prosocial, integrating one's social, emotional, and cognitive experiences within a developmental framework. Of particular importance in this approach is the role of empathy (an emotional response) to the development of a moral compass. What arouses empathy and then how it is applied to thinking and action are at the core of moral development, according to Hoffman. From birth, stages of prosocial moral development unfold. The tasks to be accomplished in order to reach higher order moral function include moving from egocentrism to the capacity to see the perspective of another. Further, the cognitive capacity to differentiate moral responses on the basis of intent, context, and character of the empathic object is critical in developing a full and sophisticated moral life. This capacity unfolds developmentally, but not simply as a linear trajectory. Rather, a series of moral scripts are inductively constructed over time through a process of cognitive-affective-social interaction.

The richness of Hoffman's theory of prosocial moral development lies in its complexity and application to biases that affect moral judgments. The relational locus between the empathizer and object of empathy is powerful in determining how the judgment will be framed and enacted. He therefore ties moral development to social justice marrying them as partners in social welfare thinking and action.

Consider Louis's moral judgment about unemployment compensation. Until he lost his job, he looked at recipients of this benefit as lazy and unmotivated. However, when he no longer had an income, he applied for support and justified it by need and contribution of his previous taxes to the fund. As his vantage point changed, his view of other recipients as moral beings did so as well.

Information Processing Over Time

We would be remiss to not include a discussion of information processing in this chapter. This theoretical approach uses the metaphor of a computer to depict the structure and processes of human thinking (Hetherington, Parke, Gauvain, & Locke, 2005;

Miller, 1956; Miller, Galanter, & Pribram, 1956; Siegler, DeLoache, & Eisenberg, 2006). Different from Piaget and neo-Piagetian predeterminists, theorists who advanced information processing models of cognition focus their explanations of cognitive development on the acquisition and precision of mental operations through experience over time, although to a greater or lesser degree, depending on the theorist, they recognize the presence of genetic structures as explanatory as well. Age related development in memory and problem-solving skills is therefore dependent on rehearsal of thinking practices as the medium through which individuals mature and are able to acquire high-level cognitive skills.

> *Consider remedial reading. Many approaches rely on intense practice of those skills that are not accomplished.*

Consistent with the computer metaphor, cognition involves the acquisition, storage, and retrieval of knowledge, as well as a series of encoding operations necessary to put information to use. Growth in these strategies, or what is referred to as *self-modification,* is the mechanism for the developmental trajectory (Hetherington, Parke, Gauvain, & Locke, 2005). Thus, development is not linked necessarily to age but to the quality of experience that one accumulates as one moves through longitudinal time (Kail & Cavanaugh, 2010; Siegler, DeLoache, & Eisenberg, 2006). So, while this approach to viewing cognition does not remand one's "normality" to a particular age or stage in human chronology, trajectory through time still takes center stage within the context of experiential-rich contexts.

> *Think of reading again. From the information processing perspective, the more time one reads, and the more varied the reading material, the more practiced one becomes, and thus, more complex reading skills can develop over time.*

Although similar to Piaget in locating time as the common denominator of development, the models of cognitive development advanced by Kail, Pellegrino, and Carter (1980) and Siegler, DeLoache, and Eisenberg (2006), along with their information-processing successors, account for individual differences in age cohorts, in that available resources and degree of cognitive practice can more readily explain variation. The same issue of tautology raised earlier is operative here. Because cognitive development in these theories is context dependent to a greater or lesser degree, the importance of thinking opportunity is critical for typical, sound, and sophisticated development. Without it, one cannot maximize cognitive maturation. However, if not able to process higher-level complex information, such thinking opportunities are not likely to be available, limiting cognitive growth, ergo circular reasoning that through this theoretical lens, truncates development.

> *A story on National Public Radio (2011) several years ago provides an excellent example of this approach to explaining cognitive development. The story recounted the benefits that preschool children derived from computerized learning toys. Attributed in large part to educational software, a disproportionately higher number of children enter kindergarten able to read. So,*

contrary to Piagetian determinism, which would lead us to explain reading as interior bio-logical readiness, the information-processing notion of rehearsal makes explanatory sense for this recent phenomenon of early reading competence in children who practice and acquire lit-eracy through computer programs.

Physical Development

Developmental theories of the corpus comprise a huge and diverse area of study and concern. Remember the discussion about mind-body dualism earlier in the book, refer-ring to the bifurcation of humans into beings whose awareness, thinking, and interior— or what we refer to as *proximal selves*—are carried in organic containers referred to as *body.* Thus, the mind thinks and the body does (Crawford, 2009). Theories of physical development, while appended to human psyche and intelligence, reflect this reduction-ism of the human into discrete parts, with the body functioning as the object of physical scrutiny.

To some theorists, including Piaget, a clear understanding of descriptive and explanatory theories of the physical, organic body is more important than any other arena of human experience in that these theorists explain health and functioning as embodied (Thelen, 1995). To others, the distinctions among mind, psyche, and body are vague (Kosut & Moore, 2010). We do not take a position here, as our work in this chapter is to critically discuss existing theories. We do, however, take on the meaning of developmental theories later in the book, in Section III. This chapter delimits our gaze to a critical overview of the lenses through which the body has been developmen-tally characterized and explained.

Before entering the theoretical world of the physical body, there is one more criti-cal issue to consider. The point at which physical description and explanation begin, end, and thus define a body are areas of great controversy. The grand theories in Chapter 4 presented a brief introduction to prenatal and postmortem thinking about the corpus, and this chapter provided snippets of this fascinating conversation. We wrestle with this in greater detail in Chapter 12, but whet our appetites with some ideas and experiences in this chapter as well. Our primary aim in this chapter is to bring attention to the two major observable areas of the proximal corpus—physical growth and physical activity, which have voluntarily or involuntarily lent themselves to devel-opmental exhibition and examination.

Similar to other areas of developmental theory discussed previously, physical growth and activity were initially approached primarily from birth through attainment of early adulthood. However, a provocateur about the limits of embodied life was an unantici-pated gift to us when we went to see a portrait exhibition by the artist Dennis Ashbaugh (Wingate Studios, n.d.). Unbeknownst to us when we entered the gallery, his portraits were depicted as genetic codes rather than external bodily features. Through this epiph-any we realized that portraiture and thus artistic rendering of human embodiment and its representation have changed significantly from depiction in classic theories of physical motor development. This exhibit factors clearly into the discussion of what is a body and when it begins and ceases to exist. Chapter 12 addresses this issue while this chapter con-tinues discussion of physical development from birth through death.

Of particular importance to describing bodily development over time is the concept of developmental milestones, in which typical appearance and activity are both described and prescribed as necessary and normative. The Apgar score (Apgar, 1953) is a well-known assessment of the viability of the newborn physical body. It provides norms for respiration, muscle tone, skin color, and reflex activity, beginning description with expected norms outside of which a child is considered to be atypical and potentially problematic. Moreover, there are numerous prescriptive and diagnostic assessments of infant physical growth and development including descriptors of size, weight, motor skill, and even sleep patterns, just to name a few, in which an atypical score, at least in countries with allopathic and osteopathic medical systems, begets immediate medical explanatory attention. In these scales, Quetelet remains alive as his construct of the normal curve underpins and dictates how a young child should look and act (DePoy & Gilson, 2007).

Expanding further forward in longitudinal time, Arnold Gesell (1880–1961) was one of the first theorists to describe chronological child motor development in detail, focusing on crawling (Gesell, 2008). Later, Byram McGraw (1899–1988) examined walking activity. Table 5.3 presents examples of important milestones for years 1 and 2 (McGraw, 1963).

Table 5.3 Child Development: Typical Ages for Milestone Development

Age	Gross Motor	Fine Motor
Year 1	Lifts head and holds head steady	Grasps objects, puts them in mouth
	Sits unsupported	Uses pincer (thumb and finger) grasp
	Rolls from back to stomach	Transfers object from hand to hand
	Crawls on all fours	Drops and retrieves objects
	Pulls to stand	
	Stands unsupported	
	Walks aided, then independently (1–15 months)	
Year 2	Walks independently	Builds towers of three blocks
	Walks backward	Scribbles
	Walks stairs with assistance	Turns knobs and pushes levers and buttons
	Removes clothing	Throws ball
	Improves balance and motor control	
	Runs	
	Kicks a large ball	

(Continued)

Table 5.3 (Continued)

Age	Gross Motor	Fine Motor
Years 2–3	Runs forward well Jumps with two feet Walks on tiptoe Stands on one foot with aid	Strings beads Turns book pages Writes using thumb and finger position Creates basic shapes in writing
Years 3–4	Walks on a line Balances one foot for 5–10 seconds Rides and steers pedaled toys Throws ball overhand Catches ball	Builds tower of nine blocks Copies basic shapes Manipulates and shapes clay
Years 4–5	Walks backward toe to heel Jumps forward 10 times without falling Walks stairs independently Turns somersault	Uses scissors to cut line Copies cross Copies square Prints some letters
Years 5–6	Runs lightly on toes Walks on balance beam Skips on alternate feet Jumps rope Skates	Cuts out simple shapes Copies triangle Traces diamond Copies first name Prints numerals 1–5 Colors within lines Has adult grasp of pencil Has handedness well-established Pastes and glues appropriately

Not unexpectedly, these classical milestone theories have formed the basis for many measures of normal motor maturation, including the Denver II (formerly the Denver Developmental Screening Test) (Frankenburg, Dodds, Archer, Shapiro, Bresnick, 1992), the Child Development Inventory (replaces the Minnesota Child Development Inventory) (Doig, Macias, Saylor, Craver, & Ingram, 1999) and the Bruininks-Oseretsky Test of Motor Proficiency-II (Bruininks & Bruininks, 2010).

As a child matures, age cohort expectations prescribe what is descriptively normative in height, weight, gross and fine motor activity, physical health, and so forth, with the normal curve allowing for some deviation, but not much. As children proceed toward adulthood, descriptive embodied expectations grow more complex both quantitatively and qualitatively, expanding both the repertoire and the efficacy of bodily growth, specialization, and competence. Thus, the descriptive theoretical focus on the typical unfolding of height, weight, and gross motor activity of early childhood is replaced with theory that characterizes typical performance in roles in which embodied descriptors are synthesized, specialized, and applied to roles and functions such as work, play, and, ultimately, reproduction (Backett-Milburn & McKie, 2006). Each of these descriptive role areas of human experience forms a field of study and application unto its own, such as vocational/career development (Crawford, 2009) and theories of play, recreation, and occupational therapy, respectively.

Current theory suggests that embodiment in young adulthood is at its peak and thus forms the comparative basis for describing decline in subsequent years (Haywood & Getchell, 2008). While other elements have been theoretically indicted for aging, developmental theories look to age as the culprit. During young adulthood, embodiment struts its excellence, beauty, potential for reproduction, and superior physical competence. Developmental description of the middle and elder years is retrospective and compared to what was. As noted earlier in this chapter, this longitudinal view of the proximal corpus does not bode well for positive growth and development posited in grand theories, as evidenced by the numerous efforts in many cultures and societies, including plastic surgery, facial adornment, and medicalization of youth characteristics masquerading as optimal health to be monitored and maximized by medical professionals (Conrad, 2007).

Those who are moving past chronological youth might be pleased to see that in some contexts, embodied aging, while reflecting the same observed phenomena as those just discussed, is imbued with a different meaning—that of growth and increasing worth rather than as decline. Furthermore, the recognition of differences in bodies through time as changing rather than as declining has been an important shift in some current developmental approaches, and allows for the descriptive focus to shift from what is physically lost to the centrality of bodily change in social, economic, political, cultural, and intellectual life (Minkler & Fadem, 2002).

Of particular importance to physical and motor developmental theories is that the acceptance of typical as normative and prescribed does not leave much room for those who have atypical bodies, in any chronological age, to be seen as physically competent. This point is discussed in more detail in Chapter 12, alongside examination of categorical descriptions and explanations of *bodies and backgrounds* views of diversity.

Explanatory theories for longitudinal physical development are diverse and form a large literature. Although problematic in contemporary postmodern and post-postmodern theories of embodiment that eschew the cleavage of Kantian dualism (a stance with which we agree), mapping current developmental theories sees them as divided into three overarching and overlapping categories: (1) proximal environment explanations, (2) distal environment explanations, and (3) interaction between the proximal body and the distal environment. These explanations are discussed in broad terms in this chapter because regardless of the causal locus, these theories still posit development as sequential and age related, and thus have inherent norms that guide our expectations for the typical body and its movement capacity. In the subsequent chapters on environmental explanations, these theories are discussed in greater detail, given their causal loci.

How might these explanatory differences contribute to the nature-nurture debate?

Proximal explanations—such as those that attribute physical maturation over time to normative neuromuscular, physiological, and so forth statuses resulting from physical growth—support the basic notion that individuals develop (with some variation) in a similar fashion. Some variables that explain degrees of difference include gender and, as artfully depicted by Ashbaugh (Wingate Studios, n.d.), genetic codes. More recently, brain maturation, perception, learning, and adaptive nature of movement have been suggested as important proximal explanations for the chronological trajectory of motor development (Adolph, Weise, Marin, 2003; Haywood & Getchell, 2008).

Theories that posit distal environment explanations for chronological physical development identify those more distant elements of environments and opportunity presented within them as the primary loci that shape proximal growth and physical competence over time. For example, Schmidt and Wrisberg (2004) linked motor activity, performance, and learning in their framework of motor development and urge professionals to facilitate motor development through providing structured external environment opportunity. Dissimilar from the proximal explanatory theories that support nature as causative of physical development, distal theories support nurture as responsible for sequential maturation. Furthermore, Berger and Adolph (2003) have identified social interaction as an important distal environment explanation for motor development. In their collaborative research, they found that parents' behavior influenced the development of skills, especially those that require risk taking by the child. Others have examined the degree to which cultural and social expectations and norms are important factors in explaining physical development.

Interactional theories explain physical-motor development as the complex interplay of proximal and distal factors. For example, Berger and Adolph (2003) identify the complementary roles of cognition and environments in the development of precise tool manipulation skills in children.

The literature on embodiment and impairment has been instrumental in expanding interactional explanations for physical development. As an example, Steele (2010) highlights the way in which one's physical appearance interacts with stereotypes to explain development of human activity. Of particular note is the interactive role of gender and physique in explaining motor development and skill acquisition (Backett-Milburn & McKie, 2006).

THINKING POINT

Provide some examples to illustrate how norms shape our notions of beauty and grace of movement.

Family Development

Developmental theories do not always refer to individuals. Developmental axioms inhere in theories of families evolving through time, of organizations, and even ideas and theories themselves (as already discussed and illustrated throughout the book). Given the centrality of family intervention throughout diverse parts of social work, we refer you to theories of family development summarized in other comprehensive texts (White & Klein, 2008) and briefly mention some ideas and critical concerns here.

While there are many approaches to defining family, including but not limited to legal, systems, social, and so on, families viewed through a developmental framework are characterized as growing not only in number of members but in complexity over time. In traditional family theory, a family was comprised of a heterosexual couple with one or more children (White & Klein, 2008). The classic trajectory of family development moved from marriage to childbearing and rearing, and grown children leaving home to begin their own family units. Of course, in the 21st century, this limited structure is no longer viable as it is monistic and builds on outdated assumptions about typical sexuality, kinship structures, economic indicators, social milieus, and global differences (Boston College, n.d.). However, we raise a major concern in this chapter about the conceptual quagmire emerging from viewing traditional family development as outdated and then applying theories of individual development to family members. From a longitudinal gaze, the ages of individual milestones are attended to in traditional fashions with children expected to grow and develop in sequence under the watchful eye of parent figures. Children are expected to outlive their parents and when they do not, family upheaval is posited. Playing hide and seek in "coping theories of child loss and trauma" are traditional and to some extent archaic definitions of families as typically developmental despite the rhetorical assertion of diverse family compositions and trajectories. Chapter 12 approaches families from contemporary viewpoints and this chapter leaves traditional family models to their own devices.

Before closing the examination of developmental specific theories, we include an example of one more type of theoretical focus: how developmental theory addresses age related life events. For example, theorists have examined career and vocational choice, sexuality and reproduction, social development and so forth (DePoy & Gilson, 2007).

Coping With Death, and Spiritual Development

Two examples of areas of particular importance to social work practice are developmental coping with death (Kübler-Ross, 1969, 1975) and chronological spiritual development (Benson, Roehlkepartain, & Hong, 2008). The development of spirituality or religion has been separated into two major domains, with development of spirituality within an individual as distinct from the development of a person as a fully spiritual being (Benson, Roehlkepartain, & Hong). Recent developmental approaches to spirituality have linked cognitive and aural development with spiritual understanding and sophistication. This area of study is obfuscated by questions about the nature of spirituality, its distinction from faith, religion and religious practice, and other abstracts such as one's consistent or purposive belief (Kwilecki, as cited in Roehlkepartain, 2006, p. 27) in a higher power and the extent to which this belief is learned, temporary, or constant (Roehlkepartain).

In theorizing about people who were aware of the imminence of their own deaths, Kübler-Ross (1969, 1975) posited a series of sequential stages through which individuals typically pass in order to cope with their own mortality and the end of their lives. Fowler, beginning with the axiom that faith is innate in humans, suggested a six-stage sequence of steps through which individuals grapple with and settle on spiritual beliefs and related behaviors (Benson, Roehlkepartain, & Hong, 2008). See Table 5.4 for brief summaries of the descriptions of Kübler-Ross and Fowler.

Recent examinations of death and dying have criticized Kübler-Ross on several points. First, her evidence was not systematic and, similar to Freud, relied on the individuals within her clinical practice as her data source. Second, the efficacy of sequential developmental stages has been questioned as well as the presence of distinctive stages that are part of a larger life perspective (Advameg, 2010; Corr, Nabe, & Corr, 2008).

Table 5.4 Longitudinal Theories: Spiritual Development and Death and Dying

Fowler's Spiritual Development	Kübler-Ross's Death and Dying
Stage 1: Intuitive Projective. Follows parental beliefs.	Stage 1: Shock and disbelief. Diagnosis or prognosis not believed.
Stage 2: Mythical-literal. Responds to religious stories literally rather than symbolically.	Stage 2: Anger and resentment. Anger at others, sometimes God.
Stage 3: Synthetic-conventional. Conformist acceptance with little self-examination. (Most do not progress past this level.)	Stage 3: Bargaining. May try to strike a deal with providers, god, whomever for longer life, better prognosis.
Level 4: Individuative-reflective. Relocation of beliefs and values from external/social to internal.	Stage 4: Depression and sorrow. Feelings of loss over the condition and consequences.
Stage 5: Conjunctive. Reliance on self for views but increased tolerance and service to others.	Stage 5: Acceptance. Accepts inevitability of death, finds peace with it.
Stage 6: Universalizing. Rare stage in which one becomes altruistic and seeks universal values such as love and justice.	

Grieving the death of another has also been posited as a normative phenomenon that can occur when an individual experiences loss (Bonanno, 2009). Although not well substantiated, stages of grieving suggested by Kübler-Ross have been applied to grieving the loss of another. The application of this conceptual framework has located grieving within typical human experience as a natural course of pain and incremental recovery. However, a recent controversy has emerged as psychopathology classifications in the fifth edition of *Diagnostic and Statistical Manual* are negotiated (Frances, 2010). Scribes of this authorative book, which enscones psychopathology as reified and treatable with pharmaceuticals, are proposing to characterize grief as major depressive disorder, eligible for psychiatric treatment and medication. This issue is addressed in more detail in subsequent chapters with analysis of the advantages and disadvantages of medicalization.

A Point to Ponder: Embodied Slivers

Different from grand developmental theories, specific theories have carved humans into slices, chards, and fragments. We refer to this phenomenon as *embodied slivers*, depicted in Figure 5.1.

Figure 5.1 Body as Slivered

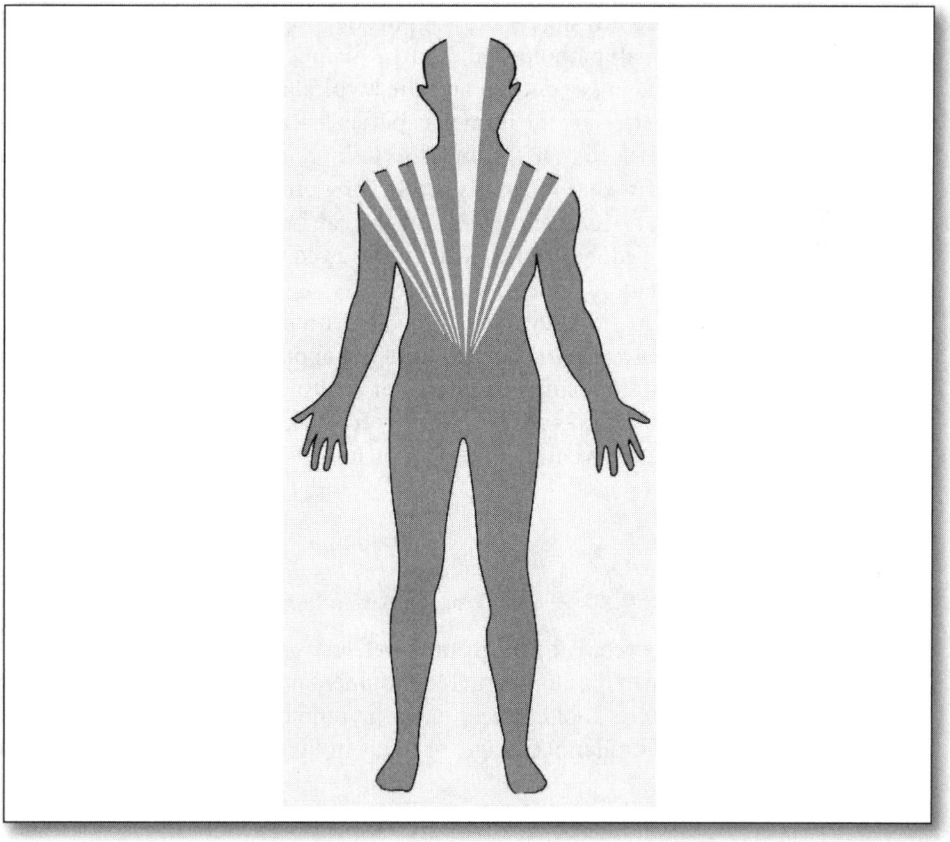

This thinking allows for depth of description and explanation, not falling prey to the indictment so often hurled at grand developmental theories as shallow in their theoretical advancement and application. Still, intellectual and practical danger lurks in reductionism, or reducing a human to slivers or parts, especially if we fail to reconstitute the fragments in our thinking and action. Observable negative outcomes of reductionism are displayed in some medical and health systems, in which specialists in one area isolate their gaze only to that area and perhaps miss the essence of human need. Thus, while reductionism allows the gift of depth, too often its application sacrifices the humanity and uniqueness of each individual and the understanding of a life as more than a single part of scrutiny.

Evidence

As discussed in the two previous chapters on developmental theory, the evidence supporting these chronological approaches is primarily derived from nomothetic methods of inquiry. What is gained by these methods is the power of prediction. Prediction lives on the establishment of a set of common rules that can be followed and anticipated. Clearly, prediction has led to many advances in science, medicine, education, and so forth, as discussed in Section III. However, on the proverbial flipside of nomothetic inquiry are the disadvantages of essentialism, homogenization, and reliance on rules out of context. What was once referred to as diverse, through the empirical methods used to investigate and support developmental specific theories, is now considered abnormal, pathological, and in many cases, undesirable. Think back to the discussions of aging as decline and the atypical body as exemplar. Rules remove context and thus eviscerate the human experience leaving only skeletons to guide thinking and action. Crawford (2009) brings this point home in his example of the car mechanic who sees two cars that will not start. Relying on context and experience rather than a book of rules, the look and travels of the car in large part determine not if the rules need to be applied, but rather which rules need to be applied and how, thus invoking human judgment.

Again, we are not suggesting one evidentiary approach over another. Rather, we refer to our master "purpose" for thinking about evidence that puts theory to work. Norms can help to identify standards of health, morality, cognition, and accomplishment, but in themselves are not the only truths about the rules, adequacy, or desirability of specific areas of human development.

Summary

This chapter covered much ground, yet just barely delved into the symphony that comprises human development. Developmental theories are both chronologically vast as well as detailed, looking deep into the human as a being who has commonalities with others of similar age, stage, or locus in life event. The chapter thus summarized developmental theories that address specific areas of human description, including cognition, moral development, and physical development over time. The pitfalls of accepting developmental-specific theories as truth were noted, because in our timeline of theories, they themselves mature and change (Kuhn, 1996; Popper, 2002). Yet unlike the view of humans posited by the theories that comprise this category, theories of development themselves can "ungrow." Discussion then moved to how developmental-specific theories reduce humans to parts and sometimes fail to reconstitute them, leading to slivers rather than human lives being addressed by different professional groups. After a discussion of the evidentiary basis of these theories, to the importance of approaching them purposively rather than prescriptively was prescribed.

References

Adolph, K. E., Weise, I. & Marin, L. (2003). Motor development. In L. Nadel, *Encyclopedia of cognitive science* (pp. 134–137). London: Macmillan-Reference.

Advameg. (2010). *Stage theory.* Retrieved from Encyclopedia of Death and Dying: http://www .deathreference.com/Sh-Sy/Stage-Theory.html

Apgar, V. (1953). A proposal for a new method of evaluation of the newborn infant. *Current Research in Anesthesia and Analgesia, 260* (July–August). Retrieved from http://apgar.net/ virginia/Apgar_Paper.html

Backett-Milburn, K., & McKie, L. (2006). *Dead end feminism.* Cambridge, UK: Polity Press.

Badrova, E. (2003). *Reference publications: Bnet.* Retrieved from Vygotsky and Montessori: One dream, two visions: http://findarticles.com/p/articles/mi_qa4097/is_200301/ai_n9199645/ pg_2/?tag=content;col1

Baltes, P. B. (1984). Discussion: Some constructive caveats on action psychology and the study of intention. *Human Development, 27,* 135–39.

Basseches, M. (1984). *Dialectical thinking and adult development.* Norwood, NJ: Ablex.

Benson, P. L., Roehlkepartain, E. C., & Hong, K. L. (2008). *Spiritual development.* Hoboken, NJ: Wiley.

Berger, S. E., & Adolph, K. E. (2003). Infants use handrails as tools in a locomotor task. *Developmental Psychology, 39,* 594–605.

Bloom, P. (2010, May 9). The moral life of babies. *New York Times,* MM44.

Boeree, C. G. (1999). *Jean Piaget.* Retrieved from http://www.ship.edu/Ncgboeree/piaget.html

Bonanno, G. (2009). *The other side of sadness: What the new science of bereavement tells us about life after a loss.* New York: Basic Books.

Boston College. (n.d.). *Sloan Work and Family Research Network.* Retrieved from Sloan Work and Family Research Network: http://wfnetwork.bc.edu/

Bringuier, J. C., & Piaget, J. (1989). *Conversations with Jean Piaget.* Chicago: University of Chicago Press.

Bruininks, R. H., & Bruininks, B. D. (2010). *Bruininks-Oseretsky test of motor proficiency (BOT-2)* (2nd ed.). Retrieved from Pearson: http://www.pearsonassessments.com/HAIWEB/ Cultures/en-us/Productdetail.htm?Pid=PAa58000&Mode=summary

Campbell, R. L. (2006, March 27). *Jean Piaget's genetic epistemology: Appreciation and critique.* Retrieved from http://hubcap.clemson.edu/~campber/piaget.html

Child Development Institute. (2000–2010). *Stages of intellectual development in children and teenagers.* Retrieved from http://www.childdevelopmentinfo.com/development/piaget.shtml

Conrad, P. (2007). *The medicalization of society: On the transformation of human conditions into treatable disorders.* Baltimore: Johns Hopkins University Press.

Corr, C. Nabe, C.M. & Corr, D. (2008). *Death and dying, life and living* (6th ed.). Belmont, CA: Wadsworth, Cengage.

Crawford, M. B. (2009). *Shop class as soul craft.* New York: Penguin.

Dehart, G. B., Sroufe, L. A., & Copper, R. G. (2003). *Child development.* New York: McGraw-Hill.

DePoy, E., & Gilson, S. (2007). *The human experience.* Lanham, MD: Routledge.

Doig, K. B., Macias, M. M., Saylor, C. F., Craver, J. R., & Ingram, P. E. (1999). The Child Development Inventory: A developmental outcome measure for follow-up ofthe high-risk infant. *Journal of Pediatrics, 135*(3), 358–362.

Frances, A. (2010, August 14). Good grief. *New York Times,* WK9.

Frankenburg, W. K., Dodds, J., Archer, P., Shapiro, H., & Bresnick, B. (1992). The Denver II: A major revision and restandardization of the Denver Developmental Screening Test. *Pediatric, 89,* 91–97.

Gesell, A. (2008). *Infant and child in the culture of today—the guidance of development in home and nursery school* (reprint ed.). New York: Harper & Brothers.

Gilligan, C. (1993). *In a different voice: Psychological theory and women's development.* Cambridge, MA: Harvard University Press.

Gruber, H., & Voneche, J. V. (1995). *The essential Piaget.* Northvale, NJ: Jason Aronson.

Haywood, K., & Getchell, N. (2008). *Life span motor development* (5th ed.). Champaign, IL: Human Kinetics.

Hetherington, E. M., Parke, R. D., Gauvain, M., & Locke, V. O. (2005). *Child psychology: A contemporary viewpoint* (6th ed.). New York: McGraw-Hill.

Hoffmann, M. (2000). *Empathy and moral development.* New York: Cambridge Univerity Press.

Huitt, W., & Hummel, J. (2003). *Piaget's theory of cognitive development.* Retrieved from Educational Psychology Interactive: http://chiron.valdosta.edu/whuitt/colicogsys/piaget.html

Infant Cognition Center at Yale University. (n.d.). Current studies. Retrieved from http://www.yale.edu/infantlab/Our_Studies.html

Inhelder, B., & Piaget, J. (1958). *The growth of logical thinking.* New York: Basic Books.

Kail, R., & Cavanaugh, J. (2010). *Human development: A life-span view* (5th ed.). Belmont, CA: Wadsworth.

Kail, R., Pellegrino, J., & Carter, P. (1980). Developmental changes in mental rotation. *Journal of Experimental Child Psychology, 29,* 102–116.

Kohlberg, L. (1984). *The psychology of moral development: The nature and validity of moral stages.* San Francisco: Harper & Row.

Kohlberg, L. (1986). A current statement on some theoretical issues. In S. Mogdil & C. Mogdil (Eds.), *Lawrence Kohlberg: Consensus and controversy* (pp. 485–546). Philadelphia: Falmer Press.

Kosut, M., & Moore, L. (2010). *The body reader: Essential social and cultural readings.* New York: NYU Press.

Kübler-Ross, E. (1969). *On death and dying.* New York: Macmillan.

Kübler-Ross, E. (1975). *Death: The final stage of growth.* Englewood Cliffs, NJ: Prentice Hall.

Kuhn, T. S. (1996). *The structure of scientific revolutions* (3rd ed.). Chicago: University of Chicago Press.

Mahoney, M. J. (2003). *Constructive psychotherapy.* New York: Guilford Press.

McGraw, B. (1963). *The neuromuscular maturation of the human infant.* New York: Hafner.

Miller, G. A. (1956). The magical number seven, plus or minus two: Some limits on our capacity for processing information. *Psychological Review, 63,* 81–97.

Miller, G. A., Galanter, E., & Pribram, K. H.(1956). *Plans and the structure of behavior.* New York: Holt, Rinehart & Winston.

Minkler, M., & Fadem, P. (2002). "Successful aging": A disability perspective. *Journal of Disability Policy Studies, 12*(4), 229–236.

Morra, S., Gobbo, C., Marini, Z., & Sheese, R. (2009). *Cognitive development: Neo-Piagetian perspectives.* New York: Taylor and Francis.

Moseley, D. (2005). *Frameworks for thinking: A handbook for teaching and learning.* Cambridge, UK: Cambridge University Press.

National Public Radio. (2011, March 11). Children's book apps: A new world of learning. Retrieved from http://m.npr.org/news/Technology/134663712

Perry, K. (2005). *Theory of child cognitive development.* Retrieved from EzineArticles: http://ezinearticles.com/ ?Theory-of-Child-Cognitive-Development&id=45 941

Piaget, J. (1954). *The construction of reality in the child.* New York: Basic Books.

Piaget, J. (1970). *Genetic epistemology.* New York: Columbia University Press.

Piaget, J. (1985). *The equilibrium of cognitive structures.* Chicago: University of Chicago Press.

Rich, J., & DeVitis, J. (1994). *Theories of moral development* (2nd ed.). Springfield, IL: Charles C Thomas.

Roehlkepartain, E. C. (2006). *The handbook of spiritual development in childhood and adolescence.* Thousand Oaks, CA: Sage.

Schmidt, R. A., & Wrisberg, C. A. (2004). *Motor learning and performance* (3rd ed.). Champaign, IL: Human Kinetics.

Siegler, R. S., DeLoache, J. S., & Eisenberg, N. (2006). *How children develop.* New York: Worth.

Smith, L. (1997). Jean Piaget. In N. Sheehy, A. Chapman, & W. Conroy (Eds.), *Biographical dictionary of psychology* (pp. 447–452). London: Routledge.

Steele, C. (2010). *Whistling Vivaldi and other clues to how stereotype affects us.* New York: W. W. Norton.

Thelen, E. (1995). Time scale dynamics and the development of an embodied cognition. In R. Port & T. van Gelder (Eds.), *Mind as motion: Explorations in the dynamics of cognition* (pp. 69–100). Cambridge, MA: MIT Press.

Thomas, R. M. (2001). *Recent theories of human development.* Thousand Oaks, CA: Sage.

White, J., & Klein, D. (2008). *Family theories.* Thousand Oaks, CA: Sage.

Williams, L. E., Huang, J. Y., & Bargh, J. A. (2009). The scaffolded mind: Higher mental processes are grounded in early experience of the physical world. *European Journal of Social Psychology, 39*(7), 1257–1267.

Wingate Studios. (n.d.). *Dennis Ashbaugh.* Retrieved from http://www.wingatestudio.com/Ashbaugh.html

Overview of Environmental Theories

Looking at Humans as Sets of Conditions

The following two chapters delve into environmental theories, or those that describe the environmental element of behavior, appearance, and experience, as well as explain these human phenomena as a function of environmental influences. But what do we mean by environment? There are numerous definitions of *environment* and until this point, what we mean by this term has not been clarified. We have used terms such as *distal* and *proximal* to denote far and near, but to what or whom? We have also used terms such as *conditions,* but what do we mean? The subsequent chapters clarify and illustrate the use of these terms related to the environment.

Drawing 6.1   Environmental Theories Word Soup

Dualism

A majority of lay understandings, and even formal definitions, follow the dualism of which we spoke in previous chapters. Remember that this enlightenment-era thinking characterized environment as a surrounding space in which a being or activity occurs and thus is a separate entity apart from the beings that inhabit or exist within it. More precisely related to humans, dualism refers to the separation between body and mind (Kazlev, 2004), giving rise to numerous classical explanatory debates such as nature-nurture, spirit-science, organic-artificial, and so forth.

More recently, however, the technology fields have redefined environments as the entire set of conditions under which one operates, broadening the definition from a location to a set of conditions.

Of course, we take another spoonful of word soup to clarify the diversity of defini- tions of the term *condition,* to illustrate its range, and thus its value for defining environments broadly. Table 6.1 presents some of the definitions that appear on the web.

Table 6.1 Definitions of *Condition*

1. A particular mode of being of a person or thing; existing state; situation with respect to circumstances.

2. State of health: He was reported to be in critical condition.

3. Fit or requisite state: to be out of condition; to be in no condition to run.

4. Social position: in a lowly condition.

5. A restricting, limiting, or modifying circumstance: It can happen only under certain conditions.

6. A circumstance indispensable to some result; prerequisite; that on which something else is contingent: conditions of acceptance.

7. Usually, conditions. Existing circumstances: poor living conditions.

8. Something demanded as an essential part of an agreement; provision; stipulation: He accepted on one condition.

9. Law.

   a. A stipulation in an agreement or instrument transferring property that provides for a change consequent on the occurrence or nonoccurrence of a stated event.

   b. The event upon which this stipulation depends.

10. Informal. An abnormal or diseased state of part of the body: heart condition; skin condition.

11. U.S. Education.

    a. A requirement imposed on a college student who fails to reach the prescribed standard in a course at the end of the regular period of instruction, permitting credit to be established by later performance.

    b. The course or subject to which the requirement is attached.

12. Grammar. Protasis.

13. Logic. The antecedent of a conditional proposition.

Source: Dictionary.com, 2010

Hanging the definitional hat of environment on the foundational pillar of *condition* therefore provides a vast scope through which to view environment, from miniscule embodied (proximal) to the abstract world of ideas and spaces (distal). The definition fits our notion of environment, since we suggest that environments can be pervasive with unclear boundaries. Yet, restricting environment to a set of variables (or conditions) still allows us to visualize and delimit it, without reverting to dualism.

THINKING POINT

 If you look at the body as environment, are the clothes that you are wearing part of it? What about a hearing aid? Does it belong to the embodied environment or to another? What about a pacemaker that is implanted within a heart?

We have no correct answer, for the location of personal items as part of the proximal embodied environment is context dependent.

THINKING POINT

 If you decided that the clothes that you wear are part of your body, what happens when you get home and take them off? Are they now part of the body environment?

Defining and delimiting the environment is thus not a simple matter. While we do not agree with dualism as shared previously, this chapter, and the next two, refer to distinctions through a continuum of proximal to distal, with proximal being home to the theories that discuss the body from a classical traditional perspective, and distal holding theories that venture further from the organic corpus than those that we classify as proximal. Later in the book, subsequent chapters discussing 21st century theories ultimately reweave these theories alongside an introduction to diverse disciplines that proceed to form unexpected intimate conceptual relationships. Before moving into the world of proximal to distal environments, note that the thinking points presented in this section already provide significant challenge to a category system in which the body is theorized as separate from its surroundings.

Temporary Return to Dualism

Moving beyond but to some extent still reflecting a duplex structure reflected in theory, we look at proximal and distal environmental theories. Proximal environmental theories are primarily concerned with the description and explanation of embodied, or what we refer to as *corporeal,* phenomena, such as internal organ systems, genetics, interior psychological structures, processes, and so forth.

Distal environmental frameworks focus their gaze primarily on the elements of human description and explanations theorized beyond the corpus, ranging from the view that behavior, appearance, and experience result directly from environmental stimuli external to the body, to the perspective of behavior, appearance, and experience resulting from distal environmental factors mediated by proximal embodied environmental factors, such as intelligence, personality, power differentials, individual values, individual beliefs, and so forth. As far as adornments and objects that are placed on the body, we suggest that their location as proximal or distal varies according to purpose and proximity to the body.

Environmental Theory Axioms

Chapters 7 and 8 illustrate how we advance axioms specific to each general environmental distance from the midline of the body. However, there are overarching axioms that unite all of the theories that we present under the category of environmental theories. See Table 6.2.

Table 6.2 Environmental Theory Axioms
1. Proximal and distal environmental descriptions, and explanatory factors that are seen as separate phenomenon, can be distinguished from one another.
2. Environments are diverse, including immediate human, physical, natural, and sensory contexts and more abstract social, indirect, and virtual contexts.
3. Environments are comprised of multiple conditions.
4. Environments create context.

The axioms reemphasize that environments are contexts created by sets of conditions.

The contexts in which we work could be delimited to workers, physical location, the social elements, the climate, and so forth. Or, consider your health context. It might include your body systems, exterior stressors, and other human and nonhuman influences that shape your health.

Note that in the examples, multiple conditions are present. Thus, even if an environment is small, such as the genetic environment, by definition, it has multiple elements and conditions.

History of Environmental Theory

In order to create a historical context for this discussion, we consulted literature on the history of environments. However, because the term *environment* is so broad, it seemed illogical to synthesize such disparate fields that used the word so differently. So, not unexpectedly, to create a historical context, we turn to word soup, etymology, to examine the derivation of the term.

The first reference to environments that we could disinter was documented in the 14th century and referred to pollution. It was not until 1603 that the word *environment*, derived from the French word *environs*, was used in its contemporary sense to denote the notion of circle. In the early 19th century, the term came to mean conditions of nature. Interestingly, after the turn of the 20th century, the term *environmentalism* emerged in psychological literature primarily in debates about the nature versus nurture explanations for human behavior. Until technology adopted the term environment to denote interior sets of conditions in human and nonhuman entities, the 20th-century use of the word referred primarily to spaces that surround humans and objects. The field of environmental psychology, a relatively new field that was developed in the later part of the 20th century, has been primarily concerned with the reciprocal interaction of natural and built conditions, and human behavior.

Evidence

Due to their diversity, multiple types of evidence generated through varied methods are used to generate and support environmental theories. For example, highly technological data such as Xray, neuroimaging, and geostatistical modeling (Pauwels, 2006) have been used to investigate and characterize bodies, brains, and physical geographies while single case study data are often taken as credible evidence for social learning theories (DePoy & Gitlin, 2011). Evidence is discussed in more detail throughout Chapters 7 and 8 with examination of specific theoretical environmental landmarks and genres.

Summary

This brief chapter defined our terms, clarifying our reasons for discussing environmental theories as a proximal to distal range, and promising to reunite them in chapters that introduce and discuss 21st century interdisciplinarity. Four axioms were then advanced and illustrated, common to the theories that we have located under this environmental theory rubric. Last, a brief etymology of the term *environment* was provided.

References

DePoy, E., & Gitlin, L. (2011). *Introduction to research.* St. Louis, MO: Elsevier.

Dictionary.com (2010). *Condition.* Retrieved from http://dictionary.reference.com/browse/condition

Kazlev, M. (2004). *Dualism.* Retrieved from Kheper: http://www.kheper.net/topics/worldviews/dualism.htm

Pauwels, L. (2006). *Visual cultures of science: Rethinking representational practices in knowledge building and science communication.* Hanover, NH: Dartmouth University Press.

7

Proximal Environmental Theories

Chapter 6 defined environment. Remember, that in concert with contemporary views that eschew dualism, the definition provided did not restrict the definition to space beyond what is considered as the traditional boundaries of the body. It will now become apparent why we chose the broader definition of environment as a "set of conditions" to frame the discussion. This chapter examines theories that describe and explain humans as a function of proximal or interior factors, or those that are delimited to the organic corpus. This is not to say that all of these theories eschew variables external to the body as causal. Rather, they range from fully proximal to interactive. It is also important to note that while we do not necessarily agree with dualist environmental classifications, we do articulate and include this approach when discussing classical theories because these conceptualizations are present and even hegemonous. The extent to which proximal phenomena explain conditions such as aging, childbirth, mental illness, and so forth has come under increasing scrutiny as theories of medicalization (Conrad, 2007) merge economics, culture, and behavior.

Categories of Proximal Environmental Theory

Not unexpectedly, there are many views that describe and explain what we label proximal environment. In order to do justice to the range of theories and their large scope, we further divide them into two subcategories: ontogeny and phylogeny (see Table 7.1). *Ontogeny* refers to the development of individuals, and thus the theories located under this subcategory focus on individual description and explanation. We further subdivide ontogeny into two categories, theories focusing primarily on observables and those addressing reportables (DePoy & Gilson, 2011). *Phylogeny* is defined as the development of the species and therefore, under the category of proximal phylogeny, approaches that examine descriptions and explanations of humans as a species reflected with each organic body are discussed. We had a hard time locating phylogeny in a particular chapter and decided that it now lies here due to its reification and primary emphasis on the corpus. However, as discussed critically, classical phylogenetic explanations are among the many that raise fundamental questions about the clarity of boundaries between distal and proximal conditions. In essence, phylogeny is not simply restricted to the proximal, but involves time-dimensional distal conditions that are represented by proximal conditions.

Table 7.1 Categories of Proximal Environmental Theories

Ontogeny		Phylogeny
Observable focus	**Reportable focus**	
Embodiment	Information processing, cognition	Evolution
Human biology, physiology	Personality traits, mental and psychological	Humanism
Genetics	Motivation	
	Identity	

Of course, the vast number of proximal environmental theories do not fit neatly or mutually exclusively into each category. So we have located each approach in the domain that we believe best reflects its central tenets.

Proximal Environmental Theory Axioms

The axioms in Table 7.2 join those listed in Chapter 6 for all environmental theories.

As you can see by these axioms, theories that fit under the proximal environmental rubric suggest that the body is discreet, can be identified and distinguished from "not body," and are most concerned with the corpus, its structures, functions, and how the organic body is causal of human description. Moreover, because no two individuals are seen as alike, even identical twins, a look under the skin, so to speak, can be important in differentiating one individual from another. However, organic similarities among subgroups of humans are also seen as important not only as identifiers and explainers, but as distinguishers between groups. As discussed subsequently, this last point is the vortex of much debate and contention, particularly in the context of contemporary scientific advancements that can manipulate the proximal environment.

Table 7.2   Proximal Environmental Theory Axioms

1. Proximal environmental theories share the concept of body as contained.
2. Proximal environmental theories are concerned with human phenomena delimited by the boundaries of the organic corpus.
3. Proximal environmental theories describe humans in terms of biological slivers of corporeal structures and processes.
4. Proximal environmental theories explain human description primarily as a function of embodied phenomena.
5. Proximal environmental theories share a focus on the organic.
6. No two humans are alike.
7. Individuals can be distinguished by their proximal environments.
8. Groups can be distinguished from one another by common organic characteristics.
9. Human behavior can be manipulated by changing the proximal environment.

Defining the Body

Note that we have used terms such as *embodied, corpus,* and *organic* to refer to the body. This section aims to clarify what is meant by these terms in the context of the proximal environment.

THINKING POINT

Think about your own body and the bodies of those around you. What characterizes it? Delimits it? Explains its appearance and behavior? Where and when does your body begin and end?

Undoubtedly, questions about describing and explaining the body are complex without a single set of answers.

Looking back into snippets of history and ingredients of word soup over time, albeit with different terms than used today, the body has been defined and represented in multiple ways, has been ascribed with diverse meanings and explanations, and has engendered responses depending on the beliefs, values, and resources of the times. As far back as ancient civilizations, conceptualization and response to bodies were complex.

In parts of ancient Greece, the limited development of scientific explanatory theory, coupled with strong spirituality, was the operational framework for ascribing parameters, meanings, and explanations to bodily appearance (Rose, 2003). While the descriptive limits of humanness were drawn at "normal" body composition at birth, it is noteworthy that infants who were physically deformed were not always considered to possess human bodies (DePoy & Gilson, 2011; Rose 2003). Rather, in certain locations throughout Greece, extreme deviance from what was considered to be typical was explained even in some of Greece's advanced intellectual contexts as monstrous and met with exclusion from the human race. While monstrosity as an explanation and eschewal as response may seem atrocious, this theme is repeated in contemporary practices, albeit dressed in different clothes labeled as scientific or as quality of life. We come back to this important point later in the book.

In the literature of early Jewish civilizations (Abrams, 1998; Olyan, 2008), references to appearances were often raised in the context of a discussion about which bodies were able to occupy sacred positions in the synagogue. Bodies considered flawed were prohibited from entering the Jewish priesthood because of spiritual beliefs linking God to earth through an ideal human conduit. Thus, the nature of a body was explained as a representation of the divine rather than a biological entity and bodies perceived as less than perfect were excluded from service to or earthly presence of God. "The blemishes which [the sages] said [disqualify a priest] are on his face, his hands and his feet" (M. Megillah, 4:7 and T. Megillah, 3:29, as cited in Abrams, 1998, p. 33).

Up through the Middle Ages, bodies were not described and explained in biological terms (Metzler, 2006). However, at the end of the Middle Ages, as scientific explanations slowly replaced beliefs in spirit and divine explanations, the definitions and depictions of human bodies revealed drastically altered conceptualizations. These conceptual changes are reflected in the literature and art throughout the Renaissance period. As an example, Francis Bacon was particularly important in advancing systematic study and representation of "corporeal reality." He asserted that bodies and the conditions that affected them were explained by biological, not moral factors. This conceptual shift can be seen in the art depicting bodies through visually representing actual knowledge of the underlying physical form (Dijck, 2005; Stiker, 1999) and accurate detailed depictions of the human anatomy. Similarly, explanations of the psyche (considered a proximal entity) and its behavioral depictions shifted over time.

Behavior, particularly that which was viewed as aberrant, in early civilizations curiously was explained as a function of the distal supernatural world affecting the corpus and its psyche. However, over the course of history, as the Renaissance influenced thinking, science, or at least pseudoscience (Specht & Courtney, 1994) emerged as the accepted explanation for observed behaviors, moods, and mental status (Mangal, 2008). Late 19th-century and contemporary theorizing defined atypical behavior and mood as proximal mental illness and laid the bedrock for the discipline of abnormal psychology and its praxis triplets, psychology, psychiatry (Mangal, 2008), and psychotherapy (Specht & Courtney, 1994) to gaze interiorly. This is not to say that moral and allegorical explanations of bodies, psyche, and corporeal difference ever disappeared as philosophers, clergy, and others continued to debate the relationship between God and nature, as exemplified by the following passage from de Cartagena (1998):

It is necessary to consider the three purposes why our Lord permits these hardships [atypical bodies], for He punishes the righteous to test them. He punishes the sinful to correct them. He punishes the wicked to condemn them. (p. 50)

As we return to the contemporary, the synthesis of several important intellectual and contextual trends has been important in shaping definitions of the body. These are: Quetelet's mathematical conceptualization of the "normal man," scientific/medical colonization of the body, complex juxtaposition of corporeal difference, and technology.

Da Vinci was known for his anatomical measurements of bodies, resulting in *Virtuvian Man* proportions as prescriptive models for desirable bodies (Gilson & DePoy, 2007). Moving forward in history, and as discussed previously, the development of mathematical statistics or concepts of central tendency added to the application of numbers to defining and characterizing bodies, among a range of other human phenomena (Davis, 1995; 2003). Once numeric observations of bodies were divided into binary categories, the description of bodies was parsed into normal and abnormal. With the mathematical proportions from *Virtuvian Man* and the foundation of the normal curve translated into scientifically supported prescriptive normalcy, and as industrialization took hold, the body became a major object to which standardized acceptable and healthy attributes were ascribed. The viable and acceptable body was described as most frequently occurring, fitting into and functioning in public work spaces, behaving as expected, and being able to use mass produced, standardized objects made for consumption (DePoy & Gilson, 2004, 2007, 2011). Further, standards of bodily and mental health and beauty were based on Enlightenment norms, and bodies that deviated from those norms were described as anomalous, devalued, and even excluded from the category of "acceptable human" through processes such as enfreakment (Thomson, 2009), construction, and labeling of insanity (Barusch, 2009) and so forth.

The second trend to note is juxtaposition of corporeal difference created in large part in the United States and Europe by immigration trends throughout the 20th and into the 21st century. Through immigration, people of different backgrounds and with clearly observable bodily and behavioral diversity moved into close contact with one another, providing the context for a range of options, from expanding acceptability to rejection of even miniscule divergence from what is expected and most frequently occurring. This trend gave rise to *diversity patina* (DePoy & Gilson, 2004), or the assumption of more fundamental differences among groups on the basis of an observable descriptive element that we refer to as *bodies and backgrounds* (e.g., skin color, ethnicity, etc.) (DePoy & Gilson, 2011).

Typical approaches to diversity provide an example. As discussed in subsequent chapters, on the basis of ethnicity, race, culture, observable gender, and other patina characteristics, assumptions are often made about other human phenomena, unrelated to the observable, that delineate membership in a diversity group.

The following chapter titles in Diller's (2011) diversity text, listed in Table 7.3, further illustrate. Inherent in this approach is that embodied observables (genetic heritage) provide the rationale for assuming other commonalities as well.

Table 7.3 Chapter Titles Illustrating Diversity Patina
Chapter 9. Working With Latino/a Clients: An Interview With Inez Souza
Chapter 10. Working with Latino/a Clients: An Interview With Roberto Almanzan
Chapter 11. Working With Native American Clients: An Interview With Jack Lawson
Chapter 12. Working With African American Clients: An Interview With Veronica Thompson
Chapter 13. Working With Asian American Clients: An Interview With Dan Hocov
Chapter 14. Working With White Ethnic Clients: An Interview With the Author

Third, with the advancement of science and entrepreneurship of the medical community throughout the 20th century, defining and colonizing the body as the purview of scientific inquiry, knowledge, explanation, judgment, and when possible, revision is an important factor in how we currently conceptualize the body and its contents (Conrad, 2007).

THINKING POINT

Think of childbirth as an example. The natural human function has become a science and medical specialty, obstetrics. And, think about medicating shyness in which chemical processes are enacted to change social behavior.

And of course, closely related to scientific and medical colonization of the body is technology as a critical factor in altering visualizations (Pauwels, 2006), conceptualizations, boundaries, and functions of bodies.

> *Consider the use of the MRI to create visual images linked to brain activity. Using this technology, the activity of the hippocampus was observed during recall activity and future planning activity. The visuals that resulted were interpreted as identifying the hippocampus as a "time traveler" (Arehart-Treichel, 2010, p.11), functioning to assist humans in future planning through invoking past memories.*

> *Now look at the role of MRI technology in advancing scientific measurement depicted in the following quotation: "John Csernansky wants to take your measurements. Not the circumference of your chest, waist and hips. No, this doctor wants to stretch a tape measure around your hippocampus, thalamus and prefrontal cortex" (Medilexicon International, 2010, para. 1).*

The previous snippets provide only exemplars of how definitions and limits of the human body have been explained in snapshots of some historical contexts. However, while not exhaustive as a history of the body, these exemplars are important because they illustrate several important points about proximal environmental theories. The binary concepts of *normal* and *abnormal,* which capture so much attention in the literature about and practice with the proximal environment, did not emerge until the Enlightenment and Renaissance joined forces with the mathematical concept of the normal curve. Binary concepts dominate contemporary discussion and explanatory analysis of the human proximal environment, whether looking at physical, observable structures or reportable, inferable human phenomena such as personality, mental status, and so forth.

> *We set standards for normal height and weight on the basis of age. Diagnoses of mental illness such as bipolar disorder, dysthymia, and even excessive shyness are considered as abnormalities to be remediated. They are based on an evidentiary foundation of observed behaviors, reported moods and more contemporarily technologically generated and interpreted images that fall outside of what is considered to be normal.*

Moreover, concepts of beauty, health, and even human value are based on conformation to a normal standard and set of ideal descriptors. This point is detailed later in the book, but now draw attention to Rothschild's (2005) and Karlberg's (2010) recent work, in which they discuss prenatal practices. Recall our point about infant deformity in parts of ancient Greece, in which infants were not considered human if, at birth, they deviated significantly from typical body structure. Rothschild (2005) notes that prenatal testing that uses science to measure and visualize "birth defects" functions as the basis for lawful abortion—in essence, to eliminate abnormal bodies and to standardize proximal environments of humans. And through her personal narrative, Karlberg (2010) suggests that prenatal testing has not only provided a mechanism for eliminating diverse bodies and brains from being born, but also has created the acceptable limits of a fetus. Do these points sound familiar? While we do not take a position on the efficacy and morality of selective abortion, we consider this practice in the context of history, and, here, present it as a window into the variable and contextual descriptions and explanations of the body over time.

Biology and Its Cousins

We now turn to biology, the hegemonous, descriptive and explanatory approach to the proximal environments of bodies. Introduced conceptually as slivers in Chapter 5, biology has further carved these slivers of proximal corporeal structures and processes into smaller fragments referred to as *systems*. Although systems are reified as "real" in biological parlance or what we label the narrative of the interior corpus, contemporary research is yielding theories that are conceptually and operationally renegotiating as these fragments as interactive. The following discussion illustrates how classical fragments are being refitted into new compounds that in the future will likely make significant shifts in understanding and management of the corpus.

Human biology and related fields such as physiology and neuroscience (Thagard, 2010) are primary chroniclers of the human body and human nature (Grene &

DePew, 2004) and provide explanations for bodily appearance, behavior, and experience. These complex fields of study span description and explanation from minute structures and inferable activity to externally observable individual description. Table 7.4 depicts the body parsed into its diverse fragments. This section presents only a brief overview of five interior, or what we refer to as *proximal environmental system*, fragments, to illustrate breadth, depth, and language of this lens in describing and explaining all aspects of humans. The references for this chapter offer further, more detailed discussions of human biology. The intrinsic descriptive taxonomy organizes system fragments according to corporeal structure and function. Through this perspective, each system is described as an entity which contains specific structures and components, and which exhibits purposive behaviors.

THINKING POINT

 Of course, there are many ways to describe and classify the proximal environment. In what other ways might you describe the organic element of human description and explanation?

Table 7.4 Proximal Environment Described and Explained Through Biology and Its Cousins

Body System Fragments	Descriptive Structures & Functions	Proximal Explanations
Neurological system (NS)	Central NS: brain and spinal cord Peripheral NS: voluntary and autonomic	Fetal neurological development influenced by factors such as sex and maternal nutrition Neurotransmitter levels and synthesis
Genetics and hereditary system	DNA, genes, chromosomes that help determine characteristics and traits	Sex, race, metabolism, size, predisposition to health and illness
Immune system	Bone marrow, lymph system, organs	Strength of immune response to perceived threats
Reproductive system	Genitals, gonads	Females: high levels of estrogen and progesterone Males: high levels of testosterone
Endocrine system	Hypothalamus and pituitary gland, adrenal glands, thymus, pineal, gonads, etc.	Heart and blood pressure function Circadian rhythms Time of puberty onset

Looking through this filter in more detail at each of the five system fragments listed in Table 7.4, the following sections include brief overviews in the narrative of the interior corpus. This linguistic style may be familiar from your coursework in human biology. Essentially, the narrative of the interior corpus describes organic structures and functions (for the most part) with evidentiary support from diverse parts of the biological scope of inquiry. Causative factors for human description are mined primarily from bodily functions, although as noted, distinguishing body from *not-body* is a difficult task. Yet, as additional research is conducted, distinguishing the systems from one another is increasingly problematic as it challenges the current system taxonomy. New terms that move toward the integration of biological fragments may ultimately revise the current system paradigm.

THINKING POINT

 Is a transplanted heart part of the body before it is relocated? After? Whose body?

Neurological System

We enter this system through the interior narrative of neurology, blended with some metaphoric license. The neurological system is structurally described as two interrelated subsystems (central and peripheral). Note that these divisions are at least rhetorically named according to their proximal location. The behavior of the nervous system is biologically and physiologically explained and visualized as a complex loop through which electricity and embodied productions labeled *neurotransmitters* travel and provoke activity. That is to say, the brain is characterized as the epicenter of human experience, perception, mental health, memory, cognition, and even meaning making (Thagard, 2010). It not only generates thought, awareness, mood, and so forth but controls embodied functions and proximally generated behaviors by sending patterned signals through its interior roadways throughout the corpus (Charney & Nestler, 2004).

Let us briefly interrupt the interior narrative to share Thagard's (2010) eloquently stated description of neurological electrical patterns:

> Whereas a lightning flash is like a single trumpeter producing a loud sound with no intended direction, the synaptic connections between neurons enable them to perform like a trained orchestra with many coordinated musicians. (p. 46)

Returning to linguistic consistency, patterns of neurotransmitted messages move centrally to the spinal cord, which acts as the major conduit to relay the brain's orders to all corporeal geographies within the interior environment by way of the peripheral nervous system (PNS). Messages from the PNS to the brain travel back via similar pathways (Charney & Nestler, 2004).

Note that the structure of the nervous system is not merely described as two large subsystems, but is further reduced into miniscule descriptive parts:

> The basic working unit of all the nervous systems is the neuron, or nerve cell. The human body has a great diversity of neuronal types, but all consist of a cell body with a nucleus and a conduction fiber, an axon. Extending from the cell body are dendrites, which conduct impulses to the neurons from the axons of other nerve cells. (Gilson, 2011, p. 90)

Next, consider the complex description of the brain and its behavior: "The human brain, which constitutes only about 2% of total body weight, may contain as many as 10 million neurons" (Gilson, 2011, p. 88). Its three major internal regions are referred to as the *forebrain, midbrain,* and *hindbrain.* Viewed from the side, the largest structure visible is the cerebral cortex, part of the forebrain. The cerebral cortex, the surface area of the cerebrum, is the seat of higher mental functions, including thinking, planning, and problem solving. The cerebral cortex is more highly developed in humans than in any other animal. It is divided into two hemispheres—left and right—that are interconnected by nerve fibers. The hemispheres are thought to be specialized, one side for language and the other for processing of spatial information, such as maps and pictures. Each hemisphere controls the opposite side of the body, so that damage to one side of the brain may cause numbness or paralysis of one arm and leg.

> The cerebral cortex has four lobes . . . [and] functions such as vision, hearing, and speech are distributed in selected regions, with some lobes being associated with more than one function. The frontal lobe is the largest, making up nearly one-third of the surface of the cerebral cortex. Lesions of any one of the lobes can have a dramatic impact on the functions of that lobe.
>
> Other forebrain structures process information from the sensory organs and send it to the cortex, or receive orders from cortical centers and relay them on down. Also in the forebrain are centers for memory and emotion, as well as control of essential functions such as hunger, thirst, and sex drive.
>
> The midbrain is a small area, but it contains important centers for sleep and pain, as well as relay centers for sensory information and control of movement.
>
> . . . Part of the hindbrain, including the cerebellum, can also be seen. The cerebellum controls complex motor programming, including maintaining muscle tone and posture. Other hindbrain structures are essential to the regulation of vegetative functions, including breathing, heart rate, and blood pressure. The brain stem connects the cerebral cortex to the spinal cord. (Gilson, 2011, p. 90)

Explanations for brain and neurological behavior are equally as complex. The connection between each axon and dendrite is actually a gap called a *synapse.* Synapses utilize chemical and electrical neurotransmitters to communicate. Nerve impulses travel from the cell body to the ends of the axons, where they trigger the release of neurotransmitters. The adjacent dendrite of another neuron has receptors distinctly shaped to fit particular types of neurotransmitters. When the neurotransmitter fits into a slot, the message is passed along.

Essentially, neurotransmitters either excite or inhibit neurological system responses. While knowledge of neurotransmitters remains incomplete there are several that have been identified and scrutinized in detail. Here are a few exemplars:

Acetylcholine (ACh): The first neurotransmitter identified (nearly 70 years ago) is an excitatory neurotransmitter active in both the central nervous system (CNS) and the PNS. Acetylcholine may be critical for intellectual activities such as memory.

Dopamine (DA): This neurotransmitter, which is widely present in the CNS and PNS, is implicated in regulation of the endocrine system. Dopamine is thought to play a role in influencing emotional behavior, cognition, and motor activity.

Norepinephrine (NE): Like dopamine, norepinephrine appears in many parts of the body. It may play a role in learning and memory, and is also secreted by the adrenal gland in response to stress or events that produce arousal. Norepinephrine connects the brain stem with the cerebral cortex (Bentley & Walsh, 2005).

Serotonin: Present in blood platelets, the lining of the digestive tract, and in a tract from the midbrain to all brain regions, this neurotransmitter is thought to be a factor in many bodily functions. Serotonin plays a role in sensory processes, muscular activity, thinking, states of consciousness, mood, depression, and anxiety (Gilson, 2011).

Amino acids: Some types of the unit molecules found in proteins are distributed throughout the brain and other body tissues. One of these amino acids, gamma aminobutyric acid (GABA), is thought to play a critical role in inhibiting the firing of impulses of some cells. Thus GABA is believed to play an important role in many functions of the CNS, such as locomotor activity, cardiovascular reactions, pituitary function, and anxiety (Bentley & Walsh, 2005).

Peptides: Amino acids that are joined together have only recently been studied as neurotransmitters. Opioids, many of which are peptides, play an important role in activities ranging from moderating pain to causing sleepiness. Endorphins are neuropeptides; they help to minimize pain and enhance adaptive behavior.

A bit more interior narrative attention is directed to the neurological system than to some others because of the growth of research in this area and attribution of so much of human experience to this proximal division.

Commentary on Neuroscience and the Neurological System

Over the past several decades, neuroscience has observed, filmed, and interpreted human experience as materialist, with the brain playing the leading role in this materialist script (Thagard, 2010). That is to say, contrary to the Kantian dualist view of mind and body as separate parts of the proximal environment, neuroscientists view the brain as the mind and visa versa, and as suggested by Thagard, this "brain revolution" has the potential to be paradigmatic in theorizing human life and meaning. Recognizable in the previous material may be some of the terms from diverse sources such as the natural food store, pharmacy shelves, and perhaps even the social work literature on psychopharmacology (Bentley & Walsh, 2005).

Neuroscience has created a grand narrative which foregrounds science as a most credible and authoritative truth teller of the human experience. Not unexpectedly, its popularity has met with conceptual and evidentiary criticisms. From the methodological standpoint, brain imaging studies have been indicted because of small associations between visual image and interpreted behavioral outcomes (Creative Commons, 2009). Because the brain has been named as the agent for almost every human experience, belief, and preference, philosophers, humanities scholars, and even many scientists have balked at the reductionist trend. In other words, attributing the sum total of human existence to proximal circuitry, while lauded by neuroscience afficianados and loyalists, has not met with overwhelming applause from brain science critics (Tallis, 2008, 2010).

Endocrine System

The endocrine system has made the news, with the term *anabolic steroids* as one of the major sports enhancing drugs of the 21st century. This drug is one of several substances found within the endocrine system, the system of the corpus to which growth, metabolism, development, learning, and memory are attributed. The endocrine system is the body's pharmacy, so to speak, in that this large system produces and regulates corporeal chemicals that oversee the proximal environment and its distal display of behavior and appearance.

Once again through the narrative of the interior corpus, structurally, this system is comprised of two basic elements, glands and hormones. Gilson (2011) discusses the descriptive process through which this system operates as follows:

> Glands secrete hormones into the blood system; those hormones bind to receptors in target organs . . . and affect the metabolism or function of those organs. Hormones travel long distances through the blood stream. . . .
>
> Endocrine glands include the pineal, pituitary, thyroid, parathyroid, pancreas, and adrenal. Endocrine cells are also found in some organs which have primarily a non-endocrine function: the hypothalamus, liver, thymus, heart, kidney, stomach, duodenum, testes, and ovaries.
>
> Similar to the nervous system, the endocrine system has its unique yet integrated form of communicating and thus doing its job throughout the body. At its most basic level, hormones "talk" through their structure, the endocrine cell, by traveling through the blood system to a target cell. A more complex form of hormonal communication however, links glands in the endocrine system directly to one another and involves multiple glands in performing the work of regulating the secretion and level of hormones. This complex system of feedback and control remains in delicate balance through "self-regulation" which

refers to hormones hav[ing] specific receptors so that the hormone released from one gland has a specific target tissue or organ. (Mader, as cited in Gilson, 2011, p. 94)

Commentary on the Endocrine System

At this point, you may be asking, "so what" about the endocrine system. To some extent, this system seems to operate in the recesses and alleyways of the proximal environment of the corpus and does not make prime time discussion until it is breached. Yet, its systematic tentacles reach throughout the corpus in areas of major significance to social work such as mental health, mood, growth, weight and so forth. Moreover, the endocrine system sits in a precarious balance that stress and other distal environmental conditions can tip, and even topple. To illustrate, in a brief web search, we stumbled upon a website that summarized articles on the endocrine system (Surfwax, 1998–2010). Among the huge range of topics included just in 2010 were: cancer, acupuncture, metabolism, nutrition, poisonous toys, the importance of singing to endocrine system health, and anger, among many others. These topics are studied through histology, or tissue studies, the primary evidentiary repository of the endocrine system. However, in addition to histological methods of inquiry, interpretations of behavioral observations can raise questions about the well-being of this system that to be answered, then move to the inquiry narrative of human biological science and medicine.

Immune System

Delving into this system, the corporeal defense department appears. If working at its peak, this system of omnipresent embodied sentries wards off interloping organisms that are determined through proximal environmental theories to be the primary causes of disease. Yet, the object of fire from the immune system is not always the interloper but sometimes may be the very environment that it is ostensibly protecting, resulting in autoimmune responses in which the body is at war with itself. We thus consider the immunity militia as it is characterized and theorized through the narrative of the interior corpus.

As summarized by Gilson (2011) through this narrative, this pervasive system is comprised of cells, organs, and fluids and uses the processes of identifying, rejecting, or deactivating antigens, which are exterior environmental agents such as a bacteria or fungi. White blood cells and the organs that produce them (e.g., bone marrow, spleen, thymus) are important descriptive components of the immune system. The immune system's response to antigens occurs in both specific and nonspecific ways (DeFranco, Locksley, & Robertson, 2007). Nonspecific immunity is more general, a process through which invading agents are surrounded and eradicated. "Scavenger" cells or phagocytes circulate in the blood and lymph, looking for attractive biochemical signals that call them to congregate at the site of a wound and ingest antigens (DeFranco et al., 2007). While this process, known as *phagocytosis,* is generally effective in basic protection, survival of bacteria and viruses and large scale attacks on the body require other tactical strategies. Thus, specific immunity is essential (DeFranco, et al., 2007).

Specific immunity, or acquired immunity, engages the lymphocytes in defense. These cells not only respond to an infection, but also develop a memory of that infection, allowing the body to launch a defense against it in subsequent exposure. Certain lymphocytes translate this memory into antibodies, protein molecules designed to attach to the surface of specific invaders. The antibodies recruit other protein substances that puncture the membrane of invading microorganisms, causing the invaders to explode. The antibodies are assisted in this battle by T cells, which destroy foreign cells directly and orchestrate the immune response. Following the primary immune response, the antibodies remain in the circulatory system at significant levels until they are no longer needed. With reexposure to the same antigen, a secondary immune response occurs, characterized by a more rapid rise in antibody levels—a period of hours rather than days. This rapid response is possible because, during initial exposure to the antigen, memory cells were created. Memory T cells store the information needed to produce specific antibodies. Memory T cells also have very long lives (Gilson, 2011).

Commentary on the Immune System

Reading and writing about the immune system invokes war analogies, and rightfully so. Not unlike groups of crusaders, in order to be operative, this system of protection requires constant attention, nutrition, and to a large extent, balance. Over the past five decades, the fragility of immunity has increasingly been visualized as more proximal environmental conditions are formalized and labeled. As Beaton (2003) notes, and reflecting efforts to realign and juxtapose the body fragments and theorized exterior factors, the field of psychoneuroimmunology studies the links between several elements of the proximal corporal environment and distal conditions.

Note that systems are still named in the new and complex world, indicating that the current paradigmatic systems remain conceptually intact as they join a complex structure; this structure is mixed but not yet theoretically transformed into a single unit. Through this multifactor but, as yet, unblended lens, recent inquiry has posited immune system causes of specific and unusual behaviors. In a recent study of obsessive compulsive behavior in mice, bone marrow transplants designed to bolster the immune system resulted in the elimination of the target behavior. This field of inquiry and practice gives social work a legitimate place setting at the medical table of immunologic treatment, as discussed in subsequent chapters on theory application.

Cardiovascular System

The interior network of highways and byways that carry "life's blood" and its power source, the heart, comprise this proximal corporeal system. Again, this system will be navigated using the vehicle of the narrative of the interior corpus.

The cardiovascular system is described as two major structures, the heart and the blood circulatory system (Gilson, 2011). The operation of the heart is described as a pump in which the heart's walls, comprised of specialized muscle, shorten and squeeze the hollow cavities of the heart to force blood throughout the circulatory system. Consider a more detailed description of the structures of the cardiovascular system:

There are three types of blood vessels:

1. *Arteries* have thick walls that contain elastic and muscular tissues. The elastic tissues allow the arteries to expand and accommodate the increase in blood volume that occurs after each heartbeat. *Arterioles* are small arteries that branch into smaller vessels called *capillaries.*

2. *Capillaries* are a critical part of this closed circulation system, as they allow the exchange of nutrients and waste material with the body's cells. Oxygen and nutrients transfer out of a capillary into the tissue fluid surrounding cells, and absorb carbon dioxide and other wastes from the cells.

3. *Veins* take blood from the capillaries and return it to the heart. Some of the major veins in the arms and legs have valves which allow the blood to flow only toward the heart when they are open and block any backward flow when they are closed (Mader, as cited in Gilson, 2011, p. 102).

The heart has two sides (right and left) separated by the septum. Each side is divided into an upper and a lower chamber. The two upper, thin-walled chambers are called *atria.* The atria are smaller than the two lower, thick-walled chambers, called *ventricles.* Valves within the heart direct the flow of blood from chamber to chamber, and when closed, prevent its backward flow.

The right side of the heart pumps blood to the lungs, and the left side of the heart pumps blood to the tissues of the body. Blood from body tissues that is low in oxygen and high in carbon dioxide (deoxygenated blood) enters the right atrium. The right atrium then sends blood through a valve to the right ventricle. The right ventricle then sends the blood through another valve and the pulmonary arteries into the lungs. In the lungs, the blood gives up carbon dioxide and takes up oxygen. Pulmonary veins then carry blood that is high in oxygen (oxygenated) from the lungs to the left atrium. From the left atrium, blood is sent through a valve to the left ventricle. The blood is then sent through a valve into the aorta for distribution around the body. (Mader, as cited in Gilson, 2011, pp. 102–103)

Contraction and relaxation of the heart move the blood from the ventricles to the lungs and to the body. The right and left sides of the heart contract together—first the two atria, then the two ventricles. The heart contracts ("beats") about 70 times per minute. The contraction and relaxation cycle is called the *cardiac cycle.* The sound of the heartbeat, as heard through a stethoscope, is caused by the opening and closing of the heart valves.

Although the heart will beat independent of any neurological system stimulation, regulation of the heart is primarily the responsibility of the autonomic nervous system (ANS). Parasympathetic activities of the neurological system, which tend to be thought of as normal or routine activities, slow the heart rate. Sympathetic activities, associated with stress, increase the heart rate.

As blood is pumped from the aorta into the arteries, their elastic walls swell, followed by an immediate recoiling. The alternating expansion and recoiling of the arterial wall is the pulse. The pulse rate is normally about 70 times per minute, the rate of the heartbeat.

Blood pressure is the measure of the pressure of the blood against the wall of a blood vessel. A sphygmomanometer is used to measure blood pressure. The cuff of the sphygmomanometer is placed around the upper arm over an artery. A pressure gauge is used to measure the systolic blood pressure, the highest arterial pressure, which results from ejection of blood from the aorta. Diastolic blood pressure, the lowest arterial pressure, occurs while the ventricles of the heart are relaxing. Normal blood pressure for a young adult is 120 millimeters (mm) of mercury systole over 80 mm of mercury systole, or 120/80.

While blood pressure accounts for the movement of blood from the heart to the body, by way of arteries and arterioles, skeletal muscle contraction moves the blood through the venous system. As skeletal muscles contract, they push against the thin or weak walls of the veins, causing the blood to move past valves. Once past the valve, the blood cannot return, forcing it to move toward the heart.

Commentary on the Cardiovascular System

Cardiovascular health is a major topic of conversation relevant to social work practice, particularly as self-help health care (e.g., health literacy and healthy behaviors) emerge as a contemporary trend. So while the heart and its network are essentially characterized through the narrative of the interior corpus as a circulatory system, their continued employment depends on careful feeding and nurturance. This point foregrounds the importance and intense relevance of proximal environmental theory to social work practice.

Another critical point about this sliver's relationship to racial and gender politics is important before leaving this system. Interestingly, cardiovascular disease has been "racialized" despite the lack of evidence supporting clear definitions of race as interior at all (Kurian & Cardarelli, 2007). This dissonance therefore illuminates the obligation of distal social and economic factors to advance conditions under which the proximal cardiovascular system can remain employed and competent in its body work. The role of social work in cardiovascular health, and thus in the proximal circulatory system, is essential.

Musculoskeletal System

This proximal system is the locus of posture and movement. In theories that parse humans into population segments, the musculoskeletal system and its activity are observable and thus major players in remanding people to categories of disabled and nondisabled (DePoy & Gilson, 2011). In essence, the musculoskeletal system comprises the robotics of the body, in that it is responsible for dynamic observable motion of the corpus. We now power walk in this system with the assistance of the narrative of the interior corpus.

The musculoskeletal system, located throughout the body, explains postural integrity and body movement. In essence, the musculoskeletal system is the body's interior environmental scaffold and propeller. The contraction and relaxation of muscles attached to the skeleton is the basis for all voluntary movements. Over 600 skeletal muscles in the body account for about 40% of our body weight. Gilson's (2011) description of the operation of this system is as follows:

> When a muscle contracts it shortens; it can only pull, not push. Therefore, for us to be able to extend and to flex at a joint, muscles work in "antagonistic pairs." As an example, when the hamstring group in the back of the leg contracts, the quadriceps in the front relax, which allows the leg to bend at the knee. When the quadriceps contract, the hamstring relaxes allowing the leg to extend.
>
> The contraction of a muscle occurs as a result of an electrical impulse passed to the muscle by a controlling nerve that releases Acetylcholine. When a single stimulus is given to a muscle, it responds with a "twitch," a contraction lasting only a fraction of a second. But when there are repeated stimulations close together, the muscle cannot fully relax between impulses. As a result, each contraction benefits from the previous contraction, giving a combined contraction greater than an individual twitch. When stimulation is sufficiently rapid, the twitches cease to be jerky, and fuse into a smooth contraction/movement called "tetanus." However, tetanus that continues eventually produces muscle fatigue due to depletion of energy reserves.
>
> Skeletal muscles exhibit "tone" when some muscles are always contracted. Tone is critical if we are to maintain body posture. If all the muscle fibers in the neck, trunk, and legs were to relax, our bodies would collapse.
>
> Nerve fibers embedded in the muscles emit nerve impulses that communicate to the central nervous system (CNS) the state of particular muscles. This communication allows the CNS to coordinate the contraction of muscles. (Mader, as cited in Gilson, 2011, p. 104)

In its entirety, the musculoskeletal system both supports the body, and allows it to move. The skeleton, particularly the large, heavy bones of the legs, supports the body against the pull of gravity and protects soft body parts. Most essentially, the skull protects the brain, the rib cage protects the heart and lungs, and the vertebrae protect and support the spinal cord.

> Bones serve as sites for the attachment of muscles. It may not seem so, but bone is a very active tissue, supplied with nerves and blood vessels. Throughout life, bone cells repair, remold, and rejuvenate in response to stresses, strains, and fractures.
>
> A typical long bone, such as the leg bones, has a cavity surrounded by a dense area. The dense area contains compact bone. The cavernous area contains blood vessels and nerves surrounded by spongy bone. Far from being weak, spongy bone is designed for strength. It is the site of red marrow, the specialized tissue that produces red and white blood cells. The cavity of a long bone also contains yellow marrow, which is a fat-storage tissue. (Gilson, 2011, p. 105)

Bones are joined together at joints. Long bones and their corresponding joints are what permit flexible body movement (Bilezikian, & Martin, 2008). Joints are classified according to the amount of movement they permit. Bones of the cranium, which are sutured together, are examples of immovable joints. Joints between the vertebrae are slightly movable. Freely movable joints, which connect two bones separated by a cavity, are called *synovial joints*. Synovial joints may be hinge joints (knee and elbow) or ball-and-socket joints (attachment of the femur to the hip bone) (Gilson, 2011, p. 10).

Ligaments hold together the bones in a joint; tendons connect muscle to bone. Cartilage caps the ends of the bones, which gives added strength and support to the joint. Fluid-filled sacs called *bursae* ease friction between tendons and ligaments, and between tendons and bones (Bilezikian, & Martin, 2008).

Commentary on the Musculoskeletal System

Dissimilar to other corporeal systems discussed so far, the musculoskeletal system is both observable and the object of judgment. Observation of this system's behavior results in movement and body carriage to which terms such as *grace, agile, powerful, clumsy,* and so forth are ascribed as descriptors and function as the object of which many assumptions about embodied health and competence are anchored. Missing from the narrative of the interior corpus is this discussion as well as recognition of the efforts that are undertaken to build and perfect movement for competition, sports, and simply public display. It is therefore not surprising that the endocrine substances in the preceding discussion (anabolic steroids) are ingested to "superhumanize" the musculoskeletal system, bringing these two systems into a partnership in movement.

Reproductive System

Similar to the musculoskeletal system, the reproductive system cleaves humans into two primary sexual categories, male and female. Because some of its elements and behaviors are observable, the reproductive system places its owners in a position to be labeled, judged, and treated as gendered. Gender is discussed in detail in Chapter 11, with a look now at the system that is indicted as organically responsible for gender, aided again by the narrative of the interior corpus.

The reproductive system is described as both proximal and distal. This chapter addresses reproductive structures as proximal and organic in composition, while other chapters expand this discussion. The proximal reproductive system behavior, although complex, is most often described in the biological literature as concerned with sexual behavior, conception, gestation, and birth. Through the biological lens, sex is described as differences in organs and related interior structures and processes, and explained as chromosomal content. Thus, from a biological explanatory perspective, sex is conferred at birth (or before in prenatal testing) on the basis of distinguishing male or female genitalia.

Gilson (2011) provides the following description of this system:

> The external male organs are the penis and scrotum. Internal organs consist of the testes; the tubes and ducts that serve to transfer the sperm through the reproductive system; and "the organs that help nourish and activate sperm and neutralize some of the acidity that sperm encounter in the vagina. The penis functions as a conduit for both urine and semen. (p. 108)

Externally, one can view the shaft and the glans (often referred to as the head or tip) of the penis. Within the shaft, three cylinders are contained. The two largest are called the *corpra cavernosa*. During sexual arousal, these become engorged with blood and stiffen. The corpus spongiosum is the third cylinder, which contains the urethra. It enlarges at the tip of the penis to form the glans. The ridge that separates the glans from the shaft of the penis is called the *corona*. The frenulum is the sensitive strip of tissue that connects the underside of the glans to the shaft. At the base of the penis is the root, which extends into the pelvis.

Three glands are part of the feedback loop that controls a constant level of male hormones in the bloodstream. The testes, male gonads, are best known for their functions in producing sperm (mature germ cells which fertilize the female egg) and in secreting male hormones called androgens. Testosterone is one of the most important hormones in that it stimulates the development of the sex organs in the male fetus and the development of secondary sex characteristics such as facial hair, male muscle mass, and a deep voice. The two other glands in the feedback loop are the hypothalamus and the pituitary gland. Both secrete hormones that serve as regulatory, primarily retaining testosterone at a constant blood level.

In the early stages, sperm cells are called *spermatocytes*, each containing 46 chromosomes including both X and Y chromosome that determine sex. As the spermatocytes mature and divide, chromosomes are reduced in half and only one (either the X or Y) sex determining chromosome is retained. The mature sperm cell is called the *spermatozoa*. This cell fertilizes the female egg (ovum), which contains only X chromosomes and thus is the determining factor for the child's sex. (Females have two X chromosomes and males have one X and one Y chromosome.)

Before ejaculation, the sperm passes through a number of tubes and glands, beginning with the testes, proceeding through the seminiferous tubules (a maze of ducts) and then to the epididymis, which is the convergence of the ducts and serves as the storage facility for sperm. Each epididymis empties into the vas deferens, which brings the mature sperm to the seminal vesicles, small glands that lie behind the bladder. In these glands, a nourishing and activating fluid combines with the sperm before it is carried through the urethra to the outside of the penis. The prostate gland through which the urethra passes produces and introduces the milky fluid to the sperm that functions to preserve the sperm and neutralize the alkalinity that is met in the female. Cowper's glands also make their contribution to the seminal fluid before it leaves the male. However, even if there is early ejaculation and the Cowper's glands do not have time to secrete fluid, viable sperm exist and can fertilize the female egg. This point is important to know because early withdrawal of the penis does not prevent the passage of some viable sperm cells that may not yet have passed through the Cowper's glands. It is also important to know that sperm only comprises about 1% of the total ejaculate, but that this small percentage of the 3 to 5 mm of total ejaculate contains between 200 and 400 million sperm. The number of sperm decreases with frequent ejaculation and advancing age.

At birth of the female, one can observe the pudendum—or vulva, *mons veneris*, which is the fatty tissue below the abdomen that becomes covered with hair after puberty—clitoris, and the vaginal opening—*labia majora* and *minora*.

Unlike the male, the female has a physical separation between excretion and reproductive organs. Urine passes from the bladder through the urethra to the urethral opening, where it is expelled from the body. The urethra is located immediately behind the vaginal opening and is unconnected to the vaginal opening. The labia majora, large folds of skin, both contain nerve endings that are responsive to stimulation and protect the inner genitalia. Labia minora join the prepus hood at the top that covers the clitoris. These structures, when stimulated, engorge with blood and darken, indicating sexual arousal. Resembling the male penis and developing from the same embryonic tissue, the clitoris is about 1 inch long and a quarter inch wide. However, unlike the penis, the clitoris is not directly involved in reproduction but serves primarily to produce sexual pleasure. The vestibule located inside the labia minor contains openings to the urethra and the vagina. It is also a site for arousal due to its richness in nerve endings that are sensitive to stimulation.

Internal structures include the vagina, ovaries, fallopian tubes, cervical canal, and uterus. The vagina is the structure that articulates with the external sexual structures. Comprised of three layers and shaped in a cylindrical fashion, the vagina both receives the penis during intercourse and is the canal through which the child passes from the uterus to the world outside of the mother. Because of its multiple functions, the vagina is flexible in size and changes climate from dry to lubricated.

The cervix is the lower end of the uterus and protrudes into the vagina. It functions to maintain the chemical balance of the vagina through its secretions. The cervical os is the opening within the cervix that opens to allow the baby to pass from the uterus to the vaginal canal and to allow sperm to swim from the vagina up through the uterus.

The uterus, also called the womb, serves as the pear-shaped home for the unborn child for the 9 months between implantation and birth. The innermost layer of three layers is called the endometrium and is the tissue that builds to form an environment for the developing fetus. If pregnancy does not occur, the endometrium is shed monthly through the process of menstruation. If pregnancy does occur, the well-muscled middle layer produces the strong contractions necessary at birth to move the fetus out of the uterus, into the vaginal canal and then into the increasingly distal world. The external layer functions as protection of the uterus within the body.

The fallopian tubes, also called the uterine tubes, connect the ovaries to the uterus and serve as a conduit for the ova (egg cells) from the ovaries to the uterus. Located on either side of the uterus, the ovaries have two major functions, the production of ova and the production of the female sex hormones, progesterone and estrogen.

Dissimilar from males who produce sperm throughout their lives, females are born with the total number of ova that they will possess. Less than half of the 2 million ova mature sufficiently to be maintained in the ovaries past puberty. Of approximately 400,000, only 400 are released in the monthly cycle.

Estrogen facilitates sexual maturation and regulates the menstrual cycle in pre-menopausal women. Progesterone, while less discussed in the media is critically important in its role of preparing the uterus for pregnancy. It also is a regulator of the menstrual cycle.

The breasts in women are considered to be secondary sex characteristics in that they do not have a direct function in reproduction. Mammary glands contained in the breast produce milk that is discharged through the nipple. It is located at the center of the areole, which is erect and is a site of sexual stimulation when touched. The size of the gland is incidental to breast size and milk production. Rather, breast size is a function of the fatty tissue within the breast (Gilson, 2011).

Commentary on the Reproductive System

More than any other system, the narrative of the interior corpus, when applied to the reproductive system, most clearly illustrates how the complexity and broader picture of embodiment becomes obfuscated in anatomic and physiologic "detailia." Facilitating medicalization of reproduction through this narrative is therefore not surprising, as discussed in subsequent chapters.

THINKING POINT

Now that you have read the section on biology, what do you think about its descriptive and explanatory potency?

Before we leave the individual, observable, organic theoretical world, let us look at a specialized and contemporary part of it, that of genetics and the human genome.

Genetics and the Human Genome

Genetics is concerned with proximal environmental structures of chromosomes, genes, and the embodied characteristics that these structures explain.

Table 7.5 provides word soup sampled from the narrative of the interior corpus definitions of four basic descriptive genetic terms. We have organized these building blocks from least observable to most obvious characteristics.

Genes and their distribution are inherited. Instrumental in first detailing the methods by which genetic structures were inherited, Gregor Mendel proposed

---

Table 7.5 Genetic Terms Word Soup

DNA: genetic material

Gene: a hereditary unit that occupies a certain position on a chromosome

Chromosome: a threadlike structure consisting of chromatin and carrying genetic information (genes) arranged in a linear sequence

Phenotype: observable characteristics of an organism produced by the organism's genetic interior interacting with the environment

during the 17th century that a sperm and each egg possessed one-half of the gene pair necessary to produce a trait. When they united, the combined genetic structure was passed from parents to their offspring. More recently, with the explosion in DNA research and the Human Genome Project, knowledge of genetics and genetic inheritance has expanded beyond this simple framework to identify complex ways in which genetic material is passed on and inherited (Lolle, Pruitt, Victor, & Young, 2005).

The question of what characteristics genetic composition actually explains has been debated for many decades. Remember the nature-nurture debate mentioned in Chapter 7, which places explanations of human behavior, appearance, and experience into two camps, influence from the distal environment or proximal inherited environment—this debate has been at the center of disagreements not only in theory but in legitimate policy, practice, and human responses to individuals.

> *Consider alcohol dependence. Some argue that it is a disease with a genetic predisposition and others assert that it is a voluntary condition attributed to lack of control and excessive alcohol intake. The way in which one explains alcohol dependence determines the worth of and responses to the individual who demonstrates this condition.*

Of particular importance to this discussion is the Human Genome Project. In 2003, a map of the genetic composition of humans was completed. It was estimated that humans possess between 20,000 and 25,000 genes that explain human description. More recently, multiple aspects of humans including disease states, syndromes such as autism spectrum disorder, and even genetic predispositions to growing rows of teeth have been revealed (News_Medical.net, 2010). Subsequent chapters throughout the book more fully discuss the implications of explaining human description in genetic terms. Some of the ethical dilemmas that emerge from this important proximal corpus view are, however, relevant here.

First, looking through a genetic lens allows for genetic manipulation. That is to say, changing genetic structures, using stem cells for medical and other purposes, and identifying the acceptable and thus the "abnormal" genetic composition to be eliminated creates opportunity as well as disadvantage. Genetic research has been extremely important in medical responses to disease, in elongating the life span, and even in the promise of cloning replacement parts for failing body structures. Yet, the dangers of genetic manipulation in homogenizing humans to the point of limiting or extinguishing diversity remains a serious concern for many ethicists.

THINKING POINT

 As you continue to explore explanations, think about your positions, and the queries and dilemmas that arise for you with regard to genetic explanations of human description.

Evidence of the Proximal Corpus

Biological knowledge and its narrative have been developed from experimental approaches of inquiry which rely on observation and measurement. Visualizing the corpus through observation of its perimeter—and through filming, extracting, measuring electricity, and so forth—from that which is contained most proximal are strategies for data collection. Biological and physiological responses are typically investigated through clinical trials and true experimentation, which seek isolated agents of change and look at the probability of their impact on specified response outcomes. Perhaps because of the methods that are used to generate this knowledge, biological descriptions and explanations appear less interpretive, and thus more clear-cut, than other theoretical fields. However, while biology can provide an observable descriptive taxonomy of body function, its explanatory power is not exhaustive, as indicated in some of the preceding system commentaries.

Reportable Ontogeny

As a reminder of what is considered reportable, recall a discussion from Chapter 1. The descriptions and explanations discussed here are by no means exhaustive, but illustrate how inferred constructs within individual humans have been approached by some of the most important proximal environmental theorists.

Now, as a basis for examination of proximal theories of cognition, it will be helpful to revisit the discussion of cognition in Chapter 5 on specific developmental theories. As noted, cognition is a construct that can only be inferred through behavior, or more recently, interpretation of brain imaging. Before technology allowed us to peek inside the skull, inferences about observable behavior, such as language acquisition and use, abstract conceptual formation and manipulation, and problem solving were the primary descriptive reportables of cognition.

Films and light show images that result from advanced technological methods, such as measuring the electrical activity, glucose use, and heat of various regions of the brain, now create visuals of brain activation which are then associated with cognitive behaviors (Cognitive Neuroimaging Laboratory, 2009).

Information processing theorists were discussed in Chapter 5. These investigators used computer and network metaphors to describe cognition as a set of thinking processes that can be explained by the activity that takes place within proximal neurophysiological fragments such as the memory. Terms such as *memory connectivity, neural network, information flow,* and so forth are monikers used to describe human thinking through this approach. As such, cognition is explained primarily as an interior process in which information is imported from the exterior environment and acted upon by biology and physiology. The extent to which genetic composition influences neurophysiologic cognitive competence remains as a point of significant and heated disagreement.

Jensen (1969) was perhaps the best known for his controversial work suggesting the inherited basis of intelligence. Relying in large part on IQ testing, Jensen criticized programs such as Head Start, suggesting that IQ was a genetic trait that was not readily modifiable from distal influences. Building on previous proximal environmental theories of cognition, Jensen used IQ tests, brain size, and other empirical measures to support his assertion that the g factor, or general intelligence, could be traced back in one's ancestry. In response, many scholars, theorists, professionals, and laypersons eschewed this notion as racist. Among them was Gould (1981), whose seminal but heavily criticized book, *Mismeasure of Man,* invalidated the evidentiary basis on which Jensen made his claims. Moreover, the recently falsified genetic explanation of race, noted earlier, further invalidates many of Jensen's initial experiments in which he distinguished lineage by racial appearance.

The debate about the genetic basis of cognition continues, particularly as applied to intelligence. A more recent yet classical exposition by Herrnstein and Murray (1994) reinvigorated the nature-nurture debate. In their controversial book, they link intelligence to class, engendering criticisms of classism and racism similar to those levied at Jensen. We are relieved to see sound discussions of proximal explanations of cognition that move away from racial, gender, and class distinctions into more complex, nondiscriminatory analyses of the interactive role of proximal neurophysiologic processes and distal environmental factors on cognitive behavior. For example, rather than looking at inheritance and group differences related to race, class, and gender to explain human thinking, Changeaux (2004), followed by numerous neuroscientists, applied a complex neurophysiologic perspective to explain the human cognitive tasks of learning and discovery. Specifically, Changeaux investigated and proposed that there is a physiological basis to the basic human activities of seeking and verifying truth.

Perhaps fueled by the study of psychopathology and the increasing focus on the neurological basis of mental illness, proximal environmental factors have been identified as explanatory of the inferable of "mental behavior," including but not limited to personality, emotions, motivation, and even vice. Medina (2000) and McGowan (2009) argue that Dante's seven deadly sins—envy, lust, gluttony, avarice, sloth, wrath, and pride—can be explained by brain science, and even more specifically by genetics.

As discussed later in the section on phylogeny, Travis (2007) looks to proximal environmental biological evolution as explanatory of human cognition. Countering genetic explanations for cognitive difference among individuals, Travis posits that all living cells are intelligent and that differences among species are adaptations to conditions necessary to survive and propogate. This is relevant here, as she and other cognitive evolutionary theorists apply concepts that advance humans as a species capable of individual intelligence and cognitive behavior.

Different from the proximal theories that explain humans in terms of physiology, some theorists identify nondevelopmental, intrinsic-inferred explanations for human description. These are referred to as *intrinsic-inferred* because the factors to which explanation is attributed or associated cannot be visualized at all. Thus, they must be ascertained through another more abstract means.

> *Consider personality, which refers to the stable intrinsic individual traits and styles that distinguish people from one another, and allow us to recognize someone on the basis of his or her personality characteristics (Schultz & Schultz, 2004). But, can we actually visualize the construct of personality, or do we make judgments about personality on the basis of cobbling together a set of observed behaviors and reported individual life experience? Personality tests such as the Myers-Briggs Inventory infer the constructs of personality type on the basis of performance on standard test items. (Myers, n.d.)*

Motivation

Looking at the construct of motivation, it is helpful to first consider what drives individuals to action.

THINKING POINT

As you read further, think about what factors explain why you do what you do.

Maslow (1970) was best known for his classic descriptive motivational hierarchy. He explained motivation to engage in specific activity as a function of interior needs. Figure 7.1 illustrates his organization of needs in a pyramidal depiction of increasing complexity as one ascends. In order to move up the pyramid, each prior need must be fulfilled from the most basic survival needs sequentially up to the most abstract.

Figure 7.1   Maslow's Hierarchy of Needs Pyramid

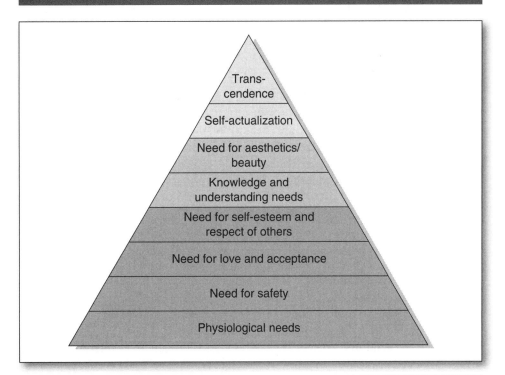

Source: Huitt & Hummel, 2003

Thus, in order to pursue self-actualization, the needs below that level must be met and secure. Curiously, a recent article in the *New York Times* (Belkin, 2010) critically reported on a suggested revision of the pyramid, in which self-actualization was redefined from an evolutionary advantage (see a fuller discussion of evolutionary theory later in this chapter) as parenting. Kenrick (as cited in Belkin, 2010), theorized that self-actualization for one's own sake has no evolutionary advantage and thus, from the perspective of continuing and strengthening humankind taken by evolutionary psychologists, redefined this high level of motivation as propagating the human species.

Maslow was not the only theorist who posited motivation as an interior environmental function. Revising Maslow's thinking, but still retaining the centrality of the proximal environment in motivation, Alderfer (as cited in Value Based Management. net, 2010) posited ERG (existence, relatedness, and growth) theory. Two of Alderfer's propositions mark the major distinction from Maslow. First, needs could be operative across levels and groups. That is to say, one can have growth and existence needs simultaneously. Second, failure to fill an upper-level need is likely to increase needs at a lower level of motivation (Value Based Management.net, 2010).

THINKING POINT

 How might Alderfer's theory explain motivated criminal behavior on the part of a chief executive officer of a large corporation?

McClelland (1985) identified three proximal factors that explain motivation to act: (1) need for power, (2) need for affiliation, and (3) need for achievement. The proximal composition and balance of these three factors, according to McClelland, explain the magnitude and nature of achievement motivation that individuals exhibit. McClelland saw reward as important to provoke action, however different from the behaviorists who identified meaningful rewards as extrinsic and thus distal, McClelland identified the satisfaction of meeting one or more of the three interior, proximal needs as the substantive reward.

Similarly, in their classic and still used conceptualization, Herzberg, Mausner, and Snyderman (1959), who studied work motivation, proposed two types of factors that explained achievement motivation, with the proximal factor being the one most responsible for genuine motivation. While they did not discount the importance of hygiene factors (e.g., salary and physical work environment) for initial satisfaction and comfort, Herzberg and colleagues distinguished "true" motivation as that which emerges from proximal factors such as the desire for personal achievement, and the intrinsic satisfaction derived from one's interest in and advancement in work itself.

> *Social workers typically do not enter the field primarily for the purpose of earning a large sum of money. Rather, they seek satisfaction through providing service to those in need.*

More recent theories of motivation (Shah & Gardener, 2008) have proposed core motives that are mediated by numerous variables including but not limited to cognition, social milieu, cultural membership, proximal corporeal structures and functions, individual and group self-regard, trust, and purpose (e.g., seeking pleasure, avoiding pain, helping others, etc.). Of particular note is the contemporary emphasis on cognition as the basis of motivation. An area of motivation theory that has engendered significant debate is the notion of *quality of motivation,* suggesting that there are "normative" and desired motives and, of course, their photographic negative, undesirable motivators. Undesirable motivators, according to Sheldon's (2008) self-concordance theory, derail an individual from setting and achieving the "correct goals."

Phylogeny

Now let us move into the theoretical world of proximal phylogeny. Theories that fall under this category focus their gaze not on individuals, but on humans as a species, and posit proximal factors as primarily explanatory of the growth and development of humans. While there are many approaches to explaining humans as a species, evolution and humanism are two essential approaches relevant to social work.

Evolutionary Approaches

Although most people identify Darwin as the first major theorist of evolution, the ancient Greeks actually posited similar ideas. Anaximander (Couprie, Hahn, & Naddaf, 2003) suggested that life evolved from inorganic matter through evolution, that life forms were related, and that humans evolved from their animal ancestors. Yet, despite Anaximander and many others, Darwin brought evolutionary theory to the forefront of biology, blazing a conceptual trail for many of his theoretical descendents.

In brief, Darwin (1859/2003) suggested that life emerged from nonlife forms, and through the process of mutation evolved from simple species to more complex animals, and then to humans. Furthermore, survival or extinction of species are explained by the proximal processes of naturally occurring random genetic mutation, in which an organism's genetic code naturally differs from its expected inherited composition. Darwin named this process *natural selection* to denote that only those mutations that are beneficial for survival, growth, and advancing complexity secure an interior stable place. Building on Darwin's ideas, Haeckel (1899) added the concept of *ontogeny recapitulates phylogeny.* That is to say, the growth and development of individuals from embryos through full maturation replicated the growth and development of the human species. Therefore, looking at the development of the human corpus from conception through physical maturation, one could obtain a mirror, so to speak, of the proximal history of humans as a species. This perspective has been debated over the years, with no agreement on the consistency between early human life and phylogenetic chronology of animals. Moreover, as briefly noted, evolutionary thinking perforates a solid perimeter between body and "not body" through rendering the corpus as a rearview mirror to the longitudinal evolution of organic life.

As briefly introduced, applying theories of evolution to the domain of psychology, the school of evolutionary psychology, or EP (Buss, 2003; Travis, 2007), arose and is prominent in contemporary psychological descriptions and explanations of humans. Evolutionary psychology is primarily concerned with the primate brain and its behavior. Through this lens, the explanation for all human thinking and action, to a greater or lesser extent, is therefore biological advancement of the human species to assure survival and evolutionary advantage. This approach, while contained within the skull, is another that lobs a huge challenge at dualist notions separating environment from body. Evolutionary theories in essence, although they gaze proximally, infer future longitudinal distal explanations as responsible for proximal human functions of advanced problem solving and adaptive abilities in that theorists claim that the human corpus behaves to both shape and insure human survival. Human phenomena such as collaboration, culture, cognition, language, music, and now parenting for self-actualization (Belkin, 2010) are explained as adaptive biological, evolutionary functions (Axelrod, 1984; Barkow, Cosmides, & Tooby, 1992; Travis, 2007). Moreover, some evolutionary theorists suggest the hidden goal of evolutionary advantage masquerading as the selection of sexual partners and the emotion of love (Pouzzner, 2000). Most recently, some theorists have revised Maslow's hierarchy of needs, replacing self-actualization with parenting as the apex of motivation and self-fulfillment (Kenrick, as cited in Belkin, 2010):

> If Hannah is attracted to Matt, the evolutionary psychologists might explain that attraction as a cognitive, neural process designed to produce the strongest offspring. Moreover, from Kenrick's vantage point, both Hannah and Matt would reach ultimate fulfillment if they had children.

THINKING POINT

 Of particular importance in this theoretical framework is the taboo on incest. Can you see why?

Incest would muddy the genetic lineage, so to speak, and disadvantage the human on the distal evolutionary continuum as a result of proximal inbreeding.

Koestler (1979), a 20th-century philosopher, integrated biological and evolutionary theory to explain atrocities committed by humans. He looked proximally to the superimposition of the frontal lobes on the lower evolutionary structure of the nonhuman mammalian brain as explanatory of the distal distinction between humans and their mammalian predecessors, and of "animal-like" behaviors such as violence and domination. He referred to human brains as *tripartite*, depicting their evolutionary structure as integrative of animal and human elements.

Evolution has been applied to numerous areas of human description. A recent application of evolutionary theory has resulted in the field of literary Darwinism (Caroll, 2004), which posits that adaption and survival explain narrative, or storytelling. That is, literature serves the purpose of advancing procreation, providing mechanisms through which humans can seek out the strongest mates, and thus produce strong and increasingly adaptive offspring.

THINKING POINT

 Can you provide an example that illustrates how creating or consuming literature has contributed to your knowledge and survival?

Humanistic Psychology

Humanism presents a completely different proximal environmental approach to explaining humans as a species. Growing out of humanistic philosophy (Grassi, 2001; Shah & Gardner, 2008), humanistic psychology was advanced in the early 1950s in response to the two major psychological paradigms of the times, behaviorism and psychoanalysis. Bugental (2008) proposed five proximal environmental tenets that are common to humanist lenses. These are listed in Table 7.6.

Maslow and Rogers were two of the seminal humanist thinkers. While Maslow was discussed in the section on ontogeny, he is also important under phylogeny, because he distinguished humans from other animal species by their higher order, abstract needs for self-actualization, and transcendence. So, Maslow too joins the host of theorists whose thoughts challenge the bifurcation of body and its context. Rogers (1980)

Table 7.6 Commonalities of Humanistic Proximal Environmental Theories

1. Human beings cannot be reduced to components.
2. Human beings have in them a uniquely human context.
3. Human consciousness includes an awareness of oneself in the context of other people.
4. Human beings have choices and responsibilities.
5. Human beings are intentional; they seek meaning, value and creativity. (Bugental, 2008)

applied humanist concepts to the practice of psychotherapy in what he named *person centered therapy.* Rogers explained all animal behavior through the concept of the actualizing tendency, or the inborn trait to develop to the fullest extent possible. Failure to reach one's fullest potential does not occur by choice, according to Rogers, but rather can be explained by the social and cultural mechanisms that are created by humans and thus distinguish humans from other animals. Because children develop in contexts in which they learn through conditional positive regard, individuals develop self-doubt, and according to Rogers, is at the root of human failings.

> *Consider your own childhood. It is probably accurate to say that you were looked upon more favorably by your teachers if you produced and behaved according to expectations. This is an example of conditional positive regard in that you would be praised when you did what was desirable but not when you behaved in an undesirable manner.*

Because Rogers suggests that humans and all organisms are innately "good," unconditional regard is necessary as the foundation to develop to our fullest potential.

> *If your teachers gave you praise with guidance no matter how you behaved, this unconditional regard would be highly associated with your fullest success.*

More contemporary humanists still proceed from the major notion that goodness inheres proximally in all humans despite the potential that negative messages being broadcast from the unconscious processes, as well as distal contexts, have to undermine dignity. Self-determination is a major value of humanists and, as such, therapy based on humanist psychology foregrounds this goal as well as positive regard for self and others (Association for Humanist Psychology, 2001). Rogers and other humanists therefore join Maslow, Bugental, and theorists in the proximal phylogenetic subdivision who perhaps unintentionally provoke debate about the mutual exclusivity of body and its environs.

Evidence

The evidentiary basis of biological and proximal environment was discussed in the preceding sections. For theories in the remainder of the chapter, diverse approaches including both logico-deductive experimental and naturalistic inductive methods of inquiry, have been employed, with humanist theorists leaning primarily toward naturalistic methods and evolutionary theorists choosing to inquire with experimental approaches. As so succinctly put in Shah and Gardner's (2008) work regarding methods and evidence for theories of motivation, "Where you stand depends on where you sit. In this case, what you posit depends on what you observe" (p. 17). We suggest that this adage applies to theories of reportable ontology as well as phylogeny discussed in this chapter. Given the grand inferences made in these theories, even when based on systematically generated data from either research tradition, the turret from which the theorist intellectualizes delimits the visible landscapes and propositions about their context and content.

Summary

This chapter examined theories that describe and explain the proximal environment, or those theories that are delimited to the corpus. To touch on a large range of proximal gazes and rationales, the discussion was divided into ontogeny and phylogeny. In the process of discussion and analysis, a focus was placed on language and evidence, and some ethical issues related to the nature-nurture debate.

References

Abrams, J. (1998). *Judaism and disability: Portayals in ancient texts from the Tanach through the Bavli.* Washington, DC: Gallaudet University Press.

Arehart-Treichel, J. (2010). Is hippocampus sometimes a time traveler? *Psychiatric News, 44*(6), 11.

Association for Humanist Psychology. (2001). Humanistic psychology overview. Retrieved from http://www.ahpweb.org/aboutahp/whatis.html

Axelrod, R. (1984). *Evolution of cooperation.* Jackson, TN: Basic Books.

Barkow, J. H., Cosmides, L., & Tooby, J. (1992). *The adapted mind: Evolutionary psychology and the generation of culture.* New York: Oxford University Press.

Barusch, A. S. (2009). *Foundations of social policy: Social justice in human perspective.* Belmont, CA: Brooks/Cole.

Beaton, D. (2003). *Effects of stress and psychological disorders on the immune system.* Retrieved from Personality Papers: http://www.personalityresearch.org/papers/beaton.html

Belkin, L. (2010, September 12). *Living to be a parent.* Retrieved from New York Times Magazine: http://www.nytimes.com/2010/09/12/magazine/12fob-wwln-t.html?_r=1&emc=eta1

Bentley, K., & Walsh, J. (2005). *The social worker and psychotropic medication: Toward effective collaboration with mental health clients, families, and providers* (2nd ed.). Belmont, CA: Wadsworth.

Bilezikian, J. P., & Martin, T. J. (2008). *Principles of bone biology* (Vols. 1–2) . St. Louis, MO: Elsevier.

Bugental, J. (2008). *James Bugental existential-humanistic psychotherapy video.* Retrieved from YouTube: http://www.youtube.com/watch?v=4-B2MVr30Yw

Buss, D. (2003). *Evolutional psychology: The new science of the mind* (2nd ed.). Boston: Allyn & Bacon.

Caroll, J. (2004). *Literary Darwinism: Evolution, human nature, and literature.* New York: Routledge.

Changeaux, J. P. (2004). *The physiology of truth: Neuroscience and human knowledge.* (M. B. DeBevoise, Trans.). Cambridge, MA: Belknap Press.

Charney, D., & Nestler, E. (2004). *The neuroscience of mental illness* (2nd ed.). New York: Oxford University Press.

Cognitive Neuroimaging Laboratory. (2009, March 10). *Cognitive Neuroimaging Laboratory.* Retrieved from Cognitive Neuroimaging Laboratory, University of Illinois Urbana-Champaign: http://cnl.beckman.illinois.edu/

Conrad, P. (2007). *The medicalization of society: On the transformation of human conditions into treatable disorders.* Baltimore: Johns Hopkins University Press.

Couprie, D., Hahn, R., & Naddaf, G. (2003). *Anaximander in context: New studies in the origins of Greek philosophy.* Buffalo, NY: SUNY Press.

Creative Commons. (2009). *The neurocritic.* Retrieved from Voodoo Correlations in Social Neuroscience: Retrieved from http://neurocritic.blogspot.com/2009/01/voodoo-correlations-in-social.html

Darwin, C. (2003). *On the origin of species* (3rd ed.). New York: Callier. (Original work published 1859)

Davis, L. (1995). *Enforcing normalcy: Disability, deafness, and the body.* London, UK: Verso.

Davis, L. (2003). *Bending over backwards: Disability dismodernism and other difficult positions.* New York: NYU Press.

de Cartagena, T. (1998). *The writings of Teresa de Cartagena.* (D. Seidenspinner-Nunez, Trans). Rochester, NY: D.S. Brewer.

DeFranco, A. L., Locksley, R. M., & Robertson, M. (2007). *Immunity.* Sunderland, MA: New Science Press.

DePoy, E., & Gilson, S. (2004). *Rethinking disability: Principles for professional and social change.* Pacific Grove, CA: Wadsworth.

DePoy, E., & Gilson, S. (2007). *The human experience.* Lanham, MD: Rowman & Littlefield.

DePoy, E., & Gilson, S. (2011). *Studying disability.* Thousand Oaks, CA: Sage.

Dijck, J. (2005). *The transparent body: A cultural analysis of medical imaging.* Seattle: University of Washington Press.

Diller, J. (2011). *Cultural diversity: A Primer for Human Services* (4th ed.). Belmont, CA: Brooks/Cole.

Gilson, S. (2011). The biological person. In E. Hutchison (Ed.), *Dimensions of human behavior: Person and environment* (pp. 79–116). Thousand Oaks, CA: Sage.

Gilson, S., & DePoy, E. (2007). Da Vinci's ill fated design legacy: Homogenization and standardization. *International Journal of the Humanities, 4.*

Gould, S. J. (1981). *The mismeasure of man* (Rev. ed.). New York: W. W. Norton.

Grassi, E. (2001). *Rhetoric as philosophy: The humanist tradition.* (A. Azodi & J. M. Krois, Trans.) Carbondale: Southern Illinois University Press.

Grene, M., & DePew, D. (2004). *The philosophy of biology: An episodic history.* New York: Cambridge University Press.

Haeckel, E. (1899). *The riddle of the universe at the close of the nineteenth century.* (J. McCabe, Trans.). New York: Harper & Bros.

Herrnstein, R. J., & Murray, C. (1994). *The bell curve.* New York: Free Press.

Herzberg, F., Mausner, B., & Snyderman, B. B. (1959). *The motivation to work* (2nd ed.). New York: Wiley.

Huitt, W., & Hummel, J. (2003). *Piaget's theory of cognitive development.* Retrieved from Educational Psychology Interactive: http://chiron.valdosta.edu/whuitt/colicogsys/piaget.html

Hutchison, E. (2011). *Dimensions of human behavior.* Thousand Oaks, CA: Sage.

Jensen, A. R. (1969). How much can we boost IQ and scholastic achievement? *Harvard Educational Review, 39,* 1–123.

Karlberg, K. (2010). Am I good enough for my family? In L. J. Moore & M. Kosut, *The body reader.* New York: NYU Press.

Koestler, A. (1979). *Janus: A summing up.* New York: Vintage Books.

Kurian, A. K., & Cardarelli, K. M. (2007). Racial and ethnic differences in cardiovascular disease risk factors: A systematic review. *Ethnicity & Disease, 17,* 143–152.

Lolle, S. J., Pruitt, R. E., Victor, J. L., & Young, J. M. (2005). Genome-wide non-Mendelian inheritance of extra-genomic information in Arabidopsis. *Nature, 434,* 505–509.

Mader, S. (2009). *Biology* (10th ed.). New York: McGraw-Hill.

Mangal, S. (2008). *Abnormal psychology.* New York: Sterling.

Maslow, A. (1970). *Motivation and personality* (2nd ed.). New York: Harper & Row.

McClelland, D. C. (1985). *Human motivation.* Glenview, IL: Scott, Foresman.

McGowan, K. (2009, October 14). *I didn't sin—It was my brain.* Retrieved from arNQ Eprints and Repository: http://www.neuroquantology.com/repository/index.php?option=com_content&view=article&id=111:i-didnt-sinit-was-my-brain&catid=99:free-will&Itemid=72

MediLexicon International (2010). *Early mental illness may be revealed by MRI mapping of brain.* Retrieved from Medical News Today: http://www.medicalnewstoday.com/articles/156992.php

Medina, J. (2000). *The genetic inferno: Inside the seven deadly sins.* Cambridge: Cambridge University Press.

Metzler, I. (2006). *Disability in Medieval Europe.* New York: Routledge.

Myers, I. B. (n.d.). *The Myers Briggs Foundation.* Retrieved from http://www.myersbriggs.org/my-mbti-personality-type/mbti-basics/

News_Medical.net. (2010, June 10). *New genetic discoveries from Autism Genome Project.* Retrieved from The Medical News: http://www.news-medical.net/news/20100610/New-genetic-discoveries-from-Autism-Genome-Project.aspx

Olyan, M. (2008). *Disability in the Hebrew Bible: Interpreting mental and physical differences.* New York: Cambridge University Press.

Pauwels, L. (2006). *Visual cultures of science: Rethinking representational practices in knowledge building and science communication.* Hanover, NH: Dartmouth University Press.

Pouzzner, D. (2000). *The evolutionary psychology of human sex and gender.* Retrieved from http://www.mega.nu/ gender.html

Rogers, C. (1980). *A way of being.* New York: Houghton Mifflin.

Rose, M. (2003). *The staff of Oedipus.* Ann Arbor: University of Michigan Press.

Rothschild, J. (2005). *The dream of the perfect child.* Bloomington: Indiana University Press.

Schultz, D. P., & Schultz, S. E. (2004). *Theories of personality* (8th ed.). Belmont, CA: Brooks/Cole.

Shah, J. Y., & Gardner, W. L. (2008). *Handbook of motivation science.* New York: Guilford Press.

Sheldon, K. M. (2008). The interface of motivation science and personality. In W. L. James & Y. Shah (Eds.), *Handbook of Motivation Science* (pp. 465–480). New York: Guilford Press.

Specht, H., & Courtney, M. E. (1994). *Unfaithful angels: How social work has abandoned its mission.* New York: Free Press.

Stiker, H. J. (1999). *The history of disability.* (W. Sayers, Trans.). Ann Arbor: University of Michigan Press.

Surfwax (1998–2010). *News and articles on endocrine system.* Rerieved from Surfwax Biology News: http://news.surfwax.com/biology/files/Endocrine_System.html

Tallis, R. (2008, April 9). *The neuroscience delusion.* Retrieved from The Times Online: http://entertainment.timesonline.co.uk/tol/arts_and_entertainment/the_tls/article3712980.ece

Tallis, R. (2010, January 25). *Neuro-criticisms by Raymond Tallis.* Retrieved from Law and Neuroscience Blog: http://lawneuro.typepad.com/the-law-and-neuroscience-blog/2010/01/neurocriticisms-by-raymond-tallis.html

Thagard, P. (2010). *The brain and the meaning of life.* Princeton, NJ: Princeton University Press.

Thomson, R. G. (2009). *Staring: How we look.* New York: Oxford University Press.

Travis, A. (2007). *Cognitive evolution: The biological imprint of applied intelligence.* Boca Raton, FL: Universal Publishers.

Value Based Management.net. (2010). *ERG theory-Clayton Alderfer.* Retrieved from Value Based Management.net: http://www.valuebasedmanagement.net/methods_alderfer_erg_theory.html

8

Distal Environmental Theories

This chapter moves from the proximal environmental theories discussed in Chapter 7 to distal environmental theories. This broad range of theories is concerned with the manner in which phenomena considered as "not body" influence human appearance, behavior, and experience. As depicted in Drawing 8.1, this humancentric set of theories proceeds down a one-way street paved by distal conditions that ultimately affect humans.

Drawing 8.1   A One-Way Street to Humans?

History of Distal Environmental Theory

Before examining current theory, a brief history will set an intellectual context for subsequent discussion. A large segment of distal environmental theories are in some way rooted in the principles that characterize the behaviorist school. These ideas suggest that, to a greater or lesser degree, bodies are manipulated, influenced, and responsive to what exists outside of them. While this tenet may be recognizable as emerging within classic behaviorism of the 20th century, Smith (2005) dates this thematic proposition back to ancient Greece, when Aristotle illuminated the power of association in prompting human behavior. Clearly reflecting Kantian dualism, separating person from environment and matter from mind, the behaviorists posited a causative relationship between observable environmental stimuli and observable behavior. The names of Pavlov and Skinner may be familiar, scholars who demonstrated direct observable behavioral changes in dogs and humans respectively, when they experimented with negative and positive environmental stimuli.

Learning theorists such as Bandura (1977) built on the work of the behaviorists, acknowledging the environmental cause of observable behavior. However, they added to the complexity of behavioral theory by identifying the mediating effect of human variation on both reported and observed descriptive responses to the environment.

> *Consider two third-grade classmates, Ian and Wallace. Both boys are taking their first reading test of the academic year tomorrow and both value good grades. Traditional behavioral theory would suggest that both boys would respond with studying behavior. However, through the lens of learning theory, we can explain why Ian studies and Wallace listens to his iPod. Each is differentially motivated by proximal factors such as preferences, cognitive style, and so forth.*

Expanding the unit of analysis to social interaction, several schools of thought were important and gave rise to two sets of theories, discussed under the distal environmental rubric, theories of interpersonal behavior and theories of intergroup behavior. We include these approaches in this chapter because of their concern with both the influence of the distal environment on proximal conditions and with observable description, primarily behavior.

The social exchange theorists, who built on behavioral frameworks integrated with perspectives of humans as rational decision makers, viewed interpersonal behavior through the explanatory lens of benefits and privileges. A brief example of this approach is provided here, followed by a more detailed discussion later in the chapter.

> *Consider a small business in which the chief executive officer, who created her company to produce fine, handmade furniture, earns $100,000 per year and artisans earn about half of that salary. Yet, no one is upset. Explained through social exchange, the artisans would see the CEO's salary as warranted in exchange for her leadership and business expertise.*

Informed by a different intellectual tradition, that of Marx and some of his contemporaries, *conflict theory* (Hirshleifer, 2001) is a framework through which description of intergroup behavior is explained as a set of changing relationships between groups and individuals with differential power. Hirshleifer suggests that humans are motivated through a balance of cooperation and conflict:

> Only if we understand threats and struggles, can we properly appreciate how, why and when mutually advantageous exchange—between husband and wife, between capital and labor, between nation and nation—can take place. (p. 11)

Clearly, built and natural physical conditions impact not only how we behave, but more expansively, where we can act. Within these sets of conditions, image, shape, navigation, and so forth influence the human experience differentially (Cuthbert, 2003). Theory about physical conditions is discussed in this and other chapters as well.

Of course, in the 21st century, conditions are not always palpable. With the hegemony of the Internet, digital environmental theories have stretched their examination beyond the physical and actual human environment to the virtual environment.

THINKING POINT

Can you think of examples that illustrate how the Internet has affected people in so many arenas of their lives?

Just to name a few, we shop, interact with family, friends, colleagues, and even those whose physical bodies we do not see. We can access paintings in museums on continents different from our own, can obtain library resources in all languages, and are bombarded by advertisements and images from unknown virtual sources.

Contemporary distal environmental theories, then, have a rich and diverse history, each emerging from a historical tradition that has shaped distinctions among how individual and group behaviors are explained through various influences.

Distal Environmental Theory Axioms

Although the thinking included under the title of distal environmental theories is diverse, they share the axioms in Table 8.1, in addition to those that we presented for all environmental theories in Chapter 6.

THINKING POINT

Compare these axioms to the axioms of developmental and proximal environmental theories. Can you detect the outward gaze that distinguishes the theories in this chapter from those in Chapters 3 and 7?

Table 8.1 Distal Environmental Theory Axioms

1. Distal environments are diverse, including immediate human, physical, natural, sensory, contexts and more abstract social indirect, and virtual contexts.

2. Theories about individuals and groups are concerned primarily with observables, that is, with human behavior.

3. While reportable variables intrinsic to humans may be acknowledged, behavior in large part is explained by influences distal to humans, including both other humans or nonhuman conditions.

4. Human behavior is motivated by distal conditions.

5. Because human and nonhuman distal conditions influence behavior, individual and group behavior can be manipulated by changing distal factors.

6. Intentional and even unintentional behavior change is in part dependent upon the degree to which an individual experiences or perceives the presence and potential of consequences.

7. Manipulation of behavior from distal environmental conditions may be tacit.

8. Consequences have diverse meanings to individuals and groups, and if ascertainable, are most potent if highly valued, and perceived as powerful.

In your comparison, can you see the outward gaze that distinguishes the theories in this chapter from those in Chapters 4 and 7? Rather than viewed as proximally unfolding in a sequential and in typical fashion, or as a function of structures and processes internal to the corpus, human description, primarily behavior, is seen as malleable. In this category of theory, the concept of actual or perceived consequence is critical in explaining behavior. In other words, if individuals and groups experience or expect consequences, their behavior is more likely to intentionally change than if they do not. If individuals are unaware of distal conditions that impact them, their behavior may change even to a significant degree, but this change may be unplanned or even not discernable by the actor. Let us turn to discussion, analysis, and illustration of representative theories now.

Behavioral and Learning Theory

As briefly noted, behavioral theory grew out of an intellectual response to the psychoanalytic school of thought. Rather than inferring the explanation for behavior, appearance, and experience, behaviorists concerned themselves with observing and explaining human action as a direct or mediated response to environmental influences (Baum, 2004). Watson, building on the work of Pavlov, developed his behavioral theory on the premise that psychology should be concerned with the observation and empirical analysis of human behavior, rather than with abstracts and inferred constructs, such as the mind and the unconscious. As mentioned earlier, Pavlov was most famous for his work with dogs. He noted that he was able to condition, or shape, canine behavior through manipulating stimuli. His most famous experiments were concerned with the observable of salivation. To produce the desired behavior, Pavlov manipulated the dogs' distal environment by introducing a food stimulus and pairing it with another sensory, nonfood stimulus, such as a bell. After an experimental trial, the food stimulus was removed and Pavlov observed that the dog still salivated when the nonfood stimulus was presented (Baum, 2004).

Watson (1998) applied this reasoning to humans through case study methods in which he would observe the behavior of a single subject, manipulate the distal environment through the creation of a stimulus in order to evoke a change in behavior, and then observe the behavior of the individual following the presentation of the stimulus. If behavior changed in the desired direction, Watson claimed that the direct influence of the stimulus on the observable behavior could explain learning. Thus, a behavior could be *conditioned* and the foundation and trajectory of two schools of behaviorism—classical and operant conditioning—were born (Watson, 1998).

Theorists who espoused classical conditioning suggested that a neutral stimulus, or one that did not provoke behavior change, could be paired with a non-neutral stimulus to produce a changed or conditioned response. Building on this work, the operant conditioning theorists, of which Skinner was perhaps the best known, explained behavior not only by immediate responses to distal stimuli, but by behavioral change in response to ongoing presentation of stimuli. Curiously, however, Skinner was considered to be a radical behaviorist rather than a behaviorist. This distinction is critical in that Skinner, although eschewing intrapsychic mechanisms, still held the proximal corpus responsible for human action. That is to say, he and the radical behaviorists who followed him saw biological and neurological structures and processes as the provocateurs of response to distal environmental conditions. Thus, one could not be an independent agent. Rather, according to this school of thought, response behavior was considered to be predetermined through the biological functioning of each organism (Moore, 2008).

We still locate Skinner and his radical behaviorist colleagues in the distal environmental theory chapter because he was most concerned with the influence of distal conditions on the corpus. By setting up an experimental design that involved the scheduled introduction of negative and positive stimuli as the experimental variable, Skinner and his successors could isolate and explain behavior changes that resulted from the presence, absence, or variation of the manipulated environmental influences. Further, the two conditions for sustained behavior acquisition and change—practice and reinforcement—could be orchestrated, observed, and verified (Baum, 2004; Moore, 2008).

To demonstrate their grasp of operant conditioning, a group of social work students developed an experiment with the desired outcome of having the professor always move to the right side of the classroom. Every time the professor approached the right wall, they sat up, and were attentive, and participatory. When the professor moved away from the desired location, they were incrementally less active in concert with the distance that the professor moved from the desired wall.

The preceding example describes a simple relationship. It was based on simple stimulus-response principles in which biology was explanatory of a reaction to distal conditions. More complex application of operant conditioning might add incremental reinforcement, make it intermittent, and pair it with other stimuli to provoke and sustain desired behaviors. Moreover, according to Skinner, one's response action itself may become a stimulus. It then becomes the *operant*—as one operates on the distal environment and produces another condition for which to respond (Moore, 2008)—and thus complicates the stimulus response connection.

THINKING POINT

Think of how parents educate their children and socialize them through concrete, attentional, or inferable negative and positive reinforcements. Now consider this a reciprocal process in which child action "operates" on the environment.

Synthesizing cognitive and behavioral approaches, Bandura (1969, 1977, 1986, 1997), a social learning theorist, identified imitation of what is sensed as the most potent environmental stimulus. He referred to this phenomenon as *modeling*. In his empirical observations of children, Bandura found that they learned by enacting the following five processes:

1. Attending to a model

2. Determining if the model should be imitated

3. Remembering what the model did

4. Copying the model's behavior

5. Ascertaining the consequences of the behavior

These five processes are complex and can occur in multiple ways.

A child does not have to observe a model directly, but can imitate what he indirectly observes. Or, a parent might tell a child about an ideal to model. Moreover, in order to adopt and inte-grate a behavior, or to change a behavior, an individual can experience the consequences directly or indirectly. For example, a teacher or parent might directly reward a child and the child will continue the behavior. On the other hand, an individual might read about someone being punished for stealing, and thus would learn not to enact the punishable behavior.

Learning through observation without directly experiencing consequences was named *vicarious learning*. What is important about Bandura's work is that he acknowledged perception and cognition, two distal processes that the behaviorists eschew, and created this proximal-distal amalgamation of vicarious learning, obfus-cating the boundary between body and its surroundings. Bandura's work is still celebrated in contemporary literature and forms the basis for the work of current theorists such as Lazaras (1989), who is renown for applying behavioral theory to therapeutic intervention.

Theorists such as Sutherland (as cited in Akers, 2009) and Akers (2009) applied and adapted social learning theory to advance explanations of criminal behavior. Akers, along with Burgess (as cited in Akers, 2009), looked at the potential for distal environmental conditions to create both conformance to and deviance from acceptable social behavior, illuminating the centrality and directionality of distal stimulants in tipping the carefully balanced scale of legal-not-legal action.

Looking at a different human geography, but similar to Akers's recognition of the nature of interaction and quality of stimuli from distal conditions, Lazarus concerned himself with emotion. Although he developed his work from multiple schools of thought, he drew on Bandura's integrative approach to support his claim that emotions could not be explained through isolating the proximal from the distal. Rather, by setting the "encounter" as his environmental unit of analysis and observing inferred, or what he referred to as *appraised emotional*, descriptors in response to diverse encounters, Lazarus was able to explain emotional development as an interaction between the distal environment and its provocation of pleasant or unpleasant proximal feeling responses. Lazaras's work expands beyond merely looking at encounters and responses, however. In an integrative fashion, he adds one's goals, personality, perceived benefit, individual motivations, anticipated long-term benefits, and other proximal factors into the explanatory stew. Still, consistent with the axioms of this class of theory, Lazarus himself separates proximal and distal domains in his investigations, but to some extent inherent in his work is the arbitrary and vague distinction between the two poles.

Consider Marci and Dan, a middle-age couple. Marci is a nurse who is studying for an advanced degree and Dan is an electrician who does not see why his wife wants to pursue this educational direction so late in her career. Through Lazaraus's approach, we can learn about them by observing and analyzing their encounters, in this case conversations.

Marci: *School went well tonight.*

Dan: *That's nice; I ate dinner alone.*

Marci: *I'm sorry, Dan. I was so excited about the class tonight that I stayed for a few minutes to talk to the professor.*

Dan: *Who is he Marci?*

Marci: *He is Susan Jones, a woman.*

Dan: *Oh, well, I ate a can of ravioli, cold.*

Marci: *What can I make for you now? I am so sorry, Dan.*

What can we see in this interaction? Dan, who disapproves of Marci's activity, communicates indirectly and Marci responds first with anger, and then with guilt.

Sharing some fundamental conceptual nourishment with Lazaras, but focusing on the domain of thinking instead of emotion, Vygotsky, a Russian psychologist and contemporary of Piaget, looked to contextual explanatory schemes to craft the social cognition learning model. He was particularly concerned with language development as central to describing cognitive changes over time (Daniel, Cole, & Wertsch, 2007; Vygotsky, 1978). We locate Vygotsky under the rubric of distal environmental theories because of the importance that he assigned to social interaction in early cognitive development. In order to develop typically in the cognitive arena, Vygotsky posited that a young child had to engage in dialectical problem solving, a distal social-interactive process in which an adult, or even an older sibling, uses language to mentor the development of problem solving in the younger counterpart. According to Vygotsky, as the child moves through time, she relies decreasingly on distal guidance through internalizing language, content, and the increasingly sophisticated tools of adaptation that have been influenced by those in the child's social world. Thus, according to Vygotsky, cognition and learning, rather than being proximal developmental processes, are enculturation phenomena that occur through social interaction. Designing the social situation is therefore the fuel for thinking, supporting the value of multiculturalism as a method for teaching and learning tolerance and pluralism (Kozulin, Gindis, Ageyev, & Miller, 2003).

> *Elijah, a Jewish male, attended Yeshiva, a school for Jewish children throughout his elementary education. When he enters seventh grade in a public school, he is confronted with diverse views from his classmates and teachers and becomes initially confused. Over the school year, he talks with new friends, learning about the way in which they live. According to Vygotsky, the change in distal environments is an alternative enculturation process through which Elijah now learns about diverse viewpoints, engages in a dialogue with himself and others, and emerges cognitively different than he would have been if he had continued his education at Yeshiva.*

Also concerned with explaining proximal processes, Mead (1934/1965, 1964) built on the work of the behaviorists and social learning theories to develop what is known as *social behaviorism.* Through a Kantian dualist lens, Mead focused on the concept of the mind. Similar to the behaviorists, Mead did not explain *mind* as an abstract psychic concept, but rather as a neural structure that can only be shaped, put into action, and acknowledged by social interaction, more specifically symbolic communication (language and human intentional gesture) with others in the distal social environment.

> *Think about how you know that you have communicated clearly to your friend. If your friend looks at you with a quizzical expression, you might think that she is not clear about what you have said, but if she responds with gestures and expressions indicating she has understood, then you surmise that you have been clear. Without the reflection of your friend's response back to you, you would not know about your own clarity.*

Mead's work has been an important foundation for the sociological distal environmental theory explanations of individual and collective thought and action, referred to as *functionalism.* Functionalism is the perspective that entities, including the mind, are defined by their purpose in relation to their context and seek to maintain equilibrium (Mead & Silva, 2011).

> *Rather than being defined by neural structures, the mind would be seen as serving the purpose of thought, moral decision making, and so forth.*

Functionalism was an important sociological theory central to many schools of social work in the mid-20th century. Social work functionalists saw social agencies as purposive in maintaining the social status quo (Bartlett, 1970). Thus, social agencies were sanctioned units of social systems responsible for certain functions that maintained societies.

> *Social welfare agencies were seen as sanctioned by the government to distribute resources on the basis of what was valued, thereby providing a safety net only for those who were deemed worthy. The agency purpose was therefore not only to provide help, but to uphold social values and social order.*

THINKING POINT

If you disagreed significantly with your agency mission and principles, how might a functionalist guide your professional behavior?

Motivation

Although motivation is frequently described as a proximal process, as discussed previously, some important theories of motivation are examined in this chapter due to their congruence with the axioms presented in Table 8.1. Specifically, attention is directed to those theories that conform to the axioms of distal environmental theories. Seminal theories of motivation, such as Maslow's hierarchy of needs, are discussed in Chapter 7 because they do not posit the importance of distal factors in provoking human behavior. However, numerous approaches to describing and explaining motivation have built on behavioral and learning theories by identifying distal environmental stimuli and consequences as central to behavior and experience.

To delimit motivation theories that foreground distal environmental conditions as explanatory, we indulge in word soup, to some extent, and adopt the definition of *motivation* proposed by Buford, Bedeian, and Lindner (1995) as an individual propensity to engage in purposive behavior in order to meet one's specified needs. Thus, this lexical approach defines motivation as an element of human description that we locate under behavior, experience, or both. Behavior can be directly observed, but the construct of motivation itself must be inferred from observation and report, and thus is experienced. So now, let us look at representative classic and contemporary motivation theories that are important in the distal environment literature.

Directed at explaining motivation to engage in a task, Deci (1975), and later Deci and Ryan (2002), entered the realm of learning theory synthesized with cognition. We include their theory of cognitive evaluation in this chapter because of the importance of consequence in provoking and describing human behavior. Individuals are more likely to engage in tasks in which they believe they can be successful (Deci, 1975; Deci & Ryan, 2002). The cognitive element of this theory occurs at the point of determining the likelihood of success. Using the "glass half empty" approach, Amsel (2006) arrived at similar conclusions through the portal of frustration rather than expectancy of success. He suggested that nonreward was equally as powerful in evoking a response as other distal environmental stimuli.

> *Think of how you make decisions to engage in a new activity. You weigh several elements, including your interest, the benefit to you and those around you, the potential for success, and perhaps the possibility of disappointment of you fail. If you are sure that you cannot succeed, it is unlikely that you would pursue the activity. But if there is an uncertainty about successful outcome, you think about the risks and benefits and make a decision on that basis. If you encounter nonreward consistent with that which you expect for your efforts, you might alter your course of action out of frustration.*

Similar to Deci and Ryan (2002) and Amsel (2006), Vroom (1995) was interested in what motivated people at work to achieve diverse levels of performance. He advanced expectancy theory in which he suggested that individuals who believe that performance will lead to positive consequences (rewards) are more likely (motivated) to engage in high performance behaviors than those who perceive neutral or negative consequences. Three cognitive concepts of expected reward coalesce to explain motivation and related performance: valence, expectancy, and instrumentality. *Valence* refers to the degree of worth that an individual attributes to an expected outcome of behavior. *Expectancy* and *instrumentality* are the perceived relationships between an individual's effort and outcome and success and outcome, respectively.

> *Suppose the work activity that you consider from the previous example is learning computer programming. Your boss wants you to learn and your coworkers are encouraging you to do so. You thus perceive this activity as important in your workplace and well-respected. But, you also know that you are both fearful of math and programming, and not very adept at computer use. So what do you do? Can you succeed? If so, how much effort do you need to expend in order to maximize the likelihood of success? If you decide against participating, what are the consequences?*

Also interested in work, Adams identified the consequence of equity as the distal influence on employee motivation. According to Adams's (1965) classic theory, *equity* is referred to an individual's assessment that he is expending an equitable amount of effort for an equivalent amount of return. Beliefs about three elements—inputs, outputs, and comparability to others—formed the basis of Adams's approach. *Inputs* include perceptions of the degree of effort, skill, and commitment that individuals put forth in their work. *Outputs* are rewards conferred upon the individual in exchange for her inputs, including but not limited to earnings, benefits, and recognition. *Comparability* refers to the maximum behavioral effort (productivity), explained by the belief that one's input will be rewarded equitably and fairly in comparison to others in one's referent group.

> *So, you decide to learn computer programming. But as you proceed, you find that you are expected to do your typical job and learn on your own time. And, no other employee is expected to work as hard as you perceive yourself to be working. Therefore, you decide to talk to your boss.*

Adams's thinking formed the foundation for numerous theorists in diverse fields, such as management, relationships, power, and social justice.

The discussion of distal environmental motivation theories ends with Herzberg's classic approach to work motivation (Herzberg, Mausner, & Snyderman, 1959). Despite its advanced age, this two factor theory remains active and vital in current contexts, perhaps because he identified proximal environmental factors as most important for work productivity, but illuminated the concept of *demotivating* distal environmental factors (Value Based Management.net, 2010). According to Herzberg and colleagues, hygiene factors—distal environmental rewards derived from work such as salary, benefits, and a comfortable work environment—were not critical as motivators of productivity and work satisfaction. Rather, the absence of these factors was important in explaining the lack of work motivation, or what Herzberg referred to as *demotivation*.

> *When you go to talk to your boss, he offers you a raise. But, he does not offer you additional time off your work duties to study and learn. So, you experience demotivation as a result.*

Each of the theories presented here has ranked diverse distal environmental factors as important in explaining motivation. Lindner (1998), in an effort to apply motivation theory to a specific work environment, tested the rankings in a sample of university staff and faculty employed in the Ohio Cooperative Extension. He found that none of the theories themselves were supported by his total sample, and thus concluded that potent motivators differ for individuals. In this sample, however, the proximal element of interest in the substance of the work was ranked highest as a motivator, and distal factors such as recognition by coworkers, income, perceived equity, and other rewards were still important but secondary to interest.

THINKING POINT

What motivates you to work? With whose theory, if any, is your motivation consistent?

Social Role Theory

Behavioral and social learning theories have also been important foundations for theories that describe and explain social roles. This literature is huge so discussion here delimits to representative elements, gender roles, normative roles, and sick roles. Although we do not address the multiple roles that individuals fulfill, the principles may be extrapolated from these theories to the explanation of role acquisition and enactment in general.

Social role theory, in some sense, is metaphoric for theater (Goffmann, 1963), in which an individual acts out scripted parts (Newman & Newman, 2008). Thus, social learning is the stage, so to speak, to social role theory in that individuals learn and enact their role-delimited behavior from those who are members of different social categories, such as male, female, sick, healthy, and so forth. These theories are included in this chapter because, for the most part, social role perspectives identify distal environmental variables as the responsible explanatory agents for transmitting the nature of acceptable behavior.

As discussed by Eagly, Baron, and Hamilton (2004), males and females learn gender-specific and gender-distinguishing description (behaviors, appearance, and experience) from distal environmental variables. Traditional gender roles and stereotypes shape description of men as agentic and women as caregivers (Eagly, Beall, & Sternberg, 2005; Schneider, 2004; Steele, 2010). *Agentic description* refers to the capacity to make and enact decisions, while *caregiving* denotes the expectation of communal behavior and nurturance of another. Who establishes and transmits social role norms is diverse among theories. From a distal-oriented developmental perspective, gender roles are learned early in the life span. Not only do children learn from watching the same sex parent, but more recent theorists have suggested that proximal preference for one parent over the other is an important influence on the acceptance and adoption of gendered behaviors and internalizing of role. Future expectancy is another powerful teacher, in that children observe and then develop cognitive schemes that shape how they proceed over the longitude of gender acquisition (Newman & Newman, 2008). In adulthood, the stage as well as sequenced auditions for roles expand as one's environments become more diverse (Jackson, 2004).

Some feminist lenses suggest that gender roles function to maintain misogyny and male dominance (Mikkola, 2008), while some economists view gender roles as a function of economic necessity (Fry & Cohn, 2010). Evolutionary theorists, discussed in more detail previously, indict procreation as purposive in shaping social roles, and as addressed in the brief overview of functionalism, functional sociologists suggest that roles are purposive and interdependent in defining the parts of social environments and in maintaining social structure and stability (Parsons, 2002).

Regardless of the purposive stance one takes, social role theorists share the common notion that social roles are learned from distal environmental variables and are further ingrained through perceived or actual consequences (Newman & Newman, 2008). Gender role description does not remain static, however. Norms for males and females and, more recently, other genders discussed in Chapter 11, are dynamic and contextual (Fry & Cohn, 2010). Distal environmental factors such as work status, marital status, sexual orientation, cultural identity, and so forth further explain differential gender role description, norms, and consequences of deviations therefrom (Newman & Newman, 2008; Riggs, 1997). O'Reilly (2010) reminds us that traditonal gender roles are changing, and may be uncoupled with proximal environmental characteristics such as sex. In her work, she examines the role of "mother" in the 21st century, noting phenomena such as men-mothering and queer-mothering.

Applying social role theory to human illness, Parsons (as cited in Cockerham, 2010) proposed the *sick role* as one which embodied socially determined rights and obligations. According to Parsons, any individuals who have been deemed a legitimate "patient" by a professional authority and who are being treated for illness by a professional are released from their normative role expectations in exchange for grateful compliance with the authority, the professional who holds the knowledge and skill to restore an individual to health. The acceptance of the sick role concept has been operational in elevating the professionals to perceived omnipotence and in locating them out of reach of skepticism or mistrust. While this stature has been somewhat eroded (DePoy & Gilson, 2004), it still in large part remains intact and has implications for legitimate professional responses.

Also concerned with the self (Goffmann & Best, 2005) and then deviant social roles, Goffman (1963) proposed a model of identity and interaction that he explained metaphorically building on the already established notion of role as dramaturgy. That is to say, he described human identity as a function of interaction, suggesting that individuals invent and reinvent the self—their identities—through enacting and then revising their social role behavior in response to scripted messages from their social stages. Without the social stage, Goffman explained that a stable identity cannot emerge. Of particular importance in Goffman's work was his analysis of the influence of the institutional distal environment on individuals and their identities. Goffman suggested that in the name of cure or community justice, deviant individuals are incarcerated, removed from civil social stages, and are subjected to exterior factors that degrade and reshape their identities. The dubious outcome of institutionalization, according to Goffman, can be explained by individual response to social input in a direction not wholly anticipated by the professionals and others who control institutions and those held within them.

Consider the movie, The Waterdance (Hurd, 1992). The social stage, so to speak, is set in a rehabilitation hospital where the characters are at various levels of rehabilitation and chronological distance from their injuries. As new residents are admitted, they learn their social roles both from other patients and staff. Unexpected by the telephone operator staff, who control outside telephone lines and regularly dismiss the requests for patients to call their friends and families, the patients, who are expected to play subservient and compliant roles, assert themselves by taking over and "occupying the telephone center."

Before leaving gender role theory, we turn to Gilligan's (1993) classic work, and recall Gilligan's introduction in Chapter 5 alongside Kohlberg's developmental theory of moral development. We now locate Gilligan's theory in this chapter because of its adherence to the axioms of distal environmental theories. Gilligan asserted that women learn and exercise moral behavior differently from men as a result of their socialization into nurturing roles. She explained moral description as gender influenced (though not gender specific) in that women are more likely to base their moral reasoning on principles of social responsibility than on notions of individual rights and justice. Further, Gilligan suggested that women make moral decisions in response to conflicting distal-generated responsibilities and roles, such as nurturer and wage earner. In light of those distal mixed messages, and different from men who look inward for moral clues, women engage in a contextual and narrative mode of moral reasoning (Gilligan, 1982; Gilligan & Attanucci, 1986; Gilligan, Ward, Taylor, & Bardige, 1986).

> *Let us look at Ann, whose son, Jason, just came home with great news. He received a scholarship of $10,000, which is $2,500 more than he needed for his college tuition and books. Ann has been struggling to make ends meet, working two jobs as a domestic and a waitress. She is torn between suggesting to Jason that he return the money that he is not using for school or saying nothing and letting Jason use the money for some personal needs. So, Ann consults with her sister and mother, both who encourage her to ask Jason to return the money. But Jason does not follow the guidance. Ann finally calls the scholarship fund to let them know about her dilemma. The basis of her decision was guidance from her family and other sociocultural messages supporting her to uphold the role of a mother as a teacher of her children.*

Similar to gender role theorists, Wolfensberger and Thomas (2007) applied behavioral and social learning theory initially to rehabilitation, and then more broadly to explain and promote social norms in populations considered to be deviant, devalued, or at risk for either. Social role valorization (SRV) theory, building on earlier normalization theory, suggests that there are socially valued descriptors that beget positive social and resource consequences. If an individual fulfills expected social descriptive norms, the individual will be rewarded. Conversely, those who deviate from the norm will be devalued and excluded from opportunity. As an example, Wong and Stanhope (2009) found that conformance to community norms even influenced the nature of available housing for people diagnosed as developmentally delayed. As they strayed further from expected norms and roles, their living options in the community were eroded, ultimately locating nonnormative individuals in group homes within ghettos comprised of those with similar diagnoses and behaviors.

SRV theory contains an action orientation. *Action orientation* means that the theory not only explains "what is" but proposes methods to change devaluation. This action element comprises valorization. That is, devalued roles can be changed or valorized through teaching role normative behavior (altering observable description) or revising social norms (changing the distal environment).

> *Andy, a young man with Down syndrome, is most comfortable wearing pajamas, and thus has frequently gone out in public dressed in these bed clothes. His social worker, however, in efforts to support his acquisition of normative behavior and appearance, takes him shopping*

for comfortable clothes that are typical in public settings, and she provides the structure and reinforcement for Andy to dress in street clothes, not pajamas, in order to appear "normal."

Thus, behavioral and social learning theory, and their derivative motivational perspectives, are important and diverse in their scope and focus. These theories underpin many contemporary educational, health, and therapeutic practices including behavior modification, health behavior intervention, applied behavioral analysis, and social marketing. Behavior modification is directed at purposive, systematically organized behavior change, using strategies such as positive and negative reinforcement.

Health behavior involves the application of behavioral and motivational principles to promoting the acquisition and maintenance of behaviors that promote health, such as smoking cessation, healthy eating, and exercise (Coreil, 2009).

Andy is very obese, in large part because he loves to eat. His social worker is concerned with his health, and thus provides nonfood rewards to stimulate his healthy eating.

In the practice of applied behavioral analysis, desired behaviors are broken down into individual tasks. Individuals who are the target of behavior change are then given opportunities to practice tasks that are reinforced. Singular tasks are added cumulatively and directed at approximating the desired response, until the desired behavioral patterns are achieved (Cooper, Heron, & Heward, 2007). This practice is known as shaping.

For Andy's eating program, the social worker begins by portion control. She helps Andy put the proper portions of food into small bags, as a first step, but does not tell him how many bags he can eat. To support his behavior of parsing his food into portions, he is rewarded. After this behavior has been learned, the social worker then works to limit the number of bags of food that he eats for each meal by color-coding them by meal and day of the week. Again, he is rewarded for the desired behavior.

Social marketing (Kotler & Lee, 2007) synthesizes marketing strategies with behavioral and motivational theory. Desired behaviors are explicated in popular media such as television, magazines, the Internet, and so forth and potent reinforcements are advanced through vicarious approaches.

Consider the messages that we get in popular media about obesity and healthy eating.

THINKING POINT

 Identify strengths and limitations of applying behavioral theory to behavior change in those who are not aware of the environmental manipulation.

Before departing from the segment of distal theories that relates to learning and roles, it is important to highlight the significance of technology in both expanding and contracting our notions of environments and their explanatory influence on human behavior. When classical behavioral and social learning theories were developed, technology as we know it today did not exist. There was no Internet, video surveillance, and so forth. Thus, theories were anchored on the premise that distal environmental factors had a profound influence on behavior since individual action could be observed and could garner consequences. In the 21st century, interaction in virtual spaces may be shaped by the rules of behavior in that space, but the extent to which consequences have any meaning beyond those spaces is unknown. Conversely, technology such as video surveillance brings observation and consequences into unexpected contexts.

Technology has also been operative in expanding our notions of observable description. In classic learning theory, the unit of observable behavior did not involve organs and internal biological structures. However, with recent advancements in neuroimaging (in which brain activity can be visualized through instruments), behaviorism has reached inside our heads for descriptive elements. That is to say, how interactive social factors explain changes in brain behavior is inferred from observation of visuals generated by contemporary instruments, and theories of social and other external explanations for brain behavior can be tested and verified (Pauwels, 2006).

Group Behavior

We now move our discussion to distal environmental theories that explain group behavior as a function of social, environmental, and even economic contextual factors. These theories reflect the axioms of distal environmental theories and thus appear in this chapter.

Social Exchange Theory

Social exchange focuses its gaze on the descriptive behavior of human interaction and exchange. Developed by Thibault and Kelley (1952), and expanded by many others, social exchange distills and applies economic explanations to how individuals and groups both experience feelings about one another and then behave in relation to each other. Although social exchange integrates theories of rational choice with behaviorism, it is included here because of its primary focus on economic behaviorism. The degree to which an individual or group believes that a reward will be maximized explains decisions about figurative or actual payment.

The two major factors that explain interactive behavior and experience are perceived costs and benefits. In other words, a group or individual weighs the cost of an interaction or longer-term relationship against its benefits, and engages in what is perceived to be a fair exchange. Person or Group A may relinquish or "pay" Person or Group B with power, money, time, and so forth, in order to receive the benefit of Group B's expertise and resources. Social exchange theory has been applied to many domains of social interaction and communication, including but not limited to marriage and family behavior, business, organizational interaction, social interactions among groups with diverse power bases, gender relations, and so forth. For example, Sprecher (1998) explained sexual interaction as a negotiated exchange between partners, each with perceptions of cost and benefit resulting from the relationship. Rusbult (as cited in Changingminds.org, n.d.) suggested that the exchange is overlooked in the early stages of a relationship. Over time, the equality of exchange becomes foregrounded and can be the demise of relationships in which one or both partners are not receiving expected benefits for what they are giving.

In classical social exchange theory, the exchange worth of an individual or group determines power. Exchange worth is the degree to which the resources individual or group possess are seen as valuable and deserving of actual or metaphoric payment. Zafirovski (2003, 2009) suggests that this view, underpinned by a simplistic binary approach, is inadequate to explain human behavior. Rather, he advances a social exchange model, which expands explanatory power beyond actual or figurative economic exchange to weighing cultural, social, and political resources and benefits.

THINKING POINT

Can you provide an example in your life that illustrates social exchange theory?

Conflict Theory

Different from social exchange theory, conflict theory has its roots in classical theories such as those advanced by Machiavelli, Hobbes, and Marx. According to Machiavelli and Hobbes, descriptive behavior in all humans could be explained by the motivation of self-interest in a social environment that contained both material goods and the threat of violence. Intergroup behavior was described as a struggle to maximize material benefit, even through violent means. Refining this cynicism, Marx was deeply influenced by what he perceived as inequities brought about by the industrial revolution and the subjugation of the majority by a few people in power. In his explanations of capitalist social behavior, Marx identified two groups, the bourgeoisie and the proletariat. The bourgeoisie was the small, wealthy segment of the population who had control over production of good and services (modes of production) and thus subjugated the laboring class, the proletariat, to external control and disadvantage. Marx posited that class divisions and antagonisms existed previously, but that the Industrial Revolution exacerbated this struggle (Layder, 2005).

Building on the notions of intergroup struggle and conflict, Rollins and Bahr (1976) developed conflict theory. They described group interaction as a struggle, explained by advancement on the part of powerful groups of policies and practices that create advantage for themselves and disadvantage for those who do not have power. According to Rollins, groups do not like to be sublimated, coerced, and controlled and thus the potential for violence inheres in social interaction between the haves and the have-nots. Conflict theory has been applied to understanding and explaining group behavior in numerous domains such as criminology, violence, marriage, and even business. In social work, conflict theory has been applied to the explanation of imbalance and friction among diverse groups.

> *A recent discussion of nursing home discharge planning characterized competing interests of individuals, the nursing home industry, and other interest groups as conflictual and suggested the application of conflict theory to this social work activity as a means for furthering understanding and efficacy. (Fogler, 2010).*

Social Movements

Particularly relevant to social work is the body of literature that theorizes the genesis, process, and outcomes of social movements, or organized group efforts to attain a common social change goal. Peculiar to social movements is voluntary membership for action but not necessarily for outcome. Mid-20th-century theories suggested that social movements emerged in the absence of formal organizations and agencies that were adequate to handle discontented groups (Goodwin & Jasper, 2009). Until the anti–Vietnam War movements of the 1960s, scholars theorized social movements as aggressive acts on the part of oppressed populations. Yet, the privilege of leaders and followers of this watershed movement changed the complexion, and thus perception, of social movements in subsequent theory. It is curious to note that social movements in the classic sense are seen as protests in which organizers evoked collective anger through diverse distal environmental stimuli as the basis for mobilizing groups to act. Thus, classical social movements such as the women's movement, civil rights efforts, and so forth were theorized to originate from the influence of creative provocation and organization skills of leaders rather than from proximal-environment motivation.

From another perspective discussed in subsequent chapters with systems theories, the term *networking* has been used even in pre-Internet 20th century as the organizational basis of social movements.

Distal Physical Environment

Looking now at the distal physical environment, remember that we see the boundaries of human and physical environment as vague. In the next section, rethink the descriptive terms *proximal* and *distal* used thus far throughout the book. This directional continuum will likely be useful in distinguishing corpus from object by the magnitude of distances between them. However, even using distance as metaphoric becomes vague as we attempt to distinguish human experience from sets of built and natural conditions.

> *Consider telemedicine through which proximal conditions can be visualized from great distances.*

In order to define the *distal physical environment,* we imbibe word soup with a web search using the key term *physical environment.* Table 8.2 presents the diverse definitions found in the results.

Table 8.2 Definitions of *Physical Environment*

1. The stuff the universe is made of (History of the Universe, n.d.)
2. The external surroundings and conditions in which something exists (Answers.com, n.d.)
3. Physical geography (Ritter, 2003–2010)
4. Climate (Ritter, 2010)
5. Decomposed materials (Massachusetts Institute of Technology, 2007)

As the five definitions in Table 8.2 reveal, there is no consensus about the essential elements of the distal physical environment. Considering our dilemma with dualism, discussed earlier, we therefore remain open and to some extent vague in defining the distal physical environment as nonhuman built and natural conditions. These conditions include fabricated objects, designed and constructed spaces, and natural spaces. Defining the distal physical environment in this fashion allows consideration of not only locations, but their contents as well. Also remember that distal physical environments have texture, movement, sound, and other dynamic elements that reciprocally interact with human experience. Given the vast expanse of this topical area, representative exemplars relevant to social work thinking and action are discussed, with an invitation to extrapolate to other content areas.

We have been particularly interested in reciprocal influence of humans and design of distal environments and objects. The history of buildings and objects is sized not only by its diversity but by its chronology and thus, limits a substantive discussion of this fascinating knowledge due to both space and the focus for this book. However, we do bring attention to stairs as exemplary of how environments were not necessarily built for function or even universal meaning. Although from a functional perspective, stairs are structures that provide a means of ascent and decent, Templer (1994) eloquently reminds us that "Stairs convey meaning and have personalities" (p. 8). Among the more esoteric functions of stairs over history have been displays of spirituality, status, and power. For example, helical stairs used in medieval European geographies were built not only as space savers but as symbols of fashion and status. Given the prevalance of elevators or escalators in contemporary buildings, helical stairs are now considered as decorative and symbolic of wealth (Templar, 1994). Of course, to many, stairs hold negative meaning in the form of social, economic, and political exclusion (Swain, French, Barnes, & Thomas, 2004).

De Dampier (2006) analyzes chairs in much the same way that Templar has approached the history of stairs. Rather than viewing the chair as a functional object on which an individual sits, she addresses the design, adornment, placement, and restricted access of sitting environments to demonstrate the proximal meaning of objects beyond their use.

The distal physical environment therefore is not simply space that surrounds the corpus and within which individuals and groups function. Rather it is the locus of diverse meanings, interactions, navigation, economics, colocations of diverse groups, exclusion, inclusion, learning, comfort, discomfort, and so forth.

As an example, the role of the distal physical environment in proximal cognitive development was raised early in the book. Cognitive theorists, whether developmental predeterminists, or information processing or scaffolding espousers, all identify *learning rich* environments as those that stimulate exploration and thinking (Cooper, Heron, & Heward, 2007). Even climate change has been fingered as a new challenge to how children learn about expectations and constructs such as constancy (Bartlett, 2008). The critical nature of accessing and manipulating distal environment and objects as the basis for learning has significant implications for those who are unable to do so typically or at all (Swain, French, Barnes, & Thomas 2004). Because of space and physical environment as meaning and symbol, this important part of human experience resurfaces in the chapters on new and emerging theories, theories that are more comfortable with allowing distal and proximal to rub elbows and become intimate.

Evidence

Due to the range of theories and substantive areas covered by distal environmental theories, methods and the nature of evidence are varied and diverse. However, with the exception of theories that propose multiple meanings, experimental-type deductive approaches are typically seen as inquiry strategies for this genre of theorists. In particular, because the classical behaviorists intellectually rebelled against intrapsychic explanations of human behavior and experience, they sought empirical support through direct observation that linked manipulation to behavioral results. Building on this experimental research tradition, social learning theorists used similar deductive inquiry approaches to support their theories, despite the inability to directly visualize proximal embodied variables that they suggested as mediating the direct relationship between stimulus and response.

Summary

This chapter examined theories that attribute explanatory importance to the social, cultural, economic, political, and built distal environmental contexts in which individuals and groups behave. Classical theories that describe human behavior as observable were introduced and explained through a system of reward and punishment. Contemporary perspectives were next discussed—perspectives that synthesize behavioral perspectives with cognitive theory, but have maintained the critical role of individual and group response to distal consequence as central to explaining human behavior and experience in selected domains. These bodies of work are founded on the view of humans as self-focused and motivated by personal interest and gain. Similarly, the classical and contemporary theories that explain human interaction as struggle view humans and group behavior as a function of perceived consequence. The chapter concluded with a brief conversation about the impact of the distal physical environment in humans.

References

Adams, J. S. (1965). Inequity in social exchange. In L. Berkowitz (Ed.), *Advances in experimental social psychology* (pp. 267–299). New York: Academic Press.

Akers, R. (2009). *Social learning and social structure: A general theory of crime and deviance.* New Brunswick, NJ: Transaction.

Amsel, A. (2006). *Frustration theory: An analysis of dispositional learning and memory.* New York: Cambridge University Press.

Answers.com. (n.d.). *Physical environment.* Retrieved from http://wiki.answers.com/Q/Define_the_physical_environment.

Bandura, A. (1969). *Principles of behavior modification.* New York: Holt, Rinehart & Winston.

Bandura, A. (1977). *Social learning theory.* New York: General Learning Press.

Bandura, A. (1986). *Social foundations of thought and action.* Englewood Cliffs, NJ: Prentice Hall.

Bandura, A. (1997). *Self-efficacy: The exercise of control.* New York: W. H. Freeman.

Bartlett, H. M. (1970). *The common base of social work practice.* New York: National Association of Social Workers.

Bartlett, S. (2008). Climate change and urban children: Impacts and implications for adaptation in low- and middle-income countries. *Environment and Urbanization, 20*(2), 501–519.

Baum, W. M. (2004). *Understanding behaviorism: Behavior, culture, and evolution* (2nd ed.). Boston: Blackwell.

Buford, J. A., Bedeian, A. G., & Lindner, J. R. (1995). *Management in extension* (3rd ed.). Columbus: Ohio State University Extension.

Changingminds.org. (n.d.). *Social exchange theory.* Retrieved from http://changingminds.org/explanations/theories/social_exchange.htm

Cockerham, W. C. (2010). *The new Blackwell companion to medical sociology* (9th ed.). Malden, MA: Blackwell.

Cooper, J. O., Heron, T. E., & Heward, W. L. (2007). *Applied behavior analysis* (2nd ed.). Englewood, NJ: Prentice Hall.

Coreil, J. (2009). *Social and behavioral foundations of public health.* Thousand Oaks, CA: Sage.

Cuthbert, A. (2003). *Critical readings in urban design.* Boston: Blackwell.

Daniel, H., Cole, M., & Wertsch, J. V. (2007). *The Cambridge companion to Vygotsky.* New York: Cambridge University Press.

de Dampier, F. (2006). *Chairs: A history.* New York: Harry N. Abrams.

Deci, E. L. (1975). *Intrinsic motivation.* New York: Plenum Press.

Deci, E. L., & Ryan, R. M. (2002). *Handbook of self-determination research.* Rochester, NY: University of Rochester Press.

DePoy, E. & Gilson, S. (2004). *Rethinking disability.* Belmont, CA: Brooks/Cole.

Eagly, A. H., Baron, R. M., & Hamilton, V. L. (2004). *The social psychology of group identity and social conflict: Theory, application, and practice.* Washington, DC: APA Books.

Eagly, A. H., Beall, A. E., & Sternberg, R. J. (2005). *The psychology of gender.* New York: Guilford Press.

Fogler, S. (2010). Using conflict theory to explore the role of nursing home social workers in home- and community-based service utilization. *Journal of Gerontological Social Work, 52*(8), 859–869.

Fry, R., & Cohn, D. (2010, Jan 19). *The rise of wives.* Retrieved from Pew Research Center Publications: http://pewresearch.org/pubs/1466/economics-marriage-rise-of-wives

Gilligan, C. (1982). *In a different voice: Psychological theory and women's development.* Cambridge, MA: Harvard University Press.

Gilligan, C. (1993). *In a different voice: Psychological theory and women's development* (Reissue ed.). Cambridge, MA: Harvard University Press.

Gilligan, C., & Attanucci, J. (1986). Two moral orientations In C. Gilligan, J. Ward, J. Taylor, & B. Bardige (Eds.), *Mapping the moral domain: A contribution of women's thinking to psychological theory and education* (pp. 73–86). Cambridge, MA: Harvard University Press.

Goffman, E. (1963). *Stigma: Notes on the management of spoiled identity.* Englewood Cliffs, NJ: Prentice Hall.

Goffmann, I., & Best, J. (2005). *Interaction ritual: Essays in face-to-face behavior.* New Brunswick, NJ: Transaction.

Goodwin, J., & Jasper, J. (2009). *The social movements reader: Cases and concepts.* Malden, MA: Blackwell.

Hall, C. (1990). *Women and identity: Value choices in a changing world.* New York: Hemisphere.

Herzberg, F., Mausner, B., & Snyderman, B. B. (1959). *The motivation to work* (2nd ed.). New York: Wiley.

Hirshleifer, J. (2001). *Dark side of the force: Economic foundations of conflict theory.* Cambridge: Cambridge University Press.

History of the Universe. (n.d.). *The physical environment.* Retrieved from http://www.historyof theuniverse.com/physical.html

Hurd, G. A. (Producer), Jimenez, N. (Writer), Jimenez, N., & Steinberg, M. (Directors). (1992). *The Waterdance* [Motion Picture]. United States: No Frills Film Productions

Jackson, P. (2004). Role sequencing: Does order matter for mental health? *Journal of Health and Social Behavior, 45,* 132–135.

Kotler, P., & Lee, N. (2007). *Social marketing: Influencing behaviors for good.* Thousand Oaks, CA: Sage.

Kozulin, A., Gindis, B., Ageyev, V. S., & Miller, S. M. (2003). *Vygotsky's educational theory in cultural context (learning in doing: social, cognitive and computational perspectives).* New York: Cambridge University Press.

Layder, D. (2005). *Understanding social theory* (2nd ed.). London: Sage.

Lazarus, A. A. (1989). *The practice of multimodal therapy: Systematic, comprehensive, and effective psychotherapy.* Baltimore: Johns Hopkins University Press.

Lindner, J. R. (1998). Understanding employee motivation. *Journal of Extension, 36*(3). Retrieved from http://www.joe.org/joe/1998june/rb3.php

Massachusetts Institute of Technology. (2007). *Mission environment.* Retrieved from http://web.mit.edu/12.000/www/m2007/teams/finalwebsite/environment/decomposers.html

Mead, G. H. (1964). *On social psychology: Selected papers* (Revised ed.). (A. Strauss, Ed.). Chicago: University of Chicago Press.

Mead, G. H. (1965). *Mind, self and society from the standpoint of a social behaviorist.* (C. W. Morris, Ed.). Chicago: University of Chicago Press. (Original work published 1934)

Mead, G. H., & Silva, F. C. (2011). *G.H. Mead: A reader.* New York: Routledge.

Mikkola, M. (2008, May 12). *Feminist perspectives on sex and gender.* Retrieved from Stanford Encyclopedia of Philosophy: http://plato.stanford.edu/entries/feminism-gender/

Moore, J. (2008). *Conceptual foundations of radical behaviorism.* East Aurora, NY: Sloan.

Newman, B. M., & Newman, P. R. (2008). *Development through life: A psychosocial approach.* Belmont, CA: Wadsworth.

O'Reilly, A. (2010). *Twenty-first century motherhood: Experience, identity, policy, agency.* New York: Columbia University Press.

Parsons, T. (2002). *Structure of social action* (Vol. 2, 2nd ed.). New York: Free Press.

Pauwels, L. (2006). *Visual cultures of science: Rethinking representational practices in knowledge building and science communication.* Hanover, NH: Dartmouth University Press.

Riggs, J. M. (1997). Mandates for mothers and fathers: Perceptions of breadwinners and care givers. *Behavioral Science, 37,* 565–580.

Ritter, M. E. (2003–2010). *The physical environment.* Retrieved from http://www.uwsp.edu/geo/faculty/ritter/geog101/textbook/about_the_physical_environment.html

Ritter, M. E. (2010, June 7). *News and commentary about issues related to the physical environment.* Retrieved from http://tpeblog.wordpress.com/

Rollins, B. C., & Bahr, S. J. (1976). A theory of power relationships in marriage. *Journal of Marriage and the Family, 38,* 619–627.

Schneider, D. J. (2004). *The psychology of stereotyping.* New York: Guilford Press.

Smith, M. J. (2005). *Philosophy and methodology in the social sciences.* Thousand Oaks, CA: Sage.

Sprecher, S. (1998). Social exchange theories and sexuality. *Journal of Sex Research, 35*(1), 32–43.

Steele, C. (2010). *Whistling Vivaldi and other clues to how stereotype affects us.* New York: W. W. Norton.

Swain, J., French, S., Barnes, C., & Thomas, C. (2004). *Disabling barriers: Enabling environments.* Thousand Oaks, CA.

Templer, J. (1994). *The staircase: History and theories.* Cambridge, MA: MIT Press.

Thibault, J. W., & Kelley, H. H. (1952). *The social psychology of groups.* New York: Wiley.

Value Based Management.net. (2010, March 29). *Two factor theory.* Retrieved from http://www.valuebasedmanagement.net/methods_herzberg_two_factor_theory.html

Vroom, V. H. (1995). *Work and motivation.* San Francisco: Jossey Bass.

Vygotsky, L. (1978). *Mind in society: The development of higher psychological processes.* Cambridge, MA: Harvard University Press.

Watson, J. B. (1998). *Behaviorism* (Revised ed.). New Brunswick, NJ: Transaction.

Wolfensberger, W., & Thomas, S. (2007). *Passing a tool for analyzing service quality according to social role valorization criteria.* Syracuse, NY: Training Institute.

Wong, Y.-L. I., & Stanhope, V. (2009). Conceptualizing community: A comparison of neighborhood characteristics of supportive housing for persons with psychiatric and developmental disabilities. *Social Science & Medicine, 68*(8), 1376–1387.

Zafirovski, M. (2003). *Some amendments to social exchange theory: A sociological perspective.* Retrieved from International Consortium for the Advancement of Academic Publishing (ICAAP): http://theoryandscience.icaap.orgf content/vol004.002/0 l_zafirovski.html

Zafirovski, M. (2009). *Liberal modernity and its adversaries: Freedom, liberalism and anti-liberalism in the 21st century.* Chicago: Haymarket Books.

Overview of Categorical Theories

Looking at Humans as Population Segments

This chapter begins a critical examination of theories that describe and explain humans as members of categories, currently and most commonly referred to under the umbrella of *human diversity*. Over the past five decades, concern with categories has not only expanded intellectually, but has become a major topic of theorizing and action outcomes. Several important trends have entered and attempted to sustain themselves in the diversity home, some more successful than others. This chapter discusses these theoretical visitors as well as those who have taken more long-term residence in this genre of theories.

Human categories can be carved in numerous directions, each providing a different texture and content. We previously harnessed dualism to look at categorization by interior and exterior characteristics. However, given the difficulty with making the distinction between these landscapes, the boundary is difficult to identify and thus do adequate theoretical work. Others have suggested analyzing categorical classifications by the degree to which one is perceived to have choice over membership, the strength and nature of identity related to the category (Copp, 2002; Guttman, 2003), the social status of the category (Guttman, 2003), the ease of moving in and out of groups, the degree of observability of the essential element of category membership, and so forth (DePoy & Gilson, 2011).

Drawing 9.1 Category Theories Word Soup

This chapter applies the diversity patina-diversity depth continuum, introduced earlier, to the analysis of categorical descriptions and explanations of humans. Diversity *patina* refers to the acceptance or assignment of diversity on the basis of an essential characteristic. Most frequently, the characteristic refers to corporeal appearance features (e.g., sexual organs, skin color, etc.), geographic location (rural, urban), origin (ethnicity, culture), and sexual preference (heterosexual or not heterosexual); we also refer to this as *bodies and backgrounds* diversity. Diversity *depth* is a human quality that belongs to every individual. This idiographic conceptualization locates diversity in the realm of varied ideas, experiences, viewpoints, habits, and so forth.

A second continuum proposed for analyzing categorical understandings of humans is proximal-distal. This continuum has been introduced already as a referent to centrality (proximal) or distance (distal), in this case applied to the degree of importance of category membership in an individual life and identity.

Categorical Theory Axioms

Table 9.1 presents the axioms that guide discussion in this chapter.

THINKING POINT

As we proceed, think about how each axiom applies to history and the representative theories that we discuss and analyze in this chapter.

Table 9.1	Categorical Theory Axioms

1. Categorical descriptions and explanations are based on nomothetic principles and methods of inquiry. As *nomothetic,* they address common characteristics of groups rather than focusing on individual uniqueness (referred to as *idiographic*). Nomothetic methods of inquiry are research strategies that seek to identify, associate, and reveal the causes of group-specific phenomena.

2. Categorical descriptions assume a collective identity and common set of experiences among members.

3. Categorical descriptions and explanations can provide positive guidance in identifying between group differences and within group similarities, but also can be misused as essentialist, overgeneralizing, stereotyping, and discriminatory. This axiom is not about theory, but rather the use of theory.

4. Categorical descriptions and explanations assume homogeneity in areas beyond the membership criterion, to a greater or lesser degree. That is, on the basis of category membership, assumptions are made about experiences, traits, and expectations unrelated to the membership criterion itself.

5. Categories and membership criteria are dynamic, and influenced by many contextual factors.

6. Categorical studies, to a greater or lesser degree, examine inequality among groups. This axiom has become increasingly hegemonous over the past several decades, because categorical studies often form the basis for civil rights and affirmative action movements.

7. Categorical studies have been referred to over the past several decades as *diversity studies.*

So, now let us move back in time to visit how earlier conceptualizations of categorical description and explanation evolved to their current thinking and action foci in human category as diversity.

History of Categorical Theory

As presented in other chapters throughout the book, and applied to categorical theories in Axiom 5, theory and understanding of human description and explanation change over time, and are dynamically shaped by the contexts in which they exist and by the foundations from which they emerge. According to Haidt (2010), the error of holding human genetics as primarily explanatory for racial, gender, and other categories based on interior environmental factors lies in the failure of the Human Genome Project to identify a constant set of human genes. Yet, Haidt suggests that this failure is actually a critical discovery, in that the "human genome is far more dynamic and variable than we thought. Gene activity varies within each person across the lifespan and in response to changing environments" (p. B10). Looking at genetics as animated rather than static eschews the notion of race and gender as unfluctuating or inscribed in historical and embodied stone. Rather, biological human variation, and thus groupings ostensibly attributed to them, over the existence of humans, reciprocally act and change with surrounding conditions. Moreover, Haidt claims that within-group variation is so great that it eclipses between-group differences, diminishing the relevance and validity of treating diversity groups as essential. While we do not necessarily agree that genes are the sole explanatory factor for human diversity, as addressed later in the chapter, some important contemporary work such as the scholarship of Painter (2010) has challenged the notion of race as heritable.

In examining the meaning of *whiteness,* Painter (2010) creates a photographic negative of *not white.* Her work looks as far back as ancient civilizations of Celts, Greeks, and Scythians to debunk the myth that a single white race ever existed. Rather, Painter refers to white races that were locally bounded and diverse in skin color. Painter's history locates the conceptual creation of a single white race as recent in chronology. In agreement with Haidt, the notion of whiteness according to Painter was not related to genetics or skin color. Rather, in concert with other diversity theorists such as Healy (2009), Painter looks to political, intellectual, and economic power relative to other groups with different appearances and skin colors as explanatory of categorical explanations for human experience.

Healy (2009) identified power in the form of the conquest of inferiors by superiors as an important foundation of race relations in Europe. Both Healy and Painter emphasize the role of enslavement of both white and nonwhite population groups as a means of establishing and maintaining difference and dominance.

Focusing on U.S. history, Steinberg (2001) pointed to the influence of European interlopers' conquest of indigenous peoples, and similar to Painter, identifies the influence of slavery on interethnic and intergroup relations in the United States, asserting that these two unfortunate historical trends set the stage for uneven and contentious relationships that link current diversity theories with negative implications of being marginalized.

From the medical historical perspective, Armstrong (2002) traced the emergence of the concept of *normal body* over the past several centuries and suggested that large-scale screening and surveillance of the body in efforts to delineate health and illness was a major contributor to notions of intergroup relations as comparisons between the ideal, desirable, and unacceptable.

Different from but complementary to Armstrong's, Healy's and Steinberg's thinking, Thomas (2001) and Warnke (2008) look to philosophy to unpack and rethink categorical theories. Warnke challenges the essentialism of categories, suggesting that they do not create exhaustive or consistent identities. Rather, in answering ontological questions such as "what is a woman," Warnke suggests that individual meanings of those categories mediate commonalities. Moreover, these meanings vary, contributing to dynamic differences in proximal to distal importance of category membership in defining personhood over the chronology of a life span.

Thomas (2001) calls upon epistemology, or the way in which we come to know about a phenomenon. He summarizes the literature challenging positivism, the notion that there is a single truth that can be known by objective "scientific" inquiry. Because postmodernists not only eschewed monism, but to a greater or lesser degree, the construct of reality itself, no one "truth" is correct, prescriptive, and desirable. Thus, the theoretical opportunity for equality of acknowledgment of all people as diverse was born.

THINKING POINT

What is the importance of this philosophical shift in theory development?

A review of classical theories of human development, such as those advanced by Freud, Piaget, and Erikson, reveals an important axiom inherent in this genre—the nature of truth as unitary and monistic. In other words, these theories did not differentiate among groups on the basis of diversity characteristics that are common parlance in today's theoretical world. Moreover, as discussed, social scientists who sought to verify and build on these classical theories used methods of inquiry that fell within the experimental-type tradition of research, which is based on positivism (DePoy & Gilson, 2011). Given the axiom of a single truth and one desirable way to come to know it, there was no conceptual room for diversity on the basis of race, class, gender, ethnicity, and so forth. And, deviation from what was determined to be the norm was considered undesirable.

Recalling what happened, theoretically, to those who did not fit within two standard deviations from the mean on Quetelet's normal curve, these outliers were considered excluded from normal, residing in the margins of the abnormal. But, with the important shifts in the social and political context identified by Steinberg and others, *theoretical marginalia* was not useful and thus postpositive and ultimately postmodern thinking gained in hegemony. With postpositivism and postmodernism as tools to frame thinking about human diversity, groups that in traditional positivist theories were considered marginal, or outside of the monistic norm, could be characterized as valued and worthy of theoretical attention, rather than simply portrayed as different and unlike the desirables.

As noted earlier in this chapter, an important intellectual trend uniting current categorical theories is their unique location under the rubric of diversity theory. Thus, diversity has become a moniker applied to those who are not typical.

Because we find the term *diversity* curious and somewhat euphemistic, we consult our word soup palette to further examine its definitions over time. A chronological review of lexical definitions of diversity reveals that in the United States in particular, the term has shifted in meaning from variety, to difference, and then to category membership.

In the 1913 edition of *Webster's Dictionary,* diversity is defined as: dissimilitude, multiplicity of differences, variety. Some prevailing and representative examples of contemporary definitions of diversity are: "the condition of being diverse: variety; *especially*: the inclusion of diverse people (as people of different races or cultures) in a group or organization (Merriam-Webster, 2010), biological difference (Wilson, 1999), racial difference (Shiao, 2004), noticeable heterogeneity (Hyperdictionary.com, n.d.), and minority group membership (Basson, 2004, 2008; Healy, 2009). These definitions are typical of current perspectives in which diversity is viewed as the proximal patina characteristic that describes and identifies predefined groups and explains appearance, behavior, and experience of group members. Moreover, in much of contemporary literature, policy, and practice discourse, the term has been further delimited to a characteristic that belongs to groups perceived as nondominant and nonprivileged, such as ethnic and racial minorities, women, nonheterosexual groups (Anderson & Middleton, 2011; Healy, 2009), and more recently, disabled groups with disabilities (DePoy & Gilson, 2011).

Given the historical and philosophical factors identified by Warnke, Healy, Steinberg, and Thomas, it is not surprising that the term *diversity* has been applied to these marginalized groups and not to populations that are considered to be the mainstream. To further understand the nature of theories of diversity, there are additional influential factors to be illuminated, including but not limited to immigration trends, civil rights movements, policy changes, technology, and increasing globalism (Healy, 2009; Painter, 2010; Parillo, 2009). We suggest, however, that a major emphasis in this shift was the failure of multicultural efforts to advance symmetry among groups, and in agreement with Shiao (2004), that an understanding of the evolution of multicultural thinking is critical to an analysis of how diversity came to be equated with categories and *otherness* (Roberts, 2007).

Multiculturalism, Category Identity, and Diversity

According to Goldberg (2009), multicultural thought moved from an assimilationist to an integrationist and then to an incorporationist approach. Table 9.2 presents the distinction among the three perspectives. Both assimilationist and integrationist schools of thought begin with the axiom that there is a dominant and desirable group of which marginal groups want to belong. The difference between assimilationist and integrationist thinking, particularly in Western thought, lies in the degree to which the marginal group, the *others* (Roberts, 2007), must take on characteristics of the dominant group. However, both assimilationists and integrationists locate power within the dominant group that sits in judgment to determine the boundaries beyond which groups are marginal, and of those who are, who is acceptable for membership, how the other must act, and the extent to which the other will be allowed to participate in and share resources of the dominant culture.

Table 9.2 Comparison of Multicultural Perspectives

Multicultural School of Thought	Viewpoints
Assimilationist	You can join us. You should join us. To join us, you need to be like us.
Integrationist	We can all live together on our world. Come and join us—we will help you *others* come into the mainstream, but you do not have to be like us.
Incorporationist	We will transform each other for the betterment of all.

THINKING POINT

Provide examples of each approach in Table 9.2.

The incorporationist approach differs significantly from its predecessors in that it asserts symmetry among groups as the basis for cultural change. That is, all groups are seen as equivalent in value and in their capacity to collaboratively transform multicultural societies for the betterment of all. Within this approach, otherness is reframed as negotiating an understanding and thus reduction of bias (Roberts, 2007).

Despite the theoretical support for group symmetry (Kukathas, 2007), we agree that multicultural efforts have remained primarily at the integrationist level of practice (Goldberg, 2009; Shiao, 2004; Roberts, 2007). Thus, diversity theory and application, in large part, have reflected segregated approaches to the promotion of civil rights for predefined groups that have been identified as diverse on the basis of diversity patina, or observable difference. While there are essential and warranted benefits to restricting diversity theory and related responses to selected diversity patina subgroups who have experienced discrimination, there are many limitations as well.

Equating diversity with oppression and marginalization has been an important intellectual and policy impetus for promoting social action that is ostensibly designed to advanced equal opportunity. Although it is beyond the scope of this book to identify all of the advances anchored on theoretical views of diversity as minority, oppression, discrimination, and marginalization, some primary examples include women's suffrage, the Civil Rights Act of 1964, The Americans With Disabilities Act of 1990 and 2008 amendments, Violence Against Women's Act, legislation prohibiting hate crimes, affirmative action, and so forth (Diller, 2011).

However, restricting diversity theory to marginalized and oppressed categorical conceptualizations has limitations. First, viewing diversity as a characteristic of otherness is a dualist approach that sets the theoretical foundation for separation and in- and out-group designations (Dallmayr, 2010; Roberts, 2007).

As Shiao (2004) states, diversity conceptualizations based on population category membership promote discrimination by "institutionalizing a closer scrutiny of non-Whites for social acceptance and asking them to be more tolerable to Whites" (Shiao, 2004, p. 17). (Note that whiteness did not become a single racial concept until the 19th century [Painter, 2010] and we acknowledge its acceptance in contemporary theory. However, considering that the United States elected a biracial president in 2008 among other changing trends, we also suggest that the term *white* is euphemistic for dominant groups which may be diverse in skin color.) Paradoxically, as noted in Axiom 3 and eloquently revealed by Roberts (2007) in her examination of narratives of alterity, population-specific conceptualizations of diversity often maintain stereotyping (Moller-Okin, 1999; Rodriguez, 2002; Schneider, 2004; Steele, 2010), ghettoizing (DePoy & Gilson, 2011), and dualist conceptions of "us and them" by positing homogeneity within the very groups that are defined as diverse. Assuming group homogeneity on the basis of a single diversity patina characteristic, such as disability or ethnicity, has the potential to promote essentialist thinking and identity politics and to restrict theory application and community responses to assumed nomothetic need. Warnke (2008) reminds us that just like membership in a group is not exhaustive and constant througout a life, needs are dynamic and changing as well.

A final point to note about equating diversity with difference is that doing so only ascribes diversity to those who lie at the extremes of the normal curve (Armstrong, 2002; DePoy & Gilson, 2011). We suggest flattening the curve as a contemporary socially just response. Expanding the theoretical paradigm of diversity beyond minority group membership to include a continuum of proximal to distal importance of belongingness in other affinity groups, while holding the uniqueness of all people as a given, provides many opportunities. These opportunities not only maintain the important theoretical and applied gains that have occurred from civil rights concepts and movements, affirmative action, and other population specific responses, but also advance new conceptualizations of similitude and difference in communities. Two important and contemporary principles help achieve this expansion: group symmetry (Kukathas, 2007) and integral pluralism (Dallmayr, 2010).

Group symmetry does not naively posit that all groups have equal opportunity and access to resources. Rather, it is an ideal that refers to the equal value and contribution of disparate groups, and their subsequent reciprocal positive transformation of multicultural environments (Kukathas, 2007). Because group symmetry has yet to be actualized in theory and its application, we agree that progressive and efficacious approaches to redress historical and constructed discrimination and contemporary injustice are necessary. However, group symmetry, as an ideal to be operationalized, has the potential of moving theory, research, and related social action beyond diversity patina to the second principle of integral pluralism (Dallmayr, 2010).

THINKING POINT

 Provide some examples of group symmetry.

Integral pluralism refers to the relocation of diversity beyond patina category membership to the larger domain of both "oneness and manyness" in which varied beliefs, ideas, and experiences as well as affinities are negotiated through dialogue. Once again, this principle is not naïve in that tension and conflict are inherent in difference (Dallmayr, 2010). Dialogue, however, confronts disagreement and thus can reposition diversity as the individuated and collective foundation for tolerance (Kukathas, 2007), transformation, and incorporation. Recognizing group membership on a proximal-distal continuum collocates individuality and group identity as equals in the diversity dialogue.

Evidence

As discussed in the next chapter, multiple forms of evidence and methods to "come to know" about diversity have been used. Nomothetic techniques relying on discerning group similarities on the normal curve have supported many diversity patina theories, while narrative provides idiographic evidence to be interpreted from varied standpoints.

Summary

This chapter discussed the history and current theoretical approaches to diversity. It then proposed that diversity be analyzed through a synthesis of group and individual identity, experience, and ideas.

References

Anderson, S., & Middleton, V. (2011). *Explorations in diversity: Examining privilege and oppression in a multicultural society* (2nd ed.). Belmont, CA: Wadsworth.

Armstrong, D. (2002). *A new history of identity: A sociology of medical knowledge.* Basingstoke, UK: Palgrave Macmillan.

Basson, L. (2004). Blurring the boundaries of diversity: Racial mixture, ethnic ambiguity and indigenous citizenship in settler states. *International Journal of Diversity in Organisations, Communities and Nations, 4,* 281.

Basson, L. (2008). *White enough to be American: Race mixing, indigenous people, and the boundaries of state and nation.* Chapel Hill: University of North Carolina Press.

Copp, D. (2002). Social unity and the identity of persons. *Journal of Political Philosophy, 10*(4), 365–391.

Dallmayr, F. (2010). *Integral pluralism.* Lexington: University Press of Kentucky.

DePoy, E., & Gilson, S. (2011). *Studying disability.* Thousand Oaks, CA: Sage.

Dictionary.com. (2010). *Class.* Retrieved from http://dictionary.reference.com/browse/class?&qsrc=

Diller, J. (2011). *Cultural diversity: A primer for human services* (4th ed.). Belmont, CA: Brooks Cole.

Goldberg, D. T. (2009). *Multiculturalism: A critical reader.* Cambridge, MA: Blackwell.

Gutmann, A. (2003). *Identity in democracy.* Princeton, NJ: Princeton University Press.

Haidt, J. (2010, September 3). Fast evolution. *Chronicle of Higher Education,* p. B10.

Healy, J. S. (2009). *Diversity in society.* Thousand Oaks, CA: Pine Forge Press.

Hyperdictionary.com (n.d.). *Diversity.* Retrieved from http://www.hyperdictionary.com

Kukathas, C. (2007). *The liberal archipelago.* New York: Oxford University Press.

Merriam-Webster. (2010). *Diversity.* Retrieved from http://www.merriam-webster.com/dictionary/diversity

Moller-Okin, S. (1999). *Is multiculturalism bad for women?* Princeton, NJ: Princeton University Press.

Painter, N. I. (2010). *The history of white people.* New York: W. W. Norton.

Parillo, V. N. (2009). *Diversity in America* (3rd ed.). Thousand Oaks, CA: Pine Forge Press.

Roberts, K. G. (2007). *Alterity and narrative.* Albany, NY: SUNY Press.

Rodriguez, R. (2002). *Brown: The last discovery of America.* New York: Viking.

Schneider, D. J. (2004). *The psychology of stereotyping.* New York: Guilford Press.

Shiao, J. L. (2004). *Identifying talent, institutionalizing diversity: Race and philanthropy in post-civil rights America.* Durham, NC: Duke University Press.

Steele, C. (2010). *Whistling Vivaldi and other clues to how stereotype affects us.* New York: W. W. Norton.

Steinberg, S. (2001). *The ethnic myth: Race, ethnicity, and class in America* (3rd ed.). Boston: Beacon Press.

Thomas, R. M. (2001). *Recent theories of human development.* Thousand Oaks, CA: Sage.

Warnke, G. (2008). *After identity: Rethinking race, sex, and gender.* New York: Cambridge University Press.

Wilson, E. O. (1999). *The diversity of life.* New York: W. W. Norton.

10

Categorical Theories Related to Race, Ethnicity, Culture, Religion, and Class

This chapter and the next two discuss seminal theoretical frames of reference addressed under the rubric of categorical theories, or those delimited by what we have referred to as bodies and backgrounds characteristics. The theories in Chapters 10 to 12 group and explain humans on the basis of corpus, origin, culture, religion, preference, or nationality. Because categories run rampant in the literature and in thinking about human description and explanation, locating this broad discussion in a single chapter was not feasible without drowning the reader under the huge ocean of bodies and backgrounds concepts and thinking. As a result, we struggled with how best to organize and divide the categories into chapters, inductively playing with the distal-proximal axis. Unfortunately, each taxonomy on this continuum led us to a dualist binary dead end. So, we made an arbitrary decision to locate material in each chapter based on the size of the "theoretical meal" that can serve as nourishment, rather than a sense of being too full.

This chapter limits discussion to the categories listed in Table 10.1. Similar to our advice in previous chapters, one can amble along the extrapolation park to apply learning from each chapter to categories that are not discussed in this book.

Table 10.1 Specific Categories
Race, ethnicity, and culture Religion Class

Note that although age can also be included in categorical classification schemes, it is not directly addressed, as we have dissected age as a critical variable in the chapters on developmental theories that foreground chronological time as explanatory of diverse human phenomena.

Race, Ethnicity, and Culture

Of course, describing and explaining humans as members of race, ethnicity, and culture categories are not easy tasks. Given its hegemony in social work and other professional fields, we looked to work on cultural competence to clarify and distinguish the terms from one another. However, this literature does not sharpen the lexical imagery. For example, Diller (2011) begins his discussion of cultural competency with statistics about the changing racial and ethnic balance of the United States, further justifying the need to be culturally competent in order to work with nonwhite racial and ethnic groups. Zack proposes eliminating the constructs of race and ethnicity altogether (as cited in Gracia, 2007). What distinguishes race, ethnicity and culture, then, is not only confusing to us but, in large part, rarely broached by others.

With conceptual boundaries equivalently unclear, the U.S. Federal Department of Health and Human Service defines cultural competence as follows:

> Cultural and linguistic competence is a set of congruent behaviors, attitudes, and policies that come together in a system, agency, or among professionals that enables effective work in cross-cultural situations. "Culture" refers to integrated patterns of human behavior that include the language, thoughts, communications, actions, customs, beliefs, values, and institutions of racial, ethnic, religious, or social groups. (Office of Minority Health, 2005, para. 1)

Further complicating theorizing about culture, race, and ethnicity is the interchangeability of ethnicity and race in some intellectual, political, and geographic regions and not in others, as the previous excerpt illustrates, along with the subsequent narrative. We therefore locate and discuss these three understandings of humans in close proximity because the distinction among them is not clear. However, for instructive purposes and because theory has been parsed into each of the three, we discuss race, ethnicity, and culture as differentiated parts of a conceptual whole. Much of the discussion and analysis overlaps but we will try not to be too redundant.

Race

For us, the major distinction between race and ethnicity lies in its history. History constructs a story that often inheres regardless of evidence to the contrary (McMillan, 2010). We emphasize that we are not distinguishing race from ethnicity and culture on the basis of genetic embodiment, but rather on its characterization as such in much of our recent history. So, we decided to discuss race first, as it seems to have the longest chronology of the three terms. Looking at definitions and theories, race is the only one of the three constructs that has been located by some theories within the corpus. That is to say, while race shares power, social, and contextual elements with ethnicity and culture, until recently, throughout history, race was theorized as genetic difference and even today, the term *human genome variation* is used to describe differences that were once considered to be fully embodied. Moreover, in the United States, different from other nations and locations around the globe, membership in the African American race was assigned on the basis of hypodescent or "blood ancestry" (Sweet, 2005). In other words, if any ancestry was considered to be black, then a child, no matter how chronologically removed from the ancestor, was classified as black. Similarly, Native Americans, Asians, and to some extent Jews have been contained within the category of race. So, not unexpectedly, as discussed in detail next, race has had and continues to sport numerous definitions within the word soup bowl. See Table 10.2 for exemplars.

Table 10.2 Definitions of Race, 1906–2005

Source	Definition
I. K. Funk. (1906). *A Standard Dictionary of the English Language.*	A primary division of the human species containing a number of groups" on the basis of biological traits including color, hair, skull teeth (p. 1471); any class of beings or animals having characteristics uniting them or differentiating them from all others. Exhibiting but slight differentiating from the typical form.
U.S. Census Bureau. (1997).	Self-identification by people according to the race or races with which they most closely identify. These categories are sociopolitical constructs and should not be interpreted as being scientific or anthropological in nature. Furthermore, the race categories include both racial and national-origin groups. White. A person having origins in any of the original peoples of Europe, the Middle East, or North Africa. It includes people who indicate their race as "White" or report entries such as Irish, German, Italian, Lebanese, Near Easterner, Arab, or Polish.

(Continued)

Table 10.2 (Continued)

Source	Definition
	Black or African American. A person having origins in any of the Black racial groups of Africa. It includes people who indicate their race as "Black, African Am., or Negro," or provide written entries such as African American, Afro American, Kenyan, Nigerian, or Haitian.
	American Indian and Alaska Native. A person having origins in any of the original peoples of North and South America (including Central America) and who maintain tribal affiliation or community attachment.
	Asian. A person having origins in any of the original peoples of the Far East, Southeast Asia, or the Indian subcontinent including, for example, Cambodia, China, India, Japan, Korea, Malaysia, Pakistan, the Philippine Islands, Thailand, and Vietnam. It includes "Asian Indian," "Chinese," "Filipino," "Korean," "Japanese," "Vietnamese," and "Other Asian."
	Native Hawaiian and Other Pacific Islander. A person having origins in any of the original peoples of Hawaii, Guam, Samoa, or other Pacific Islands. It includes people who indicate their race as "Native Hawaiian," "Guamanian or Chamorro," "Samoan," and "Other Pacific Islander."
	Some other race. Includes all other responses not included in the "White", "Black or African American", "American Indian and Alaska Native", "Asian" and "Native Hawaiian and Other Pacific Islander" race categories described above. Respondents providing write-in entries such as multiracial, mixed, interracial, Wesort, or a Hispanic/Latino group (for example, Mexican, Puerto Rican, or Cuban) in the "Some other race" category are included here.
Helms (as cited in R. M. Thomas, 2001). *Recent Theories of Human Development*	Individual acknowledgment of common ancestry and culture.
W. Zelinsky (2001). *The Enigma of Ethnicity*	Collective perception of race as social construction.
C. D. Royal & G. M. Dunston (2004). *Commentary: Changing the Paradigm From "Race" to Human Genome Variation*	Human genome variation.
Biology On-Line. (2005).	The descendants of a common ancestor; a family, tribe, people, or nation, believed or presumed to belong to the same stock; a lineage; a breed.

THINKING POINT

Compare and contrast the scope and values that are inherent in each definition in Table 10.2.

Reflected in the word soup in Table 10.2, over the years and even contemporaneously, the construct of race morphed through disparate abstracts and applications that emerge from a range of descriptive and explanatory lenses, including corporeal endogamy through self-assignment. We reiterate that as cautioned by Gracia (2007), we are not suggesting a simplistic view of race as embodied and ethnicity as nationality. Rather, we look to the history as a distinguishing factor with particular emphasis on the history of genomic variation that belongs primarily to race.

Race as Description

According to Healy (2009), race was not a concept until the 1500s, the point at which Europeans ventured into geographic areas in which the indigenous people both shared common physical characteristics among themselves and differed in appearance from the shared observations of continental populations. Superimposed on observable difference was the attribution of inferiority, setting the stage and providing the rationale for colonialism, conquest, oppression, and the contemporary analysis of racial category membership as a power differential. The elaborate study and taxonomic organization of humans into racial groups and subgroups became an important area of descriptive study and inquiry (Gould, 1996), but ultimately failed to hold its truth value when race was subjected to genetic or biological (Sweet, 2005), or even legal, explanation (Warnke, 2008). Still, evolutionary biologists such as Moran (2007) remain skeptical and suggest that genetic racial differences, while not absolute, do exist. His claim is based on disease prevalence data, which identify some pathologies, such as high incidence of prostate cancer, as peculiar to African American populations.

The eschewal of biological race is not the only complicating factor in describing racial categorization in that the boundaries that separate racial descriptions were unclear historically and remain so now. Sweet (2005) attributes this phenomenon in large part to leakage of color across intermarital lines. Others, such as Warnke (2007) and Gracia (2007), challenge the essential characteristics of race through vexing questions such as what criteria classify humans according to race, how dark does one's skin have to be in order to be considered black, and how does black differ from African American?

Preceding and in agreement with Sweet (2005), Zelinsky (2001) noted that with the exception of isolated communities such as San, Ainu Innuit, and Laps (Sami), humans are intermixed, and cannot be separated into discrete races. Classifying even these groups as single racial categories is still questionable, however (Painter, 2010).

It is therefore curious that in the United States, census data (Population Reference Bureau, 2010) are still organized according to diversity patina descriptive, observable conceptualizations of race.

Descriptive theories of race have also posited race as a set of reportables, or experiences, that are shared by a group or the identification with a group on the basis of ancestry (Helms, as cited in Thomas, 2001; Warnke, 2008). For example, *Africology* refers to understanding the unique experiences of Africans, and recent doctoral programs have been established to study this field (Hunt, n.d.). Descriptive elements under this theoretical rubric include actual or acknowledged language, common behaviors, customs, music, food, location, and so forth, rather than biological and appearance comparisons to other groups (Hunt, n.d.; Thomas, 2001). Thus, Africology crosses over the boundaries of race as observable to defining race as culture. Jewish populations travel similar vagary. In 1980, the U.S. Supreme Court ruled that Jews were a distinct race (Rich, 2001–2006), yet category members often describe themselves as a culture, as discussed in the section on religion.

Yet, even with its vagueness, the descriptive element of race has and continues to form the basis for intergroup relations that began in the United States with slavery, oppression, and segregation of African Americans and others, such as Native Americans, Asians, and other indigenous and immigrant groups. The rich but contentious history of intergroup relations on the basis of descriptive racial categories continues today. As noted in Table 10.2, the U.S. government adheres to diversity patina descriptive understandings of race through its color-based taxonomy.

THINKING POINT

Can you think of advantages and disadvantages of maintaining a census taxonomy on the basis of diversity patina?

Explanatory Theories of Race

As noted, and what separates race from ethnicity and culture for us, are the major historical debates about the nature and existence of race as genetic and embodied. Theorists advance strong perspectives and disagreements about what factors explain commonalities in appearance and the behaviors and experiences that are described as common to those members who share or acknowledge the same physical or ancestral characteristics. And, as examined and will be discussed in detail in subsequent chapters, which explanatory theory or theories are accepted forms the foundation for the way in which communities and individuals ultimately respond to race.

Explanatory theories of race span the continuum from race as innate, inherited biological traits (Moran, 2007), to the notion of race as a socially constructed human phenomenon (Ore, 2005; Warnke, 2008), to the denial of race at all and the assertion that it should be eliminated as a human category (Zack, 2007).

Historically, theorists posited biological explanations for race and asserted the existence of common sets of genes inherited from one's ancestors that determined race and distinguished among racial groups (Graves, 2001; Unander, 2000). However, biological explanations in and of themselves were not necessarily negative. The acknowledgment of biological similarities and differences among groups was productive in identifying and providing positive health and medical responses to diseases such as Tay-Sachs and sickle-cell anemia, common to Jews and blacks respectively.

THINKING POINT

What other positive outcomes of biological similarities can you think of?

However, as we have noted, biological explanations for race and human difference created the backdrop on which essentialism, oppression, discrimination, and even genocide could be anchored. This occurred through the suggestion that inferior intelligence, character, capacity, and worth could be inferred, and even asserted, on the basis of diversity patina such as one's skin color or other observable physical characteristics (Painter, 2010). In his classic book titled the *Mismeasure of Man,* although criticized on epistemic grounds, Gould (1996) traced the numerous ways in which biological explanations have been used to diminish and discredit so many groups. Consider, for example, the historical practice of craniometry that involved using skull size as a measure of intelligence. Similarly, during the early 1900s, workers were trained to observe people who immigrated to the United States, entering through Ellis Island, and on the basis of identified atypical facial characteristics, determined intellectual inferiority (Gould, 1996). It is no surprise that these practices had no supportive evidence, yet in some sense remain implicit today in policy, community, and professional response and treatment, and result in stereotyping, profiling, and discrimination (Schneider, 2004; Warnke, 2008).

Over the past several decades, despite assertions by scholars such as Moran (2007), advancements in human genomics have failed to identify a complement of genes that can definitively explain commonalities of appearance in racial groups such as those defined in Table 10.2. The term *human genome variation* (HGVbaseG2P, 2010; Royal & Dunston, 2004) has therefore been substituted for race and other genetic groupings to clarify that phenotypes, observable corporeal commonalities, do exist between members of common ancestry but that there is no evidence for the exclusive existence of genetic explanations for distinct racial subgroups. Eschewing that common descriptive phenomena shared by group members can be explained by phylogenetic subspecies, while retaining the importance of genetic variation and phenotype to explain human difference and commonality, for us, seems to best allow clear and productive discourse. The concepts of phenotype and genomic variation do not deny the ongoing existence of oppression and discrimination on the basis of diversity patina such as skin color or other physical traits, but rather allow for advances in health, social, economic, and political status on the basis of genomic variation.

> *Cancer and cardiovascular research has made significant strides as geneticists describe and explain the genetic predisposition to both pathologies and unravel the genetic programming that can be interrupted to reverse the growth of these deadly cells.*

On the opposite end of the spectrum of race, explained as biological, is the set of theories that overlap with culture and ethnicity, positing that race is a construction with no embodied basis (Ore, 2005; Painter, 2010). Under the constructed rubric, many factors have been advanced to explain racial membership, including but not limited to political, economic (Steinberg, 2001), cultural (Maryland College Institute of Art, Center for Race and Culture, 2011), legal (Warnke, 2008), linguistic (Diller, 2011), and social (Royal & Dunston, 2004) contexts. As such, belonging in a racial group is explained as dynamic and changing in response to external influences. Omi and Winant's classic (1994) definition of race illustrates: "Race is a concept which signifies and symbolizes social conflicts and interests by referring to different types of human bodies" (p. 55).

We have certainly seen the feasibility of this explanation over the years, as noted in the move from viewing racial category membership as genetically determined to the recognition of race as ancestral, locational, legal, cultural (Hunt, n.d.; Fernando, 2006), power-motivated, or social. Further, even biological explanations have differed and changed according to their placement on the globe and chronological time. Two examples highlight this point.

> *Consider the one-drop rule, occurring before the U.S. Civil War. People were assigned to the category of* Negro *if they had even one metaphoric drop of African American blood (Warnke, 2008). It is curious to note that even current references to this rule imply the undesirability of African American racial heritage. Sweet (2005) discusses this important point in his analysis of descriptions of a 2003 movie,* The Human Stain. *In addition to the title of the film, all 14 representative media summaries and criticisms in some sense refer to the main character as a light-skinned African American who attempts to pass as white, and thus lives a "lie."*

Over the years, biological explanations have changed their focus from blood relation to genetic characteristics and then to phenotype in the United States. However, in countries such as Brazil, appearance rather than biological ancestry distinguishes racial category membership, although this trend is changing as globalization provokes homogenization of classification. In some cases, Brazilian children have worn different racial monikers than their parents, explained by their observable skin color (On-Line Encyclopedia, 2010).

It is particularly important to note that theories that explain racial category membership and experience as a construction become partially consumed by minority, ethnic, and cultural concepts as they move into the culturescapes of customs and politiscape of intergroup power differentials. For example, in 1998, the American Anthropological Association explained race as a worldview or an ideology that has resulted in inequality of "access to resources, jobs, and the rights of citizenship" on the basis of skin color. Bell's (1992) classic critical race theory explained race as economic disadvantage rather than embodied, and untouchable by current law because the legal system is an institution riddled with racism itself. Interestingly, showing the malleability of race theory, in 2007, the American Anthropological Association (2007) changed its 1998 definition to a view of race as multifaceted and understood through three explanatory lenses: historical, genomic variation, and lived experience.

Integrative theories, such as those implicit in both American Anthropological Association approaches (American Anthropological Association, 1998, 2007) neither ignore the importance of skin color and other observable patina characteristics in differentiating groups nor neglect the importance of social, political, economic and cultural factors in explaining race. These theories span a continuum from attributing identity to membership in a racial category (Appiah, 2005) to analyzing racial belonging as a global phenomenon. Consider, for example, Helms's (as cited in Thomas, 2001) theory of racial identity development. She explains racial identity as the interaction of common ancestry and the developmental process by which individuals come to see themselves as members of a racial group. Furthermore, Helms distinguished differences in the sequence of racial identity development initially between blacks and whites and then later among other groups of common ancestry.

> *Consider Mohammed and Lorenz, two black men in their late 30s who grew up together in an urban area. Mohammed recently converted to Muslim. Mohammed went to a historically black college (HBC) for his undergraduate work and then to an urban school for law. Lorenz went to a rural school as an undergrad and then to an urban school to study law. Mohammed, who grew up as a Baptist, decided at the age of 29 to convert to Muslim. He also wears traditional African robes to demonstrate his pride in his African American descent. Lorenz, who married a white woman, does not experience the same pride in his African ancestry, and he and Mohammed, still dear friends, often discuss the issue of black identity and the differences between them.*

> *Looking at Mohammed's racial identity development, we see that his family of origin strongly identified as black, and he therefore chose an HBC to please his parents. It was therefore not difficult for Mohammed to extract customs, rituals, and notions about cultural belonging from his surroundings and to adopt those which were comfortable and fit for him. He believes that his friend Lorenz is struggling with his black identity, despite Lorenz's assertion of comfort.*

Warnke (2008) reminds us that, similar to other group membership and identity, racial identity can take many paths at multiple depths, depending on how it is recognized, explained, assigned, and demonstrated by its owners.

Ethnicity

Once again stirring the word soup pot, an examination of the etymology of the word ethic reveals its origin in the Greek term for nation, *ethnos*. In the 14th century, its usage denoting "pagan" appeared in Scotland. More recent meanings include "peculiar to a race or nation" in the 19th century, and in 1935, as "racial, cultural or national minority group" (Harper, 2001–2010). From this word soup history, it is not hard to fathom how the overlap of the three terms in this discussion (*race, ethnicity,* and *culture*) occur, at least lexically. However, as noted, although definitions of *ethnicity* retain some elements of embodiment, throughout history, the body has not been the primary basis on which ethnicity is and has been theorized.

In the United States, concepts of ethnicity emerged from immigration trends, and thus, in large part, ethnicity has come to signify members and descendents of minority immigrant groups whose language, customs, or religion are not characteristic of the majority of citizens. Yet, categories such as Jewish, which can be defined as ethnicity, race, religion, or culture (Goldstein, 2006) and others such as Latino, which do not have universal commonalties continue to lob (Gracia, 2007) challenges into the court describing ethnicity.

In his own word soup review of diverse definitions, Zelinsky (2001) suggests that the common elements of most descriptions on the basis of ethnicity, although problematic and vague, include membership identity, behavior, and beliefs that differentiate a subgroup of a population from other groups in that same population. We particularly like Thomas's (2001) description, and adopt it to clarify the descriptive elements of ethnicity. He states:

> I would prefer to use the term ethnic to designate a group whose members (a) share a distinctive culture that includes such characteristics as customs, language, appearance and/ or religion and (b) are assigned their ethnic identity by other people and/or adopt that identity for themselves. (p. 219)

Note that this description has several important explicit and implied elements. First, asserted membership confers belonging on the basis of knowing and displaying the descriptors that are attributed to an ethnic group. Conversely, those who do not share the descriptors are excluded. Second, and most important, is that ethnic identity does not have to be accepted by ethnic group members in order to be assigned. So if one looks like, acts like, or even thinks like members of a particular group, ethnic identity can be assumed regardless of one's asserted identity. We are not suggesting the ethical stance of this definition, but rather, like it for clarity and transparency, particularly in geographies in which appearance and behavior confer identity regardless of one's personal perspective. Such definitions assist in laying bare ethnicity as an important basis of intergroup power relations, stereotype, and discrimination, particularly in the post–9/11 world of profiling. (Note, however, that the term *culture* is contained in this definition, fusing culture and ethnicity together in almost a seamless fashion.)

> *Consider Quansheng, a 44-year-old man of Chinese descent whose first language is Cantonese. He recently converted to Judaism, but his ethnicity using Thomas's (2001) definition would be Chinese.*

The explanatory theories of ethnicity reveal to us why ethnicity, despite its vague descriptors, is critically important to consider in understanding human categorization.

Similar to other essentialist categories, once an individual is identified as a member of an ethnic group, assumptions about commonalities beyond the descriptive factors are made. And, responses to ethnic group members then follow.

Consider Mohamed. As he boards the airplane, he is pulled aside for extra security.

THINKING POINT

 On the basis of ethnicity, what career would you guess Quansheng chose? Why?

Explanations for ethnic category membership include but are not limited to individual choice; alterity based on nationality, citizenship, and immigrant status; socialization, political power; and census categorization.

Due to his Asian appearance, we see Quansheng as "other," categorize him as Asian American on the census, and then assume that he is steeped in the exotica of distant geographies. We expect that he speaks with a Chinese accent and are surprised when he speaks Yiddish fluently.

By individual choice, we refer to the purposive adoption of behaviors or appearance of the group to which an individual aspires to belong. Alterity on the basis of nationality, citizenship, and immigrant status explains ethnicity as belonging to the *other* who relocates and interacts within populations from which the individual is differentiated by national origin. Explanations based on socialized *otherness* locate ethnicity in the realm of learning how to look and act from one's ethnic group members.

The thinking of Kertzer and Arel (2002) further illustrates the usefulness of defining ethnic membership as conferred. They suggest that political power and census explanations are inextricably linked. These explanations focus on the role of political advantage in creating and reifying ethnic census categories through counting. Consistent with ideas advanced by Bell (1992), Rodriguez (2002), and Gracia (2007), among others, Kertzer and Arel assert that ethnicity is constructed. However, they explain the construction as politically motivated and further identify how the census and ethnicity are tautological. Tautology in this context refers to the circular logic by which the census constructs ethnic categories and their attributes and then validates them through counting how many people contain the attributes and thus occupy each creation.

Consider Rodriguez to clarify. According to Rodriguez (2002), the ethnic category of Hispanic is constructed and brown skin color denotes the diversity of interethnic groups, many of which cannot be categorized by a single ethnicity. Thus, the term *Hispanic* implies no common ancestry, rituals, and even language, yet it is defined and then counted as if it exists, reifying its presence and even its magnitude.

Many contemporary theorists thus tend to identify human construction as explanatory of legitimate ethnicity and its category membership. That it to say, ethnicity is not embodied or natural. Therefore, to a greater or lesser degree depending on the factors that are theorized as explanatory, ethnic group membership is dynamic and boundaries are permeable.

Selecting individual choice as explanatory of ethnicity suggests that ethnicity is changeable, under the control of individuals who elect to occupy an ethnic space, and can be tried on and acquired so to speak by anyone. On the other hand, if you adopt national origin as explanatory, movement in and out of ethnicity is not as fluid. Yet, regardless of where one is born, there is always the potential to change appearance and behavior and adopt the customs of another geographic location. Thus, ethnic identity, even if explained by birth, is possible to change at least on the surface. However, if ethnicity and race are equivalent and conferred, as suggested by Diller (2011), the ease of identification recedes as one's appearance is increasingly consistent with stereotype.

We now move on to a discussion of culture. Keep in mind that the boundaries among culture and its kin, race and ethnicity, are fuzzy.

Culture

Not only is there a substantial historical and contemporary literature on culture, but also academic disciplines such as anthropology and sociology have devoted much of their research agenda to defining, characterizing, and looking at culture as descriptive and explanatory of human experience from diverse perspectives over many years.

As Fox and King (2002) look into word soup, they acknowledge multiple definitions of culture and what legitimately describes and explains it. Hylland-Eriksen (2002) clearly links ethnicity and culture in his statement, "in social anthropology it [ethnicity] refers to aspects of relationships between groups that consider themselves and are regarded by others as being culturally distinctive" (p. 4). Further, Spikard's (2005) book title, *Race and Nation: Ethnic Systems in the Modern World,* reveals his perspective on the unclear relationships among race, ethnicity and nationality.

While our intent is not for you to become experts in cultural literature and research, here we focus our discussion toward an understanding of how diverse conceptualizations of culture have been used to illuminate the human phenomena of classification on the basis of bodies and backgrounds patina. Before reading this section of the chapter, review of the discussions on multiculturalism and cultural competency (Diller, 2011) may be helpful. As noted, culture, and then multiculturalism, have been important constructs in parsing groups of humans into those who share a common language, set of rituals, beliefs, behavioral conventions, nationalities, appearance, and so forth.

Culture as Description

Culture is a complex construct that has taken on expanded meanings over time. In order to tackle the task of distilling cultural descriptions down to a meaningful discussion within our domain of concern, we once again plunge our lexical spoon into word soup history.

The word *culture* derives from the Latin root *colere*, which means "to inhabit, to cultivate, or to honor" (Harper, 2001–2010). Interestingly, culture in the 16th century referred to agriculture, or the cultivation of land and tilling for crops. It was not until the 19th century that the term was applied to intellectual and artistic cultivation of a particular group. Further foregrounding the emerging group-specific nature of culture, in the late 19th century, the meaning of the word *acculturation,* derived from the word *culture,* was recognized as the adoption of an "alien" or nonbirth-based culture (Harper), which we now name *assimilation* in the multicultural literature.

Historically, traditional anthropologists such as Tylor (1877), Mead (1934/1965), Geertz (1973), and Boas (1940/1995) described culture as the set of beliefs, symbols, moral imperatives, artistic practices and tastes, rituals, language, and customs that are both exhibited by and shape the lives of members of a group. Hylland-Eriksen (2002) noted that these seminal anthropologists were not interested in intergroup relations but rather investigated the "essence" of what they considered to be singular groups, leaving outside influences to sociologists. For these scholars, the culture of relatively isolated and circumscribed non-Western civilizations was of interest as it had the potential to unearth and aggregate universal essential elements of all cultures, and could best be inferred by observing individuals and groups acting within the limits of their own environments (Hylland-Eriksen, 2002).

Boas (1940/1995) was particularly influential in popularizing ethnography, an empirical method designed to learn about cultures other than one's own. Ethnographers were world travelers, so to speak. In order to characterize the essence of cultural membership, ethnographers would spend years living within the civilization that they sought to study. Many cultural anthropologists—including Benedict, Malinowski (Young, 2004), Spradley (1979), and Geertz (1973)—immersed themselves in these so-called foreign cultures, observed behaviors and interaction, interviewed members of the cultures, and drew conclusions based upon their findings that they claimed characterized the particular culture under scrutiny. Due in large part to intellectual, technological, political, and globalization trends, contemporary ethnographic and related techniques of inquiry have been applied to diverse groups, including but not limited to groups who interact in physical settings. For example, cultural status has been bestowed upon groups who share common characteristics such as disability (DePoy & Gilson, 2004, 2011), pain (Morris, 1993), youth (Bennett & Kahn-Harris, 2004), and even sewing (Beaudry, 2006).

THINKING POINT

Can you think of other groups who could be studied through ethnographic approaches?

The word soup in Table 10.3 illustrates the diversity of current definitions of *culture*.

Table 10.3 Definitions of *Culture*

1. A particular society at a particular time and place; "early Mayan civilization."

2. The tastes in art and manners that are favored by a social group.

3. Acculturation: all the knowledge and values shared by a society.

4. (Biology) the growing of microorganisms in a nutrient medium (such as gelatin or agar); "the culture of cells in a Petri dish."

5. (Bacteriology) the product of cultivating micro-organisms in a nutrient medium.

6. Polish: a highly developed state of perfection; having a flawless or impeccable quality; "they performed with great polish;" "I admired the exquisite refinement of his prose;" "almost an inspiration which gives to all work that finish which is almost art," —Joseph Conrad

7. The attitudes and behavior that are characteristic of a particular social group or organization; "the developing drug culture;" "the reason that the agency is doomed to inaction has something to do with the FBI culture."

8. The raising of plants or animals; "the culture of oysters."

Source: Dictionary.com, 2010

THINKING POINT

Compare the scope and values inherent in each definition.

Because of the overwhelming complexity of the concept of culture, Fox and King (2002) have suggested that attempts to agree upon a single understanding, and thus its universal elements, are no longer useful in advancing our understanding of human phenomena. However, given the importance attributed to multiculturalism and cultural competence, we suggest that a broad definition of culture is not only useful but also essential to the lives and practices of professionals. We therefore synthesize multiple perspectives to describe culture as group specific rules (explicated or tacit) that guide one or more of the three elements of human description of group members—appearance, behavior, and experience—and locate individuals within self-proclaimed or externally imposed groupings. This definition can apply to any group, but is more expansive than the political discussions that equate culture with minority, ethnic, and racial status. Because we believe that it is critical to define what we describe, explain, and then act upon, we advance this definition to clarify our perspective as comprehensive but not exhaustive of a host of ideas and views.

> *Consider the Hernandez and the Goldstein families. The Hernandez family is Catholic, speaks Spanish in their home, and they consider themselves as part of the Hispanic culture on the basis of those descriptors and their ancestry. The Goldsteins, a Jewish family, observe the Sabbath on Friday evening, send their children to Hebrew school to learn Hebrew and study for their bar mitzvahs, and joke about their love of bargain shopping as a cultural trait.*

> *The Goldsteins have two children, David, who is about to turn 13, and Ron who is 11. David now considers himself to be part of the teen culture. He listens to the same music that his friends enjoy, he dresses in fashions that his friends wear, and he hangs out with his friends at the local Internet café. He text messages his friends on their cell phones and receives text messages back.*

Each family, and David, considers themselves as part of a larger culture with rituals, language, and even jokes about traditions and stereotypes. But as the exemplars illustrate, culture does not have to have a religious or ethnic ancestry.

> *Different from the Hernandez's and the Goldstein's language descriptor, David speaks the language of text messaging to his friends and shares music, appearance, and experience as a teen as an important part of his identity.*

THINKING POINT

To what cultures do you belong? What describes them?

In his classic work on black urban experience, Kelley (1997) reminds us, however, that when thinking about and characterizing culture from a bodies and backgrounds context, one runs the risk of essentialism.

> Thinking of the black urban ghetto in the singular opened the door for the "underclass." Once culture is seen as a static measurable thing-behavior that is either part of an old African or slave tradition of product of dire circumstances, it is not hard to cast black people as pathological products of broken families, broken economies and/or broken communities. (Kelley, 1997, p. 3)

THINKING POINT

As you think of a culture and what it's members holds in common, now identify the diversity within it.

Explanatory Theories of Culture

With such diverse descriptions alongside the broad scope of definitions for culture and cultural membership, it is not surprising that explanations have been equally as complex. We have bisected our discussion into two categories: explanations at the distal metalevel and explanations of culture at the proximal individual and group level.

Distal metalevel explanations have looked at culture as an entity in itself. Rather than focusing on how individuals and groups acquire and act within cultures, these explanations have posited reasons that culture exists and functions. Table 10.4 presents prevalent distal metalevel explanations.

Table 10.4 Distal Metalevel Explanations of Culture

Culture as a function of adaptation: Culture exists in order to provide the structure and processes in which its members can function in diverse environments.

Culture as a function of geography: Cultural hearths, or major cultural centers, transmit to adjacent locations, also referred to as *diffusion*.

Culture as genetic disposition for learning: Humans have an innate capacity to learn the language, symbols, and rules that shape the lives of group members.

Culture as evolutionary: Cultures are purposive in preserving the survival of their members; they are dynamic and change over time in response to the diverse elements of the contexts in which they exist.

Culture as independent innovation: Culture is created from ideas within a single group itself.

Consider the Goldstein and the Hernandez families to illustrate each explanation in Table 10.4.

Culture as adaptation: Jewish history is plagued with a long trail of persecution from ancient Egypt through World War II and beyond. The cultural values of the primacy of family, the narratives that are passed on through the generations, along with the ritual observances such as the Sabbath service, function to link the present to the past, to transmit cultural values and beliefs, and to create a distinct identity for the survival of the Jewish culture (Gevirtz, Sarna, & Krasner, 2008).

Culture as geography: Spanish culture pervades much of the globe. The explorations and conquests of the Americas on the part of Spain have served to expand the reach of the Spanish culture throughout the New World, where a significant number of countries speak Spanish as a first language and others, such as the United States, have a large number of Spanish-speaking families, such as the Hernandezs, who were all born in the United States. It is curious to note, however, that Spanish culture, despite its wide diffusion, does not carry with it ubiquitous pride and esteem, in that many who are considered to be "Hispanic" do not enjoy equality of opportunity and often experience discrimination (Schmidt-Norawara & Nieto-Phillips, 2005).

Culture as genetic: Within the past several decades, the notion that genetics explains culture has emerged (Haviland, Prins, & Walrath, 2008). From this perspective, the propensity to learn and adopt cultural descriptors in both the Hernandez and Goldstein families would be explained by family ancestry and proximal environment. However, culture as not defined by family lineage begs the question of genetic inheritance. The teen culture experienced by David could be explained as a genetic trait to learn and acquire distal-environment patterns as the basis for fitting in and survival, although this explanation crosses over to the next list, culture as evolutionary.

Culture as evolutionary: This perspective suggests that through the processes of selection, inclusion, and exclusion, cultures provide the forum in which members adapt, strengthen, survive, and evolve (Gontier, Bendegem, & Aerts, 2006). The survival of the Jewish culture could be explained through this lens, as the Goldsteins often talk about the Israelis as a culture of survivors.

Culture as independent innovation: Jose Hernandez is a computer engineer who designs computer games. While he may be considered a member of the Hispanic culture, his professional culture is an example of culture as innovation. Through specialized communication unique to his profession, Jose and his cultural peers invent virtual worlds and new cultures that then recruit other cultural members (Haviland, Prins, & Walrath, 2008).

As Table 10.4 and the exemplars illustrate, numerous perspectives have been advanced to suggest why and how cultures and their membership develop and change. Some theories (Haviland, Prins, & Walrath, 2008) explain humans as cultural members on the basis of an adaptive global process, while others explain culture as purposive and influenced by variables such as proximity to other groups (Schmidt-Norawara & Nieto-Phillips, 2005).

Of particular importance here is the geographic lens, which is not only focused on individual cultures but on the interaction between and among cultural groups. Emerging from studies of global space and resource distribution, geographers have set the foundation for thinking about how diverse groups who come into contact with one another affect and change the nature and members of each group individually, and then both collectively. Recalling the discussion of multiculturalism, groups may interact and change voluntarily or not. The colonialists and postcolonialists have discussed cultural interaction in great detail and posed numerous paradoxes that emerge with increasing globalization of culture and cultures. For example, think of how art and music from one country have influenced populations in other countries. They have competed as well as globally morphed (Gannon, 2008).

THINKING POINT

 Can you think of music, art, media, and other cultural artifacts that have global influence and thus create global change?

The second level of cultural explanations is concerned with how and why group members and groups themselves acquire and perpetuate culture. Acquiring the elements that are necessary for cultural membership has been explained as both voluntary and involuntary. While some theorists explain culture as instinctive, others suggest that it is learned by living within a group whose members, artifacts, and context purposively and tacitly transmit cultural descriptors. And, with the increasing emphasis of neuroscience, acculturation has been attributed to interior-environment neurofunctioning (Chaio, 2009). The degree to which one is aware of one's cultural descriptors, and by extension, the degree of choice that individuals have over cultural membership, is not agreed upon.

Religion

This chapter distinguishes religion from similar concepts, such as faith and spirituality, by membership in a formal, institutional group known publicly by members and non-members for its common theological beliefs, practices, and customs. What we mean here is that different from spiritual beliefs and faith, which we located under the descriptive category of diversity depth, membership in a religious category is recognized by an individual's espousal of a formal world religion and acceptance as a member of a religious sect by those who are already members. Thus, we have located religion under diversity patina. We are aware that this distinction has been implicated in diminishing the value of religion (Cline, n.d.) while elevating spirituality, and further, according to Cline (n.d.), spirituality as divine belief is not a construct that is global—being more present the United States than in other geographies. Yet, the definition of *religion* as formal institution, for us, categorically adheres to the axioms of categorical theories, while the idiosyncratic personal beliefs that are encased in the term *spirituality* do not.

THINKING POINT

Distinguish your spirituality from your religion.

To further clarify the institution of religion, we parse explanations for religious category into two subgroups (divine and not divine) to indicate that spirituality and religion can and often do coexist, overlap, and become one another. Divine explanations are not discussed here in that they are personal and inconsistent with the axioms of categorical theories. Rather, spirituality is encountered in other chapters.

Similar to ethnicity, explanatory factors of religious affiliation that are not divine include individual choice, socialization, and birthright. Choice and socialization were discussed earlier in this chapter. For religious group membership, suffice it to say that, in large part, individuals can choose to move in and out of groups by purposively adopting the descriptive criteria for membership or exclusion. However, exclusion may not always be voluntary, bringing us to the birthright explanation.

Birthright refers to the extent to which descent determines religious group membership. Typically, children follow the religious practices of their parents, at least until adolescence. However, different religious groups ascribe membership on diverse birthright criteria and some groups exclude volunteers on that basis.

> *Bob was born into the Catholic religion. And, although he was baptized and went to church with his family every Sunday, he was never comfortable with his Catholic identity. Because he believed in God and wanted to belong to a formal religion, he decided to explore other faiths. Over a period of several years, Bob became familiar with the teachings and customs of Judaism, and decided to go to synagogue. It was at that point that he learned that without a Jewish mother, he was not considered to be Jewish. Pursuing formal conversion, Bob was required not only to study, but to also select a Jewish name as part of the ritual conversion.*

Furthermore, some of the roles that one takes in a religious group, such as rabbi or Catholic priest, may require different explanatory criteria than others.

> *Women cannot become Catholic priests.*

THINKING POINT

Consider the diverse explanations for inclusion and exclusion in formal religions and religious roles.

We return to religion as institutional in the section on legitimacy.

Class

While the term *class* is familiar and commonly used, similar to other categories that describe and explain humans as group "innies and outies," class has multiple definitions depending on context, discipline, and focus. Some theorists even suggest that it is an outdated construct because so many proxies for class have been used. For example, social stratification, family status, occupational value, and wealth have all been stand-ins for class (Lareau & Conley, 2008). Despite the vagueness and pluralism of the category, we include class in this chapter because of its frequent appearance in cultural competence literature, its relevance to social work diversity dialogues, and the conformance of its varied definitions to the axioms of categorical theories. Because of the large girth of literatures on class, an initial critical discussion is provided here, with further referral to primary sources and other collections that concern themselves with class.

We thus dive into word soup once again to explore the varied definitions of *class*.
Table 10.5 presents the first 25 definitions of the term from Dictionary.com (2010).

Table 10.5   Definitions of *Class*

1. A number of persons or things regarded as forming a group by reason of common attributes, characteristics, qualities, or traits; kind; sort: a class of objects used in daily living.

2. A group of students meeting regularly to study a subject under the guidance of a teacher: The class had arrived on time for the lecture.

3. The period during which a group of students meets for instruction.

4. A meeting of a group of students for instruction.

5. A classroom.

6. A number of pupils in a school, or of students in a college, pursuing the same studies, ranked together, or graduated in the same year: She graduated from Ohio State, class of '72.

7. A social stratum sharing basic economic, political, or cultural characteristics, and having the same social position: Artisans form a distinct class in some societies.

8. The system of dividing society; caste.

9. Social rank, esp. high rank.

10. The members of a given group in society, regarded as a single entity.

11. Any division of persons or things according to rank or grade: Hotels were listed by class, with the most luxurious ones listed first.

12. Excellence; exceptional merit: She's a good performer, but she lacks class.

13. Hinduism. Any of the four social divisions, the Brahman, Kshatriya, Vaisya, and Shudra, of Hindu society; varna. Compare caste (def. 2).

14. Informal. Elegance, grace, or dignity, as in dress and behavior: He may be a slob, but his brother has real class.

15. Any of several grades of accommodations available on ships, airplanes, and the like: We bought tickets for first class.

16. Informal. The best or among the best of its kind: This new plane is the class of the wide-bodied airliners.

17. Biology. The usual major subdivision of a phylum or division in the classification of organisms, usually consisting of several orders.

18. British University. Any of three groups into which candidates for honors degrees are divided according to merit on the basis of final examinations.

19. Drafted or conscripted soldiers, or persons available for draft or conscription, all of whom were born in the same year.

20. Grammar. Form class.

21. Ecclesiastical. Classis.

22. (In early Methodism) one of several small companies, each composed of about 12 members under a leader, into which each society or congregation was divided.

23. Statistics. A group of measurements that fall within a specified interval.

24. Mathematics. A set; a collection.

25. The classes, the higher ranks of society, as distinguished from the masses.

Source: Dictionary.com, 2010

Stratification, grouping, and valuation are common to all 25 definitions, even when referring to class as academic course or grade, with the underlying explanation for membership in each stratum as diverse. In the United States, class is particularly complicated because the United States is often described as a class-less society. But, is it really? According to Lareau & Conley (2008), as we proceed through the 21st century, class is becoming more rigid. What about group differences related to economic description, lifestyle description, birthright, and prestige? And, what about the choices that one makes in appearance and behavior to display a certain "class"? All of these elements are important in distinguishing groups from one another, all imply value, and all are central or related to class-based descriptions and explanations of humans.

THINKING POINT

Before you begin to read this section, think of class description. To what extent do you believe that class is observable?

To briefly consult historical word soup, although distinctions and ranking of worth on the basis of social, economic, intellectual, and descent variables have been documented throughout written history, the term *class* did not take on its current meaning in the English language until the late 18th century. And, it was not commonly and frequently used to depict social stratification until the 19th century. Numerous seminal thinkers over the last two centuries have taken on the challenge of describing and explaining class (Harper, 2001–2010). Weber and Marx were two of the most influential contributors to this body of scholarship. Both described class as an economic phenomenon. For Marx, the focus was on one's work role and for Weber, one's class membership was both a function of economic status and other less central non-economic factors (Levine, 2006).

More recently, Lakoff and Johnson (as cited in Penelope, 1994, p. 23) directed their description of class to values reflected in language. They posited the view of orientational metaphors as descriptive of class. Orientational metaphors organize "a whole system of concepts with respect to each other" (p. 14). For these scholars, *orientational metaphors* are defined as descriptors that use spatial direction and location as comparisons, such as *up* or *upper class* and *down* such as *downtrodden,* and *high class* and *low class* to position people in comparison to one another. The concept of vertical direction in these metaphors is apparent, within the vertical positioning inherent in the words describing class, offering an important hint about what class is and is not. Synthesized with definitions from other theorists (Foster, 2003; Lareau & Conley, 2008), class can thus be described as a hierarchical organizing framework in which group members are located in comparison to one another. Even when using the word as a quality, as in the example "she has class," high value and what high value is not are implicit. The explanatory criteria for group belonging differ, however, as discussed later in this chapter.

THINKING POINT

What values are suggested by orientational metaphors?

Because class as a human category explains comparative membership as intergroup ranking, more than one class must exist to create the hierarchy. On the diminutive numeric side of the continuum, class is described in two groups, the haves and the have-nots, the "high-brow and the low-brow" (Foster, 2003), or the upper and lower class. Members of the haves, or the upper class, experience power, prestige, and advantage, while members of the have-nots, or lower class, experience subordination and lack of access to power and resources. Most theorists would not omit the middle class in the United States and in an increasing number of non-Western countries around the world such as India (Fernandes, 2006). So, models that stratify populations into classes typically have three or more divisions. Still, other theorists suggest many more than three classes, such as Fussell (1983), who, in his classic work, proposed the following nine classes, distinguishable by the appearance, behaviors, and possessions of the members:

1. Top out-of-sight: the super-rich, heirs to huge fortunes

2. Upper class: rich celebrities and people who can afford full-time domestic staff

3. Upper-middle class: self-made well-educated professionals

4. Middle class: office workers

5. High prole: skilled blue-collar workers

6. Mid prole: workers in factories and the service industry

7. Low prole: manual laborers

8. Destitute: the homeless

9. Bottom out-of-sight: those incarcerated in prisons and institutions

Recent work has looked at class descriptions in abstract virtual settings. According to boyd (n. d.), social networking sites signify classes by member choice. MySpace, for example, has been frequented by "lower" classes more than Facebook, although this virtual stratification is a moving target that appears and disappears from one's computer or mobile phone screen with nothing left but an electronic footprint of one's class designator at a slice in time.

Before leaving description of class, consider one more important descriptive element, the nature and flexibility of classes themselves. Similar to boyd (n.d.), but in physically palpable settings, Bertaux and Thompson (2006), in their ethnographic examinations of social mobility, found that class is not only flexible but unstable. Class membership follows suite. Bertaux and Thompson paint a moving lexical picture that details travels through and to distant geographies, work opportunity, education, and social imagination as change agent stars surrounded by the ogres of prejudice and resource inequity that limit mobility. In countries such as India, which had and to some extent still have well-developed and institutionalized social ranking systems, class entrance and permanent membership are conferred by one's ancestry. Yet, even within its formal stratification history, with India still as an example, is developing a middle class, maintaining formalized caste census categories ostensibly as data to identify and redress historical political and social discrimination. In the United States and other Westernized countries, class boundaries are often seen as permeable providing that one takes on the characteristics that denote group membership.

> *Consider Debbie, a middle-aged, urban black woman who grew up in government subsidized housing with her two brothers and her mother. Looking at her today, we see a tall, thin attorney, dressed in an expensive navy-blue wool suit. Her hair, which she wears tied back, has been straightened and her nails are carefully manicured. She carries a fine leather brief case with a matching shoulder bag. From her description, we would not know her socioeconomic background, and on the basis of her observable descriptive elements, would most likely locate her in the middle class. Reflecting back on her life, Debbie shares that she made a conscious decision at the age of 23 to change her appearance. She cut her dreadlocks and transformed her observable appearance in to what she considered to be middle class "professionalism" because she was concerned about being discriminated against on the basis of negative descriptive stereotypes that may have been attributed to how she dressed as a student.*

Explanatory Theories of Class

Explanatory theories of class are diverse in the factors that they illuminate. Moreover, what influences and creates class membership for different individuals are not agreed upon. Table 10.6 presents the variables that are most frequently used to explain class membership. They are diverse, play solitaire or a team sport, and address varied descriptive elements.

Table 10.6 Explanatory Schemes for Class

- Economic status, wealth
- Bodies and backgrounds patina
  - Family background
  - Religious affiliation
  - Educational background
  - Occupation or work status (no collar, blue collar, pink collar, white collar, independently wealthy, land owner, etc.)
- Branding
- Virtual and physical neighborhood

Class as Economic Status and Wealth

Marx and those who followed his tradition explained class membership as a function of one's relationship to modes of production. That is to say, the extent to which individuals owned what they produced determined their membership in a class. Of particular importance to Marx were the class divisions comprised of the bourgeoisie (capitalists) and the proletariat (laborers). The bourgeoisie dominated the proletariat in that they controlled what was produced, how, and by whom, while the proletariat labored for wages under the exploitive control of the capitalists (McClelland, 2000). As relayed in Chapter 8, Marx's thinking forms the foundation for conflict theory in which humans are seen in conflict with one another for personal gain. Given that the bourgeois are the class who control resources and production, Marx and those who built on his theory explained class as a struggle between the haves and the have-nots.

> Bill, a 60-year-old man, worked in a steel fabrication plant until 2 years ago. Over his 40 years of employment in the same job, Bill was a union member, and had always perceived the management as the enemy. Because of this struggle, Bill did not feel that his frequent exaggerated claims of injury and request for workers' compensation were wrong. Rather, he felt that he was owed whatever he could get from the "man." When the management decided to offer Bill early retirement, he took it and began a small carpentry business of his own. Bill has not missed a day of work, but has had a string of employees whom he considers to be irresponsible because they are not reliable.

From a Marxist class perspective, Bill's change in behavior could be explained by his move from the proletarian to the bourgeois class.

Marx is not the only theorist who explains class through an economic lens. For example, Weber (1958a, 1958b) explained social class as an individual's location in the economy (owner, employee). The census term *socio-economic status* has become widely used to denote social stratification on the basis of income or occupation.

Looking at Bill's socioeconomic status, we would most likely locate him in the working or lower middle class on the basis of his income and skilled labor occupations.

Zweig (2004) suggests that income and wealth are not in themselves explanatory of class membership. Rather, the political and economic power that those who possess wealth can purchase provides the explanatory basis for social stratification.

Bodies and Backgrounds Patina

This large slice of class explanations serves up an interactive patina foundation for explaining class and membership in each stratum. Numerous bodies and backgrounds characteristics have been linked to class individually, in pairs, and in multiples beyond duos. Each constellation produces a diverse refraction of class, as discussed subsequently. The patina triumvirate—race, class, and gender—comprise much of the diversity dialogue, and while we acknowledge that these categories are often brought to bear on analysis of oppression and discrimination, we dice them apart for clarity and refer to our discussions on race and gender for analysis of these two constructs. We now peer more deeply into class membership explained by landscapes that we have not yet toured.

Family Background

As noted earlier, inheritance was one of the major explanations of social class and legitimate membership in the early 1900s. Throughout the globe, it is still considered an explanation of class today, to a greater or lesser extent, in that those from privileged classes are likely to be disproportionately more advantaged than their counterparts from devalued stratifications (Beller, 2006; Fernandes, 2006; Fussell, 1983). Of particular centrality in differentiating wealth and family background as explanatory of class are the classic works of Fussell (1983) and Bordieu (1984). In agreement to some extent with one another, both scholars illuminate the role of "taste" in establishing and projecting class. Bordieu suggests that class-specific aesthetic sensibilities are transmitted, for the most part, through family to children who then internalize and display these symbols of class to their social spaces. Similarly, Fussell indicates that the look of "things" in households and such are class distinguishers more than wealth, income, or other proxies for membership in a social stratum. Thus, taste in accoutrements and sense of aesthetics are transmitted through family and create a collage of class indicators lending themselves to statements such as "he has class" or "she is uppercrust" and phrases such as "high-brow and low-brow" referring to design (Foster, 2003).

THINKING POINT

Several principles, some conflicting, are inherent in the inherited explanation of class. Can you think of some?

Consider Ralph for analysis. Ralph came from a poor family. His mother worked as a domestic and his father worked as a coal miner. Neither parent had completed high school. Ralph went to the local public school with children from families with similar incomes and educational backgrounds. Along with his friends, Ralph learned to roller skate on the street and preferred skating over reading or studying. He also preferred to dress like his dad in coveralls with a black leatherette wallet on a chain. So, when he dropped out of school at the age of 16, no one was surprised or dismayed.

Through the lens of the inherited perspective, the social status of Ralph's family of origin may explain his class. Moreover, his dress and chosen street sport were indicative of both Bordieu's and Fussell's claims about the role of aesthetics and "stuff" as explanatory of social class.

But, evidently, family background is a contentious and unclear explanation, and thus is not a popular perspective in contemporary class theory (Lareau & Conley, 2008). Is family background associated with or causal of class membership?

Looking at Ralph, we might surmise that his parent's educational backgrounds, tastes, or occupational status were operative in Ralph's occupational choices and other descriptive behaviors that are inferred as class designators and transmitters.

Of particular note is the extreme position of eugenics that can result in identifying inheritance as causal of class because of the potential, from a proximal-environment perspective, to explain class as a genetic function. Quigley's (1991) perspective illustrates as follows:

The eugenicists argued that the United States was in immediate danger of committing racial suicide as a result of the rapid reproduction of the unfit coupled with the precipitous decline in the birthrate of the better classes, and proposed a program of positive and negative eugenics as a solution. (para. 1)

THINKING POINT

Identify historical events that reflect the eugenic perspective.

Religion, Education, and Occupation

Explanations of class on the basis of religious affiliation, education, and occupation are anchored not in stratification of income, but on attitudinal sets about the worth of each of these diversity patina categories. Warner (Warner, Meeker, & Eells, 1949) was perhaps one of the most seminal theorists to illuminate the explanatory role of attitudes in social stratification. He was best known for positing three general class stratifications—lower, middle and upper—explained by social attitudes about the nature of one's occupation.

> *Looking at Bill and Ralph, even if they made enough money to be economically classified as upper middle class, according to this approach, their skilled labor occupations would locate them in a lower stratification.*

As Christiano, Swato, and Kivisto (2001) note, there are many perspectives on the intersection between class and religion. Even Weber (1958a, 1958b) suggested that religious beliefs could distinguish members of social classes. The contemporary research, however, is conflicting about which religious affiliations are associated with diverse social strata (Christiano, Swato, & Kivisto, 2001). It is therefore not surprising that current theory and inquiry have moved beyond single diversity patina variables as explanatory of class to a more complex elaboration of determinants of class within delimited contexts. Elitism linked to occupation and the education necessary to assume such positions has become prominent in the class discussion (Beattie, Arum, & Ford, 2010). What remains important to consider is that through the lenses of occupation, education, and religion, social attitudes—not diversity patina variables themselves—are the basis for social stratification.

> *If we look at Bill through this lens, we might be surprised that he loves opera and has season tickets to the ballet.*

Branding and Neighborhood

Before we venture from class, we raise an important explanatory framework for the 21st century. Although not directly indicted by Fussell and Bordieu, both made allusions to the role of appearance as a brand of one's class so to speak. Foster (2003) provides direct reference to design and branding as indicative of social status, implying that cultivating and displaying a particular "high-brow" taste can open doors for upward mobility. O'Guinn, Allen, and Semenik (2010) are not tangential or shy in explicating the role of purshases in an advanced capitalist, consumption-oriented global world. They state,

> Markers of social class would include what one wears, where one lives and how one speaks. . . . Stratification-related consumption preferences reflect value differences and different ways of seeing the world and the role of things in it; they reflect taste. (p. 179)

This quote provides a segue to the final patina explanation of class—location. Neighborhood of residence and networking, as discussed, are symbols of stratification and value. Gated communities abound adjacent to less affluent locations, imbuing value on those who have the key to enter the gated perimeter. Similarly, as boyd (n.d.) reflects, one's virtual haunts are abstract inferences of class. These points are developed further in the chapters on new and emerging descriptions and explanations, as they are of primary importance in understanding human experience in the 21st century.

Evidence

Not surprisingly, the evidentiary basis for theories of categorical distinction are as diverse as the theories themselves. We suggest, however, that many of the essential elements that lead categorical carvings are vague and falsely assume that terms such as *race, class,* and *religion* have universal meanings that are understood as monistic to all. So, in looking at the evidence to support the existence of these categories, notwithstanding their validity in explaining human difference, savoring word soup can once again clear your lexical palette.

Summary

This chapter examined descriptions and explanations of human phenomena through the lens of categories—race, ethnicity, culture, religion, and class. The advantages and disadvantages of each diversity patina perspective were analyzed, concluding where the chapter started, with word soup as the basis for a clarifying examination of patina and its meanings.

References

American Anthropological Association. (1998). *American Anthropological Association statement on "Race."* Retrieved from http://www.aaanet.org/stmts/racepp.htm

American Anthropological Association. (2007). *Race: Are we so different?* Retrieved from http://www.understandingrace.org/home.html

Appiah, A. (2005). *The ethnics of Identity.* Princeton, NJ: Princeton University Press.

Beattie, I. R., Arum, R., & Ford, K. (2010). *The structure of schooling: Readings in the sociology of education.* Thousand Oaks, CA: Pine Forge.

Beaudry, M. (2006). *Findings: The material culture of needlework and sewing.* New Haven, CT: Yale University Press.

Bell, D. (1992). *Faces at the bottom of the well: The permanence of racism.* New York: Basic Books.

Beller, E. (2006). *Families and mobility: A re-conceptualization of the social class of children.* Berkeley: University of California Press.

Bennett, A., & Kahn-Harris, K. (Eds.). (2004). *After subculture: Critical studies in contemporary youth culture.* New York: Palgrave Macmillan.

Bertaux, D., & Thompson, P. R. (2006). *Pathways to social class: A qualitative approach to social mobility.* New Brunswick, NJ: Transaction Publishing.

Biology On-Line. (2005). *Race.* Retrieved from http://www.biology-online.org/dictionary/race

Boas, F. (1995). *Race, language, and culture.* Chicago: University of Chicago Press. (Original work published 1940)

Bordieu, P. (1984). *Distinction: A social critique of the judgment of taste.* Cambridge, MA: Harvard University Press.

boyd, d. (n.d.). *danah boyd.* Retrieved from http://www.danah.org/

Chaio, J. Y. (2009). *Cultural neuroscience: Cultural influences on brain function.* Amsterdam: Elsevier.

Christiano, K. J., Swato, W. H., & Kivisto, P. (2001). *Sociology of religion: Contemporary developments.* Walnut Creek, CA: AltaMira Press.

Cline, A. (n.d.). *Religion v. spirituality.* Retrieved from About.com: http://atheism.about.com/od/religionnonreligion/a/spirituality_2.htm

DePoy, E., & Gilson, S. (2004). *Rethinking disability.* Belmont, CA: Brooks/Cole.

DePoy, E., & Gilson, S. (2011). *Studying disability.* Thousand Oaks, CA: Sage.

Dictionary.com. (2010). *Condition.* Retrieved from http://dictionary.reference.com/browse/condition

Diller, J. (2011). *Cultural diversity: A primer for human services* (4th ed.). Belmont, CA: Brooks/Cole.

Fernandes, L. (2006). *India's new middle class: Democratic politics in an era of economic reform.* Minneapolis: University of Minnesota Press.

Fernando, S. (2006). *Mental health, race and culture* (3rd ed.). New York: Palgrave MacMillan.

Foster, H. (2003). *Design and crime* (and other diatribes). New York: Verso.

Fox, R. G., & King, B. J. (Eds.). (2002). *Anthropology beyond culture.* Oxford, UK: Berg.

Funk, I. K. (1906). *A standard dictionary of the English language.* New York: Funk & Wagnalls.

Fussell, P. (1983). *Class: A guide through the American status system.* New York: Summit Books.

Gannon, M. J. (2008). *Paradoxes of culture and globalization.* Thousand Oaks, CA: Sage.

Geertz, C. (1973). *The interpretation of cultures: Selected essays.* New York: Basic Books.

Gevirtz, G., Sarna, J. D., & Krasner, J. B. (2008). *Jewish history: The big picture.* Springfield, NJ: Behrman House.

Goldstein, E. L. (2006). *The price of whiteness: Jews, race and America.* Princeton, NJ: Princeton University Press.

Gontier, N., Bendegem, J. P., & Aerts, D. (2006). *Evolutionary epistemology, language and culture: A non-adaptationist, systems theoretical approach.* New York: Springer.

Gould, S. J. (1996). *The mismeasure of man* (Rev. ed.). New York: W. W. Norton.

Gracia, J. J. (2007). *Race or ethnicity: In Black and Latino identity.* Ithaca, NY: Cornell University Press.

Graves, J. L. (2001). *The emperor's new clothes: Biological theories of race at the millennium.* New Brunswick, NJ: Rutgers University Press.

Harper, D. (2001–2010). *Ethnic.* Retrieved from On-Line Etymology Dictionary: http://www.etymonline.com/index.php?search=ethnic&searchmode=none

Haviland, W. A., Prins, H. E., & Walrath, D. (2008). *Cultural anthropology: The human challenge.* Belmont, CA: Thomson.

Healy, J. S. (2009). *Diversity in society.* Thousand Oaks, CA: Pine Forge Press.

HGVbaseG2P. (2010, September). *About HGVbaseG2P.* Retrieved from Human Genome Variation Database: http://www.hgvbaseg2p.org/index

Hunt, L. (n.d.). *UWM establishes a new doctoral program in Africology.* Retrieved from University of Wisconsin, Milwaukee: http://www4.uwm.edu/news/stories/details.cfm?customel_datapageid_11602=359454

Hylland-Eriksen, T. (2002). *Ethnicity and nationalism.* Sterling, VA: Pluto.

Kelley, R. D. (1997). *Yo' mama's disfunktional! Fighting the culture wars in urban America.* Boston: Beacon Press.

Kertzer, D., & Arel, D. (2002). *Census and identity: The politics of race, ethnicity and language in national census.* Cambridge, UK: Cambridge University Press.

Lareau, A., & Conley, D. (2008). *Social class: How does it work?* New York: Russell Sage.

Levine, R. F. (2006). *Social class and stratification: Classic statements and theoretical debates.* Lanham, MD: Roman Littlefield.

Maryland Institute College of Art, Center for Race and Culture. (2011). Retrieved from: http://www.mica.edu/Research_at_MICA/Research_Centers/Center_for_Race_and_Culture.html

McClelland, D. C. (2000). *Karl Marx: Selected writings.* Oxford, UK: Oxford University Press.

McMillan, M. (2010). *Dangerous games: The uses and abuses of history.* New York: Random House.

Mead, G. H. (1965). *Mind, self and society from the standpoint of a social behaviorist*. (C. W. Morris, Ed.). Chicago: University of Chicago Press. (Original work published 1934)

Moran, L. (2007, Nov. 1). *Is race biological?* Retrieved from Sandwalk: http://sandwalk.blogspot.com/2007/11/is-race-biological-concept.html

Morris, D. (1993). *The culture of pain.* Berkeley: University of California Press.

Office of Minority Health. (2005, October 19). *Office of Minority Health.* Retrieved from U.S. Department of Health and Human Services: http://minorityhealth.hhs.gov/templates/browse.aspx?lvl=2&lvlID=11

O'Guinn, T., Allen, C., & Semenik, R. J. (2010). *Advertising and integrated brand promotion.* Belmont, CA: Cengage.

Omi, M., & Winant, H. (1994). *Racial formation in the United States.* New York: Routledge.

On-Line Encyclopedia. (2010). *Brazilian racial formations.* Retrieved from: http://encyclopedia .jrank.org/articles/pages/6027/Brazilian-Racial-Formations.html

Ore, T. (2005). *The social construction of differences and inequality: Race, class, gender, and sexuality.* New York: McGraw-Hill.

Painter, N. I. (2010). *The history of white people.* New York: W. W. Norton.

Penelope, J. (Ed.). (1994). *Out of the class closet.* Freedom, CA: Crossing Press.

Population Reference Bureau. (2010). *The 2010 census questionnaire: Seven questions for everyone.* Retrieved from Population Reference Bureau: http://www.prb.org/Articles/2009/questionnaire.aspx

Quigley, M. (1991). *Our refractory human material: Eugenics and social control.* From PublicEye.org: http:jjwww.publiceye.orgjracismjeugenicsjmq%20eugenics%20paper.html

Rich, T. (2001–2006). *What is Judaism.* Retrieved from Judaism 101: http://www.jewfaq.org/judaism.htm

Royal, C. D., & Dunston, G. M. (2004). Commentary: Changing the paradigm from "race" to human genome variation. *Nature Genetics, 36,* 55–57.

Schmidt-Norawara, C., & Nieto-Phillips, J. (2005). *Interpreting Spanish colonialism: Empires, nations, and legends.* Albuquerque: University of New Mexico Press.

Schneider, D. J. (2004). *The psychology of stereotyping.* New York: Guilford Press.

Spikard, R. (2005). *Race and nation: Ethnic systems in the modern world.* New York: Routledge.

Spradley, J. (1979). *The ethnographic interview.* Belmont, CA: Wadsworth.

Steinberg, S. (2001). *The ethnic myth: Race, ethnicity, and class in America* (3rd ed.). Boston: Beacon Press.

Sweet, F. (2005). *The legal history of the color line.* Palm Coast, FL: Backintyme.

Thomas, R. M. (2001). *Recent theories of human development.* Thousand Oaks, CA: Sage.

Tylor, E. B. (1877). *Primitive culture: Researches into the development of mythology, philosophy, religion, art, and custom* (2nd American ed.). New York: H. Holt.

Unander, D. (2000). *Shattering the myth of race: Genetic realities and biblical truths.* Valley Forge, PA: Judson Press.

U.S. Bureau of the Census. (1997). *Race.* Retrieved from http://www.fedstats.gov/qf/meta/long_68183.htm

Warner, W. L., Meeker, M., & Eells, K. (1949). *Social class in America: A manual of procedure for the measurement of social status.* Chicago: Science Research Associates.

Warnke, G. (2008). *After identity: Rethinking race, sex, and gender.* New York: Cambridge University Press.

Weber, M. (1958a). Class, status and party. In H. Gerth & C. W. Mills (Eds.), *From Max Weber: Essays in sociology* (pp. 180–195). New York: Oxford University Press.

Weber, M. (1958b). *The Protestant ethic and the spirit of capitalism.* New York: Scribner.

Young, M. (2004). *Malinowski: Odyssey of an anthropologist, 1884–1920.* New Haven, CT: Yale University Press.

Zack, N. (2007). Ethnicity, race and the imporance of gender. In J. Gracia (Ed.), *Race or ethnicity* (pp. 101–123). Ithaca, NY: Cornell University Press.

Zelinsky, W. (2001). *The enigma of ethnicity: Another American dilemma.* Iowa City: Iowa University Press.

Zweig, M. (2004). *What's class got to do with it? American society in the twenty-first century.* Ithaca, NY: ILR Press.

11

Categorical Theories Related to Sex, Gender, and Sexual Orientation

T his chapter delves into the contentious world of differentiating people by diverse "gendered" descriptions and explanations. One of the most challenging and fundamental questions concerns the origins, foundations, and commonalities of gender and related studies. With so many of the contemporary layers of theory casting aside, obfuscating or eliminating the sexual-embodied environment from the spotlight, what is the underlying bedrock for categorization and response? Looking back to ancient Greece and then forward to current theory to find an answer, Diotima (1995–2010), a website on gender studies in classical Greece, concerns itself with diverse views of sexuality, women, queer studies, and gender relations. Of course, looking at current interpretive literature to answer historical questions opens the revisionist sinkhole, but limited options exist to access work on that area from the vantage point of 2010 (Brizee and Tompkins, 2010a, 2010b). The following quote from contemporaries, Brizee & Tompkins (2010a, 2010b), provides a viable response to the quandry:

> Gender studies and queer theory explore issues of sexuality, power, and marginalized populations (woman as other) in literature and culture. Much of the work in gender studies and queer theory, while influenced by feminist criticism, emerges from post-structural interest in fragmented, de-centered knowledge building (Nietzsche, Derrida, Foucault), language (the breakdown of sign-signifier), and psychoanalysis (Lacan).
>
> A primary concern in gender studies and queer theory is the manner in which gender and sexuality is discussed. (p. 59)

In this narrative, sexuality is central but in concert with the axioms for all categorical theory—gendered conceptual understandings of humans seek to identify group commonalities within the framework of current diversity approaches. That is to say, the interpretation of sex, body, and role occurs through differential lenses, each concerned with group membership and its consequences.

Not only do the theories in this genre argue with one another, but the definitions of sex, gender, and sexual orientation join the boxing match as well. So, similar to race, ethnicity, and culture, we group these three categories together because the boundaries that distinguish them from one another are not at all clear.

We also decided to include feminist and queer theories in this chapter due to their concern with gendered phenomena. As discussed next in more detail, but noted here for ongoing reflection, it is curious that the male-female binary remains inherent in progressive feminist and queer thinking despite its eschewal in contemporary theory and the assertion of multiple genders in the histories, as well as current contexts in diverse geographies across the globe. Phrases such as *in-betweens* have been coined to expand the bifurcation of humans beyond two gendered categories, but references to masculine and feminine still occur as the bookends against which the others lean and are compared as partial or nonexample.

Now, let's make our way through the conceptual morass of sex, gender, and sexual orientation. The categorical theories in this chapter will examine how determination of membership on the basis of proximal environment features, gendered behavior, or the meanings of gendered categories have been described, explained, and challenged.

Sex and Gender

Because sex and gender do not have clear and consensual definitions, once again, we turn to the derivation brand of word soup, etymology, to understand word usage over time. According to Harper (2001–2010), since the early 1400s, the term *sex* has referred to male and female genders originating from *seco,* two sections or division in half. Gender emerges from the Latin word *genus,* which means kind, sort, or gender. Harper distinguishes the usage of sex from gender in the 20th century by suggesting that the precarious erotic or embodied tenor of the word *sex* opened the door for gender to describe male or female sexuality. He also notes the presence of other genders with the pop term *gender bender* that was first used to describe David Bowie.

In proximal environmental literatures, sex is both assigned and recognized according to typical anatomical sexual reproduction characteristics and further described as biologically determined differences in areas such as weight, strength, physical capability, and so forth. A claim of clear binary distinction, made by Justice David Brewer of the Supreme Court (as cited in Abraham & Perry, 2003) illustrates as follows:

> The two sexes differ in structure of body, in the functions to be performed by each, in the amount of physical strength, in the capacity for long-continued labor, particularly when done standing . . . the self reliance which enables one to assert full rights, and in the capacity to maintain the struggle for subsistence. (p. 466)

But, what has happened to sex through the gaze of uncertain proximal environmental characteristics?

Consider this exemplar from Warnke (2008):

> David Reimer's doctors thought that without a penis he could not be a boy. His parents and psychologists worried that he was not really a girl. (p. 1)

Or, consider the Indonesian Bugis (Davies, 2007), a sect of Muslims who list five genders as typical in this Indonesian culture. Furthermore, Spade and Valentine (2011) dicsuss historical exemplars of nonbinary genders in the United States; they chronicle the documentation of the Native American *berdache* grouping, first through the skeptical eyes of European colonialists and then forward in time. Spade and Valentine suggest that because this gendered group did not fit neatly into male or female camps, the derogatory term *berdache*, meaning male prostitute and illustrative of the importance of sexuality in defining identity, was conferred by European visitors on men who were known as *effeminate.* More recently, analysis of the berdache foregrounds their spiritual functions and alternative gender over sexuality.

From just these three exemplars, the vagueness as well as extension of contemporary views of sex, gender, and as discussed subsequently, orientation, beyond male and female make sense. Adding to the complexity of membership in gendered categories is the assertion that experience does not have to be consistent with one's biological sex characteristics (Siragusa, 2001; Stryker & Whittle, 2006). That is, progressive definitions of gender identity suggest that rather than being a biological phenomenon, gender is a function of comfort as a member of a particular gendered group (Siragusa, 2001; Stryker & Whittle, 2006). Some constructed approaches, particularly those that fall within feminist viewpoints, suggest that gender has little to do with biology or individual experience, but rather is a set of social relationships which position women as socially and politically inferior to men (Mikkola, 2008). However, others such as Sterling (2005) urge theorists to repossess biology and sex as indistinct from gender. We do not take a position other than to suggest that the distinction between gender and sex remains both unclear and in flux.

To make sense of the large literature on sex and gender as descriptive and explanatory categories, presented next are representative examples of sex or gender are as biologically determined, followed by a discussion of other conceptualizations that suggest multiple explanations for the construct.

Sex and Gender as Description: How Many Genders?

Although, in Westernized geographies, gender is typically depicted as male and female, the latter part of the 20th century saw the number of biologically described embodied configurations expand to five: (1) heterosexual male, (2) heterosexual female, (3) homosexual male, (4) homosexual female, and (5) transsexual (UN Habitat Conference, 1996) and then six: (1) the feminine, (2) masculine, (3) androgynous, (4) transsexual, (5) cross-dresser, and (6) culturally specific genders (McDermott, 2006). Table 11.1 provides word soup descriptive definitions of each of these terms, quoted from Siragusa (2001).

Table 11.1 Descriptive Definitions of Gender Terminology

Gender	Definition
Feminine	Term used to describe the socially constructed and culturally specific gender behaviors assigned to biological females.
Masculine	Term used to describe the socially constructed and culturally specific gender behaviors assigned to biological males.
Androgynous	From the Greek roots for male (*andro*) and female (*gyne*). An androgynous person may identify and appear as both male and female, or as neither male nor female, or as in between male and female. This person also may or may not exhibit the behaviors of the two traditional genders, thus making it difficult for others to place them into a specific gender category.
Transsexual	Individuals who do not identify with their birth-assigned sex, and sometimes alter their bodies to reconcile their gender identity and their physical body and/or biological sex.
Cross-dresser	One who dresses, either in public or private, in clothing that society assigns to the opposite sex. Cross-dressing is not an indication of one's sexual orientation or gender identity. The formerly used term, *transvestite*, is now considered offensive by some.
Culturally specific genders	The principle that gender is not so much natural as it is cultural and historical.

Source: Siragusa, 2001

In addition to specific observables, remember that *gender-bending* was introduced as a term to describe individuals who identify as male or female, but do not embody and exhibit all of the typical observable and reportable descriptors of a gender.

Consider the terms girly men *and* genderqueer.

THINKING POINT

Can you think of other examples of gender-bending?

Terms such as *effeminate* and *girly men* expose the underlying essentialism about what behaviors males "should" exhibit. An effeminate or girly man is therefore considered "too female," bending gendered behaviors beyond the limits of maleness.

Complementary to biological, observable characterizations of gender is description of gender as role. This descriptive scheme discusses gender according to observable, behavioral, and social expectations associated with naturally occurring physical sex characteristics (Rathus, Nevid, & Fichner-Rathus, 2010). Thus, through observation, one should be able to recognize typical feminine and masculine roles such as mother, housekeeper, and caregiver, or father, laborer, and football player respectively.

A third important descriptive approach is gender as reportable or experiential. As we discussed, gender is described as an individual's sense of and identity as a particular gender regardless of biology (Rathus, Nevid, & Fichner-Rathus, 2010; Siragusa, 2001).

Some feminist theories, while diverse in their scope and foci, have been important in this arena of gender description. All have a common descriptive perspective of gender as an experience of fundamental inequality between groups distinguished by biological bodies of women and men, with women being at greater disadvantage than men (Daly, 1984). Moreover, descriptive gendered variations range among diverse feminist schools. For example, the Amazon feminists (Tandon, 2008) use Greek mythological symbolism to depict the physiques of women, while material feminists focus description on gender differences in economic, political, and other resources (Tandon, 2008).

Warnke (2008) however, reminds us that similar to changing proximal-distal identity of other categories, gender follows the same rules. The importance of one's gender as definitive of personhood ebbs and flows as does one's concern with behaving in gendered role–specific ways.

Explanatory Theories of Sex and Gender

Similar to description, the vast number of explanatory theories of sex and gender attest to the importance of this genre of categorical theorizing. Physiology, genetics, and psychology are the primary proximal explanatory theories of gender along with the appearance, behavior, and experience of individuals who are contained within each gendered category. Within the proximal corpus, physiology and genetics establish male or female sex in the embryonic phase, initially as a function of genetic inheritance of the correct complement of X and Y chromosomes. With the "proper" genetic structure in place, physiological processes determine the direction of the development of ana-tomical and physiological sexual reproductive and related gender characteristics of category membership (DePoy & Gilson, 2011). If two genders, male and female, are accepted as the typical descriptive scheme, physiological and genetic explanations serve to normalize only male and female categories of gender, and other more recently asserted gender category members are remanded to the atypical, emerging from incor-rect or abnormal genetic and physiological processes. For example, some have high-lighted hormones as the locus of "normal" gender development and assignment in that they are seen as responsible for "masculinizing or feminizing" the brain (Rathus, Nevid & Fichner-Rathus, 2010).

Although numerous psychological theories have been advanced to explain various descriptive aspects of gendered category members, this discussion occurs later in the chapter when gender conceptualizations move outside of the corpus. The criteria for proximal environmental notions of gender and sex, however, places cognitive psycho-logical gender explanations within the confines of the brain (Galotti, 2009; Sanes, Reh, & Harris, 2006). In the 1960s, Kohlberg advanced the concept of gender typing, com-prised of three elements: (1) identity, (2) stability, and (3) constancy. *Identity* is defined as one's sense of self as a gendered individual with a particular identification as male or female. *Stability* refers to the degree to which the acquired identity remains intact over time, and *constancy* refers to the nature of one's gender identity being consistent regardless of influences from both distal and proximal sources. These three concepts unfold longitudinally and sequentially, with identity acquired first, followed by stabil-ity, and then constancy. A review of Kohlberg's (1986) and Piaget's (1970) stages of cognitive development reveals that both Kohlberg and Piaget located gender within this framework as one of many cognitive schemes to unfold in a predetermined man-ner and explain human behavior.

As proximal focused theories of cognition themselves have grown and matured, gendered explanations of thinking have been proposed and investigated. Galotti (2009) reminds us that "to present one approach if in fact there are several is to ignore human diversity" (p. 407). Explanatory differences related to male and female gender in language, moral structures, and cognitive organization have been assigned as well as commonalities in male/female group-specific cognitive performances and maturation over time. From a proximal environmental viewpoint, explanatory gendered factors include hormone effects on brain function, diverse neurological structures, and so forth. More recently, cognitive differences attributed to genders other than males and females have been studied. Implicit in the research, even if coated with a cultural enamel, is that there are fundamental embodied differences in neurology attributable to gender, regardless of where the reasons are located on the proximal-distal contin-uum. Nonetheless, with cognition considered to be a brain function, the establishment of cognitive differences "proximalizes" the basis of gendered membership at least in part through this inquiring lens. A significant part of the March 2010 issue of the *American Journal of Public Health* (American Public Health Association, 2010) is devoted to gender and sexuality. A perusal of just the table of contents reveals that diverse areas of health and health behavior are parsed by gender category. Among the topics are institutional discrimination, gendered responses to public health surveys, mood and anxiety disorders, substance dependence, mental health, HIV risk reduction behavior, and adolescent smoking.

Researchers have been on the hunt for differences in genetic explanations for gendered appearance, behavior, and experience other than male and female. Some have suggested that no gene for homosexuality has been identified, while others have found the politically unpopular role and contribution of genes to this contentious area of human description (Långström, Rahman, Carlström, & Lichtenstein, 2008).

Distal Environmental Theories of Sex and Gender

Numerous fields—including psychology, sociology, and anthropology—have advanced distal environmental explanatory theories of gender category and membership. Not surprisingly, the literature on gender in these fields is enormous and could not be treated with justice in this small space. The References provide many resources for further reading and examination beyond this discussion.

Distal explanatory factors that shape categories and their residents have examined the range of influences from concrete behavior modifiers in one's immediate environment, as proposed by the behavioral psychologists, to the grand milieu of culture. Within this range of environmental milieus, sociologists have been an important influence on explaining gendered social role behavior as shaped by social customs and institutions; these include but are not limited to families, workplace, governments, and institutional practices such as marriage.

Historically, in the United States, families have served two important functions, economic sufficiency, and socialization. The classical heterosexual, two-parent family was in large part held responsible for the initial social unit in which traditional instrumental male and nurturing female gender roles were learned and maintained (Mischel, Shoda, & Smith, 2002). Staggenborne (2010), however, argues that looking to families in isolation of macroconcerns is shortsighted. She draws attention to the intersection of economy, organization, and family to explain gendered behavior and socialization. In other words, she asserts that organizations, particularly corporations, still create time and location structures for work that mediate against coparticipation of fathers in child care.

Mary and Troy just had a baby boy. Troy is an executive in a large computer company, and is expected to travel and keep long hours, often entertaining business partners in the evenings. Because of his role in a corporate environment, Troy cannot be home much of the week.

THINKING POINT

How has your family influenced your gendered identity, behavior, and role acquisition?

Gender roles and gendered behavior are thus complex, with multiple factors that influence not only one's sense of one's own gender, but additionally, the nature of gendered interactions. As social change continues to alter these descriptions and explanations for gender, the explanatory power of a unitary theory or approach dwindles and requires a more in depth view through a wider diameter, at the host of explanatory interactions that delimit and explain the construct of gendered category and membership.

Interactional Theories of Sex and Gender

This genre of explanatory theories, in our view, once again, provides the richest scaffold for analysis of gendered identity, development, and behavior. Interactional theories look at a range of gender issues through a lens which illuminates the intersection of the proximal embodiment of gender with distal environmental factors as explanatory of human phenomena.

Beginning with environments most proximal to individuals, two psychological explanations for gendered development and identity are particularly significant: intrapsychic and gender schema theory.

Although many see intrapsychic theories as interior to the corpus because they focus on the conscious and unconscious processes of gender development, identity, and gendered behavior, as previously noted, we see these theories as integrative in that they explain gender as the intersection of biology and family dynamics. Looking through Freud's stages of development, while ostensibly biologically predeterministic, the major marker of adulthood is differentiation from same-sex parent and intimacy with a partner of the opposite sex. So, despite the inward focus of the process to the typical unfolding of healthy gender description and category assignment, according to Freud, membership in the "normal" category of male or female cannot occur without the correct parenting, with particular attention on the mother figure (Freud, 1966). The controlling, distant mother has been indicted as the cause of many diversions from what Freud and other psychoanalysts considered to be typical and desirable (Jonte-Pace, 2001).

Gender schema theory, originally proposed by Bem (as cited in Chrisler & McCreary, 2010), asserted that male and female self-perception, and thus category membership, is a function of cognitive processes. Within input from the environment on the proper and typical cluster of gender descriptions, cognitive patterns guide one's gender identity, role function, and gendered assignments. Common in this approach to intrapsychic and biological explanations is the definition of the category of gender and its membership as stable and unchangeable. Theories, however, challenge those two notions.

In an approach that integrates learning theory with biology, Bandura and Bussey (2004) explain gendered development and behavior as social input into gendered biological characteristics. Further, within this explanatory framework, individuals themselves can change the behavioral and appearance elements of their gender, and thus, in large part are responsible for broadening the system of gender expectations and ultimately movement in and out of gender categories.

Gender role theory suggests numerous explanations for the development and enactment of one's theatrical gender part. Eagly, Wood, and Diekman (2000) looked back in history to the time when embodied characteristics of men and women were mainly responsible for explaining the division of labor along with child bearing and rearing expectations. Given these assignments on the basis of proximal corporeal features, role expectations were institutionalized and males and females were socialized into them (Wood & Eagly, 2002). Of course, as the social context and economy change, gender roles and who occupies them follow suite.

> *Marjorie and Ken just gave birth to a baby boy, Todd. They dressed Todd in baseball-themed clothing throughout his infancy and toddlerhood, assuring his appearance would be clearly explained as male. When Todd turned 5, he asked his parents for ballet lessons as a present. Both Marjorie and Ken were concerned that Todd might be perceived as "effeminate" and planned to enroll him in football camp. Alana' son, William, a classmate of Todd's, also asked Alana for ballet lessons. He had seen* Swan Lake *on television and wanted to leap in the air like the men who danced. In their conversations, Alana, Marjorie, and Ken agreed that ballet could be acceptable as male gendered, considering the strength and power of male dancers. They thus decided that both boys could go to ballet lessons once each week.*

The example illustrates stereotype and role perception. Although Todd's parents were initially skeptical, the three parents allowed their sons to take ballet because it did not threaten the gendered assignment of "male" to their sons.

Sexual Orientation

Closely tied to and overlapping with sex and gender as explanatory of human experience is the construct of sexual orientation. Sexual orientation refers to an individual's preference for and arousal by an actual or potential sexual partner or practice (McDermott, 2006). On first blush, of the three terms, this phrase seems to be most clear. However, as expected, the usages of *sex, gender,* and *sexual orientation* to refer to the same construct of gendered description and explanation has become more prevalent.

Sexual Orientation as Description

Looking at the way theories have described sexual orientation, it is first important to note that because sexual orientation is not as observable as some other proximal categories, it is most frequently inferred from reportable behavior and observation of appearance. And, although there are many descriptive views of sexual orientation, two primary descriptive elements, partner preference and practice preference, are most prevalent. Looking through the lenses of both partner and practice preferences, theorists have claimed a range of sexual orientations numbering from 2 to 400 (McDermott, 2006).

Consistent with the recent postulation of five genders, five descriptive categories of sexual orientation explicated as partner preference have been suggested: (1) preference for a partner of the opposite sex (heterosexual), (2) preference for a partner of the same sex (homosexual), (3) preference for a partner of either sex (bisexual), (4) preference for oneself as a partner (masturbation), and (5) preference for an animal partner (bestiality) (McDermott, 2006).

From a practice perspective, sexual orientation has been described by one's preferred sexual behaviors. These include intercourse, masturbation, oral sex, equipment or paraphernalia-assisted sex, anal sex, and so forth. It is understandable, then, how McDermott came up with 400 sexual orientations on the basis of sexual practice (McDermott, 2006).

While preference for partner and practice have previously been central to sexual orientation description, more recently, this category has joined others that are used euphemistically to depict alterity and foreground discrimination. As an example, Badgett and Frank's (2007) work focuses on international employment discrimination against the lesbian, gay, bisexual, and transgender (LGBT) population, despite their book titled more broadly as *Sexual Orientation Discrimination*. Moreover, identity has been added to the decriptive definitive elements of sexual orientation, moving preference and sexual action into the locations inhabited by sex and gender (McAnulty & Burnette, 2006).

Similar to other categorical theories, descriptions in and of themselves are not the locus of value judgment and response. Rather, explanatory theories create the platform for debate and judgment.

Explanatory Theories of Sexual Orientation

Similar to gender explanations, genetic, physiological, and psychological lenses have been posited to explain biological-proximal factors that cause, shape, and or influence sexual preference and practice. Traditional theories, which accept heterosexuality as the only typical "normative" description of sexual orientation, have looked not only for explanations but for cures of what are considered as atypical and undesirable sexual preferences and practices (McAnulty & Burnette, 2006).

Through the biological perspective, membership in a sexual orientation category is about corpuses, their anatomy, and their hormones. Over the years, explanations categorizing heterosexuality as the only acceptable sexual orientation have given way to more inclusive schemes (Roughgarden, 2004). Yet, researchers still seek answers to the questions regarding biological explanations for human membership in "alternative" sexual orientation categories. For example, despite the omnipotence of homosexuality in both the animal kingdom and throughout the history of humans, numerous studies have focused on the identification of a "gay gene," or other biological and structural causes for what is considered to be atypical sexuality. In 1994, Friedman and Downey (as cited in Rathus, Nevid, & Fichner-Rathus, 2010) sought to determine the extent to which testosterone levels were explanatory of sexual orientation category membership. They and their successors found no association in adulthood, but did raise some questions about the effects of exposure to prenatal hormones on the development of sexual orientation and self-assignment to an alternative category.

Researchers have also looked to brain anatomy, evolution, and other aspects of biological-proximal conditions to ascertain the development of sexual orientation, but have no conclusive causal results (Poliani, 2010; Rathus, Nevid, & Fichner-Rathus, 2010).

Despite documented prevalence and acceptance of bisexual and homosexual activity in the animal world (Poliani, 2010), biological explanations for those same categories of human sexual orientation locate members in the atypical and less desirable part of town. And, although such devaluation has been challenged through comparative biological lenses (Roughgarden, 2004), traditional views still dominate the literature on proximal explanations for sexual preference category.

THINKING POINT

Should sexual orientation be analyzed as a biological phenomenon? If so, why? If not, why not?

Similar to gender, numerous external explanations have been advanced to explain sexual orientation. However, dissimilar to sex and gender if considered distinct from sexual orientation, critical moral and religious issues are invoked when assigning members of alternative orientations to the categories of normal and not normal, and particularly over the past several years in light of contentious debates about the legitimacy of same sex marriages. This legitimacy issue and response is discussed in greater detail in Chapter 18.

Relevant to this chapter's focus on explanations, we highlight moral perspectives for diverse positions on sexual orientation. Several explanatory rubrics of sexual orientation related to procreation are important in informing the moral questions raised by locating sexual orientation within the diversity dialogue: evolutionary obligation, along with the economic, social, and political value of sex for the purpose of procreation.

Because evolution theoretically obligates people to transmit and perpetuate their genetic structures, it categorizes the set of moral imperatives for heterosexual orientation as most desirable (McAnulty & Burnette, 2006). Curiously in opposition to the evolutionary rationale, yet with the same desired outcome, many religious groups espouse heterosexual membership for procreation. As suggested by Rathus, Nevid, and Fichner-Rathus (2010), these perspectives have tentacles reaching not only to religious beliefs over centuries of human history, but to economic, political, and social contexts as well. Considering there are so many explanations for sexual orientation category membership, many of which are even competing, but all of which are rooted in context, those who espouse a constructed framework have significant support for their views.

Postmodern thinking has promoted a paradoxical acceptance of diverse sexual orientations. This means that because postmodernists view the world as a cornucopia of meaning attributable to any single symbol, the existence of a category (conceptualized as a symbol) and thus diverse categories in and of themselves is questionable. Because of the postmodern espousal of interpretive diversity, existence, meaning and value of group members cannot be generally affirmed. How, then, can any explanation

of a category be acceptable if existence is not concrete? To a large extent, gay and lesbian studies, and more expansively queer theory, suggest that all sexual orientation
categories are social constructs, and thus do not have monistic explanatory meanings.
So, while postmodernists have removed stigma and devaluation, they have not replaced
it with substance. Through marrying traditional disciplines as strange partners, post-
postmodern thinking promises to replace substance and meanings without being
monistic or prescriptive.

> *If Joshua sees himself as a member of the heterosexual orientation, what must his life exhibit
> in order to be a category member? From a postmodern approach, no single theory either
> characterizes heterosexuality or membership criteria. So, does he qualify as heterosexual if
> he is now married to a woman but has a history of attraction to men? Within postmodern-
> ism, the meaning is variable, so he might or might not, depending on the diverse interpreta-
> tions of his life. However, once we move into post-postmodernism, integrative theories might
> suggest brain biology, fashion, and history as definitive of sexual orientation and locate him
> in the heterosexual category because of his biological maleness, branding as male through his
> fashion choices for male clothes, and emergence from a homosexual to heterosexual life over
> his own history.*

This very current trend is discussed in Chapter 12.

Interactional Theories of Sexual Orientation

Turning to theories that explain sexual orientation category membership through
the interactive range of proximal-distal elements, we suggest that despite their pen-
chant for the proximal, many psychological explanations hold the interaction between
corpus and distal context as explanatory of sexual orientation category membership.
Beginning with psychoanalytic theory, as noted above in the section on gender, Freud
and his successors look to the intersection of biology of the child and the nature of
parenting as the explanation for the development of sexuality. In order to reach the
hallmark of adult maturation, heterosexual intimacy, one had to navigate psychosexual
stages efficaciously. Sexual orientations other than heterosexuality were explained as
the inappropriate emergence in adulthood of infantile sexuality and youth sexual characteristics as a function of poor parenting (Freud, 1938).

Interestingly, despite the reluctance to accept proximal explanations for sexual
orientation category membership (McAnulty & Burnette, 2006), there is limited evidence to support the learning theory basis for sexual orientation categories (Golombok
& Tasker, 1996). However, implicit in the notion that sexuality is learned and reinforced, social learning theory does illuminate the potential for all sexualities to be
"learned" through reinforcement (Bohan, 1996). Studies supporting this perspective,
however, are difficult to come by.

Similar to the preceding point about the complexity of gender explanations,
McAnulty and Burnette (2006) suggest that numerous factors coalesce to explain sexual orientation, including but not limited to biological predisposition, social and cultural context, and political, intellectual religion, economic trends and evolution.

THINKING POINT

Which approaches explaining sexual orientation seem most viable to you? Why?

Feminisms

Discussion now moves to feminist and queer theories. Because each theoretical genre is a field of study in its own right, this chapter aims to whet the appetite for further reading in these broad and diverse approaches to describing and explaining humans.

We use the term *feminisms* to highlight the complexity, pluralism, and multiple conceptually based meanings of feminist symbolism in different eras as well as to diverse individuals and groups. Although met with some criticism for its linearity (Aikau, Erickson, & Pierce, 2010), feminism has been discussed in three chronological waves. The first wave spans time from the 18th to the mid 20th century, during which inequality on the basis of gender category was formally identified by scholars such as Mary Wollstonecraft, Susan B. Anthony, and Victoria Hull. Women's suffrage and Amendment 19 (the right for women to vote) were major action outcomes of these progressive, vocal feminist thinkers. The 1960s, when civil rights became a major liberal intellectual and political agenda, ripened the equality pastures for second wave feminism or what is referred to as the women's movement. During this tumultuous era, women joined the ranks of other *marginalia groups* claiming their rights for equality of opportunity in the workplace, scholarly world, and even in the bed. The third wave of feminism was seeded in postmodernism of the 1990s and beyond, in which diverse roles and goals were posited, and bring us to feminisms today as a set of ideas and actions that are pluralistic, including views of interpretation of symbolic and substantive relations among genders (Brizee & Tompkins, 2010a, 2010b).

Commonalities among feminist waves and theories within each type are excerpted in Table 11.2.

The paradoxical bedrock of feminisms was suggested previously, noting the importance to read critically with the inherent binary in mind. As revealed in the common principles in Table 11.2, despite rhetorical acceptance of diverse genders in 21st century theory, inherent in feminism, because of its concern with patriarchy, is the binary of male and female. Queer theory, to some extent, attempts to redress this limitation as discussed later in this chapter.

Although concentrated on male-female inequity, feminist theories range far and wide (Thomas, 2001) in their consideration of what variables are important determinants of power differentials and of what needs to be done in order to eliminate gender-based disparities. Thomas distilled feminist approaches into five schools of thought.

Table 11.2   Commonalities of Feminisms

1. Women are oppressed by patriarchy economically, politically, socially, and psychologically; patriarchal ideology is the primary means by which they are kept so.

2. In every domain where patriarchy reigns, woman is other: She is marginalized, defined only by her difference from male norms and values.

3. All of Western (Anglo-European) civilization is deeply rooted in patriarchal ideology, for example, in the biblical portrayal of Eve as the origin of sin and death in the world.

4. While biology determines our sex (male or female), culture determines our gender (masculine or feminine).

5. All feminist activity, including feminist theory and literary criticism, has as its ultimate goal to change the world by prompting gender equality.

6. Gender issues play a part in every aspect of human production and experience, including the production and experience of literature, whether we are consciously aware of these issues or not.

Source: Brizee & Tompkins, 2010a, 2010b

Table 11.3 summarizes Thomas's central explanatory ideas of each with regard to gender description. The legitimate responses that each approach demands are discussed in Chapter 17.

As Table 11.3 illustrates, feminist theories explain the descriptive experiences of gender categories and female disadvantage in many ways, but to a greater or lesser extent, all posit agents that both cause and can be the salvation for gender discrimination.

Table 11.3   Feminist Theories

Theory Type	Major Points
Liberal feminism	Gender role imbalance disadvantages women through formal and informal institutions and social customs respectively, and provides the forum for male domination of women in all social spheres.
	Claims of natural gender differences in gender development and comparative capacities are unsubstantiated.
	Males and females who accept traditional theories of gender difference are responsible for perpetuating inequity.
Radical feminism	Gender role imbalance disadvantages women through formal and informal institutions and social customs respectively, and provides the forum for male domination of women in all social spheres.
	Claims of natural gender differences in gender development and comparative capacities are unsubstantiated.

Theory Type	Major Points
	Males and females who accept traditional theories of gender difference are responsible for perpetuating inequity.
	Traditional notions of gender differences should be eliminated along with traditional sexual orientations.
Multicultural feminism	Women from diverse cultural backgrounds experience oppression and discrimination in differential ways.
	Oppression in all cultures is caused by men who curtail female rights, women who accept this plight, and women who fail to recognize cultural embeddedness and differential treatment of women in diverse cultures.
Marxist feminism	Oppression and disadvantage experienced by women is caused by patriarchal, capitalist, political, social, and economic systems
Ecofeminism	Humans are part of the natural order and must be responsible for its health.
	Because women are more connected to nature than men, women have a greater understanding of the natural world.
	Western cultures are characterized by male domination of nature, including domination of women.

This important area of scholarship is worth pursuing, as it has been critical in informing social work practice approaches to diversity and women's issues. The application of feminisms to social work theory, research, and praxis are discussed later alongside categorical legitimacy.

THINKING POINT

Compare the feminist approaches in Table 11.3, and apply them to explain the gendered element of someone you know.

Queer Theory

Queer theory builds on the feminisms binary of male and female by including all genders, at least lexically. We could not resist the fascinating etymological journey in queer word soup. According to Harper (2001–2010), in the 1500s, *queer* was used as an adjective to describe qualities such as "strange, peculiar, eccentric," and "oblique, off-center." "Spoil and ruin" joined these lexical meanings in the 19th century and at the beginning of the 20th century, queer turned sexual to refer to homosexuality. The etymology implies a history of marginalia that continues to be implicit in the term *queer* as it is used in its theoretical context today.

Although queer theory emerged from gay and lesbian studies, theorists ostensibly have expanded their gaze more broadly to challenge the notion of human genders and experience as categorical. As such, queer theorists assert that theory is amorphous in its scope, criticizing normativity in institutions, communities, social context, and so forth as exemplified by Sullivan's description of his own work (2003). "Rather than focusing narrowly on sexuality and sexual practices, this book aims to consider critiques of normalizing ways of knowing and being that may not be evident as sex-specific" (p. vi).

Thus, embedded in Sullivan's (2003) critical project, despite claims to look more broadly, is sexuality as his central hub. Queer theory is thus included in this chapter, because in its effort to dismantle human categorization, we would suggest that queer theory itself bifurcates thinking into normative and not-normative categories with gender as its primary concern.

Queer theorists suggest that symbolic meanings attributed to category members by themselves and others outside of the group, rather than proximal material bodies, should be the explanation for identity. Eschewing both the traditional, typical descriptive category of sexual orientation (heterosexual) and essentialist traditional biological, evolutionary, and religious explanations for the acceptability of heterosexuality as hegemonous, queer theorists illuminate sexual orientation as a complex set of social, political, economic, and religious symbols, practices, and mores; these locate typical or most frequent heterosexual orientation as normal and assert anything else as both atypical and deviant. Similar to feminisms, queer theory is a set of theories, each which foregrounds different factors as explanatory of human description.

Evidence

Given the diversity of the theoretical frameworks discussed in this chapter, the evidence and methods to generate data to support theory have a large expanse. Traditional theories lean towards nomothetic methods and statistical techniques to reveal within category commonalities and between category differences. Contemporary constructionist and postmodern theories, such as many queer theories, rely in large part on narrative, literature, and symbol.

Summary

Covering much gendered ground, this chapter first discussed the difficulty in distinguishing sex, gender, and sexual orientation. Within a vague context, the etymology of each term was viewed, and then diverse approaches to each of the overlapping descriptions and explanations highlighting gender were examined. The chapter concluded with brief discussions of two major gendered theoretical frameworks, feminisms and queer theories. This large body of knowledge is revisited in the legitimacy chapter (Chapter 18) that addresses responses to gendered views of humans.

References

Abraham, H. J., & Perry, B. A. (2003). *Freedom and the court: Civil rights and liberties in the United States.* (8th ed.). Lawrence: University Press of Kansas.

Aikau, H., Erickson, K., & Pierce, J. (2010). *Making trouble for the binary in second and third wave feminism: Reconceptualizing "waves" and "generations".* Retrieved from All Academic: http://www.allacademic.com/meta/p21023_index.html

American Public Health Association (APHA). (2010, March). *American Journal of Public Health 100*(3).

Badgett, M. V., & Frank, J. (2007). *Sexual orientation discrimination: An international perspective.* New York: Routledge.

Bandura, A., & Bussey, K. (2004). On broadening the cognitive, motivational, and sociostructural scope of theorizing about gender development and functioning: Comment on Martin, Ruble, and Szkrybalo (2002). *Psychological Bulletin, 130,* 690–701.

Bohan, J. S. (1996). *Psychology and sexual orientation: Coming to terms.* New York: Routledge.

Brizee, A., & Tompkins, J. C. (2010a, April 4). *Feminist criticism (1960s–present).* Retrieved from Purdue Online Writing lab: http://owl.english.purdue.edu/owl/resource/722/11/

Brizee, A., & Tompkins, J. C. (2010b, April 21). *Gender studies and queer theory (1970s–present).* Retrieved from Purdue Online Writing Lab: http://owl.english.purdue.edu/owl/resource/722/12/

Chrisler, J. C., & McCreary, D. R. (2010). *Handbook of gender research in psychology.* New York: Springer.

Daly, M. (1984). *Pure lust: Elemental feminist philosophy.* Boston: Beacon Press.

Davies, S. G. (2007). *Challenging gender norms: Five genders among Bugis in Indonesia.* Belmont, CA: Thomson.

DePoy, E., & Gilson, S. (2011). *Studying disability.* Thousand Oaks, CA: Sage.

Diotima. (1995–2010). *Diotima.* Retrieved from Materials for the Study of Women and Gender in the Ancient World: http://www.stoa.org/diotima/about.shtml

Eagly, A. H., Wood, W., & Diekman, A. B. (2000). Social role theory of sex differences and similarities: A current appraisal. In T. Eckes & H. M. Trautner (Eds.), *The developmental social psychology of gender* (pp. 123–174). Mahwah, NJ: Lawrence Erlbaum.

Freud, S. (1938). *The basic writings of Sigmund Freud.* (A. A. Brill, Trans.) New York: Modern Library.

Freud, S. (1966). *The complete introductory lectures on psychoanalysis.* (J. Strachey, Trans.) New York: W. W. Norton.

Galotti, K. M. (2009). *Cognitive psychology: In and out of the laboratory.* Belmont, CA: Cengage.

Golombok, S., & Tasker, F. (1996). Do parents infuence the sexual orientation of their children: Findings from a logitudinal study of lesbian parents. *Developmental Psychology, 31*(6), 3–11.

Harper, D. (2001–2010). *Ethnic.* Retrieved from On-Line Etymology Dictionary: http://www.etymonline.com/index.php?search=ethnic&searchmode=none

Jonte-Pace, D. (2001). *Speaking the unspeakable: Religion, misogyny, and the uncanny mother in Freud's cultural texts.* Berkeley: University of California Press.

Kohlberg, L. (1986). A current statement on some theoretical issues. In S. Mogdil & C. Mogdil (Eds.), *Lawrence Kohlberg: Consensus and controversy* (pp. 485–546). Philadelphia: Falmer Press.

Långström, N., Rahman, Q., Carlström, E., & Lichtenstein, P. (2008). The genetics of homosexuality. Genetic and environmental effects on same-sex sexual behavior: A population study of twins in Sweden. *Archives of Sexual Behavior, 36* (1), 75–80.

McAnulty, R. D., & Burnette, M. M. (2006). *Sex and sexuality* (Vol. 1). Westport, CN: Greenwood.

McDermott, l. (2006). *Human sexuality.* Saddle River, NJ: Pearson.

Mikkola, M. (2008, May 12). *Feminist perspectives on sex and gender.* Retrieved from Stanford Encyclopedia of Philosophy: http://plato.stanford.edu/entries/feminism-gender/

Mischel, W., Shoda, Y., & Smith, R. E. (2002). *Introduction to personality: Toward an integration* (7th ed.). Hoboken, NJ: Wiley.

Piaget, J. (1970). *Genetic epistemology.* New York: Columbia University Press.

Poliani, A. (2010). *Animal homosexuality: A biosocial perspective.* New York: Cambridge University Press.

Rathus, S. A., Nevid, J. S., & Fichner-Rathus, L. (2010). *Human sexuality in the age of diversity* (8th ed.). Englewood, NJ: Prentice Hall.

Roughgarden, J. (2004). *Evolution's rainbow: Diversity, gender, and sexuality in nature and people.* Berkeley: University of California Press.

Sanes, D. H., Reh, T. A., & Harris, W. A. (2006). *Development of the nervous system.* St. Louis, MO: Elsevier.

Siragusa, N. (2001). *The language of gender: A discussion and vocabulary list for educators on gender identity.* Retrieved from Gay Lesbian Straight Education Network: http://www2 .hawaii. edu/N Igbti/The%20 Language%200f%20Gender.pdf

Spade, J. Z., & Valentine, C. G. (2011). *The kaleidoscope of gender: Prisms, patterns, and possibilities* (3rd ed.). Thousand Oaks, CA: Pine Forge Press.

Staggenborne, S. (2010). *Social movements.* New York: Oxford University Press.

Sterling, A. F. (2005). The bare bones of sex: Part 1—sex and gender. *Signs: Journal of Women in Culture and Society, 30*(2), 1492–1527.

Stryker, S., & Whittle, S. (2006). *The transgender studies reader.* New York: Routledge.

Sullivan, N. (2003). *A critical introduction to queer theory.* New York: NYU Press.

Tandon, N. (2008). *Feminism: a paradigm shift.* New Delhi, India: Atlantic Publishers.

Thomas, R. M. (2001). *Recent theories of human development.* Thousand Oaks, CA: Sage.

Warnke, G. (2008). *After identity: Rethinking race, sex, and gender.* New York: Cambridge University Press.

Wood, W., & Eagly, A. H. (2002). A cross-cultural analysis of the behavior of women and men: Implications for the origins of sex differences. *Psychological Bulletin, 128,* 699–727.

12

Categorical Theories Related to Disability

his chapter looks at the hotly contested and debated category of disability. Disability is discussed last in the chapters on categorical theories because it was the most recent newcomer to the categorical axioms.

As stated earlier in this book, our previous work categorized disability as proximal. However, a conceptual bind emerged from the complexity of descriptive and explanatory theories ranging from their location of disability as within the miniscule structures of genes, to larger corporeal elements up through disability as situated in social and cultural meanings. By now, this range is likely a familiar refrain as we try to orchestrate an understanding of theories that incise parts of humanity into slivers (DePoy & Gilson, 2011). This chapter thus examines disability category membership from diverse scenic viewpoints but again refers to the large literature for more concentrated study of this elaborate lexical construct.

Disability as Description

Throughout this chapter, we use the terms *typical* and *atypical*, rather than *normal* and *abnormal*, to refer to appearance, behavior, and experience. Consistent with the axioms and reflecting Quetelet's bell-shaped curve in the background, normal and abnormal terminology prescribe "what should be" on the basis of what most frequently occurs. And while Quetelet is foundational to some views of disability, he is not on the top ten with other progressive scholars who take the position that disability and corpus have little to do with one another. So, to avoid the conceptual quicksand and to remove the value judgment from the normal-abnormal binary, our word choice is purposive.

This conversation continues with a deeper dive into word soup. The term *disability* has only recently become a signifier for the grand category of atypical bodies. Early Islamic literature does not contain a single term for embodied conditions, but rather tethers what today would be considered as disabled to illness of the body and heart (Rispler-Chiam, 2007). In the Western world, disability's predecessor, *handicap*, was alleged to have emerged from the cap-in-hand proclamation, in which Henry VII in 1504, recognizing the plight of injured soldiers, formally allowed these worthy citizens to beg in the streets as a means to their own subsistence. More broadly, the recognized use of the term *handicap* is an equalizing scoring system in which less competent or accomplished persons are artificially advantaged to increase the likelihood of their success when positioned against a superior opponent. In the early part of the 20th century, the term was apprehended by medicine and ascribed to individuals with bodily differences that ostensibly placed them at a disadvantage. Ultimately the word *handicap*, in this sense, came to mean a specific embodied condition such as a "physical or mental handicap."

Given the current pejorative notion of bodily inferiority, it is no surprise that a euphemistic term to replace handicap was sought to describe bodies that did not conform to the "typical." It is curious that the term *disability* was selected as a respectful replacement for handicap, given that the prefix *dis* emerged from Dis, the name given by ancient civilizations to the ruler of Hades, or the underworld. Dis was portrayed as punishing mortals by extracting their health, wellbeing, and capacity to function in their environments (DePoy & Gilson, 2011).

Moving to fresh ingredients for word soup, Table 12.1 provides current definitions of *disability*.

Table 12.1   Definitions of *Disability*

1. Lack of adequate power, strength, or physical or mental ability; incapacity.

2. A physical or mental handicap, esp. one that prevents a person from living a full, normal life or from holding a gainful job.

3. Anything that disables or puts one at a disadvantage: His mere six-foot height will be a disability in professional basketball.

4. The state or condition of being disabled.

5. Legal incapacity; legal disqualification.

Source: DePoy & Gilson, 2011

In a recent talk, video-recorded by TED, a nonprofit organization dedicated to dissemination of innovation in ideas, technology, and design, Mullins (2010) discussed disability definitions. She lists the following synonyms from her research:

Crippled, helpless, useless, wrecked, stalled, maimed, wounded, mangled, lame, mutilated, run down, worn out, weakened, impotent, castrated, paralyzed, handicapped, senile, decrepit, laid up, done up, done in, counted out . . . (para. 2)

Mullins (2010) adds the following antonyms:

healthy, strong, capable (para. 2)

A foray into disability word soup might send many people quickly through the exit door in escape from this conversation, as the devaluation implicit in these terms is clearly apparent and not likely to be a category to which many would prefer to belong. Yet, as the theory illustrates, many scholars and individuals with atypical bodies have posited descriptions and explanations for disability that depart from this ghetto, while others with typical bodies proclaiming disability membership have taken up residence. We travel back briefly to set the context and then return to contemporary description and explanation to see why.

History of Categorical Theory Related to Disability

Looking backwards in time, before disability was used to describe a group of people with permanent medical-diagnostic classifications that affected their daily activity in atypical ways, words such as *cripple, blind, deaf, handicapped,* and so forth were often articulated. These terms differentiated the atypical from the typical individual on the basis of a physical, sensory, cognitive, or mental difference, most frequently an absence or diminished capacity to perform a function compared with the typical.

An investigation of historical text directly or indirectly focusing on disability reveals the following commonalities:

1. What is atypical differs according to context.

2. In each era, there have been several potential assumed and accepted explanations for a single atypical human characteristic.

3. These explanations form the basis for legitimate categorization and subsequent response to category members.

4. The responses proffered provide an analytic window on the beliefs, values, politics, economics, intellectual trends, and level of technological development of the times, as well as a reflective platform on how current definitions of disability influence how we interpret history (Rose, 2003).

From early civilizations through contemporary times, attention to the atypical as a curiosity or undesirable to be eliminated has been thematic. As stated in the commonalities across chronological eras, however, the nature of the atypical and responses to it vary with context. In a more detailed history, DePoy and Gilson (2011) provide a view of disability for civilizations throughout the world during the Middle Ages. Many explanations for the atypical floated outside of the organic proximal body into the ethereal world of spirit and divinity, with punishment as the most common explanation for difference. It is therefore not surprising that, in general, what would be considered today as disability was met with disdain through exclusion and even premature death in some contexts. Yet, in the Middle Ages, the notion that people with atypical bodies were placed on earth purposely by a divine being for typical counterparts to show charity, and thus moral behavior, was prevalent and still inheres in charitable responses to disability today, as discussed in Chapter 18.

As Enlightenment thinking replaced its predecessor in the Western world, scientific explanations for corporeal function and appearance were sought, shifting reasons for the atypical from religious or divine punishment to proximal embodied pathology. This is not to say that religion or moral explanations for disability membership ever disappeared, as reflected in such frequently articulated statements such as "I was injured because I sinned," or "I must deserve this fate."

Scientism, technology, and professionalism of the 20th century have been instrumental in assigning and restraining disability within the proximal corpus and as object of professional scrutiny, treatment, and cure (DePoy & Gilson, 2011). While the prevailing public view of disability remains medical, the disability studies community has concocted alternative views related to human rights and diversity. Consistent with the axioms of categorical theories, reframing disability within a diversity dialogue in which disability is characterized as victim of discrimination is possible due to the contextualized intellectual landscapes that contemporary conversations and ideas traverse.

Returning to the present, two grand perspectives come into view that battle with one another for hegemony, with a third approach emerging from our own thinking. We colocate description and explanation together under each approach, being careful to differentiate them. The rationale for this organization will be evident, in that description always lies in the atypical.

Medical-Diagnostic Descriptions and Explanatory Theories

Within this grand approach, atypical appearance, behavior, or appearance invoke disability description, which then catches the attention of a medical or health professional. Reference to the International Classification of Function (ICF), the most recent revision of the *International Classification of Functioning and Disability (ICIDH-2)* (World Health Organization, 2010) characterizes the breadth and depth of medical-diagnostic description. This classification system measures functioning in what are claimed as universal activity categories listed in Table 12.2, and distinguishes health, illness, impairment, and disability. As discussed in Chapter 18, there is much debate about this measurement tool. Although its authors locate it globally and assert its universal relevance, as well as its consideration of context, others do not agree and see it as a tool to count disability from a proximal embodied perspective. We tend to agree with the last group, although we do suggest that analysis of this tool is more complex than imprisoning it in a single category. We come back to this discussion later, and for now, return our attention to the embodied activities in Table 12.2 that form the basis for typical or atypical measurement.

Table 12.2   ICF Activity Areas
Learning and applying knowledge
General tasks and demands
Communication
Mobility
Self-care
Domestic life
Interpersonal interactions and relationships
Major life areas
Community, social, and civic life

In the ICF, each of these broad activity areas is then divided into subcategories and tasks, and the descriptive element of disability is determined by the nature of one's capacity to act in a manner typical for the individual's reference group in a hypothesized standard environment—one that would not influence the activity in any way. Capacity is then compared to expected or typical performance and assessed along with contextual correlates to determine the efficacy of an individual's activity (World Health Organization, 2010).

If an atypical suspect emerges, the medical explanatory triumvirate (biology, physiology, psychology) is alerted and activated for diagnosis and response. Medical-diagnostic explanation thus locates disability internal to the body, characterizes it as pathologically generated, and then goes into action to decrease or eliminate it. Why some medical conditions are accepted as legitimate explanations for disability (i.e., mobility impairments in which individuals cannot walk) and others are not (mild nearsightedness), despite being correctable with adaptive equipment, is a fundamental question providing a segue to disability as constructed.

Constructed Descriptions and Explanatory Theories

As indicated by the term *constructed*, disability from this vantage point is described and explained as a phenomenon built on factors and forces in the exterior environment, rather than by an interior medical condition (DePoy & Gilson, 2004).

Descriptively, disability as constructed can take many forms ranging from atypical proximal conditions to no presence of a discernable atypical condition. Thus, while a proximal medical condition may be acknowledged as causative of atypical appearance, function, or experience, from the constructed perspective, it is not necessarily undesirable, in need of remediation, or even relevant to understanding the circumstance of "disabled people." We have put quotation marks around the term "disabled people" since this moniker attaches to an unstable grouping who change according to explanations, and discussed in Chapter 13, to the degree of "stick-to-itiveness" to the group.

Constructed explanations impute a range of political social, economic, and other factors that portray disability as exclusion, discrimination, truncation of rights, and devaluation (Nussbaum, 2007; Scully, 2008; Stein, 2006). Negative social attitudes, limited or nonexistent physical and communication access, and the denial of rights and privileges are examples of just some of the social practices that explain disability in these perspectives (Albrecht, 2006). Thus, within the constructed approaches there are many different emphases, each which has been posited as an explanatory model of disability in itself. For example, looking at the political construction of disability, the barrier creating the disabling condition is disempowerment due to unequal earning opportunity for individuals with undesirable conditions (Davis, 2006).

The cultural approach suggests that all individuals who define themselves as disabled belong to a unique group and share a common cultural disability identity (Siebers, 2008). Membership in the culture is not attributed to a proximal diagnostic condition, because diagnosis is irrelevant in this approach to determining who is disabled. Those individuals who perceive their conditions to be treated unfairly and constructed as undesirable by dominant social institutions are members of the culture of disability in that they share disadvantage and curtailment of civil rights (Siebers, 2008; Stein, 2006).

> *Consider Gary. In his late 20s, he broke his hip in a skiing accident and now walks with a limp. Under medical diagnostic explanations his descriptive walking style (limping with a cane) would be explained by a medical condition that is permanent, and thus he would be classified as disabled. But he skis, bikes with one leg, and is not "unable" to do what he wants to do. Is he disabled? Gary does not consider himself disabled, but others who see him locate him in the disability category because his limp sets him apart from those who walk typically. To illustrate further, a few years ago, he went into car dealership and no one waited on him. When he asked why, the salesperson said that no one thought he was a qualified car purchaser because they assumed, on the basis of his limp and cane, that Gary did not work. He quickly corrected the misperception and bought his car.*

Because constructed explanations lay blame on the distal environment, not the atypical corpus, as explanatory of disability, there is significant debate between the medical and constructed camps about which is accurate and correct. Theorists such as Miceli (2010) and DePoy and Gilson (2011) suggest that bypassing the body does not do any theoretical work to guide responses to disability, because the atypical proximal corpus is the object and change target. Proponents of the constructed approach eschew proximal embodied models of disability because they devalue, medicalize, and pathologize those who are legitimate members of the disability category (DePoy & Gilson, 2011).

In an effort to respect both explanatory approaches, more terms have surfaced in the word soup tureen. Impairment is now used to name an embodied condition while disability refers to the discrimination and negative treatment afforded to those with impairments (DePoy & Gilson, 2011; Henderson, 2006).

Given the continuing debate and confusion, we proposed a third integrative explanation for disability, disjuncture. We turn to it now.

Disability as Disjuncture

The initial thinking about disjuncture emerged from a conversation in a disability studies class in which we asked students to reflect on the rationale for the current "disability" standards for built and virtual distal environments. The students indicated that they just took these environmental features for granted, and had not thought about why doorways, chair heights, computer access, and so forth could not be reconceptualized differently. This conversation prompted our investigation into distal environmental design history and the rationale for disability standards that comply with the Americans With Disabilities Act (1990). Informed by much reading in human factors theory (Salvendy, 2006) and by research into design and architectural practices and standards, we heeded Davis's (2003) caution about disability as an unstable category and thus one in need of reconceptualization. Davis posited the revision of the category to include every "body" regardless of its current status. Thus, Davis retained the proximal environment as the entry point into the disability club, referring to Christopher Reeve as exemplary of how quickly one can change disability status.

Building on this work and the work of other theorists who explain disability as interactive, we have posited disjuncture as one of many explanations that could form a solid axiological, as well as praxis, foundation for disability category membership and the responses discussed in Section III of the book. Unlike Davis (2003), however, we do not look to the proximal environment for the initial entrance into disability. Moreover, dissimilar to human factors theory (Salvendy, 2006), the proximal material corpus may be, but is not necessarily, the home of disability. Rather, we recognize proximal and distal environment as equal entryways and suggest that a potent explanation of disability is not simply an interaction but rather an ill-fit between the two.

Figure 12.1 depicts a visual of disjuncture explanations.

As represented in Figure 12.1, both moderate or compliance juncture to us is still explanatory of disability due to an area of poor fit that remains between proximal embodied and distal environments. Note here that referring to proximal and distal environments, rather than body and surrounding space, eliminates dualism. For example, an ill-fit could be explained as pathology, a distal environmental barrier, or even dissatisfaction with one's goal attainment. Explaining disability in this manner allows for multiple entry points, locations, and thus responses as discussed

Figure 12.1   Full Juncture-Disjunction Continuum

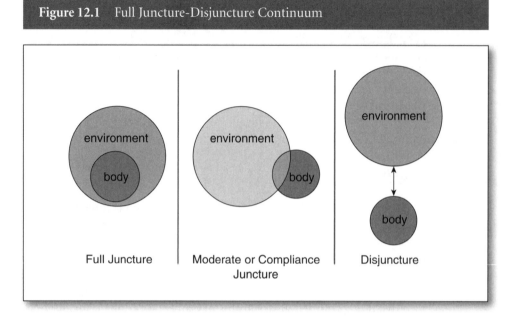

in Section III. Moreover, the medical-constructed binary is transcended without neglecting either explanatory scheme.

> *Consider Gary once again. Gary includes his cane in his "interior" because it is part of his movement through space. And, while his proximal body is atypical, he does not experience ill-fit with distal environmental conditions. While he disdains negative stereotyping and has devoted his career to eliminating its ill-effects on so many people, he considers himself in full juncture. Others however, might locate him as disjunctured, as he must use a cane for ambulation and often has to make efforts to participate that others do not.*

As our application to social work will reveal, viewing disability as disjuncture does not devalue individuals with atypical proximal conditions, nor hold designers of distal products, environments, and services as fully responsible for creating juncture. Moreover, eliminating disjuncture does not provoke the constructed argument about the devaluation of disabled "bodies." Rather, reduction and elimination of disability from this approach refers to eschewing the ill-fit, and not the person who is considered disabled.

Evidence

Once again, the evidentiary basis for categorizing humans within the disability group is diverse. Medical-diagnostic descriptions and explanations tend towards deductive approaches such as epidemiology, or counting the number of individuals who have specific medical conditions, and experimental-type strategies to support theory and predict disability as well as its treatment outcomes (Drum & Krahn, 2009).

Those who espouse constructed models lean more towards narrative and other nonnumeric evidence inductively analyzed, to support claims of discrimination

(Kuppers, 2003, Siebers, 2008; McRuer, 2006). We suggest that mixed methods, along with multiple forms of evidence (e.g., images, architecture, film, virtual sources, performance, and so forth), be used to characterize, posit, and then test ways to eliminate it.

Summary

This chapter scrutinized disability. Word soup from the past and the present provided an initial context, followed by a brief historical journey, and then a look at disability within the medical or constructed debate. An integrative explanation was next proposed, disability as disjuncture, with discussion about why this approach leaves the door open for multiple legitimate responses. The chapter concluded with some comments on evidence for categorizing humans within the disability group.

References

Albrecht, G. (2006). *Encyclopedia of disability.* Thousand Oaks, CA: Sage.

Davis, L. (2003). *Bending over backwards: Disability dismodernism and other difficult positions.* New York: NYU Press.

Davis, L. (2006). *The Disability studies reader.* New York: Routledge.

DePoy, E. & Gilson, S. (2004). *Rethinking disability.* Belmont, CA: Brooks/Cole.

DePoy, E., & Gilson, S. (2011). *Studying disability.* Thousand Oaks, CA: Sage.

Drum, C., & Krahn, G. (2009). *Disability and public health.* Washington DC: American Association on Intellectual and Developmental Disabilities.

Henderson, B. (2006). Impairment. In G. Albrecht (Ed.), *The encyclopedia of disability studies* (pp. 920–922). Thousand Oaks, CA: Sage.

Kuppers, P. (2003). *Disability and contemporary performance.* New York: Routledge.

McRuer, R. (2006). *Crip theory.* New York: NYU Press.

Miceli, M. (2010). The disavowal of the body as a source of inquiry in critical disability studies: The return of impairment? *Critical Disability Discourse, 2,* Retrieved from http://www.library.yorku.ca/ojs/index.php/cdd/article/view/23855/28103

Mullins, A. (2010, Feb). *The opportunity of adversity.* Retrieved from TED: Ideas Worth Spreading: http://www.ted.com/talks/aimee_mullins_the_opportunity_of_adversity.html

Nussbaum, M. C. (2007). *Frontiers of justice: Disability, nationality, species membership.* Cambridge, MA: Belknap Press.

Rispler-Chiam, V. (2007). *Disability in Islamic law.* Dordrecht, Netherlands: Springer.

Rose, M. (2003). *The staff of Oedipus.* Ann Arbor: University of Michigan Press.

Salvendy, G. (2006). *Handbook of human factors and ergonomics.* Hoboken, NJ: Wiley.

Scully, J. L. (2008). *Disability bioethics.* Lanham, MD: Rowman & Littlefield.

Siebers, T. (2008). *Disability theory.* Ann Arbor: University of Michigan Press.

Stein, M. D. (2006). *Distributive justice and disability: Utilitarianism against egalitarianism.* New Haven, CT: Yale University Press.

World Health Organization. (2010). *International classification of functioning, disability and health (ICF).* Retrieved from WHO Classifications: http://www.who.int/classifications/icf/en/

13

Classical and Contemporary Systems Theories

Parts and Wholes

This chapter examines systems theories, a set of frameworks that drive much of social work thinking and action.

Systems Approaches as Description

Cooking up word soup for the term *system*, there is an overwhelming number of disciplines and fields in which systems frameworks are considered as guidelines, illustrated in Table 13.1.

Table 13.1 Definitions of *System*

1. A group or combination of interrelated, interdependent, or interacting elements forming a collective entity; a methodical or coordinated assemblage of parts, facts, concepts, etc: *a system of currency; the Copernican system.*

2. Any scheme of classification or arrangement: *a chronological system.*

3. A network of communications, transportation, or distribution.

4. A method or complex of methods: *he has a perfect system at roulette.*

5. Orderliness; an ordered manner.

6. (*Often capitalized*) *the system:* society seen as an environment exploiting, restricting, and repressing individuals.

7. An organism considered as a functioning entity.

8. Any of various bodily parts or structures that are anatomically or physiologically related: *the digestive system.*

9. One's physiological or psychological constitution: *get it out of your system.*

10. Any assembly of electronic, electrical, or mechanical components with interdependent functions, usually forming a self-contained unit: *a brake system.*

11. A group of celestial bodies that are associated as a result of natural laws, esp. gravitational attraction: *the solar system.*

12. *Chem.* See also phase rule a sample of matter in which there are one or more substances in one or more phases.

13. A point of view or doctrine used to interpret a branch of knowledge.

14. *Mineralogy.* Also called crystal system, one of a group of divisions into which crystals may be placed on the basis of the lengths and inclinations of their axes.

15. *Geology.* A stratigraphical unit for the rock strata formed during a period of geological time. It can be subdivided into series.

Source: Dictionary.com, 2010

Related to the scope of concern here, systems frameworks describe and explain human phenomena as a set of interrelated parts. There are many variations and applications of systems approaches, ranging from those that look at the proximal corpus as a system, to those that examine humans' systems comprised of proximal and distal elements, and even extending to systems which do not contain embodied elements.

Consider these systems: your nervous system, your family system, your school or workplace, the weather, a barn full of animals, a cell phone system.

System Theory Axioms

Table 13.2 helps illustrate what various examples of systems have in common.

Table 13.2   System Theory Axioms

1. Systems theories posit that all systems are comprised of component parts, which, to a greater or lesser degree, interact with one another.

2. Systems are dynamic. That is to say, all systems change, albeit in different ways. Some change in a predictable manner and some do not.

3. Some theories posit that systems can be influenced by distal factors (open systems), while others examine system immunity from elements exterior to their protective battlements (closed system).

4. Regardless of the parts and what influences them, systems theory addresses relationships.

5. While all systems are dynamic, the nature and causes of change and movement differ according to the perspective.

6. Systems theories span a full scope of description from miniscule to universal.

As the axioms illustrate, systems theories all address an entity no matter how large or small, as comprised of subparts. Change is a central tenet in systems theory, in that systems are described as dynamic and relational. Many of the theories located in this chapter could also be categorized under other rubrics. For example, organizational systems, which examined next, could fit well within exterior environmental theories. While discussions on biological and cultural systems could also fit under systems approaches, we located them in the chapters on environmental theories due to their primary substantive focus.

In this chapter, we delimit our discussion to theories that extend distally beyond embodiment, and thus, do not address biological systems exclusively. To organize this vast literature, we begin a brief discussion of the history of systems theory and then move from exemplars of systems organized from most proximal (close) to humans to most distal (distant).

History of Systems Theory

What is particularly interesting to us about the history of systems theory is the way in which diverse methodology and equipment have influenced the nature of these ideas. Specifically, the development of systems theory over the years has moved from simple description of the linear interaction of two or more related parts of a whole to nonlinear conceptualizations of systems as complex in structure, interaction, and degree of vagueness within system elements. Recently, computer models have been able to discern how seemingly disparate and chaotic phenomena are actually part of extensive longitudinal systems. The capacity of computers to move human thinking beyond the chronological time, not only of our planet or universe, but into the infinite, has been elegant in creating images of systems concepts that could not be cogitated without these time extenders. Fuzzy systems, or fuzzy set theory, is also significant here, which views a system and its subsets as variable in their degree of membership and clarity of systemic and subsystem boundaries (Rangin, 2008). Both of these contemporary approaches are discussed later in the chapter. We now return to Greece to briefly visit the brains of antiquity.

THINKING POINT

Identify ways in which the computer as a system has changed human description.

The conceptual roots of systems theory can be traced back to Aristotle, who in ancient Greece coined the phrase, "the whole is more than the sum of its parts." Of particular note is Aristotle's proposition of a binary within this logic—that of true or not true. So either an element was or was not part of a system (Brule, 1985), building the scaffold for closed systems thinking. Numerous inventions and ideas over chronological time demonstrated elements of closed systems theory, such as a feedback loop, or the mechanism through which one part of the system receives information from another and then responds.

For example, clocks and early cisterns were structured as closed feedback loops, in which all the parts responded to information communicated throughout and within the system parts to other parts, but any influences outside of the boundaries of the system itself were not considered to affect them.

Yet, it was not until the mid-20th century that classical systems thinking was articulated as formal theory. Among the most renown classical systems theorists were Parsons (1951), Luhmann (2011), and then von Bertalanffy (1968). All adhered to the Aristotelian binary, suggesting that systems, their elements, and interactions could be ascertained and represented.

Parsons was a functionalist and viewed systems through that lens. By *functionalism,* Parsons (1951) meant that the descriptive behavior of small and large social groups could be explained by the human drive to meet four functional tasks:

1. Adaptation to the physical and social environment

2. Goal attainment

3. Development of an integrated and sound society.

4. Creating the expectancy and incentives for individuals within social systems to carry out their functions.

The behavior of enrolling and studying in college, if viewed through functionalism, would be explained by an individual's need to seek education in order to adapt to expected adult roles, expected goals, and a future stable place in one's social group.

THINKING POINT

What does functionalism have to do with systems? Can you see the embedded interaction of humans and social environments in functionalism?

Further building on this important school of thought, Parsons (1951) sought to characterize social action through a systems approach, in which environments and processes were seen as subelements of social action. Briefly, he suggested that social action could be explained by humans (behavioral organisms) interacting with proximal environmental elements of ideas and expectations (culture), within proximal physical environments (space, objects, locations).

The behavior of the college student (behavioral organism) is a function of abstract and concrete influences from the social, cultural, and physical elements of the system (college).

In the history of social work theory, functionalism was central to the mid-20th-century debates, which pitted diagnostic (Freudian) explanations against functional frameworks. Based in large part on the thinking of Rank (as cited in Dore, 1990), functionalist social work was proposed and advanced by the Pennsylvania School of Social Work. Through this interactive lens, the *helping relationship* was the provocateur of change, not the intrapsychic maturity of an individual client. Moreover, functionalists identified the helping relationship as part of a social agency constrained by time, and the view of agencies as formal and sanctioned parts of large social systems. Thus, the social worker was a system element whose work was sanctioned by the agency subsystem within the larger social system that the agency served. Much of functionalist thinking inheres in contemporary social work practice theories, including the construct of client self-determination, time, and relationship as the pivot points for client assessment and intervention (Dore, 1990).

Focusing systems theory on interaction while walking in the Aristotelian footsteps of binary logic, Luhmann (2011) characterized systems as communication entities which had distinct identities. He described systems as separate from their environments and explained their function as the extraction and use of limited distal information to communicate meaning. Luhmann himself acknowledged the convolutions in his own theory. This is mentioned here because of its emphasis on communication and relationship as the basis of systemic interaction—concepts relevant to social work practice and similar to other theorists who forged interaction as a critical element in changing systems.

Building on multiple disciplines including but not limited to philosophy, biology, and physics and the work of his contemporaries, von Bertalanffy (1968) advanced general systems theory. Simultaneously, cybernetics, the application of mathematical concepts to describing and explaining communication and feedback mechanisms within systems, was also born. According to von Bertalanffy and his contemporaries, a system is described as a set of interacting parts or activities that form a whole and interact. Thus, while components of a system can be identified, they cannot be reduced to individual and discrete elements, ergo keeping Aristotle alive and present in contemporary systems thinking. Yet, von Bertalanffy is perhaps best known for his work in open systems. A critical advancement in systems theory, given its acknowledgment of influences from the universe beyond the system boundaries as identified, is the concept of open systems as penetrable. Thus, open systems can benefit from or become victims—or both—of influences that lurk outside.

> *Consider a family system comprised of a 3-year-old boy, a 2-year-old girl, and a mother. Each individual can be seen as separate, but the behavior of one affects the others and shapes the system. As mom goes to work, she both brings resources into the family as a benefit but loses time with her children as a result of social and economic invasions.*

Von Bertalanffy further described systems as dynamic, changing, and complex. Thus, the nature, shape, and balance of the system can be explained by movement in one or more components, communication of that change to other system elements, and then responsive change within the system. The process of communication is called *feedback*.

> *Returning to the family, suppose the 2-year-old girl gets a head cold and mom takes her daughter to the physician. That change in one system component, the girl, is communicated to and affects not only the other components, mom and brother, but the shape and nature of the whole family system. Brother is too young to be left alone and a babysitter has to be found and paid. The mom, a subsystem of the family system, takes a sick day from the work system, affecting the economic viability of the family system and also influencing the work environment. Because the family is an open system, mom and the family system have to consider the economy and work influences in decisions and actions.*

Classical Systems as Description and Explanatory Theories

Classical systems theories have been applied to explaining a range of units of analysis from family systems to organizational, social, cultural and virtual systems. Most images of classical system elements and their interactions have been primarily portrayed as static slices in time.

With the omnipotence of the computer, computer modeling, and the hegemony of postmodern thinking, systems theory has undergone important conceptual and visual changes. Current systems theories describe the behavior and appearance of complex and unclear systems and explain and depict these through interdisciplinary lenses in motion. Among the most important are chaos theory, complexity theory, and fuzzy set theory. Complexity and chaos explain change in complex systems or those that are not reducible and predictable.

Two complex systems that function according to principles of chaos include the nervous system and the Internet. Both systems are influenced by numerous unpredictable factors and function in ways that require computer-aided mathematical technology to describe.

THINKING POINT

Compare linear systems theories with complex systems approaches.

Fuzzy systems or fuzzy set theory proposes a different logic than the binary of belonging or not belonging. According to this curiously named systems approach, elements have a range of membership in a system.

Think of in-laws. Are they part of a nuclear family, or not?

As the brief history illustrates, descriptions and explanations of systems have moved from conceptualizing them in determinist and predictable ways to understanding them as complex behaviors. Multifaceted mathematical, digitally generated, models can explain these complex behaviors. In essence, the generation of systems theories is an open and fuzzy system itself.

THINKING POINT

Explain how the generation of systems theories is an open and fuzzy system itself.

Changes in methods of inquiry, technology, and mathematical complexity influence the nature of description and explanation of systems, creating a complex, open system of knowledge in which the fit of particular theories can range from partial to full.

Contemporary Systems as Description and Explanatory Theories

We are back to the present so let us now examine systems theories that have been useful in describing and explaining humans in their diverse environments. Bronfenbrenner's bioecological theory (2005) helps organize the proceeding discussion within the five levels of systems theory that he proposed. These elements are placed on a proximal to distal continuum, noting that they are embedded as well as "fuzzy" (although Bronfenbrenner does not use this terminology or conceptual framework).

Bronfenbrenner's System Levels

According to Bronfenbrenner's original framework, humans develop within the context of four systems, from proximal to distal: (1) micro, (2) meso, (3) exo, and (4) macro. More recently, he proposed a fifth system, chrono, which refers to embeddedness in and process through the element of time. Thus, development itself is explained as a systems phenomenon blurring the boundaries between systems and developmental theories and illustrating the conceptual quagmire of parsing theories into a taxonomy. Table 13.3 provides descriptions of each level (Bronfenbrenner, 2005).

Table 13.3 System Levels and Exemplars

Proximal--Distal				
	Micro	**Meso**	**Exo**	**Macro**	**Chrono**
Definition	Immediate surroundings	Sets of microsystems	System that indirectly influences an individual	Abstract system that guides and shapes systems that are distal	System of time and history
Exemplar	Family, home, school, work	Community, neighborhood	Mother's workplace, sister's school	Economy, culture, policy	Maturation and location in an historical era

In Bronfenbrenner's original model, the human organism is described as nested within four system components. Adding the fifth level allows a view of this system as it changes within the abstract of history and the span of a life. Incorporating and building on the functionalist concept of timing (as cited in Dore, 1990), Bronfenbrenner reminds us that time is not only measured by an individual's chronological aging but additionally as chronological movement within the systems themselves (e.g., family, national history). The addition of sociocultural history to systems theory is parallel to and thus strengthens the rational for the inclusion of human capabilities and development of nation states (Nussbaum, 2007; Sen, 2007) in developmental theories, as discussed in Chapters 3, 4 and 5.

Consider Jose, an 18-year-old male who lives in an urban area. Jose is graduating from high school and deciding on his future as either a student or an actor. Examples of systems that effect Jose are his family (micro), his friends (micro), his teachers, to a greater or lesser degree (micro), his neighborhood (meso), his father's recent job promotion (exo), and the expectation from his extended family and his culture that he go to college immediately following his high school graduation (macro). Each of these systems will influence Jose's decisions and, in turn, his choices influence the systems in which he is nested.

THINKING POINT

What if Jose chooses not to go to college? How will this violation of cultural expectations reflect on his father, friends, and so forth? And then, how do his decisions interact with the chronological fluctuations in the economy (chrono)?

Over the past several decades, Bronfenbrenner (2005) expanded the description of the microsystem to include the individual and language and symbols to which an individual attributes meaning, thus creating the concept of the *biopsychosocial* human.

Microsystem theories describe and explain immediate distal environments in which individuals behave and act, such as work, family, sports teams, support groups, and so forth. This chapter covers family systems theory, word processing, and organizations as examples of microsystems, while the concepts extrapolate to other microsystems as well.

THINKING POINT

What do families, word processing, and organizations have in common?

Bowen (1985) was instrumental in developing family systems theory and applying it to therapeutic work with families. Different from theories which point to individuals as the locus of change as well as blame, Bowen removed individual portrait of function, replacing it with a wide angle lens containing the family in dynamic interaction. He suggested that families are emotional systems. From this broad imagery, family members are characterized by networks of feelings and emotions that profoundly influence each member, but cannot be reduced to a snapshot of any one individual member as responsible for system operation (Gilbert, 2006). Interaction within the family unit is a choreographed dance of seeking and receiving feedback in the forms of support, attention, approval, connection, affirmation, distance, estrangement, and so forth. Consistent with classical systems theory, change in one member element affects change (Bronfenbrenner, 2005) throughout the family system despite the degree of distance among family members.

The number and configuration of family members, as well as the degree of tension within the system, are important in explaining its stability. Moreover, the degree of individuality of each member, or what Bowen (1985) called *differentiation*, explained the manner and extent to which a family is influenced by other family members and interactions. Thus, Bowen explained the complexity of the family system by the multiple influences and processes occurring within the system and on each member. To depict these complex system interactions, Bowen developed a graphic that came to be known as a *genogram*. Different from a family tree, which portrays lineage, the genogram represents not only family relationships, but also influences on family elements and on the system itself. Although there are variations, genograms use static geometric symbols to depict family systems.

> *Consider Mario and Cathleen in 2010. They met in 2006 and began living together in 2007. Using a genogram graphic, their relationship would be depicted as shown in Figure 13.1. The square represents the male, and the circle represents the female. The broken line denotes that both are linked in an intimate relationship but are not married.*

Figure 13.1   Mario and Cathleen, 2007

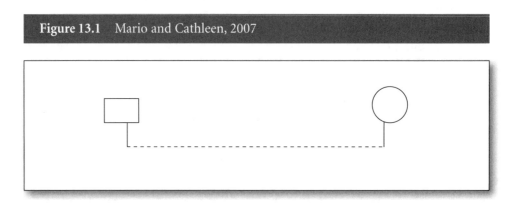

Mario and Cathleen married in 2008, as depicted in Figure 13.2. Note that the line is now solid to indicate formal marriage.

Figure 13.2   Mario and Cathleen, Married in 2008

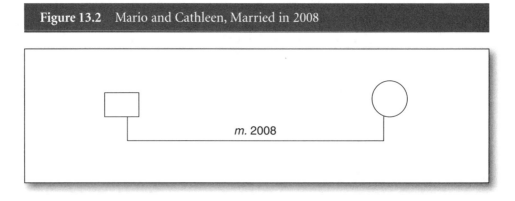

In 2008, Cathleen became pregnant, as depicted by the solid triangle in Figure 13.3.

Figure 13.3   Mario and Cathleen, Cathleen Pregnant in 2008

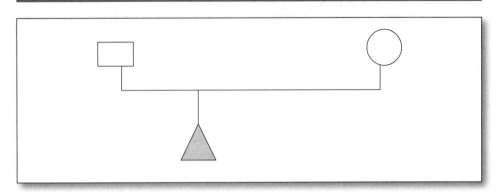

Cathleen, an only child, has two living parents who were divorced. Figure 13.4 represents her family of origin. Note that the straight marriage line is slashed with the year of divorce, and Cathleen's birth year of 1988 is also represented.

Figure 13.4   Cathleen's Family of Origin

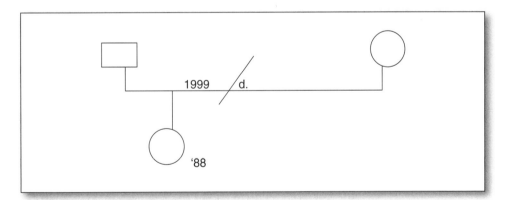

THINKING POINT

What are the similarities and differences between Figures 13.1, 13.2, 13.3, and 13.4?

As these simple genograms illustrate, graphics of families become increasingly complex as the system grows and changes.

THINKING POINT

What uses can you suggest for the graphic of a genogram?

Now consider the computer as a microsystem. As we were typing on our computer today, we noticed that some misspelled words corrected themselves in our word processing function. How is the computer a microsystem? It is comprised of structures which interact, change, and engage in a feedback loop. If we type teh *instead of* the, *the computer receives input (the incorrectly typed word), processes it, and corrects it (output) in response. The nature of the document is changed as well as its reception by those who read it. Of course, if your computer is connected to the Internet, the extent to which it remains micro is arguable. In some sense, the Internet responds directly to individuals while also providing the opportunity for participation in system elements that are extremely distal and abstract.*

Consider advertising. If you shop online, software outside of your individual hardware unit surveils your purchases and voila, advertisements "just for you" appear on your screen. Amazon, for example, sends recommended reading based on what you as an individual have browsed and ordered. The direct interaction between the Internet and you straddles and thus challenges the distinction among system sizes and proximity, suggesting that even theory developed in the mid-20th century needs to be reconsidered.

Although organizations can also be mesosystems or exosystems, we locate and discuss them under microsystems, because so many individuals work and conduct other activities directly in organizational contexts. According to Daft (as cited in Zastrow & Kirst-Ashman, 2010, p. 43), four essential elements can describe organizations. First, organizations are social systems. That is to say, they are comprised of humans who are guided by the rules and expectations of the organizational system. Second, organizations are purposive and goal directed. At least rhetorically, organizations have a mission statement that guides all organizational behavior. Third, organizations are developed, designed, and structured to achieve one or more stated goals through specified activities. And fourth, organizations exist within larger environmental systems.

Systems concepts can thus be readily applied to organizations, in that they are whole entities, comprised of smaller, interdependent parts, they undergo change, each part influences the other, and there are one or more systems of communication or feedback that inhere within the organizational system. Of course, the nature and mission of organizations change the complexity of the system. As an example, Zastrow and Kirst-Ashman (2010) assert that social service systems, because they focus on service to humans, are way more multifarious than systems that produce innate "things." Senge's (1990, 1994) work, to some extent, illustrates Zastrow and Kirst-Ashman's point. In focusing on learning environments, Senge proposed *systems thinking*, or the application of systems principles to describing, explaining, and improving organizations and their functions, as one of the critical components in developing and advancing learning capacity.

> *Consider the Urban Counseling Center, a local urban agency providing mental health services to a range of clients. From the systems perspective, the individuals involved in the interior social system would include clients, employees, and others involved in agency activity. The purpose could be found in the mission statement and might look something like "improve the mental health of the community by providing direct services to individuals and families, and through advocacy functions." Structurally, the physical plant is comprised of office space, meeting rooms, waiting rooms, and hygiene facilities, along with space and objects related to the achievement of the agency goals. The organizational chart provides the personnel and reporting structure in order to achieve the agency goals. The environmental context includes both the geographic area surrounding the agency, the areas from which clients and employees come, and the macrolevel of policy, laws, rules, insurance governance, and so forth. Within the agency, there are multiple feedback loops, including formal meetings, documents, and informal communications. Looking at the agency as a learning community according to Senge's (1990, 1994) model, the system's infrastructure and processes would be developed to define and then maximize learning for targeted organizational social participants, who might include providers and clients.*

Figure 13.5 depicts an organization system reporting hierarchy of the mental health agency in the preceding example.

Figure 13.5 Organizational Chart of the Urban Counseling Center

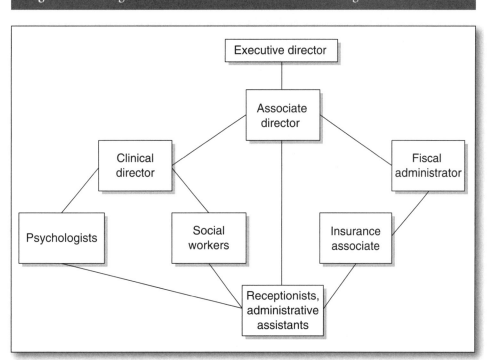

Note that in classical systems theories, although distal environment is acknowledged, the dynamic relationship between human and nonhuman elements is not often discussed in microcontexts. We find this omission as a major flaw in using these theories to inform action. Thinking back to the discussion of disability, for example, architecture is a critical element within microenvironments that influences navigation, emotion, and functioning. Thus, architecture should be considered in family as well as in more distal systems.

Returning to Bronfenbrenner's (2005) model, microsystems exist within mesosystems, such as communities, neighborhoods, and so forth. This system level is comprised not only of individual microsystems but of intricate relationships among them. Furthermore, mesosystems may unite microsystems under a conceptual mesoumbrella, so to speak. That is, in addition to being concretely delimited, as is the case in communities or neighborhoods, mesosystems can be bounded within conceptual perimeters, such as adolescents, elders, Americans, and so forth.

THINKING POINT

How many other conceptual mesosystems can you name?

Mesosystems are endless but all have in common that they organize, shape and are shaped by systems levels in which they are nested and which they contain.

Exosystems are those that are related to and influence a micro unit of analysis but are indirectly connected to it.

Consider how the closing of a retail outlet in which you do not shop can affect you. Individuals in your neighborhood may become unemployed and the overall economic well-being of your community may be affected. You may know a family who has to move to seek work elsewhere. While these are not intense and direct "hits" on your life, they are nonetheless whirling adjacent to your systems atmosphere.

We refer to this system level as *tangential-influential*, which denoting its important place in the systems model. Even though critical, the exosystem is often omitted from explanations of human behavior, family behavior, and organizational behavior. DePoy and Gilson (2008), in their evaluation practice model of programmatic and professional practice evaluation research, have built in the critical step of examining exosystems among all system levels. This decreases the likelihood of overlooking unintended and unanticipated influences to explain the process and outcome of social work activity.

Returning to the mental health agency, suppose an expected outcome for a depressed client is mood stability after six counseling sessions and a regimen of antidepressant medication. The microsystem in this example is the agency in which the client is a biopsychosocial subsystem and the social work professional is another subsystem. The professional sees the client making good progress over 4 weeks, and then notices that the client's mood has plummeted unexpectedly. The social worker carefully asks the client questions about his family system, work, and other systems in which he is directly involved, but neglects to consider the influence on the client's mood of the Chilean miners who were trapped underground in September 2010. While not directly affecting this urban area, the client's despondency is abstract and related to the exosystem of devastation and worker vulnerability in another part of the world. Without that information, the social worker cannot explain the despondency and the failure of the client to meet outcome expectations.

Consider one more example from the virtual world. Each day at work, an off-site computer technician backs up our computers. Yet, we are aware of his tangential but influential presence only when he captures our computers to reconfigure software.

Looking more fully at the macrosystem level, according to Bronfenbrenner (2005), macrosystems are described as abstract systems of ideas and practices that guide behavior and activity in exo, meso, and micro systems. Further, Bronfenbrenner asserts the importance of understanding the macrosystem level, in particular social policy, in explaining behavior at other system levels. Macrolevel systems are not limited to formal policies and rules however. Cultural systems, abstract social systems, communication and media systems, and now virtual systems may be part of the macrolevel analysis.

Looking beyond the screens of our individual computers, the macrosystems—many of which are hidden—govern not only the way in which individual computers operate, but shape the networks that link computers in large systems. For example, consider the Internet. The macrosystem rules, whether the computer user is aware of them or not, directs all network activity. Now think of a virus. This macrosystem introduces unwanted change into micro–, meso– and exo–virtual systems.

The macrosystem is particularly important in illuminating the interaction between laws, policies, cultures, and global trends, along with all systems embedded within this large system expanse.

Think of the federal, state, local, intellectual, and corporate policies and ideas that influence the mental health agency. Of particular importance are policies that determine reimbursement for services. This important economic macropolicy is a critical influence on mental health practice. For example, one major practice model, brief counseling, resulted in large part from restrictive fiscal support for ongoing mental health intervention (Corwin, 2002). Or, consider the recent effort on the part of the DSM-V revision team to decrease the time for nonclinical bereavement, adding a new diagnosis for social work and other clinicians to handle.

The rational model of policy analysis (Stone, 1986) fits well under this system level. This analytic model views policy formulation as a democratic negotiation among multiple system interests.

THINKING POINT

Can you identify how rational models assume a linear relationship between identification of a social need and response?

System components are viewed as differential entities with varying degrees of competing interests and power bases. As these interest groups interact and provide feedback, policies that best emerge from needs are developed, implemented, evaluated, and revised according to system feedback.

Looking at mental health again, over the past decade, mental health providers, one subsystem, have sought parity with physical health insurance coverage, a competing subsystem of care. The insurance industry, a third competing subsystem, has lobbied against parity as a means to contain costs and maximize profit. In order to advocate for parity, the mental health system introduced additional information into the macrosystem, conceptuality equating mental and physical illness as medical concerns rather than psychological, social issues. The linear and logical desired outcome is policy that mandates equivalent reimbursement rates and schedules for both types of services. Resulting policy varies throughout states in the United States, depending on negotiated terms and interactions among systems of varying power, influence, and so forth.

Looking at the chronosystem level, the history of a system over time can be traced and its future informed. At this level, rather than a "slice in time" static portal, subsystems are put into longitudinal maturation within events and concepts comprising the distal layers of the system.

Consider 9/11, an event just in the past decade. This was a critical historical turning which not only profoundly changed family microsystems of those who died, but which created a new historical context for the globe in which security, intergroup relations, and community mesosystems' interactions all changed in an instant. The event itself was a macrosystem element, but the maturational processes of social, economic, navigational, and intercultural relations over chronological time are exemplary of the chronosystem level of concern. Further, response and adaptation within all system levels over time are part of the chronosystem. What has happened to the families of those who died as they travel longitudinally beyond the actual event? What has happened to communities who, over time, have debated the building of a mosque adjacent to Ground Zero?

Chronosystems thus take static system views and energize them from a developmental perspective, but still within a classical systems framework. Thus, Bronfenbrenner's (2005) systems theory lens describes and explains both snapshots and full video images of system behavior, yet still retains a linear and reductionist personality. *Reductionist* means that systems can be reduced into their component parts and analyzed according to direct influences among them. Rational policy analysis illustrates this point. The expected outcome of policy negotiation directly links back to identified social issues and needs, and negotiation proceeds in a logical sequence. Similarly, positivist methods of inquiry are useful in understanding systems and system parts as linear and correlated. However, traditional systems theories have not provided the explanatory power to understand complex systems or those that cannot be characterized through linear relationships. Along with the simple lines of classical systems theories, nonlinear frameworks are necessary to capture and explain labyrinthine 21st century phenomena.

THINKING POINT

 Think of how difficult simple systems, such as your own family, are to predict. Can you see how systems with many more parts, influences, and properties require more complex theories?

Complex Systems

Several contemporary approaches to describing and explaining the behavior of complex systems have been developed. Because these theories are mathematically complex and require computer-generated models to explain their behavior (Wolfram, 2010), a detailed discussion of their principles is beyond the scope of this book. However, some basic tenets and how their explanation has informed human behavior are useful as well as a discussion of complex systems.

Chaos Theory

Chaos theory, a contemporary explanatory theory, has been important in advancing analysis of complexity and unpredictability. Through this lens, system behaviors, which before computer-generated mathematical models seemed random, nonrepetitive, and unrelated, have been observed and explained as complex behavioral patterns that have extreme fluctuations. However, these perturbations, while sending a system on a wild ride, still can be observed within boundaries that do not deviate too far from an attraction point (Peat, n.d.). Of particular emphasis are the roles of cumulative miniscule movements and slight variations in starting points in influencing system motion. The butterfly effect has been used metaphorically to depict the effect of tiny events through following the wing movement of multiple butterflies as they eclipse catastrophic intensity in locations extremely distal to the movement (Gleick, 2008). Slight variations in starting points indicate differences in the initiation point of behavior, which catapults systems in diverse directions despite the almost undetectable distinction among systems. So, the role of single events in creating turbulence is acknowledged, and important to understanding human description and explanation.

Thinking back to the discussion of induction and deduction, in essence, similar to induction, chaos theory begins from points of what appear random and unrelated, as systems ebb and flow and organize themselves just to disassemble, grow, and restabilize. The capacity to visualize and ascertain patterns from seemingly unconnected phenomena is thus emergent with prolonged engagement through computer modeling, a logical process through which the computer induces patterns over time, as computers can be programmed to depress the time throttle beyond human cognitive capacity (Peat, n.d.).

Chaos has been applied to understanding and intervening with diverse human systems. In his application of chaos theory to group behavior and development, McClure (2005) illuminates how the unpredictable sequence of order-upheaval-order is not only characteristic of human interaction, but is essential for growth. According to McClure, when systems are stable, linear systems theories may be sufficient for explanation. However, when disruption necessary for growth and change occurs, chaos theory is particularly cogent as it replaces simplified deductive thinking with higher–order complex processes.

Returning to policy analysis to illustrate, in macrosystems theory, as noted, rational policy analysis and formulation are directly linked to social problems and needs, and the expectation that policies will ultimately produce desired outcome. However, within the contemporary global economy, the relationship between policy and outcome is not simple or predictable, suggesting the need for nonrational models of analysis in which outcomes are seen as a function of complexity (Stone, 1986).

> *Consider the complication of the erosion of national economies, which have given way to global corporate structures that oversee health insurance. It is possible that approval for client coverage may be outsourced to India or the Philippines, where policies, cultures, and values—despite corporate rules—influence how determinations are made. Systems are large, complex, and unpredictable. Further, corporations that provide insurance products may also be involved in other businesses, rendering traditional macrolevel systems theory and rational policy analysis obsolete in explaining multinational corporate economics.*

Network Theory

THINKING POINT

Think of how the shoe-bomber changed security policy in airports throughout the globe.

Network theory, a related approach to chaos, grew out the field of computer science. It too is concerned with complex systems, or networks of multiple, interrelated subelements that function in nonlinear and often unpredictable ways. Network science has befriended many fields, including but not limited to communications, marketing, social science, power, and even air travel (Lewis, 2009). Three basic elements comprise networks: nodes, ties, and flows. *Nodes* are the contact points between which *ties* carry *flows*.

> *Consider your phone. In this example, the phone is a node, the phone linkage to others is the tie, and the voices, traveling as electric or digital messages, are the flows.*

> *Now apply network theory to humans. Staying with the phone example, the individuals talking to one another on the phone are the nodes, communication itself is the tie, and the flows are the messages that are delivered and received through communicating.*

Von Hipple (2005) applied network theory to innovation, showing how significant innovations in product design, social welfare, policy, and many other arenas can be exponentially superior to non-networked systems. Facebook, for example, illustrates how behavior of a complex social network, while a system, cannot be easily predicted, as it depends on so many threads that undergo processes of entrance, engorgement, activity, hibernation, departure, and so forth. According to von Hipple (2005), network theory has great power in being actualized for group thinking by those who come together in somewhat of a chaotic fashion, and ultimately stabilize for invention. The Center for Collective Intelligence at MIT (Karagianis, 2010) is a prime exemplar of network theory applied to global problems. Multiple people are brought together through networks of information and communication technology to tackle problems such as "climate change, poverty, terrorism, healthcare, or crime—problems too big to be solved by any one expert or group" (para. 2).

Fuzzy Systems Theory

Different from chaos and network theory, fuzzy systems or set theory locate the complexity of systems in the degree of membership of each subset or subsystem (Rangin, 2008). Thus, fuzzy systems take into account vagueness and degrees of variation. For example, the discussion of race in Chapter 10 highlighted Brazil's classification into racial categories based on skin color. Superimposing Gracia's (2007) question of how dark does one have to be in order to be considered black, fuzzy systems become palpable and important. The process by which social workers come to assess client mental health is another example. Despite the presence of a medical diagnosis, assessment is an art that locates an individual centrally or peripherally within a category. The relatively new category of autism spectrum disorders illustrates even further, with a range of phenomena that fit somewhere within this grouping. So, rather than asking the likelihood of membership, fuzzy thinking addresses degree and thus differs from probability. This point is relevant to evidence and research. While fuzzy sets can be modeled with numbers representing range of membership and belonging, the numbers have different meanings than probability statistics, which propose how likely the occurrence of an event will be. While fuzzy systems have been criticized for their acceptance of vagueness (Rangin, 2008), we would suggest that they are useful in explaining group membership and system embeddedness as complex and varied in intensity.

As a child, Harry was devoted to his family, yet as he entered adolescence at age 13, he strayed in his emotional attachment as well as willingness to spend time with them, accept their values, and even attend family holiday events. This behavior can be explained as "adolescent" from a developmental perceptive, but may also be seen as fuzzy, with regard to the changes as a subsystem of his family system. When Harry apologized to his mother at age 13 and once again assumed a close and central position in his family, his membership in the systems of family and adolescence changed, with membership increasing and decreasing in intensity respectively.

As the discussion and exemplars reveal, complex, fuzzy systems or networks are abstract, unpredictable, and variable and allow unanticipated factors to introduce vagueness and unpredictable change.

Evidence

Evidence has been discussed throughout the chapter. The application of systems theories has met with criticism because of the limited data to support the application of these amorphous classical practice conceptualizations to social science, and substantively to explain human experience (DePoy & Gilson, 2008). However, the appearance of contemporary complex theories on the social work scene is pleasing to us, along with the richness that can result from the use of mixed methods and a mix of diverse data sets for discovery, prediction, and outcome assessment. The evidentiary basis for theories, as well as their application, should be carefully examined before assuming that systems guide practice.

Summary

This chapter examined multiple systems approaches to describing and explaining humans. Beginning with a brief history of systems thinking, Bronfenbrenner's (2005) five system levels then provided a framework in which to think about linear systems. Discussion and illustrations then highlighted how each system level is described and applied to explaining human phenomena. Systems theory was then applied to diverse aspects of humans within systems contexts, including virtual milieus. The limitations of linear systems thinking was noted before venturing into the 21st century, where contemporary nonlinear systems approaches can be used to describe and analyze complex human phenomena. The chapter concluded with a comparison of traditional and complex system theories and a brief statement about evidence.

References

Bowen, M. (1985). *Family therapy in clinical practice.* Lanham, MD: Jason Aronson.
Bronfenbrenner, U. (2005). *Making human beings human: Bioecological perspectives on human development.* Thousand Oaks, CA: Sage.

Brule, J. (1985). *Fuzzy systems: A tutorial.* Retrieved from http://www.austinlinks.com/Fuzzy/tutorial.html

Corwin, M. (2002). *Brief treatment in clinical social work practice.* Belmont, CA: Brooks/Cole.

DePoy, E., & Gilson, S. (2008). *Evaluation practice.* Boston: Taylor & Francis.

Dictionary.com. (2010). *Condition.* Retrieved from http://dictionary.reference.com/browse/condition

Dore, M. M. (1990). Functional theory: Its history and influence on contemporary social work practice. *Social Service Review, 64*(3), 358–374.

Gilbert, R. (2006). *The eight concepts of Bowen theory.* Falls Church and Bayse, VA: Leading Systems Press.

Gleick, J. (2008). *Chaos: Making a new science.* New York: Penguin.

Gracia, J. J. (2007). *Race or ethnicity: In Black and Latino identity.* Ithaca, NY: Cornell University Press.

Karagianis, L. (2010). *Collective brainpower.* Retrieved from Spectrum: http://spectrum.mit.edu/articles/normal/collective-brainpower/?utm_campaign=email10su&tr=y&auid=6425928

Lewis, T. (2009). *Network science: Theory and practice.* Hoboken, NJ: Wiley.

Luhmann, N. (2011). *Introduction to systems theory.* New York: Polity Press.

McClure, B. (2005). *Putting a new spin on groups: The science of chaos.* Mahwah, NJ: Lawrence Erlbaum.

Nussbaum, M. C. (2007). *Frontiers of justice: Disability, nationality, species membership.* Cambridge, MA: Belknap Press.

Parsons, T. (1951). *Toward a general theory of action.* Cambridge, MA: Harvard University Press.

Peat, F. D. (n.d.). *Non-linear dynamics (chaos theory) and its implications for policy planning.* Retrieved from http://www.fdavidpeat.com/bibliography/essays/chaos.htm

Rangin, C. (2008). *Redesigning social inquiry: Fuzzy sets and beyond.* Chicago: University of Chicago Press.

Sen, A. (2007). *Identity and violence: The illusion of destiny.* New York: Penguin.

Senge, P. (1990). *The fifth discipline.* New York: Doubleday.

Senge, P. (1994). *The fifth discipline fieldbook.* New York: Doubleday.

Stone, D. (1986). *The disabled state.* Philadelphia: Temple University Press.

von Bertalanffy, L. (1968). *General system theory: Foundations, development, applications.* New York: George Braziller.

von Hipple, E. (2005). *Democratizing innovation.* Cambridge, MA: MIT Press.

Wolfram, S. (2010, April). *Stephen Wolfram: Computing a theory of everything.* Retrieved from TED: http://www.ted.com/talks/stephen_wolfram_computing_a_theory_of_everything.html

Zastrow, C., & Kirst-Ashman, K. K. (2010). *Understanding human behavior in the social environment* (10th ed.). Belmont, CA: Brooks/Cole.

14

New and Emerging Theories

Theory of the 21st Century

Thus far, the book has introduced many contemporary theories, some from traditional disciplinary foundations (e.g., neuroscience, biology, developmental approaches, and anthropology) and some from interdisciplinary fields (e.g., systems theory, network theory, complexity theory, fuzzy sets, and categorical approaches). This chapter dives into the ocean of theories that can be framed within postmodern and post-postmodern lenses, or those that locate descriptions and explanations of humans within the multidisciplinary world of symbols, networks, cyber-phenomena, constructions, social change, and reintroduction of substance.

Let us briefly reflect on today's world to contextualize the work discussed in this chapter. We live in communities no longer defined by their geographic or even physical boundaries, and thus, we can be in several places at one time (Bugeja, 2005). We now have models to answer to how light can pass through diverse locations simultaneously. The miniworld of atoms and particles collide to inform us about physics undetectable through human vision. Time is accelerated within networks of chips and wires. We can increasingly participate in global events when they happen through viewing them in action. Work no longer needs to take place in a physical workspace. We can create and revise our own virtual identities and communicate with great immediacy across the globe. We text message, e-mail, podcast, read on screens that mimic and perhaps will replace book pages, and "friend" on two-dimensional screens. We can access libraries across the globe from our homes and can meet face-to-face even if we are physically situated in different continents. We live among people who originated from geographic locations throughout the globe. We challenge the intellectual status quo of separate disciplines and discuss concepts such as intersectionality, symbols, and constructed realities.

Given these contemporary trends, and as stated in previous chapters, it is no surprise that traditional theories describing and explaining humans, such as those that are deterministic, are no longer adequate to legitimately apply to human experience. And so, we come full circle theoretically to our last rubric of human description and explanation, new and emerging theories.

The chapter concludes with the theoretical framework that organizes the discussion throughout the text, explanatory legitimacy. This chapter provides the theoretical and experiential rationale for a legitimacy worldview, which does not eschew traditional theory but places it in a larger linguistic, symbolic, and interdisciplinary framework from which to think about our contemporary universe. So now, after spending much time in the world of theory-past, let us come up to date to theory-present and theory future.

New and Emerging Theory Axioms

Table 14.1 presents the axioms that bind the theories in this chapter under a single rubric.

As the axioms in Table 14.1 illustrate contemporary theories reflect the pluralism, complexity, flexibility, and sometimes even uncertainty, brought about by technology, the simultaneous shrinking and expanding of the globe, and the rubbing of elbows, so to speak, of so many diverse ideas, experiences, and worldviews. We refer to this phenomenon as *diversity depth,* as introduced previously. That is, contrary to diversity patina, which locates difference in a single variable, diversity depth is seen as

Table 14.1   New and Emerging Theory Axioms

1. New and emerging theories share the characteristics of multidimensionality, pluralism, and complexity.
2. New and emerging theories range from describing and explaining order to disorder.
3. New and emerging theories are supported by multiple ways of knowing.
4. New and emerging theories move beyond binary concepts of normal and abnormal to describe and explain heterogeneity.
5. Individual new and emerging theories do not claim to be the single dominant worldview or truth.
6. New and emerging theories eschew traditional concepts of objectivity, eliminating them or replacing them with new understandings or re-understandings.
7. New and emerging theories are embedded in social, political, economic, geographic, intellectual, or cultural contexts.
8. New and emerging theories trend towards interdisciplinarity, dismantling and reorganizing the boundaries and corpuses that distinguish the classical academic and practice fields.

a universe of ideas and worldviews (DePoy & Gilson, 2004, 2011). These theories provide the permission to be uncertain and to hold purposive and multiple ways of thinking about our worlds. They allow us to be human and to see other humans through our own values and views. They acknowledge and integrate context as an important element to consider, rather than attempting to neutralize it as a biasing factor.

Theories are dissected and parts situated within interdisciplinary other disciplinary homes, authoring new and rich fields of inquiry that select the most feasible, rather than the only true, ideas as residents. And finally, the theories that reside in this genre do not prescribe human description and explanation but rather map "fuzzy" possibilities for debate and resonance with one's worldview. Our thinking spaces expand to accommodate multiple explanations, forms of evidence, and debate. Wow, we love these ideas and see them as most productive to guide our interactions and work with diverse humans within complex contexts.

Postmodernism as Description and Explanatory Theory

Every work that attempts to define and characterize postmodernism will acknowledge the inherent challenge of this task. In essence, postmodernism is not a theory, but a set of ideas that views the world and universe as a pastiche, or collage, of disparate beliefs, views, experiences, cultures, and practices (Powell & Lee, 2007). Perhaps the best-known postmodern theorists are Derrida, Lyotard, and Foucault. A detailed discussion of the philosophical works of these and other theorists who influenced, and were influenced by, these three contemporary thinkers is beyond the scope of this text. However, in this chapter, we discuss basic tenets, and of course, urge you to read further.

"What postmodernism teaches is not new. Heraclitus said, 'You cannot step into the same river twice' and his student added, 'not even once, since there is no *same* river'" (University of Chicago, 1998). As this quote illustrates, different from substantive schools of thought theorizing about human phenomena as constant—such as the developmentalists, behaviorists, linear systems theorists, and so forth—postmodernists deny or deconstruct the existence of a single truth, or cultural story, that unites humans under an explanatory umbrella. Rather postmodernists refer to the concept of grand narrative, or a linguistic, narrative text, set of images, or symbols that can be interpreted in many ways. Grand narrative thus holds no meaning by itself other than its reference to other symbols and words. To some extent, the term *grand narrative* can be pejorative as it implies manipulation and tomfoolery, or the use of words to derail more fundamental expressions of ideas. Moreover, as postmodernism looks in on itself, for example, some suggest that even postmodernism is simply a meaningless symbol, as it implies that modernism has ended, and thus oxymoronically, a different reality must follow (Toplu & Zapf, 2010).

We disagree that postmodernism is meaningless; it has invited healthy skepticism and questioning for many enlightenment era concepts that are long overdue for scrutiny. Nevertheless, we do empathize with those who grieve the intellectual loss of objectivity and reality (Moya & Hames-García, 2000), but suggest that, in essence, theory and knowledge development follows a dynamic nonlinear path as depicted in chaos theory. Thus, in order for new relevant theorizing to emerge, older systems of knowledge needed to be destabilized and replaced with new hybrid branches, which themselves will not remain static over time. We celebrate such an elegant image of knowledge as a complex system that changes in anticipation of or response to the universe or parts that it seeks to elucidate. Postmodernism serves the destabilizing purpose as it eviscerates enlightenment reality, leaving room for new ideas to fill the void. But, let us return to postmodernism, now with exemplars, before we move on to discuss the tides that are rushing in to nourish the hunger for the return of substantive knowledge.

Consider freedom of speech. Some postmodernists might view freedom of speech as a grand narrative in the United States, and thus would argue that the concept is no more than a story that does not describe the lived experience of American citizens. Rather, it obfuscates the existence of power mongering and inequality through verbal disguise.

Thus, postmodernism suggests that the myth grand narrative designs masks the economic and rights disparities of individuals and groups (DePoy & Gilson, 2009; Michaels, 2006).

THINKING POINT

Who in the United States might not experience freedom of speech? Contrast the ideal of freedom of speech with the experiences of those groups.

Another grand narrative that postmodernists reject is that of science as truth (Powell & Lee, 2007).

Consider race. As discussed, scientific inquiry before the Human Genome Project parsed humans into distinct racial groups that are now reflected in census categories. However, new information has suggested that racial categories cannot be verified. The scientific evidence of the past, which was accepted as truth, is no longer relevant today despite the continuation of counting racial categories as "real."

Postmodernists value local narratives—or small, context-embedded stories. Considering how postmodernism can fit with contemporary multicultural societies, rather than applying general description and explanation to all humans, postmodernism acknowledges difference and pluralism, and rejects a single reality.

Think about the concept of multiple intelligences. While Gardner (1999) does not identify it as a postmodern concept, we do. Here is our rationale. Unlike previous theories of cognitive development, in which intelligence is defined in a restrictive and universal way for all people, multiple intelligence theories posit different types of intelligence (Gardner, 1999). Table 14.2 identifies the areas that Gardner included under the rubric of "smart."

Table 14.2 Eight Intelligences

Linguistic intelligence: word smart
Logical-mathematical intelligence: number or reasoning smart
Spatial intelligence: picture smart
Bodily-kinesthetic intelligence: body smart
Musical intelligence: music smart
Interpersonal intelligence: people smart
Intrapersonal intelligence: self-smart
Naturalist intelligence: nature smart

Source: Gardner, 1999

According to Gardner (1999), the logico-mathematical definition of intelligence is not purposive, thus we see Gardner's work encased in a political perimeter in which he analyzes and expands the valued type of being smart. In other words, there is no single concept of smart, and other purposive narratives now enter the fray of "scientific" theory of intelligence.

Unlike the modernists—who rebelled against and detested the order and form of Enlightenment theory, art, music and drama, and mourned the fragmentation and disorder in the world (Toplu & Zapf, 2010)—the postmodernists accept and celebrate the world as a carnival, so to speak. In other words, the postmodernists describe the world as a set of juxtaposed, fragmented, diverse ways of being within an advancing context of technological and language symbols (Toplu & Zapf, 2010). Extreme postmodernists, such as Baudrillard (1995), see nonsense rather than sense in our world, and thus play with ideas, words, and images without assigning meaning or substance to them. Baudrillard used the term *simulacra* to describe symbols (*signifiers* in postmodern speak) that have no foundation or original source.

Consider the Office Assistant avatar on versions of Microsoft Word prior to 2004. The avatar was the paper clip or dog in the help screen. It was a symbol with no referent. It was not a photo of anything, it just existed in cyberspace, emerging when programmed to do so, but depicting a helpful character.

THINKING POINT

Can you think of more examples of simulacra? And, can you see why the postmodernists describe the universe as symbols with no grounding?

Powell and Lee's (2007) words further clarify:

The mapmakers of the past centuries superimposed a fictitious grid upon the globe-the meridians-the lines of latitude and longitude. They charted narrow straits, far-flung exotic archipelagos, dark continents, prevailing winds, waves and currents. Similarly, postmodern intellectuals have attempted to map the contours of our rapidly changing world, its mix of identities, realities, cultures, races, gender roles, technologies, economies, cyberspaces, mediascapes. (p. 4)

As reflected in Powell and Lee's passage, postmodernism does not discard the existence of knowledge, but rather, concerns itself with the construction of knowledge as a pluralistic set of symbols within a purposive, political, and local framework. Viewing knowledge as diversity of ideas, or what we introduced as diversity depth, is appealing to us in that there is no prescribed worldview and there are many bodies of evidence, beyond traditional positivist designs but including them as well, that can support individual claims. Moreover, postmodern knowledge is considered purposive.

Consider the distinction between bench, or basic, research and applied research. DePoy and Gitlin (2011) do not make this distinction any longer, and see all research and evaluation methods as purposive and applied. They suggest that multiple methods of inquiry should be used to study complexity of human description and explanation within a political, value-laden, purposive context.

What if you were the director of an alcohol abuse treatment agency, studying the outcome of your intervention on clients being treated or previously treated for alcohol dependence? If you wanted to know about long-term outcomes, you might study the incidence of relapse in clients. But, what if your agency funding were dependent on successes of your clients? Would you study sobriety, something that your program could not control or promise, or would you look at intermediate indicators, such as social skill acquisition, that are associated with the long-term goal of sobriety?

In postmodern terms, the choice of mininarrative, the research design and focus, in the preceding example would depend on the function of the activity. Both outcomes, sobriety and social skill acquisition, are relevant to treatment of alcoholism, but the choice of one over the other as the topic of investigation is framed within a political context.

THINKING POINT

Apply this research example to other topics in your professional domain. How would you investigate these topics for two different purposes?

Of particular importance to postmodern thinking is the role of technology. The omnipotence of computers, cell phones, and other information and communication technology is central to much of postmodern thinking in that this technology has changed the way in which we conceptualize, characterize, organize, store, and disseminate knowledge (Nel & Kroeze, 2008). Technology has created digitized information, which can be easily changed with no discernable record of what came before. And, some suggest that the demise of the "book" as we know it is not only desirable but necessary in order to meet the expanding enterprise of knowledge dissemination.

> Paper-and-ink books are more expensive to produce (and reproduce) than their digital doubles, and more difficult to disseminate, search, and recycle. In short, digital books are more affordable, accessible, and environmentally friendly. (Leo, 2010, para. 2)

Thus, information and communication technology (ICT) has ratcheted up the consumer element of knowledge. Knowledge is linked to advertising, can be purchased at an affordable price, and can be consumed. The number of websites that exist and then cease to exist without a visible trace is a key illustration. And then, who decides about what qualifies as knowledge and what does not? In postmodern societies, multiple forms of knowledge are acknowledged, beyond simply that which is supported with the "scientific narrative." The Dalia Lama XiV's early 21st-century book is another prime example. In the prologue of his recent work on the intersection of spirituality and science, the Dalai Lama (2005) says, "I was never trained in science. My knowledge comes mainly from reading news coverage of important scientific stories in magazines like *Newsweek*, or hearing reports on the BBC World Service and later reading textbooks on astronomy" (p. 1).

Yet, the Dalai Lama's writing is considered by many to be the pinnacle of scholarship and knowledge. Further in concert with postmodern thinking, the Dalai Lama identifies the functional capacity of science as transformative, but then suggests that because of its limitations, science fails to produce a full understanding of humans. For this purpose, other knowledge sources are identified such as spirituality, moral discourse, and ethical analysis (Dalai Lama XiV, 2005).

THINKING POINT

Given this example of the Dalai Lama, why do you think so many postmodern thinkers espouse Buddhism?

We have spent some time discussing postmodernism, and now you might be asking why. While postmodernism cannot yield truth or prescribe what we should do in our professional lives, it is valuable in informing our thinking and action. In our opinion, the postmodernists have opened the discourse about pluralism in many domains, including the professional world. For example, what is the acceptable knowledge base for professional practice? Is it evidence-based practice or narrative? And, what theoretical frames of reference are viable, sound, and purposive? These issues are reintroduced later in this chapter. And most important, as noted earlier, postmodernism destabilized a system of knowledge that was and is in need of change, leaving ahead the great opportunities for knowledge now being harnessed.

Now let us look at some other emerging theories that we believe to be important in studying and responding to humans.

Social Constructivism

Social constructivism, a flavor of postmodern thinking, views humans as the creators of "reality." We place the quotation marks around reality because, according to the social constructivists, reality does not exist by itself to be known by objective observation. Rather, humans invent "reality" within social contexts, and it thus does not dwell outside of human thought and action. By engaging in interaction and discourse, humans construct knowledge through sharing and attributing meaning to symbols.

THINKING POINT

Can you see some of the elements of postmodern tenets in the social constructivist worldview? If so, what are they?

There are multiple realities and with the focus on symbols, social constructivists challenge the notion of truth. Instead of truth, humans exist within contexts of meaning (Kim, 2001; Lock & Strong, 2010). For example, recent literature in the field of disability studies suggests that disability is not a medical condition but rather one that is socially constructed (DePoy & Gilson, 2011). Human description and explanation further illustrate.

> *Suppose we describe Aaron as an individual who moves through space using a wheelchair. A medical approach to disability would explain his use of a wheelchair on the basis of a medical-diagnostic condition, such as paraplegia (paralysis of the lower limbs). However, through a social constructivist lens, although Aaron would still be described as a wheelchair user. Thus the concept of disability, his disability, would be explained in terms other than medical. His disability might be attributed to barriers in the built environment that do not allow him to move and participate in his community in the same way that typical people can. Or, his disability might be explained as an attitudinal stereotype. The socially constructed explanation for disability therefore would locate disability in the social context, not inside of an individual.*

This example highlights the importance that social constructivists place on culture, meaning, and context. Knowledge is subjective, viewed and interpreted through individual bias, value, and worldview. The question then arises about how anyone can come to know anything. While some social constructivists would suggest that one cannot, we agree with Lock and Strong (2010) who refer to the "intersubjectivity," or prelinguistic "stirrings" (p. 9). That is to say, different from positivists, who espouse a single truth about the essentials of humans, or some postmodernists who suggest no truth, social constructivists describe human knowledge as communication, negotiation, and consensus within and among the living of a human life.

> *A few years back, we received a grant to study the meaning of independence and quality of life for youth with special health care needs and disabilities. The study was intended (in concert with postmodern notions, mind you) to inform services and community supports to assist youth to become productive in their communities. So, we set out to study the views of youth, their parents, their teachers, service providers such as health and social service professionals, and policy makers who develop funding and legislative guidelines for services and community supports.*
>
> *The findings posed quite a postmodern dilemma. Parents saw the meaning of independence and quality of life for their children as living independently away from parents in a home of their own. The teachers defined independence and quality of life for the youth as their acceptance and actualization of responsible self-care. Providers did not agree on the meanings, and policy makers delimited the concepts of independence and quality of life within fiscal constraints of public support. Most unexpected was the view of the youth themselves who seemed to achieve "intersubjectivity" without negotiation. They saw independence and quality of life as equal opportunity. That is to say, they wanted the same opportunities that their nondisabled counterparts had for their futures.*
>
> *Not only did the two terms,* independence *and* quality of life, *then, have differing descriptors depending on the context and people who were asked, but the definitions were diverse, context*

embedded, and needed to be negotiated if the knowledge gained from the study was to be useful in refashioning community services and supports (DePoy & Gilmer, 2000). In other words, both terms are grand narratives.

The example raises another important point about social constructivism—the inquiry methods used to support knowledge through this lens. Research methods based on the traditions of experimental design are not relevant to this school of thought. Thus, social constructivists call into question the grand narratives of science and scientific inquiry. Because experimental methods are based on the philosophical foundation of monism and objectivity, research that seeks to find a single truth through implementing procedures claiming that human bias does not interfere with the knowledge generated are not used. Rather, narrative strategies, which can yield multiple views, such as the inquiry described earlier, provide the evidence on which constructed claims are based. Narrative, storytelling, and other inductive methods therefore form the constructivist epistemology, or the way in which we come to know anything (DePoy & Gitlin, 2011). Once again, the terms *bias-free* and *objective* are grand narratives.

The methodological point creates a good segue to the contemporary use of fields such as political theory, economics, literature, and visual culture as lenses through which to describe and explain humans. Obviously each of these important fields cannot be discussed, so visual culture was chosen, in large part because of visual hegemony in contemporary imagery, symbol, and, in particular, technology such as the computer screen. Again, the concepts discussed can be extrapolated to other fields.

Visual Culture

Visual culture is a relatively new field that seeks to describe visual images and explain them in terms of cultural and social meanings (Rampley, 2005; Sturken & Cartwright, 2009). More expansive than the study of art or art history, visual culture is concerned with a broad scope of visual images, including art but hosting digital, electronic, craft, film, mass media, advertising, photographic, and other images that inhere throughout our environments. In addition to describing and explaining this wide range of images, visual culture theorists cover an expanse of human appearance, behavior, and experience—from proximal to distal. We begin our discussion with the proximal and expand outward.

Looking at the proximal, not too long ago, it was atypical to conceptualize the visual arts as theories of humans, that is, about individual human description and explanation. But, think about the notion of visualizing personhood through visual pictures generated by brain scans (Dumit, 2003). This visual image reveals new implications about human description and explanation. In a single glance, different from understanding humans as behaving beings, the behavior can now be linked to an image that ostensibly depicts the proximal corporeal environment of one's humanity. Extending further is genetics, in which human forms are depicted in essence by barcodes and maps rather than bodies viewed from outside of the organic corpus (Heiferman & Kismaric, 2005).

Appiah (2010), in his most recent work illuminating foot binding among Chinese women, illustrates the role of bodily adornment. His work reveals an intense social meaning of visual image that transcends the desire to avoid pain. He states, "The mechanism that had made foot binding attractive to those of lower socio-economic status depended on its being practiced by those of higher social status" (p. 44). In other words, social identity lives in image. Clearly, visualizing is powerful, as seen in the practices of the ancient Maya who flattened the heads of royal infants to depict their status (Fashion Encyclopedia, 2010), and in contemporary practices of plastic surgery.

These points bring us to fashion in general as identity. Anderson (as cited in Rampley, 2005) proposed that fashion takes on the status of an academic discipline due to its potency and increasing presence in theorizing about humans. She asserts that fashion, defined proximally as bodily dress and adornment, is both descriptive of individual identity and explanatory of individuality. What she means by this point is that individual selection of fashion displays a descriptive image of the fashion "consumer" to others and provides important explanatory meanings, such as one's cultural context, gender identity, wealth, status, and sexuality. More distally, within the complex contexts of the information age in the Western world, fashion has been explained as a critical factor in selecting a social group, along with establishing and illustrating one's group membership.

Think of how you react to two men, one wearing a suit and tie, and the other wearing a pair of jeans. Their visual descriptions would certainly differ and it is likely that the explanatory meanings that you attribute to each will be vastly variable. Each could belong to multiple groups, but the man wearing a pair of jeans might be excluded from belonging to social groups in which casual dress is not acceptable, and the man wearing a suit might be excluded from membership in a social group of those who only coalesce around casual descriptions.

Consider also the adornment of what previously was considered to be medical equipment. Because of the importance of fashion to individual identity and group membership, and in light of the aging of the baby boomers in the United States, it is not uncommon to see items such as mobility aids (canes, crutches, and even wheelchairs), now adorned with fashion images and/or luxury fabrics sporting texture and design, and thus included in the category of fashion accessories.

Our computers allow a final, but vague, proximal visual image. For the past several years, we have been giving our students the assignment to create an avatar that displays their identities. Some have chosen alternative genders, some craft nonhuman-appearing bodies, and so forth.

The image, its selection, and keyboard control are proximal, as is the meaning of the image to each individual. Yet, the image is distal from embodied visuals and performance, and can communicate meaning to the other ends of the globe.

Moving into more distal space, as discussed previously, Fussell (1983), in his examination of social class, explained the selection of household items as a class indicator.

Consider two families. The Smiths live in an apartment in Atlanta, Georgia, in a working-class section of town. Mr. Smith earns his living as a brickmason and Mrs. Smith drives the public bus. The Jeffersons live in an apartment across town, in an area close to the university campus where they are both professors. Both families earn an equivalent income. The Smith's living room is comfortable, housing two recliners, a coffee table, a couch, and a large screen television. In the Jefferson household, the coffee table is the location for several books of modern art and a Kindle e-reader. On one wall of their living room, hardbound classic books rest in between items that they have collected from their global travels.

As Fussell (1983) advances, both families purchase and display their social class through visual culture, despite income. Of particular note within the field of visual culture is the construct of visual rhetoric (Olson, Finnegan, & Hope, 2008).

THINKING POINT

Does the term *visual rhetoric* sound like an oxymoron?

Beginning with word soup to look closer at the meaning of visual rhetoric, in the 1500s, *rhetoric* referred to one's expressive eloquence, and thus a *rhetorician* was one who practiced the art of elegant communication, most typically through public oration (Harper, 2001–2010). More recently, rhetoric has come to mean a narrative to be interpreted. Considering how visual images tell stories, socialize us, and communicate cultural expectations, values, and differences, the meaning attributed to and communicated by visual images is the subject of visual rhetoric.

THINKING POINT

What does Photo 14.1 tell you about the homeowners who decorated their room as shown in the image?

Photo 14.1   The Home Library

The stories that advertisements tell also illuminate the significance of visual rhetoric. Through visual image, we can learn about a product, its use, and why we need it. We can be convinced of the narrative of need, after which we run out to purchase a product that is visually marketed to us.

Also useful examples are logos and symbols such as Mickey Mouse ears or the Nike swoosh, that by themselves, mean nothing, but we are socialized to recognize their designated meaning. A photo of the image below (Photo 14.2) was taken in Jerusalem. This image depicts the Nike swoosh logo being used to convince passerbys to practice the Jewish Orthodox prayer practice of tefillin, a curious juxtaposition of tradition with "cool."

Coinciding with the Jeffersons, who tell stories of their travels through items in their home, Melonie Bennett (2005), a photographic artist whose work was displayed in several Maine galleries "My photography is an ongoing visual diary of my family and friends and the times we share together" (para. 3). And, in the virtual world, blogging has created continuous narratives in cyberspace depicting the diversity depth of individual bloggers.

Visual images are thus powerful public descriptors and communicators of social norms, cultural expectations, marketing messages, among myriad other meanings. How these images interact and produce outcomes, and how they often conflict and miscommunicate have been topics of contemporary examination (Barthes, 1978; Rampley, 2005). Even the visualization of another's expression is considered an image that explains behavior.

Photo 14.2   Just Do It: A Call to Religion?

Think about how seeing the faces of an audience can explain the behavior of a performer. Or, what about the image of an angry parent to a child?

Currently, amidst investigation of architecture's visual rhetoric on university campuses, the range of cultural messages is of particular interest (Gilson & DePoy, in press). These messages range from welcome through rejection in the knowledge creation and consumption enterprise communicated through architectural rhetoric, image, and navigation. Thus, in addition to the built structures, visual rhetoric of campuses gets put into motion as spoken by who can and cannot navigate, in what mode, and through what spaces (Gilson & DePoy, in press). So, visual rhetoric is not simply about static image or object, but refers to movement and performance as well.

Performance itself speaks volumes about humans. As an example, how one performs on an IQ test identifies the individual as an intelligent being, or perhaps not. Sandahl and Auslander (2005) have synthesized the work of visual rhetoric with disability studies, suggesting that any observable impairment provides a performance spectacle to which the viewers attribute meaning. Meanings typically include pity, stigma, difference, and other judgements about undesirability. Hahn's (1988) classical work referred to the onlookers' phenomeon as *aesthetic anxiety*, referring to such thoughts as "Oh no, what if I looked like that?" when visualizing a body using a wheelchair for mobility or with other atypical visual difference.

For our final synthetic exemplar, we accompany Harry through his day.

> *Harry, a legal secretary, goes to work every day. He leaves his one bedroom, ground floor apartment in Brooklyn, New York dressed in suit and tie, gets onto the subway, travels to Manhattan, gets off the subway, and walks half a block to his office on Madison Avenue. He then enters the 30-story building, passes through a metal detector, and takes the elevator to the 24th floor. He exits the elevator and walks through the hallway to his office, where he spends the day in a space filled with papers, books, e-books, office furniture, iPod, phone, fax and computer equipment, and artifacts necessary for his work. For most of his day, Harry sits at his desk doing legal research and preparing reports. After work, he retraces his steps back to Brooklyn, where he goes home, changes into his exercise clothing, and takes the bus to his health club. At the health club, Harry runs on the treadmill for an hour, listening to music on his iPod, while enjoying the mural of a beach scene painted on the wall of the gym.*

THINKING POINT

Think of all of the physical elements that might be described throughout Harry's day.

Through the explanatory lens of visual culture, one might begin to look at the construction of Harry's urban living and working environments as artificial and fashioned in order to be economically manipulative. By the term *economically manipulative*, we refer to one's curiosity of contemporary postindustrial cultures, the removal in daily life of the natural resources essential to meet human needs. This then must be refilled through purchasing a constructed product or service that produces significant corporate profit.

Looking at Harry's world, his sedentary job, public transportation, and even elevators eliminate the natural capacity to fulfill the human need for exercise. Harry must then purchase a membership to the health club in order to get the exercise to keep his body healthy, as conceptualized in large part by the congruence of his appearance with marketed images of health.

Harry wears a suit and tie to work, but to the gym, wears clothes that fall under the descriptive umbrella of "active wear." Is he manipulated by the power of the fashion design industry to spend his money on symbols of his activity?

According to Rampley (2005), the answer is yes. Fashion is a powerful industry that wields significant influence and advantage not only in terms of profit, but as noted, creates and publicizes identity. Note the numerous magazines, websites, and other media that tell us what to wear for success, romance, sports, and so forth.

Now look at navigation through Harry's daily life.

As Harry descends into the subway, the stairs are separated into two sections by a middle rail, denoting the expected foot-traffic pattern. The token booth is surrounded by glass and gates, telling us to stay away, and revealing the history and current threat of theft. On the subway trains, seats are positioned so that people are not facing one another, facilitating solitary activity and gazing at advertisements, rather than conversation. In the city, visual symbols such as traffic lights, street signs, and painted lines on the pavement direct pedestrian and vehicle traffic. Stores signify their style and class and invite targeted groups of consumers through window displays, signs, doors, and architecture. Buildings divulge their age, grace, and preferred interlopers through their architecture.

In addition to the built environment and human-made objects, visual culture expands to natural objects and their manipulation.

Consider the bananas that Harry purchases on his way home. Banana producers separate their banana crop into three divisions, A, B, and C on the basis of color and shape. The bananas that are classified into the A category are exported from Costa Rica to the United States and to other countries for sale in grocery stores. The bananas that fall into the B category are mashed into baby food and other edible products made from bananas, while those in the C category are sold for animal feed. So, Harry's visual image of a "good banana" is constructed and what he pays for these fruits has little to do with taste, quality, and nutritional value.

Now, let's peek into Harry's virtual visual culture. In the morning, he is awakened by the same voice on his cell phone that awakens his brother who lives 3,000 miles away. As Harry gets out of bed, he smells the coffee that he "made" before he awakened that morning by virtue of technology. Shortly after he gets up, Harry's mother calls him and while he is talking to her on his cell phone, he logs onto his computer to instant message his friends. At work, Harry does his legal research in the Harvard Law library, without even being in the same city. When he goes to the health club, he works out on a virtual mountain simulated by his treadmill. And, in the evening, Harry and his partner get together at home over a glass of wine and Pavarotti singing opera that they downloaded to their iPod a few days before. Before bed, they make reservations on the Internet to go on a vacation in Hawaii and then shop for bathing suits online.

Barney (2004), in his explanation of the virtual world, suggests that networks, or nodes of humans tied together through virtual space, are isolating mechanisms that are designed to alienate people from social contact and then refill empty lives with the ability to purchase interaction. However, DePoy and Gilson (2004) see the virtual element of visual culture through a more positive lens, as a means to level the playing field among diverse people and to advance tolerance and acceptance by reducing discrimination on the basis of diversity patina.

At work, Harry calls a client, Juanita, who cannot hear at all, and through text telephone (TTY) technology, they have a phone conversation. In his health club, Harry runs on the treadmill next to his best friend, Lian, a man who is unable to see but knows how far he runs because his treadmill speaks to him. Lian works full-time from his home as a technology support person for a small firm. Through the virtual environment, Lian can work on the firm's computers, network, and server, and also back up all work, whether or not he is physically present. Lian belongs to an online chat room where diversity is expressed through exchange of ideas, not by one's appearance or other palpable symbols of visual culture.

The palpable and virtual worlds through the theoretical lenses of visual culture are a waltz between image and meaning, with humans both as leaders and followers, as manipulators and manipulated. Visual culture theories draw from multiple disciplines and methods of inquiry, including but not limited to anthropology, philosophy, rhetoric, sociology, and design. Given these disciplinary roots, it is not surprising that inductive inquiry methods such as semiotics, the analysis of the meaning of symbols, and narrative are particularly central to knowledge generation in visual culture theories (Chandler, 2004). Reference to interdisciplinarity now brings us to a critical turning in new and emerging theories, the movement beyond postmodernism.

Beyond Postmodernism: Post-Postmodernism

We loved this quotation from the introduction to a conference held in the late 20th century, at the University of Chicago, that began to address the "now what" of postmodernist thinking.

> If we absorb postmodernism, if we recognize the variety and ungroundedness of grounds, but do not want to stop in arbitrariness, relativism, or aphoria, what comes after postmodernism? (University of Chicago, 1998)

The quotation highlights the abundance, as well as the vacancy, of postmodernism. As previously noted, postmodernism fills us with provocation such that we make room for diversity depth, debate, and unending questions. Yet, we are left with no substantive answers or theoretical guidance.

Rebelling aginst rebellion has the potential to rebuild, re-understand, and reconstitute the knowledge that has been dismissed, albeit in ways which are most relevant to context. Clearly, return to Enlightenment thinking and disciplines, while "retro," would not advance theory and knowledge to make sense of human life in the 21st century.

Rather, as Kirby (2010) suggests, one major trend from postmodernism to post-postmodern thinking lies in the shift of cultural production from author to receiver. With technology and instantanous dissemination, anyone can develop and transmit knowledge, and it must be consumed in order to exist. Social networking, in which large numbers of individuals form collectives that circumvent authority and materiality, is a prime illustration.

A second, and meritable, difference between postmodernism and the next intellectual era, according to Kirby (2010), is the emphasis on individual as consumer. Given the advanced market economy that is globalizing consumption, the student, reader, or receiver of theory is the target of marketed material in the name of profit. While Kirby laments these trends and others which, for him, characterize post-postmodernism or what he refers to as *pseudomodernism,* we are not as pessimistic.

To the contrary, in our opinion, contemporary thought has great potential to introduce new theoretical friends by breaking down disciplinary boundaries, and by harnessing the market-based economy for social change.

THINKING POINT

Think about how interdisciplinary trends are increasingly needed to describe and explain humans in our complex, technologically advanced, global, multicultural worlds.

Jefferson (2005), an economist, wrote a recent essay highlighting the importance of biological experimentation in helping him to understand the more abstract narratives and theories in his own field. Having spent time in a microbiology laboratory participating in an effort to reduce the "balkanization of disciplines" (p. B5), Jefferson was able to extrapolate inquiry principles to explaining economic phenomena.

Carmen (2004) integrates political theory and genomics. According to Carmen, the scientific enterprise derived from the generation of descriptive and explanatory knowledge of the human genome and its application to human behavior are, and should, be examined within the disciplines of political theory and axiology (values and ethics). Through his discussion of genomics, Carmen reminds us that science of human biology and physiology exist within an interpretative theoretical framework in dynamic and diverse contexts, and thus is not a singular discipline.

A third difference between postmodernism and post-postmodernism lies in terminology. Terms such as *interdisciplinary, multiple, diverse, inter-relatedness, realities, multiples, narrative, construction, embedded, culture,* and so forth resound in post-postmodern literature, illuminating an advance rather than return to substance through remixing theory (Shields, 2010), or what we refer to as *strange theoretical bedfellows.*

With great optimism, we see contemporary theory of humans as interdisciplinary and embedded within a foundation of relevance and purpose, with a broader authority than previous knowledge productions. Creative interdisciplinarity holds the promise for advancing knowledge that can be put to use in addition to being observed and consumed. DePoy and Gilson (2011) illustrate the promise of contemporary theory, recent work that synthesizes design, marketing, and branding with disability studies to produce much needed social and cultural change. This synthetic theoretical lens can be used to explain the breadth of human experience, not simply those who are constrained within the disability club. Other work (Gilson & DePoy, 2007) provides a broader discussion of these points, with analysis here focused on disability for instructive purposes.

Design, Branding, and Disability

As discussed previously, social workers and other health professionals in the 20th century conceptualized and responded to disability as an embodied deficit.

Postmodern thinking deconstructed the linguistics of decrepitude to suggest that disability was not necessarily an atypical body riddled with illness metaphors, but rather was a product of social attitudes that located atypical bodies as excluded and objects of discrimination. As divulged, this debate, while potentially productive, remained in the world of symbol and discussion, leaving the term *disability* delimited to an essentialist, but for us, amorphous, lexical category.

Post-postmodernism brings us beyond the opposing word soup viewpoints of disability as medial or socially constructed to think about disability from multiple perspectives, each of which can be addressed within a purposive context. Given the hegemony of the three 21st-century trends—technology, the market economy, and visual culture—design and branding provides a set of theoretical foundations that will not replace other understandings of disability, but provide another synthetic lens to drive action. We are not suggesting that individuals do not have diverse conditions and functionality, but rather that the term *disability,* which was indicted with no meaning in postmodernism, now denotes multiple meanings as the marketplace designed. Tracing how this viewpoint evolved, and exploring its value in crafting social action to redress negative valuation and life experiences of those categorized as disabled, is covered in Chapter 20 alongside the legitimacy of new and emerging theories.

As an extension of visual culture, we suggest that design and branding within the 21st-century global market economy are critical in shaping identity, category, and place. Thus, these lenses can refract a view of disability that can form a direction for purposive action.

Design is a complex construct increasingly used to describe human intention and activity, and to name a property of virtual, physical, and even abstract phenomena.

Cooking with word soup once again, Table 14.3 presents multiple, representative lexical definitions of *design.*

As reflected in the definitions and consistent with post-postmodern thought, design is purposive and may refer to decoration, plan, fashion, functionality, and influence. What is evident in the diverse definitions is the broad scope to which design applies, including but not limited to the activities of conceptualizing, planning, creating, and claiming credit for ones ideas, products, and entities, as well as the inherent intentional or patterned characteristics of bodies, spaces, and ideas (Margolin, 2002; Munari, Eames, Eames, Guixe, & Bey, 2003). Despite the post-postmodern ubiquitous and diverse use of the term, of particular note is the post-postmodern commonality in all definitions of design as purposive and intentional, two other hallmarks of post-postmodern thinking. Design, then, is not frivolous, but rather, is cultural iconography—it is powerful, political, and is both shaped by and explanatory of notions of standards, acceptability, membership, and desirability (Munari et al., 2003; Foster, 2003).

In contemporary Western economies, design is closely related to branding. Given the emergence of branding from the fields of marketing and advertising, brands within this constrained conceptual framework are defined as the purposive design and ascription of logos to a product for the intent of public recognition, addition of value, and consumption. More recently, scholars have enlarged the definitional scope of branding as a critical culturally embedded symbolic set of icons that commodify and reciprocally

Table 14.3 Definitions of *Design*

1. To create, fashion, execute, or construct according to plan: devise, contrive (Merriam-Webster, 2006–2007).

2. Any design, logo, drawing, specification, printed matter, instructions or information (as appropriate) provided by the Purchaser in relation to the Goods (Magneteco, n.d.).

3. A set of fields for problem-solving that uses user-centric approaches to understand user needs (as well as business, economic, environmental, social, and other requirements) to create successful solutions that solve real problems. Design is often used as a process to create real change within a system or market. Too often, Design is defined only as visual problem solving or communication because of the predominance of graphic designers (Nathan.com, n.d.).

4. The plan or arrangement of elements in a work of art. The ideal is one where the assembled elements result in a unity or harmony (EvoWiki, 2008).

5. Both the process and the result of structuring the elements of visual form; composition (Ackland Art Museum, n.d.).

6. A clear specification for the structure, organization, appearance, etc. of a deliverable (TenStep, 2001–2010).

7. To intend or have as a purpose; "She designed to go far in the world of business" (Farlex, 2010).

8. A plan for arranging elements in a certain way as to best accomplish a particular purpose (Munari, Eames, Eames, Guixe, & Bey, 2003).

represent and shape values, ideas, and identities. Thus, through the process of choosing and accepting cultural iconography in the form of products, fashions, food, music, and so forth, one ostensibly defines the self and displays value to others (Holt, 2004).

Building on design and branding theory, the conceptual portal of design and branding is potent for unpacking and analyzing the purposive, political, and profit-driven nature of embodied labeling, identity formation and recognition, stereotyping, and responses that explain disability and can give a specific meaning to it as a category. The explanatory importance of this conceptual framework lies in the processes and purposes of design and branding as deliberate, complex, and potentially able to manipulate meaning of self, others, and categories (Licht & O'Rourke, 2007).

As noted, while product branding is part and parcel of popular visual culture, it looms larger and more powerful in explaining populations and affixing their value. Visual logos are only one type of branding. The space that one occupies, those who provide services, and simply the performance of disability, as discussed by Sandahl and Auslander (2005), are branding phenomena that confer identity (Pullin, 2009; Riley, 2005, 2006).

Looking at disability brands as exemplary, specific "disability" products are designed as functional, recognizable, identity assigning, and manipulative of those who use them and those who view them. In essence, the aesthetic design and distribution outlets of these products brand and thus explain the user as disabled.

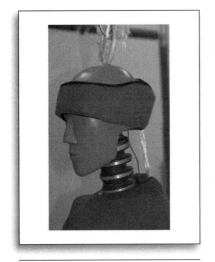

Photo 14.3   Medical Protective
Headgear

The photos of protective headgear in Photos 14.3, 14.4a, 14.4b, and 14.5 help illustrate. Despite identical functionality, the item in Photo 14.3 is designed as prescribed, clearly discernable medical equipment, while items in Photos 14.4a, 14.4b, and Photo 14.5 are designed as fashion items that would not brand those who wear them as atypical, disabled, or sick.

The power of creatively informing action through post-postmodern "re-understanding" through divorce and remarriage of traditional disciplines becomes observable. Note that the fields of neurology, medicine, fashion, visual culture, branding and marketing, and human rights have come together resulting in the development and distribution of this new product. Medical headgear is no longer segregating and a symbol of deviance.

Different from postmodernism, which provided limited local theoretical guidance, post-postmodernism has gone global, gifting us with both intellectual and utilitarian richness.

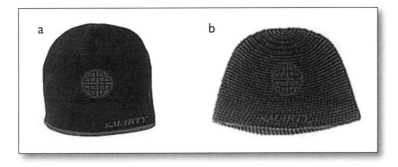

Photo 14.4a and 14.4b   Well-Designed Protective Headgear

Photo 14.5   Well-Designed Protective Headgear

As we promised, however, we now discuss explanatory legitimacy as a post-postmodern theory. So let's turn to this discussion now.

Explanatory Legitimacy as Post-Postmodern Theory for Social Work

Although we originally conceptualized explanatory legitimacy as postmodern because of its acceptance of multiple explantory frameworks within an axiological context, we suggest that legitimacy thinking about humans provides the opportunity for reconciling and rejoining theories that have not been previously united. This point brings theoretical synthesis to inform contemporary and progressive local through global legitimate response. Theoretical wealth and informed, productive, and negotiated social action can result when both monism and skepticism are transcended as opposites and invoked solely or in concert with one another for purposive use.

> *Recently, we wrote a project titled "Social Work Robotics" in which we proposed to use social robots for clinical functions. Post-postmodern "logic" guided our creative synthesis of engineering, social learning, and counseling intervention.*

THINKING POINT

Can you think of other examples? They are infinite and span the spectrum of all human experience.

Evidence

Methodological issues have been addressed throughout the chapter. To summarize, mixed methods follow the logical reordering and fusion of the research traditions. Yet, purposive choice about the nature of evidence (and how to generate and apply it) is the guiding principle for the evidentiary basis of post-postmodern thinking.

Summary

This chapter covered a range of new and emerging theories. Analysis delimited to theories that fit within postmodern and post-postmodern ideas, such as pluralism and diversity depth and interdisciplinarity. Exemplars from disability studies illustrated key concepts, followed by a summary of the evidentiary elements of new and emerging theory as purposive rather than prescriptive.

References

Ackland Art Museum (n.d.). *Glossary.* Retrieved from www.ackland.org/tours/classes/glossary .html

Appiah, K. A. (2010). *The honor code: How moral revolutions happen.* New York: W. W. Norton.

Barney, D. (2004). *The networked society.* Malden, MA: Polity Press.

Barthes, R. (1978). *Image, music, text.* (S. Heath, Trans.) New York: Hill & Wang.

Baudrillard, J. (1995). Radical thought. *Canadian Journal of Political and Social Theory, 18,* 1–3.

Bennett, M. (2005). *Artist's talk: Melonie Bennett.* Retrieved from Bates College: http://www .bates.edu/x63819.xml

Bugeja, M. (2005). *Interpersonal divide: The search for community in a technological age.* New York: Oxford University Press.

Carmen, I. H. (2004). *Politics in the laboratory.* Madison: University of Wisconsin Press.

Chandler, D. (2004). *Semiotics: The basics.* New York: Routledge.

Dalai Lama XiV. (2005). *The universe in a single atom: The controversy of science and spirituality.* New York: Morgan Road Books.

DePoy, E. & Gilmer, D. (2000) Adolescents with disabilities and chronic illness in transition: a community action needs assessment. *Disability Studies Quarterly, 20*(1), 16–24.

DePoy, E., & Gilson, S. (2008). *Evaluation practice.* Boston: Taylor & Francis.

DePoy, E., & Gilson, S. (2009). Designer diversity: Moving beyond categorical branding. *Journal of Comparative Social Welfare, 25,* 59–70.

DePoy, E., & Gilson, S. F. (2011). *Studying disability: Multiple theories and responses.* Thousand Oaks, CA: Sage Publications.

DePoy, E., & Gitlin, L. (2011). *Introduction to research.* St Louis, MO: Elsevier.

Dumit, J. (2003). *Picturing personhood: Brain scans and biomedical identity.* Princeton, NJ: Princeton University Press.

EvoWiki. (2008). *Intelligent design is wrong.* Retrieved from http://evolutionwiki.org/wiki/Intelligent_Design_is_Wrong

Farlex. (2010). *Intend.* Retrieved from the Free Dictionary: http://www.thefreedictionary.com/intend

Fashion Encyclopedia. (2010). *Head flattening.* Retrieved from http://www.fashionencyclopedia .com/fashion_costume_culture/Early-Cultures-Mayans-Aztecs-and-Incas/Head-Flattening .html

Foster, H. (2003). *Bright minds, beautiful ideas.* Amsterdam: BIS.

Fussell, P. (1983). *Class: A guide through the American status system.* New York: Summit Books.

Gardner, H. (1999). *Intelligence reframed: Multiple intelligences for the 21st century.* New York: Basic Books.

Gilson, S. & DePoy, E. (2007). Da Vinci's ill-fated design legacy: Homogenization and standardization. *International Journal of the Humanities, 4.* Retrieved from http://www.Humanities-Journal.com

Gilson, S., & DePoy, E. (in press). The student body: Research in social science and disability. *Research in Social Science and Disability.*

Hahn, H. (1988). The politics of physical differences: Disability and discrimination. *Journal of Social Issues, 44*(1), 39–47.

Harper, D. (2001–2010). *On-line etymology dictionary.* Retrieved 2010 from On-Line Etymology Dictionary: http://www.etymonline.com/index.php?search=ethnic&searchmode=none

Heiferman, M., & Kismaric, C. (2005). *Paradise now: Picturing the genetic revolution* [Art exhibit]. Retrieved from http://www.genomicart.org/pn-intro.htm

Holt, D. (2004). *How brands become icons: The principles of cultural branding.* Cambridge, MA: Harvard Business School Press.

Jefferson, P. N. (2005, October 7). The economist as biologist. *Chronicle of Higher Education*, p. B5.

Kim, J. (2001). *Social constructivism. Emerging perspectives on learning, teaching, and technology.* Retrieved from Georgia College of Education: http://www.coe.uga.edu/epltt/Social Constructivism.htm

Kirby, A. (2010, Aug–Sept). *The death of postmodernism and beyond.* Retrieved from Philosophy Now: http://www.philosophynow.org/issue58/58kirby.htm

Leo, J. R. (2010). The cult of the book—and why it must end. *Chronicle of Higher Education,* Retrieved from http://chronicle.com/article/From-Book-to-Byte/124566/

Licht, A., & O'Rourke, J. (2007). *Sound art: Beyond music, between categories.* New York: Rizzoli.

Lock, A., & Strong, T. (2010). *Social constructionism: Sources and stirrings in theory and practice.* New York: Cambridge University Press.

Magneteco. (n.d.). *Design.* Retrieved from http://magneteco.co.uk/terms.aspx

Margolin, V. (2002). *The politics of the artificial: Essays on design and design studies.* Chicago: Chicago University Press.

Merriam-Webster. (2006–2007). *Design.* Retrieved from http://www.merriam-webster.com/dictionary/diversity

Michaels, W. B. (2006). *The trouble with diversity: How we learned to love identity and ignore inequality.* New York: Metropolitan.

Moya, P. M., & Hames-García, M. R. (2000). *Reclaiming identity: Realist theory and the predicament of postmodernism.* Berkeley: University of California Press.

Munari, B., Eames, C., Eames, R., Guixe, M., & Bey, J. (2003). *Bright minds, beautiful ideas.* Amsterdam, Netherlands: BIS Publishers.

Nathan.com. (n.d.). *An evolving glossary of experience design.* Retrieved from www.nathan.com/ed/glossary/

Nel, D. F., & Kroeze, J. H. (2008) *Information technology as an agent of post-modernism.* Retrieved from Cogprints: http://cogprints.org/6207/

Olson, L. C., Finnegan, C. A., & Hope, D. S. (2008). *Visual rhetoric.* Thousand Oaks, CA: Sage.

Powell, J., & Lee, J. (2007). *Postmodernism for beginners* (2nd ed.). New York: Writers and Readers Publising.

Pullin, G. (2009). *Design meets disability.* Boston: MIT Press.

Rampley, M. (2005). *Exploring visual culture: Definitions, concepts, contexts.* Edinburgh, Scotland: Edinburgh University Press.

Riley, C. (2005). *Disability and the media: Prescriptions for change.* Lebanon, NH: University Press of New England.

Riley, C. (2006). *Disability and business.* Lebanon, NH: University Press of New England.

Sandahl, C., & Auslander, P. (2005). *Bodies in commotion.* Ann Arbor: University of Michigan Press.

Shields, D. (2010, March 14). *David Shields's post-postmodernism.* Retrieved from Biblioklept: http://biblioklept.org/2010/03/14/david-shieldss-post-postmodernism/

Sturken, M., & Cartwright, L. (2009). *Practices of looking: An introduction to visual culture.* New York: Oxford University Press.

TenStep. (2001–2010). *Glossary—terms and definitions.* Retrieved from http://www.lifecyclestep.com/open/miscpages/490.1Glossary.htm

Toplu, S., & Zapf, H. (2010). *Redefining modernism and postmodernism.* Newcastle Upon Tyne, UK: Cambridge Scholars.

University of Chicago. (1998). *Conference on after postmodernism.* Retrieved from http://www.focusing.org/apm.htm

Section III

Application to Social Work

Thinking, Knowledge, Values, Ethics, and Practice

15

Guidelines for Application to Social Work

❖

The part of the book that activates theory for social work practice has finally arrived. The previous chapters concentrated on a critical presentation of theory, and provided some illustrations of how each might look through an applied lens. We also shared our own theoretical preferences and which ones we put to work for ourselves in practice. This chapter advances guidelines for theory selection as purposive and legitimate for social work practice. So, let's jump in and begin to harness the universe of theory to inform social work action.

Scope of Social Work Thought

According to the Council on Social Work Education (2008),

> The purpose of the social work profession is to promote human and community well-being. Guided by a person and environment construct, a global perspective, respect for human diversity, and knowledge based on scientific inquiry, social work's purpose is actualized through its quest for social and economic justice, the prevention of conditions that limit human rights, the elimination of poverty, and the enhancement of the quality of life for all persons. (para. 1)

As likely apparent by now and as advanced in the preceding paragraph, the universe of theories about human experience that inform the broad range of what we do size the scope of social work thought.

Social work has undergone major longitudinal changes since its first graduating class in 1898 (Hepworth, Rooney, Rooney, Strom-Gottfried, & Larsen, 2009), from its roots in charity and poverty work (Ambrosino, Heffernan, Shuttlesworth, & Ambrosino, 2008) through its psychoanalytic-functionalism debate in the mid-20th century (DePoy & Gilson, 2007), and now arriving in the technological age of the 21st century with the vision expressed by Council on Social Work Education in the previous paragraph, and the National Association of Social Workers (2009), as follows:

> Technology competence is becoming integral to competent and responsible professional practice. Thus, it is imperative that the social work profession immediately develop a set of competencies for the use of technology in social work practice, based in direct practice, management, social work education, and research, and that NASW members actively seek opportunities for ongoing education and training in technology use. Training should include legal, ethical, and competency-based standards concerning the risks and benefits to clients and to the profession. It is equally important that NASW take a lead role in using various technologies, such as e-mail, the World Wide Web, and distance learning opportunities to improve members services, fulfill its mission, and achieve its goals. (para. 1)

Regardless of the content or context, as this brief journey from the origins of social work in charity to the contemporary recognition of technology as omnipotent reveals, social work thinking has been and is explicitly bounded by its values and ethics. Thus, a theoretical framework that foregrounds values and guides social work to think within this axiological perimeter is not only critical, but fundamental, to the profession of social work. We assert that explanatory legitimacy meets that challenge.

Through explanatory legitimacy, social work thinking is activated when the initial judgment about the legitimacy of a phenomenon for social work attention and response is verified and embedded within values applied to the theoretical explanation. So we turn to legitimacy now to clarify its definition and role in social work.

What Is Legitimacy?

As already introduced in Sections I and II, legitimacy is the third part of our conceptual framework. In this element, we make judgments regarding the scope of human description (activity, appearance, and experience) and explanations that fit within our professional domain, and the responses to those whom we accept as legitimate recipients of social work activity. Although description forms the initial basis for catching professional attention so to speak, decisions of legitimacy are based primarily on value judgments rendered about the fit and adequacy with social work values and scope of theoretical explanations for human behavior, not on the descriptive behavior, appearance, and experiences themselves.

> *When Dimitri was in high school, his atypical behavior, initially reported by the librarian, garnered a social worker's attention. According to the librarian, Dimitri was reclusive, disrespectful, and a troublemaker. These three characteristics are descriptive because the explanations for them were not clear to the social worker. But, these descriptors were sufficient for professional attention. Because the social worker explained these behaviors through the medical*

proximal-environment lens of "mental illness," she determined that Dimitri was a legitimate candidate for being excused from school for psychiatric assessment and then prescribed group therapy. In other words, he was a member of the category of "youth with emotional problems," and thus worthy of the response of therapy. But, consider what might have happened if the explanation for Dimitri's behaviors had been located within criminal justice theory as petty criminal activity? While the social worker's attention would have been caught by the same description as noted previously, students whose behavior was explained by unlawful intent would not have been legitimate recipients of therapy within the school. Rather, Dimitri might have been categorized as member of a different group, juvenile delinquents, and would have been sent to an alternative service system for a different and punitive response, and perhaps even another school.

Thus, building on current literature and theory (DePoy & Gilson, 2011; Jost & Major, 2001), we suggest that the attribution of legitimate membership status to an individual or group is a dynamic, value-based categorization that has little to do with the description but rather with judgments and beliefs about the explanations for human behavior, appearance, and experience.

THINKING POINT

Think of a category or group to which you belong. What criteria are used for membership? For exclusion? What values are inherent in these criteria?

We are not suggesting that people or groups who are determined to belong to any category do not share common actions, appearances, or experiences. We are, however, suggesting that we see description as diversity and explanation as pluralistic. As noted throughout the book, many explanations can be attributed to the same description, and all, some, or none may be accurate.

What if the accurate explanation for Dimitri's behavior was intent to commit petty crime, and the social worker responded to him through the explanatory lens of mental illness? Or what if both explanations were accurate?

These two questions illustrate the importance of determining the evidentiary basis for attributing explanations to description, as discussed throughout the book. Thus, description and explanation are evidence-based or, at least for the purpose of informing professional practice, should be based on credible knowledge and rigorously verified information, albeit pluralistic in nature.

There are numerous ways in which the social worker could verify the accuracy of her judgment about Dimitri, including looking into his history, administering a formal assessment, or seeking anecdotal information from others who know him. This information would be critical to affirm any explanation and then response to Dimitri's behavior.

Another example helps show the critical, and sometimes life and death need for verification of explanation.

Edna, an 86-year-old woman, lives alone in a small apartment and goes to a senior center each day. On a Tuesday, Edna's friend noticed that she seemed sad and called the social worker to ask what to do. The social worker decided that Edna qualified for social work attention, and conducted a clinical assessment. Edna's appearance and behavior were consistent with the explanation of clinical depression, a legitimate rationale within the social work scope of concern, and so the social worker's response was to refer Edna to a psychiatrist for medication and then work with Edna in a clinical setting. But, the night before Edna was to be seen by the psychiatrist, she lost consciousness in her home. Luckily, Edna's friend stopped over and found Edna, called the ambulance and saved her life. In the ER, the medical explanation of diabetes was attributed to explain Edna's behavior and appearance, and the response was hospitalization until her blood sugar was stabilized. Had the social worker verified her initial explanation of depression, she would have found that Edna was not depressed, but rather was medically unstable.

Why did the social worker miss this important piece of information, and thus choose the incorrect explanation? Because of her value on psychiatric explanations for behavior, the social worker delimited the range too narrowly, and missed the correct medical explanation, legitimacy determination, and response for Edna's condition.

As depicted in both examples, judgments and beliefs about the viability and correctness of explanations create the platform on which determination of group belongingness and response are made. Related to professional practice, the value judgment occurs at the point of deciding who belongs to the category of legitimate social service recipient and what professional response should be given on the basis of the explanation. But, importantly, it is a professional obligation to verify to the extent possible, that explanations are feasible and relevant.

Returning to Dimitri to illustrate, as previously presented, many youth exhibit a range of behaviors, similar to Dimitri's. The first question to be asked is how aberrant does behavior have to be before it attracts attention as something atypical? If we see youth behavior in categories of normal and not-normal, the categorical boundaries are drawn and individuals fit in one or the other. However, if we see behavior as a continuum of diversity, then responses can be afforded to all.

This point is discussed in detail in the chapters on legitimacy. Similarly, the host of reasons that humans behave in the ways that they do are vast and diverse as well. Expanding our explanatory tools not only increases our understandings, but has the potential to enhance our appreciation of the multiplicity of intentions and reasons for human activity, appearance, and experience. The explanations we choose are a function of knowledge framed within an axiological set of preferences.

What Are Values?

Debates about the definition and nature of human values have been recorded from antiquity through current times. So, we indulge in a meal of word soup once again. Table 15.1 illustrates the range of definitions revealed in a recent Google search.

Table 15.1   Definitions of *Value*

1. The quality (positive or negative) that renders something desirable or valuable; "the Shakespearean Shylock is of dubious value in the modern world" (Farlex, 2010b).

2. The amount (of money or goods or services) that is considered to be a fair equivalent for something else; "he tried to estimate the value of the produce at normal prices" (Lexipedia.com, 2010b).

3. Prize: hold dear; "I prize these old photographs" (Lexipedia.com, 2010a).

4. Respect: regard highly; think much of; "I respect his judgment"; "We prize his creativity" (HSBC Business Network).

5. Measure: place a value on; judge the worth of something; "I will have the family jewels appraised by a professional" (Farlex, 2010a).

6. An ideal accepted by some individual or group; "he has old-fashioned values" (Farlex, 2010b).

7. Value is a term that expresses the concept of worth in general, and it is thought to be connected to reasons for certain practices, policies, or actions (Wikipedia, n.d.).

8. The power of a thing to command other goods in exchange; the present worth of future rights to income and benefits arising from ownership (Office Finder Information and Referral Network, n.d.).

9. The monetary worth of property, goods or services (NC Buy, n.d.).

10. An expression of monetary worth of a particular piece of real estate (New York City Real Estate .com, n.d.).

11. Our sense of what something is "worth," financial benefits (Nathan.com, n.d.).

12. Value is the respondent's estimate of how much the property would sell for on the current market. For vacant units, value is the sales price asked for the property at the time of the interview and may differ from the price at which the property is sold. The "sales price asked" includes the price of a one-housing-unit structure and the land on which it is located. The "sales price asked" may also include additional structures such as garages, sheds, barns, etc (U.S. Census Bureau, 2005).

13. Is not only what the Museum was or would be willing to pay for the object. It also reflects the return on that investment, in the number of visitors that choose to see it, the number of students that wish to refer to it, the number of images that are sold or licensed throughout the world. It is a measure of demand for that particular work. It also should contain an element of what economists call Net Present Value (Ashley-Smith, 1995).

And, although diverse in their scope and nature, what all definitions of value have in common is the core foundation of value as human beliefs.

THINKING POINT

What distinguishes values from other beliefs, and why do values and not just any set of beliefs weigh in most heavily on legitimacy decisions?

The answer to the Thinking Point questions lies in the nature of values as beliefs about what is good, correct, moral, and ethical. Looking at historical word soup, *value* denoted belief about worth dating back to the 13th century (Harper, 2001–2010). Thus, inherent in values are rights and wrongs. The terms *values* and *ethics* are often used interchangeably, but there is distinction. Ethics are standards, and values are the belief in what standards should apply. Because of the ethical and moral foundation of values and value determinations, the context and shared beliefs are essential in asserting what is right, sound, and good in shaping our professional decisions.

> *Consider Dimitri again. If the explanation of intent to commit crime was attributed to his behavior, he would be seen as less valued than if his behavior was explained by mental illness despite the equivalence of his behavior. Each explanation begets a different category membership and response. Membership in the category of mental illness elicits treatment, while membership in the category of petty criminal is met with punishment.*

Now, let us clarify exactly what we mean by values and the contextual elements that surround them. As visited in our global tour of theories of human behavior, each lens carries with it an explicit or implicit definition of value. Building on the classic value scholarship that informs our legitimacy framework (Rokeach, 1973) and on the word soup recipes, we define *values* as the set of beliefs about the desirability and worth of descriptions and explanations (DePoy & Gilson, 2011). In agreement with Lewis (2000), we further distinguish values from other types of beliefs by their moral and action orientations. Applied to legitimacy, values guide who or what human behavior will qualify for social work attention and what professional action will ensue.

> *Dimitri, a few years later as a young college graduate, experienced what many youth report, a feeling of being lost. The social worker who encountered him did so within the value perimeter congruent with proximal interior-environment medicalization. Given Dimitri's history, the social worker applied the explanations that he valued to understanding the causes of Dimitri's current behavior, and thus determined that Dimitri's picture was explained by a diagnosable mental illness. But now, consider another scenario. What if the social worker valued religion as explanatory and curative rather than medicine? Dimitri's behavior might be explained by divine causes and his willingness to pray might have been the criterion for legitimacy as a client. From this explanatory alternative, the legitimate response might have been a spiritual retreat.*

Truth or Credibility

We have engaged in a wrestling match with this question throughout the book. Instead of asking if theory and its explanatory outcome are true, refer back to the previous chapters to see what is viable, purposive, and resonant with your professional and personal values. Through explanatory legitimacy, abductive rather than deductive logic is the keystone that provides stability and confidence in the pluralistic theoretical context of the 21st century. From this perspective, credibility of theory and support for professional decision making emerges from well-informed, rather than true, claims and actions. This principle transports us to the next value encased portal, that of evidence.

What Evidence Is Legitimate?

In social work, as in many other professional and academic fields, recent trends have favored scientifically generated evidence as the only worthy body of knowledge on which professional judgments should be made. However, remember that we introduced the postmodernists who pummeled science and repainted it as lexical symbol. They only added more fuel to the smoldering debate about the nature and role of science in social work and other practices based on social science theory (Sonnert & Holton, 2002). Numerous terms have been used in these discussions to describe professional activity that in some way uses or generates knowledge based on the principles of "scientific" inquiry. In part, the disagreement about what constitutes science and by extension, scientific inquiry, and how or even if science should form the foundation of social work judgment have contributed to the conflict about scientifically driven professional decision making (Gieryn, 1999). We would assert however, the systematically developed evidence, pluralistic in nature but following one or more of the three logic structures (deductive, inductive, abductive), is essential for selecting and applying theory to guide legitimate response decisions. (Refer back to Chapters 1 and 2 for a discussion of these structures.)

Each year in our research methods classes, students question the role of research in social work practice. As already discussed, we do not hold evidence-based practice models as the pinnacle of knowledge, and to the contrary, see the mechanical application of evidence-based knowledge as gross misuse of this logico-deductive framework. However, we still cling to the rigor and necessity of evidence, despite the diversity of its substance, framed by systematic logic as the valued way to come to know about and support practice. Remember that we referred to systematic evaluation as the relevant approach to social work knowledge. For us, evaluation research posits social problems, verifies them through systematic thinking, examines what we do from a logical eye, and then characterizes the result of social work through accepted thinking and action traditions. Thus, evaluation research in explanatory legitimacy is the valued and purposive amalgamation of knowledge for use and knowledge from use.

Purpose and Legitimacy

Of course, within the explanatory legitimacy home, professional judgment relies not only on systematically and logically generated evidence, but also on pluralism comprised of numerous contextual factors and professional and personal beliefs.

Look at Dimitri once again. If we accept the logico-deductive model of evidence that is prescribed by evidence-based practice as the only legitimate form of knowledge, then informal history, anecdotal information from high school, and Dimitri's values would not be as important as "objectively" generated evidence to consider in professional judgment and response. A strict evidence-based practice model would have directed the social worker to select a formal assessment to measure the magnitude of Dimitri's mental illness. The results of the assessment would be the primary basis for legitimate determination and response. Based on the results of the assessment, goals and objectives for professional intervention would be established, and the professional response would be selected from evidence based practice literature that demonstrated successful achievement of the specified goals.

It is next helpful to consider why this model is too restrictive to support social work professional judgments in the 21st century. First, social workers engage in practice in order to address social problems and issues. However, because a problem is a value statement about what is undesirable (DePoy & Gilson, 2008), empirical evidence does little to support opinion in the form of problem claims. A closer analysis of the role of deductive models of inquiry in illuminating social problems reveals that approach to research can examine and document the magnitude, frequency, and even predictors of a theorized social phenomenon. Inquiry can even examine the degree to which people view such social phenomena as problematic. However, deductive models of inquiry cannot attribute problem status to social phenomena. Because we suggest that the role of empirical evidence in social work practice is encased in a value perimeter, problem ascription and the relevance of problems for social work practice are variable and depend on who is seated in the definitional power seat, so to speak.

Second, in evidence-based models, the empirical evidence to underpin judgment and response is based on dualistic models of inquiry (Gambrill, 2006; Smith, 2008), that is to say, by researchers who use etic and "objective" logical approaches. Therefore, inconsistent with contemporary pluralistic methodologies, reliance on experimental-type traditions diminishes other forms of knowledge as acceptable and valid evidence (DePoy & Gitlin, 2011; Smith, 2008). The criterion of objectively generated knowledge continues to support a knowledge hierarchy that harkens back to the Enlightenment and is no longer canonized as the single way of coming to know.

A third and critical limitation of evidence-based practice is the application of nomothetically derived knowledge to idiographic concerns. We remind you that nomothetic knowledge aims to describe and explain common characteristic of groups and differentiate them from one another on that basis, while idiographic knowledge describes and explains uniqueness and difference. While we believe that nomothetic knowledge is one essential pathway to predicting the outcome of professional activity, we suggest that it is insufficient as the sole source of evidence for contemporary professional judgment. Given the growing emphasis on diversity, pluralism, and interdisciplinarity in social work and other fields, knowledge of group commonalities does not necessarily capture a full range of varied and unique experiences and needs necessary to inform value-based social work thinking and action. Considering the purposive context of knowledge generation in itself, the assertion that experimental-type design rigor and structure determine quality is a myth that limits the critical assessment of knowledge for use in social work judgment.

Denise is a social worker, and thus engages in clinical practice. In a recent interview with students, she defined child neglect and poverty as the social problem that she most frequently encounters. Yet, she provides cognitive behavioral therapy to youth so that they can feel more positive about themselves and feel confident. Her rationale for this intervention is that evidence-based practice has shown that cognitive behavioral methods are the best brief methods to alleviate or derail depression. So, Denise values therapy as her intervention and turns to evidence-based practice to support her choice of techniques, but is left on the dock as the social-problem boat sails away and nothing is done about poverty and neglect.

The nature of evidence itself continues as an important area of debate. Because social work practice theories (Kirst-Ashman & Zastrow, 2009; Toseland & Rivas, 2002) stress use of self and the relationship between client and professional, the incompatibility of logico-deductive thinking with the relational foundations of practice is often raised. Moreover, different groups value different forms of evidence as credible. For example, the legal profession bases decisions on anecdote, precedent, and logical argument, not experimental-type evidence, and the clergy holds liturgy as the evidentiary basis for judgment. Thus, different forms of evidence are credible for different professional and other interest groups (DePoy & Gilson, 2008). Nomothetic models of evidence-based practice borrowed from fields such as medicine do not necessarily address these issues in the hierarchy of worthy evidence, and thus are often antithetical to the commitment to respect for diversity as it applies to acceptable evidence for professional judgment and response in the world of the 21st century.

> *Looking at Dimitri again, suppose that the strategy supported by purposive, evidence-based practice defining therapeutic outcomes is group therapy and medication. But, what if Dimitri is shy because he stutters, and thus values art and visual representation over verbal communication? Idiographic, not nomothetic, knowledge would reveal this important piece of evidence.*

Finally, and perhaps most important to consider, evidence-based practice is focused on what content to use as the basis for legitimate judgment and response. While the nature of knowledge is important, how one uses knowledge in decision making is the more critical concern for social work (Gambrill, 2006). However, we suggest that critical thinking must be applied to all professional judgment, including the evidence that is legitimate to support judgment and response.

Legitimate Evidence for Social Work

Throughout the book, we suggest that evidence (defined broadly as knowledge to support a claim) be used as the basis for judgment and response in a purposive, expansive, pluralistic, and reflective manner. That is, we suggest that all forms of evidence should be considered, but not necessarily accepted, as supportive of professional judgment. Six axioms advance thinking about legitimacy judgment and choosing a cogent response, presented in Table 15.2.

We suggest that professional judgment occur through the purposive application of diverse sets of logically generated and selected evidence to the definition and clarification of description, explanation, and legitimacy determination and response. Consistent with the explanatory legitimacy frame of reference, this approach is not a significant departure from current approaches, but rather provides an organizational foundation through which to evaluate the credibility, scope, and purpose of evidence and to consider multiple forms of evidence to describe, select, and verify viable explanations, and make legitimacy determinations. Because each of the three elements of explanatory

Table 15.2 Legitimacy Judgment and Response Axioms

1. Social workers should be vigilant in scrutinizing their professional decisions and the rationale for them.
2. Professional knowledge and its use are purposive, contextual, and value-encased.
3. Professional knowledge is pluralistic, with multiple forms of credible evidence, theory, and methods for knowledge generation.
4. Professional evidence should be systematically generated and used with one or more logic structures as the foundation for thinking and action.
5. Professional social work evidence for social work thinking and action should not be sloppy or vague.
6. Why and how a body of knowledge is used should be clearly understood and articulated when a social worker is asked for or thinks about a rationale for intervention.

legitimacy call for different forms of evidence, no single type of knowledge suffices to support professional thinking. Description involves multiple sources, including knowledge derived from systematic observation (observables), from logical inference (reportables), or from narrative (reportables). Explanation requires knowledge of the scope and range of literature and theory that can provide a sound, relevant rationale for description, not for preferred intervention. Legitimacy requires the careful, purposive, and reflexive integration of acceptable evidence, values, and ethics to the logical and systematic selection of intervention and articulation of process and outcome.

Reconsider the options of the social worker who initially approached Dimitri in high school. Description was ascertained through observation, explanation through knowledge of theory, and legitimacy judgment and response on the basis of evaluation of the worth of the explanation for Dimitri's unacceptable behavior.

But, also consider Denise, who defined the intervention before ever seeing clients.

Taxonomy of Legitimacy: Proximal to Distal Environments and Ideas

Now that we have discussed and illustrated legitimacy and suggested a set of axioms and model for thinking about description, explanation, and legitimacy judgment and response, we reiterate the brief taxonomy for our discussions of legitimacy from previous chapters. As discussed throughout the book, we have organized descriptive and explanatory theories into the following divisions: developmental, environmental, categorical, systems, and new and emerging theories. Each has implications for professional judgment at multiple levels of concern, from judgments and responses proximal to human environments through the full range of elements, and then to the range of proximal through distal environments and the abstract universe of ideas. Legitimacy proximal to humans focuses on judgment and response that are designed to change elements of individuals. Distal environmental legitimacy is concerned with judgment and response to change environments distal to the corpus, and legitimacy of ideas is concerned with judgment and response to abstracts such as policy, theory, research, values, and other forms of knowledge. The theory genres exemplify this point. Thus, each of the following chapters on legitimacy begins by discussing legitimacy of proximal to distal environments and ideas inherent in the specific category of theory. The relationship between theoretical values and social work values are then examined, concluding with exemplars of how each theory division could be used in social work practice. Before we conclude this chapter, we turn to the value base of social work.

Social Work Values

There are numerous perspectives on what constitutes the value base of social work practice. Two different, but central, approaches include the value base that appears in the National Association of Social Workers (NASW) *Code of Ethics* (Table 15.3) preamble and the value foundation that is advanced by the Council on Social Work Education (CSWE) (Table 15.4).

Table 15.3   Social Work Values as Stated in the NASW *Code of Ethics* (2010)

The primary mission of the social work profession is to enhance human well-being and help meet the basic human needs of all people, with particular attention to the needs and empowerment of people who are vulnerable, oppressed, and living in poverty. A historic and defining feature of social work is the profession's focus on individual well-being in a social context and the well-being of society. Fundamental to social work is attention to the environmental forces that create, contribute to, and address problems in living.

Social workers promote social justice and social change with and on behalf of clients. "Clients" is used inclusively to refer to individuals, families, groups, organizations, and communities. Social workers are sensitive to cultural and ethnic diversity and strive to end discrimination, oppression, poverty, and other forms of social injustice. These activities may be in the form of direct practice, community organizing, supervision, consultation, administration, advocacy, social and political action, policy development and implementation, education, and research and evaluation. Social workers seek to enhance the capacity of people to address their own needs. Social workers also seek to promote the responsiveness of organizations, communities, and other social institutions to individuals' needs and social problems.

The mission of the social work profession is rooted in a set of core values. These core values, embraced by social workers throughout the profession's history, are the foundation of social work's unique purpose and perspective:

- service
- social justice
- dignity and worth of the person
- importance of human relationships
- integrity
- competence

This constellation of core values reflects what is unique to the social work profession. Core values, and the principles that flow from them, must be balanced within the context and complexity of the human experience.

Table 15.4 CSWE Value Statement
Service, social justice, the dignity and worth of the person, the importance of human relationships, integrity, competence, human rights, and scientific inquiry are among the core values of social work. These values underpin the explicit and implicit curriculum and frame the profession's commitment to respect for all people and the quest for social and economic justice.

Source: Council on Social Work Education, 2008

The social work value perimeter advanced by NASW defines "good" societies within general characteristics. These elements provide the targets for social change at multiple levels. The CSWE value statement lays out the elements of professional education and professional obligation of social workers to accept these commitments.

Using the NASW values as guidelines, social work practice would strive to engage in service at multiple levels of concern in order to achieve social justice, and to promote the dignity and worth of clients. All social work relationships would embody integrity and social workers would exercise competence in all professional activity. Adhering to CSWE values, social workers would subscribe to similar values but would add inquiry to their toolbox. As postmodernist theory foregrounds, however, the terms that are used in value statements have multiple interpretations and can serve as grand narratives. In other words, what do social justice, integrity, and dignity mean? As already evident throughout previous chapters, the meaning of these value statements and how they are operationalized in practice are local and largely dependent on the theoretical flavors through which we taste the terms.

Looking at the term *social justice,* for instance, does it mean that individuals should all have equality of opportunity to behave as they choose? Or, does it mean that social groups should lay out expected behaviors for all who want to remain within or join the group? Both are examples of different approaches to social justice, one respecting the rights of individuals and the other respecting the rights of the majority.

How do we interpret social work values to assure that we are practicing efficaciously, respectfully, and competently within the professional domain? Our answer is to know and be able to articulate why we are acting; to be vigilant in assuring that our reasons are logical; to clearly identify the knowledge base that frames our view of humans, that identifies what is good and desirable, and what is not; and to clearly state the evidence rationale for engaging in Plan A over Plan B.

Summary

This chapter defined legitimacy as determination for professional acceptance of a "client" or phenomenon for legitimate social work response. The role of values in determining membership and eligibility in the club of social work concern was examined, and then applied to eligibility for social work services. The second part of legitimacy, response, was then discussed and its application to social work action was analyzed. The chapter concluded with an examination of the value bases of social work that guide our professional scope and decision making.

References

Ambrosino, R., Heffernan, J., Shuttlesworth, G., & Ambrosino, R. (2008). *Social work and social welfare: An introduction*. Belmont, CA: Thomson.

Ashley-Smith, J. (1995). *Definitions of damage*. Retrieved from Conservation Online: http://cool.conservation-us.org/byauth/ashley-smith/damage.html

Council on Social Work Education. (2008, November 17). Retrieved from Education Policy and Accreditation Standards: http://www.cswe.org

DePoy, E. & Gilson, S. (2008). *Evaluation practice: How to do good evaluation research in work settings*. New York: Routledge.

DePoy, E., & Gilson, S. F. (2011). *Studying disability: Multiple theories and responses*. Thousand Oakes, CA: Sage Publications.

DePoy, E. & Gitlin, L. (2011). *Introduction to research: Multiple strategies for health and human services, 4th ed.* St. Louis, MO: Mosby.

Farlex. (2010a). *Ideal*. Retrieved from the Free Dictionary: http://www.thefreedictionary.com/ideal

Farlex. (2010b). *Monetary value*. Retrieved from the Free Dictionary: http://www.thefreedictionary.com/monetary+value

Gambrill, E. (2006). *Social work practice: A critical thinker's guide*. New York: Oxford University Press.

Gieryn, T. F. (1999). *Cultural boundaries of science: Credibility on the line*. Chicago: University of Chicago Press.

Google.com. (n.d.). *Value definitions*. Retrieved from http://www.google.com/search?hl=en&lr=&client=safari&rls=en&oi=defmore&defl=en&q=define:value

Harper, D. (2001–2010). *On-line etymology dictionary*. Retrieved from http://www.etymonline.com/index.php?search=ethnic&searchmode=none

Hepworth, D. H., Rooney, R. H., Rooney, G. D., Strom-Gottfried, K., & Larsen, J. A. (2009). *Direct social work practice: Theory and skills*. Belmont, CA: Cenagebrain.

HSBC Business Network. (n.d.). *The value of you!* Retrieved from http://network.hsbc.co.uk/topic/Open-Talk/Value/1700003308&

Jost, J. T., & Major, B. (2001). *The psychology of legitimacy: Emerging perspectives on ideology, justice, and intergroup relations*. New York: Cambridge University Press.

Kirst-Ashman, K. K., & Zastrow, C. H. (2009). *Understanding human behavior and the social environment* (8th ed.). Belmont, CA: Brooks/Cole.

Lewis, H. (2000). *A question of values: Six ways we make the personal choices that shape our lives*. Crozet, VA: Axios Press.

Lexipedia.com. (2010a). *Appreciate*. Retrieved from http://www.lexipedia.com/english/appreciate

Lexipedia.com. (2010b). *Nuisance value*. Retrieved from http://www.lexipedia.com/english/nuisance+value

Nathan.com. (n.d.). *An evolving glossary of experience design*. Retrieved from www.nathan.com/ed/glossary/

National Association of Social Workers. (2010). *Code of ethics*. Retrieved from www.socialworkers.org/pubs/code/default.asp

NC Buy. (n.d.). *Credit center*. Retrieved from www.ncbuy.com/credit/glossary.html

New York City Real Estate.com (n.d.). *Glossary V.* Retrieved from http://www.new-york-new-york-real-estate.com/v1.html

Office Finder Information and Referral Network. (n.d.). *Glossary of real estate terms.* Retrieved from http://www.officefinder.com/gloss2.html

Resnik, D. B. (1997). *Some definitions of key ethics concepts.* Retrieved from http://www.scicom.lth.se/fmet/ ethics_03.html

Rokeach, M. (1973). *The nature of human values.* New York: Free Press.

Smith, Q. (2008). *Epistemology.* New York: Oxford University Press.

Sonnert, G., & Holton, G. (2002). *Ivory bridges: Connecting science and society.* Cambridge, MA: MIT Press.

Toseland, R. W., & Rivas, R. F. (2002). *An introduction to group work practice* (4th ed.). Upper Saddle River, NJ: Pearson Education.

U.S. Bureau of the Census. (2005). *Housing vacancies and home ownership.* Retrieved from http://www.census.gov/hhes/www/housing/hvs/qtr105/q105def.html

Wikipedia. (n.d.). *Value.* Retrieved from en.wikipedia.org/wiki/Value

16

Application of Developmental Theory to Social Work

❖

C hapters 3 through 5 discussed two categories of developmental theory, grand and specific. Both categories inform our understanding of humans as they pass through chronological time. This chapter embarks on the "so what" about these theories and tries to answer, within the framework of explanatory legitimacy, how bathing in this genre of theoretical knowledge can be analyzed and used to make professional decisions and to inform professional action.

Remember, we assert that legitimacy decisions are value determinations based on explanations, not descriptions. That is to say, legitimacy is a determination of the appropriateness and worth of an explanation for professional response. So, before illustrating theory-specific legitimacy, the first step, as a foundational task, is to examine the values inherent in development theories. The next task is to examine the congruence of these values with the value base of social work.

Common Developmental Theory Values

The last chapter conveyed that theories informing and advancing understanding about humans are built on values, whether or not explicated, about what is human, the limits of "humanness," and what is desirable and undesirable about humans. Developmental theories are particularly vocal in defining the desirable parameters of human description and explanation in diverse chronological cohorts. They broadcast theorized norms, and to the contrary, what is not normal, implying a desirable manner for human unfolding and floating across the chronology of a life.

If we look at psychoanalytic theory, we see that babies are supposed to explore through putting objects in their mouths, but adults are not. Thus, based on this explanation, if we saw an adult sucking his thumb, that descriptive behavior through the explanatory psychoanalytic lens would be considered as abnormal, infantile, and undesirable—sufficient to warrant professional attention and change.

THINKING POINT

Think about how developmental theory has influenced your life in school and at home. How did developmental theory influence those who taught you and took care of you?

Although developmental theories are diverse in their foci, they are all relatives by virtue of sharing the values listed in Table 16.1.

Table 16.1 Common Developmental Theory Values

1. Average is desirable.
2. Conformity to averages is desirable.
3. Average is prescriptive.
4. Orderly, prescribed progression through chronology is desirable.
5. Quantitative and qualitative growth are associated over time.
6. Experience-rich environments produce learning and growth.
7. Proximal through distal environments should be age appropriate.
8. Supportive, appropriate learning environmental conditions produce learning and growth.
9. Maturation, learning and growth up to the point of decline are expected.
10. Nomothetic evidence (generated by examining groups) provides the systematic nourishment for verification of theory.

Looking closely at the narrative of developmental theories, the inherent value on averages is typically the leading character. In other words, developmental theories hold what is typical and most common for an age cohort as generally desirable and what is not typical as anomalous and for the most part undesirable (that is, of course, unless one is ahead of one's age group in valued areas of growth). Moreover, as individuals age over time, they should exhibit similar trajectories that increasingly build on previous experience, skill, and capability.

Thus, the example of psychoanalytic explanations for thumb sucking would suggest that infants should engage in this behavior in order to grow and develop during their oral phase, while adults should not. In order to learn and integrate adult behaviors, as children proceed to age, they should relinquish oral behavior and replace it with other forms of more mature exploration and satisfaction. Note that the word should *reveals a value judgment.*

To a large extent, these values have much to do with the epistemology, or way in which we come to know about and document developmental elements of life. This is discussed further under the section of this chapter on developmental legitimacy of ideas.

Proximal Environmental Developmental Legitimacy

Remember that we defined *proximal environmental legitimacy* as the element that is most concerned with the individual human. One of the most important elements of concern to social work decision making and response informed by developmental theories is the comparative unfolding of an individual human over time. Developmental descriptions tell us what is desirable, developmental explanations tell us why. And, refracted through explanatory legitimacy, it is the "why" that determines if the description will catch the social work gaze, be deemed legitimate for social work response, and that shapes the response that we proffer.

Consider the life of Larry, a 24-year-old man who can be described as atypical in his appearance, behavior, and experience. At birth, Larry's facial features looked different from those of typical white neonates. His eyes were almond shaped and he had an atypical crease on the palms of his hands. As he matured over his first 2 years of life, compared to his age counterparts, he walked at a much later age than the average, he was not toilet trained at 4-years-old, an atypical age for this task, and his muscle tone was floppier (weaker) than the average expected of his age. At the age of 4, his intelligence test showed a lower than average score for his age group. These longitudinal descriptions identify what is different about Larry in relation to his age and ethnic cohorts. But, the descriptors do not tell us why, and thus legitimacy decisions cannot be made simply on description.

Because of his corporeal and behavioral descriptors, Larry was diagnosed with Down syndrome shortly after his birth. This proximal corporeal explanation provided a well-accepted rationale for Larry's differences, and located him clearly in the realm of social work concern. As an individual whose descriptive patina was explained by a genetic syndrome, Larry was characterized and responded to as developmentally delayed. Because the social worker applied Piagetian and Eriksonian explanations to predicting Larry's future, and thus expected Larry to follow a slower learning and social developmental trajectory than his age counterpart, Larry was placed in specialized child care with others who were similar to him in intelligence and task achievement.

But now, consider Andy, who, like Larry, demonstrated slower than average descriptors over his first 2 years of life, compared to his age counterparts. He walked at a much later age than the average and was not toilet trained by 4. Also like Larry, Andy's intelligence test at age 4 showed a lower than average score for his age group. Thus, Andy's developmental description was equivalent to Larry's. But unlike Larry, the explanation for Andy's atypical description was explained by developmental delays because of an impoverished environment. And thus, unlike Larry, the professional response to the explanation for Andy's descriptive picture was different. Andy was placed in Head Start, which is founded on the developmental theoretical value that stimulating environmental learning conditions distal to the corpus produce cognitive and social growth and development. Although both boys exhibited equivalent descriptions that caught the eye of the social worker, the legitimacy determination and response were different for each on the basis of the explanation.

Now consider Maria and Juanita, twin sisters, both now 12 years of age. According to their mother, Rosa, Maria has always been a "model child" and Juanita has always been the "problem child." These two terms reveal the value placed on each girl's description. Maria, the model child, exhibited the desired behaviors of commitment to studying, enjoying productive sports activity outside of school, and engaging willingly in helping her mother around the house. Juanita, although loving to her family and friends, spent most of her time playing the piano at the expense of her academic grades. Thus, in this family, desirable behavior appropriate for age 12 was characterized as helping, achieving in school, and engaging in productive sports, all behaviors which are considered to be developmentally typical and worthy of early adolescence classification. Because she was worried about Juanita, Rosa took Juanita to see a social worker. After determining that the explanation for Juanita's behavior was a great talent in and love of classical piano, the social worker advised Rosa not to worry and to support her child as she developed her music career.

In this example, developmental descriptive expectations framed Rosa's concerns but also shaped the explanation for Juanita's perceived deviance from the desired norm, and provided the basis on which the social worker made her recommendation. What if the social worker had learned that Juanita turned to music because she was afraid to compete with her sister? That explanation would certainly have elicited a different response, since a fear rationale for developmental description is considered aberrant and restrictive of future normative growth and development.

The examples provide a segue to the values that developmental theories place on distal environments. Developmental theories prescribe the "proper conditions" in which humans should live. As noted in Table 16.1, stimulating and socially supportive conditions are valued over stressful, sparse distal environments.

Look at the responses to both Larry and Andy. Because the explanation for Larry's atypical developmental description was believed to be unchangeable, the expectations for "slower than average" growth and development located response in learning conditions in which his pace fit that of others. Thus, Larry was "normalized" so to speak, not by stimulating the pace of his individual growth, but through changing the social conditions around him so that he fit and was typical in that social cohort. Andy, on the other hand, was placed in a distal learning environment that adhered to valued conditions inherent in developmental explanations. Through stimulating and supportive features, Andy's individual growth and development was predicted to accelerate to the point of achieving at the level that is typical for his age cohort.

THINKING POINT

 Remember back to your elementary school. How tall were your peers? What did they like to do? What artifacts were in your classrooms? Think of the nature of children's books, children's television, clothes, movies, and so forth. Now, think of your high school peers, classroom, books, clothes, and resources.

Considering the importance of age appropriateness in environments, we suspect that both sets of descriptors you identified in the Thinking Point are very different, given the different age cohorts who are expected to learn and interact in each. In our practice experience on a short-term, adult mental health inpatient unit, one of the major issues of concern to the staff was to assure that the unit artifacts and decorations were age appropriate. Looking at that concern through the lens of developmental legitimacy, we did not want the clients to feel "infantilized" or remanded to a less mature period of time by hanging juvenile images on the walls.

To summarize so far, in identifying the values about environments proximal through distal that are common to developmental theories, the "average" trajectory over time is desirable, and that the most acceptable distal environments are those in which typical description is fostered through stimulation and support. Moreover, in the absence of responses that are believed to move atypical individuals closer to the average, the valued response is to homogenize the distal social environment so that no one is too aberrant. At this point, you might be wondering how knowledge based on this set of values emerges and becomes central to professional thinking. Let us turn to legitimacy of developmental ideas to enhance our understanding.

Developmental Theory Legitimacy of Ideas

First, we revisit the derivation of developmental theories to understand what is valued as their evidentiary basis. As noted in the last chapter and in Table 16.1, most of the theories that characterize growth and development are nomothetic. That is to say, they are based on the commonalities that are observed in groups of people, not on the lives of individuals.

THINKING POINT

Identify how the theories in Chapters 3 through 5 are nomothetic.

The nomothetic process of inquiry involves observation of groups by researchers and theorists, verification of hunches through measuring the magnitude of what is observed and related to those observations, and then ascription as "truth" of those observations that stand up to this type of scrutiny.

The Wechsler Adult Intelligence Scale (Weschler, 2010), or what is commonly known as the WAIS-IV, measures adult intelligence in four theoretical spheres of cognition, verbal comprehension, perceptual reasoning, working memory, and process speed. The test yields total and subscale scores that compare individuals against the total group of those who take the test. To derive and finalize the most recent iteration, 2,200 subjects from the United States, ranging in age from 16 to 90 years of age, and 688 Canadians in a similar age span, participated. This sample was chosen to be as "representative as possible" of the whole population in the United States and then extended beyond U.S. borders to render the test more "global." By representative, we mean that the sample of 2, 200 + 688 was selected to exhibit the proportion of gender and other categorical population characteristics (or what we refer to as diversity patina*). Based on the performance of the subjects, the average intelligence scores for specified age cohorts were established.*

Thus, from theory of what is most common to group members, we derive theory of what is typical and normal, and then on that basis, assert theory of "what should be." Further, based on this approach to knowledge generation and then prescription of desirable averages, developmental theories provide a scaffold for expected growth and maturation over time. They allow us to locate individuals within their age groups and compare them to others within that same slice of the life span. They prompt us to distinguish the characteristics of different age cohorts from one another. The desirable human is theoretically cooked up to be one who fits within what is typical for the individual's similar age buddies and follows a trajectory through chronology in a manner that is not too far from how age mates proceed.

Applying developmental legitimacy of ideas to the selection of research methods, the experimental-type tradition (DePoy & Gitlin, 2011) would be most valued in developmental theory development and verification. This tradition, as described, seeks to test theoretical constructs and principles on a sample of subjects primarily through defining, isolating, and then measuring phenomena. The results in the form of numeric statistics about group averages and deviations from those emblems of normalcy are then interpreted to describe, relate, or predict the phenomenon under study. Groups can be compared against one another to exhume and predict the causes of differences in findings.

Suppose you observed that as people age, they seem to acquire social wisdom that they did not have in young adulthood. Using the legitimate research tradition of developmental theory, you would define wisdom, *and determine a strategy to measure it. Then, in two samples, one representing young adulthood and one representing middle adulthood, you would test and compare scores on your wisdom assessment. Based on the results, you would verify or falsify your hunch about acquisition of wisdom over time.*

THINKING POINT

Can you describe how the experimental-type research tradition leads us to look at commonalities, and thus averages, as valued?

Individuals are not considered as the unit of analysis, but rather, the legitimate aim is to differentiate group characteristics.

THINKING POINT

As you think about the preceding example, note another point about the logic sequence. Theory development begins with observation of commonalities. Then, those commonalities are named and defined, and then verified and venerated through testing what was observed. In this logical sequence, can you see any circular thinking? We begin by defining what we observe and then seek to observe what we define.

Developmental legitimacy of ideas is an important influence on another set of ideas, policy. Consider the U.S. policies that are based on age. Among the many national, state, local, and corporate policies are those governing education, social resources and benefits, voting, driving, health and health insurance, criminal justice, employment, and so forth.

Consider public school. Throughout the United States, public school is organized into grade levels, typically beginning at kindergarten and then proceeding sequentially up through 12th grade. Normative expectations for entrance into each grade are based on age and the extent to which a student's skill conforms to expectations that are age specific.

THINKING POINT

Can you describe how the public schools' grade system is based on developmental explanations for social and cognitive skill acquisition and development?

If an alternative theoretical explanation such as behaviorism were at the root of public school organization, grade levels arranged on the basis of age would be replaced by distal environmental explanations and students might be divided by the type reinforcements that we prefer (e.g., praise, monetary reward, recreation time). We do not mean to imply that behavioral theory is not used to structure and explain learning and guide pedagogy. Rather, this example illustrates the primacy of developmental explanations in shaping school organizations and the legitimate criteria for advancement from one grade to another.

THINKING POINT

How might schools be structured if they were based on categorical theories? Compare and contrast your vision to the current public school policy based on developmental theory.

Developmental explanations form the legitimate foundation for policy decisions in many arenas, particularly those that assume eligibility for resources and privilege on the assumptions that one's passage through time explains social, cognitive, and moral maturation.

Consider eligibility to drive, drink alcohol, vote, get married without parental permission, give consent for medical intervention, receive social security, retire, and enter into legal contracts.

To tease out the legitimacy determination and response for these policies, consider Peter, a 17-year-old male, and Steve, an 18-year-old male. Both Peter and Steve want to join the army. Both young men have graduated from the same high school with 3.0 grade point averages, both have worked at the local hardware and paint shop since they were 16, and both have equivalent physical, social, cognitive, and other skills. For the most part, Peter and Steve are equivalent in behavior, appearance, and experience. However, Peter must get parental permission to join the army, and on the basis of age explanation, Steve does not. The assumption that a youth at age 18 is more socially mature than a youth at age 17 derives from developmental theories that explain maturation as cumulative over chrono-logical time.

Now, to raise some important cautions about developmental legitimacy, consider a recent article in the New York Times *(Social Security, 2010) that discussed the threats to the pen-sion system in the United States. A major factor in the potential bankruptcy of the pension system is the increasing life span, and thus years of supported retirement of the American employee. If we look at this problem through developmental legitimacy, we see that eligibil-ity for retirement and pension is based on the explanation of years worked and chrono-logical age. However, the failure to adjust the explanatory age criterion for benefit eligibility has created a situation in which many workers who retired after 30 years of employment (e.g., automobile manufacturing) are living longer as retirees than as workers. Using the developmental explanation of age as the basis for retirement has increased the dollars paid out beyond the dollars paid into the system, thereby creating a crisis in pension stability for many American workers.*

The example of retirement policy suggests two points about the use of develop-mental explanations for legitimacy determinations and responses. First, it is important to continue to study longitudinal demographics and to verify the contextual accuracy of developmental descriptions and explanations on a regular basis. What may have been a sound developmental rationale for legitimacy determination and response, at one time, may no longer be relevant and accurate today.

Second and most important, if using developmental theory for legitimacy deci-sions, it is necessary to recognize that developmental legitimacy of ideas refers to developmental theory as well as ideas informed by it. What we mean is that the viabil-ity of developmental theory for application should be judged within its own matura-tional time frame, so as not to apply theory from a different context to contemporary societies that have evolved beyond the explanatory power of the theory itself. This gets ahead of our theoretical genres here, suggesting context be considered. However, espousal and cogent use of developmental theory warrants its advancement into the 21st century such that factors other than the unfolding of the corpus be engaged.

THINKING POINT

Have you noticed how, over the past several decades, women's shoe stores tend not to have sizes below a U.S. size 6? Can you explain how contemporary developmental approaches would have informed this business decision?

Revisiting the pension policy example, had the policy makers been as astute as the shoe corporations, perhaps developmental theory would have been revised to increase the age at which people are theorized to desire termination of full-time, remunerative work.

Now that we have examined and analyzed the application of developmental theory to legitimacy decisions and actions regarding humans, distal environments, and ideas, let us consider the fit of developmental theory with social work values.

Fitting Developmental Legitimacy With the Value Base of Social Work

Table 16.2 illustrates the articulation of social work and developmental legitimacy values.

Table 16.2   Social Work Values and Developmental Legitimacy

	Social Justice	Integrity	Respect for Individual Dignity and Worth
Developmental legitimacy	Responsibilities and rights are linked to conformity to age appropriate behavior, with increasing responsibility accruing over the life span until perceived decline. As one proceeds through orderly development, benefits of citizenship are increasingly earned until perceived decline.	Adherence to moral principles are the basis for decision making, and behavior evolves over chronological time until perceived decline.	Dignity and worth inhere in all stages and ages, within the acceptable limits of age appropriate behavior.

As depicted in Table 16.2, through the lens of developmental legitimacy, each of the central social work values acquires three boundaries: age appropriateness; increasing attribution of worth as an individual matures chronologically up to the point of perceived decline; and conformity to a greater or lesser extent to what is typical, common, and thus expected.

In criminal justice, one major factor in determining who belongs to the category of criminal, and then what the legitimate response should be, is one's age. If an individual perpetrates

harm against another, age is an important factor in determining the extent to which an individual is held responsible for his or her actions and integrity, the extent to which dignity and worth should be conferred upon an individual, and the extent to which rights should be conferred or removed. Through the developmental portal, individuals whose moral development is considered to be incomplete are not held as responsible for their own integrity as those who are expected to have acquired adulthood and adherence to mature and accepted moral standards.

Minor children who commit crimes become legitimate members in the category of juvenile delinquency, begetting responses that curtail their rights to some extent. However, in comparison to adults, minor children are not held as accountable for their actions and the moral decisions that underpin them, and thus are afforded more lenient responses than adults who perpetrate equivalent behavior. As we often read in the news, decisions on how to try youth who are embarking on adulthood, but are not yet of majority age, are often contentious; they also depend on the legitimate determinations of the perpetrator's assumed capacity to know the scope and boundaries of socially acceptable morals, and intent to violate them.

THINKING POINT

Think of an example to illustrate the intersection of social justice and developmental values.

Developmental Social Work Legitimacy: A Case Illustration

Now let us turn to an example to illustrate the use of developmental theories for social work legitimacy in the domains of the proximal to distal environments and ideas.

Consider the application of developmental legitimacy to the social work practice domain with humans. Rachel is 78 and lives in her own apartment. Five years ago, she had a major stroke which left her unable to walk or care for her daily needs. Until his death from a massive heart attack last month, Rachel's husband Lev took care of her with the assistance of two personal care attendants, Barbara and Karen.

Now, after Lev's death, Irving, their 51-year-old son, comes to you for clinical intervention. Descriptively, Irving exhibits sadness about the loss of his father and anger toward his mother, whom Irving describes as a major burden for his father, and thus, in large part holds her responsible for his father's death. Using a longitudinal explanatory lens, you locate Irving's descriptive symptoms within chronological stages of grief. On that developmental explanatory basis, you determine that he is a legitimate client for an ongoing response aimed at helping him negotiate the chronological stages of grief and acceptance of his father's death. Moreover, using a developmental lens for age appropriate behavior, you further explain Irving's reported sadness by his perception that he is now entering the "older generation" in his family. Given the theoretical evidence that individuals adjust to loss over time, you expect that with support from weekly counseling, he will improve.

As time goes on, you notice that Irving is not adhering to predicted chronological grief stages of behavior and emotions, and that contrary to becoming less angry, he plans to place his mother in a nursing home, unbeknownst to her and despite her competence and autonomy. Assessing him for integrity, and then weighing the social justice issues of aging relevant to his mother's rights as an individual who has aged without cognitive decline, you search for another explanation for Irving's intended plans.

As a generalist social worker, after your clinical encounter with Irving, you become concerned with developmental legitimacy applied to the domains of the distal environment and policy. Because of your commitment to social justice, integrity, and individual dignity and worth, you decide to work within your social service agency environment not only as a clinician, but also as a program developer. You aim to expand options for elder care and limit unnecessary and unwanted institutional care. You first look at developmental legitimacy to set expectations for chronological change in aging. Based on developmental theory, you work within your own agency to delimit the acceptable boundaries for membership in the categories of elder competence and incompetence to live in the community and make independent autonomous decisions about one's life. Based on your developmental analysis of legitimacy for competence and response, you then collaborate to develop programs to support aging in place, until developmental cognitive change, interpreted as decline through some developmental lenses, occurs and explains the movement from the category of competent to incompetent. Once an elder joins the ranks of incompetence, different responses related to living placement and support would ensue.

Given your developmental analysis of aging, competence and choice, you work at the policy level toward expanding age specific funding for social service alternatives to nursing home care for those who are legitimate members of the class of competent elders.

As the next legitimacy chapters illustrate, approaching social work practice through lenses other than developmental provokes different determinations and responses.

Summary

This chapter discussed developmental legitimacy in all domains of social work practice. The inherent values of developmental theories were examined, exploring their fit with social work values and then applying developmental theory to a case example.

References

DePoy, E., & Gitlin, L. (2011). *Introduction to research.* St. Louis, MO: Elsevier.

Social Security. (2010, April 1). *Times topics.* Retrieved from New York Times: http://topics .nytimes.com/top/reference/timestopics/subjects/s/social_security_us/index.html?scp=1- spot&sq=social%20security&st=cse

Weschler, D. (2010). *Wechsler adult intelligence scale (WAIS–IV)* (4th ed.). Retrieved from Pearson: http://www.pearsonassessments.com/HAIWEB/Cultures/en-us/Productdetail .htm?Pid=015-8980-808&Mode=summary

17

Application of Environmental Theory to Social Work

❖

C hapters 6 through 8 discussed environmental theories. With this, the proximal distal continuum of environmental theories was posited to reflect that we do not agree with a clear dualist distinction between body and its surrounding. Yet, in order to analyze and do justice to those theoretical frameworks, which still subscribe to the notion of the body as separate from its surroundings, we organized the chapters according to the distance of environmental conditions from the organic corpus. We took this approach while attempting to use language to best reflect a contemporary critical approach to theories that hold environmental conditions as explanatory of human description.

In this chapter, we remain constant with our proximal-distal continuum language to analyze and apply environmental theories to social work practice. Included among environmental conditions are the host of proximal to distal tangibles and abstracts that comprise and interact with humans. This chapter looks at the "so what" of environmental theories and tries to answer, within the framework of explanatory legitimacy, how this ocean of knowledge about environments can be harvested and used to make professional decisions and to inform professional action.

THINKING POINT

To refresh yourself on the issue related to dualism and environmental theories, list the theories in each environmental theory chapter, and compare and contrast the theories with regard to their similarities and differences.

Common Environmental Theory Values

Table 17.1 presents the values of environmental theories, some of which sit on the surface and some which dive below what is articulated.

Table 17.1   Common Environmental Theory Values
1. "Healthy" environments produce desirable behavioral results.
2. Desirable environments are comprised of healthy structures and healthy processes.
3. Environments that harm and impede growth and development should be changed.

If we examine environmental theories for their inherent values, we see these value statements as implicit or explicit in all of them to a greater or lesser degree. Environmental theories identify the set of conditions that are valued, the specific outcomes resulting from desired conditions, and frequently advance the processes through which these conditions can be created to produce preferred outcomes.

Consider successful performance on an exam in college as the desired outcome. Environmental theories suggest various conditions that can be created and manipulated in order to enhance the greatest likelihood that the outcome will occur. Depending on the theory and the desirables posited, you might see grades, instructor praise, special privilege, and so forth as reinforcements, or distribution of candy during the exam to stimulate and satisfy proximal corporeal environmental conditions, and thus produce the preferred outcome of successful test performance.

THINKING POINT

What type of environmental conditions best stimulate your productivity and why? What theory or theories describe and explain your experience?

Thus, environmental theories are particularly potent in explaining causes of human behavior and identifying ways in which to change behavior through manipulation of proximal to distal conditions. Because of this principle, environmental theories and their application are both central to and often contentious within social work practice.

Think of the practice of behavior modification. As explained previously, carefully structuring the distal environment and the rewards for desirable behavior can shape an individual's behavior. But who chooses what behaviors are desirable and through what means these behaviors will be supported or extinguished? Now, consider the proximal practice of psychiatric medication and the critical ethical dilemmas presented by its ability to introduce conditions that chemically alter or eliminate many types of human behavioral variation.

THINKING POINT

Identify the ethical dilemmas present when the individual who was the target of behavior change disagrees with the desired outcome.

Proximal to Distal Environmental Legitimacy

One of the most important elements of concern to social work decision making and response informed by environmental theories is proximal behavior change of individuals. Environmental theories tell us what, why, and how.

Consider Mike, a 32-year-old male who decided to return to college to get his bachelor's degree in engineering after working as a large equipment operator for the state highway department. Mike lives with his wife, Alana, a high school teacher, and his two school age children. On two incomes, Mike and Alana were financially comfortable, but now that Mike has relinquished his salary, the family must tighten their belts, so to speak. After Mike's second week at college, he came home feeling blue. Over the next few weeks, his blue mood worsened to the point of interfering with his concentration on his academics.

Through the lens of environmental theories, numerous causes could be hypothesized for the change in Mike's proximal conditions of mood and scholarly behavior, including limited meaningful distal reinforcements from his new school environment, limited ability to enhance his and his family's distal environment with purchases, proximal discomfort in his new social environment, and so forth. Description of the new school environment supports the explanatory accuracy of all of these conditions. Numerous distal conditions could be manipulated to evoke a change in Mike's descriptive behavior and experience. It would be possible for him to talk to his instructors (learning conditions) to request additional help and more frequent feedback as reinforcement. Or, he might decrease the time spent in his school environment to work part-time and change the conditions in his home environment. He might also seek to find new social conditions, such as a study group at school, that provide the feedback for comfort and improved performance.

From a proximal environmental perspective, there are also numerous descriptors and potent explanations for Mike's recent changes. Consider, for instance, just one proximal element that would be of interest to clinical social workers, Mike's psychiatric status. Looking through a biological lens, it is likely that his mood is a function of chemical changes and imbalances that antidepressant medications, along with counseling, could manipulate. From a proximal environmental theory of motivation, it may be possible that without comfort needs being met, he is not motivated to engage in higher-order functions such as education. Changing his income or that of his family's can manipulate this condition to assure that comfort needs are met.

THINKING POINT

Can you identify other similar exemplars?

Now consider the possibility that Mike has a history of depression in his family. Recent research supports the genetic predisposition to mood.

This explanation opens the floodgate to genetic engineering. As introduced in Chapter 7, the Human Genome Project has been considered as a legitimate member of two opposing philosophical groups, health productive and genocidal. Those who see genetic engineering as the potential cure for much of the illness that plagues the proximal human genetic environment are ardent supporters of genetic research and intervention to identify and conduct, respectively, health-producing manipulations as the basis for eliminating unhealthy genetic conditions. Stem cell research has been held not only as a fountain of youth, but also as a potential cure for human pain and suffering. However, opponents of genetic research and intervention argue that it should be curtailed because of its potential to manipulate and homogenize human diversity, and thus lead not only to a reduction of difference and variation, but to genocide.

Prenatal testing has the potential to identify many proximal conditions that are considered to be undesirable to the medical and biological fields. Susan, a 42-year-old woman, and her husband Isaac have been trying to conceive for 15 years, but with no positive results. Finally, after many years, Susan became pregnant. Upon her first prenatal checkup with a new obstetrician, she was advised that because of her age, she was at high risk of having a child with Down syndrome (and thus could have a child with an intellectual impairment). Her obstetrician suggested amniocentesis. When she went home that night and spoke to Isaac, he opposed the test, indicating that any child was welcome as his. However, Susan disagreed on several points, but most vigorously with regard to her assertion of the devaluation of people with intellectual impairments in their distal social environments. In their debate, Isaac asked Susan what conditions she would not abort and where the line is drawn on what an acceptable proximal corporeal environment is for a human. As they talked over time, each was able to see the values of the other and come to an agreement.

As this example illustrates, there is no right or wrong position. But, the answers to what constitutes a healthy proximal environment emerge from the values that inhere in one's theoretical frame of reference.

Susan looked at the distal social environmental conditions as the basis for judging the efficacy of the proximal environment, and Isaac looked through the lens of diversity to define proximal environmental health.

THINKING POINT

Under what environmental circumstances would you approve of abortion? What values are inherent in your perspective?

Extrapolated to other proximal conditions such as intelligence, mood, weight, and so forth, the features that are theorized to occupy the position of health, and then to manipulate proximal to distal environments to conform, are powerful ones indeed.

We raise another environment value conflict that is critical to social work practice, psychiatric pharmacology. As the practice of medicating behavior and emotions increases its hegemony, diagnostic criteria and related practice to produce valued bio-chemical conditions in the proximal corporeal environment become more contentious. Pharmacological manipulation promises the extensive benefits of creating comfort and even prolonging life through reversing suicidal ideation. So why then would anyone oppose its use? Opponents of psychiatric medication to manipulate the conditions of mood and personality suggest that there is a high price to pay not only for the individual who is medicated, but for our more distal social and cultural environmental conditions as well (Conrad, 2007; Greenberg, 2010). The benefits of psychiatric medications often accompany serious and undesirable side effects such as weight gain, memory loss, inability to concentrate, sleep alteration, and even toxicity. Moreover, chemical manipulation has met with severe criticism from proponents of maintaining and advancing human variability who suggest that diversity of behavior, and even mood, should be celebrated, not truncated (Greenberg, 2010). Of particular note is the construction of illness, *medicalization* in Conrad's (2007) moniker, in the name of chasing maximum profit for pharmacology and the health industrial complex.

Let us look at Samantha. Samantha, an art student at a large university, has recently experienced some disturbing phenomena. At night, before she falls asleep, she hears voices, and when she gets up to look for people talking, she sees no one. Because she is afraid that people are hiding in her house, she tries to stay awake as long as possible and only falls asleep when she is so exhausted that she can no longer force herself to do anything else but sleep. Over a 2 month period, Samantha has noticed that she is exhausted, afraid to unlock her door, and fearful of telling anyone about her experiences. She forces herself to attend classes, but has difficulty concentrating. Her best friend, Hallie, finally convinces her to see a clinical social worker. Upon hearing about her experiences, the social worker sends Samantha to a psychiatrist who evaluates her and places her on antipsychotic medications. Samantha experiences relief from her symptoms and continues to see the psychiatrist for ongoing medication.

Over the next year, Samantha does well, but she notices her decreasing ability to produce paintings for her classes because of two new experiences, tremors in her hands and the inability to generate innovative ideas for her work. To help her, the psychiatrist prescribes medication to decrease the tremors and to increase her ability to concentrate. However, in a few weeks, she finds that she is unable to sleep again. Because she is taking amphetamines prescribed by the psychiatrist to help Samantha concentrate, the psychiatrist adds a sleeping medication to the chemical regimen. Finally, Samantha decides that she needs to change her major because she is not successful in her painting classes anymore, and because she is unable to get up early enough to attend studio art classes held in the early morning.

In this example, it is clear that manipulating Samantha's proximal environmental conditions was immediately relieving and continued to produce ongoing benefits to reduce her undesirable psychiatric conditions. However, although often silenced until they speak, the long-term implications of psychopharmacology are important to illuminate and weigh against the benefits, and are thus the object of debate and disagreement. Emotive and creative proximal corporeal environmental manipulation, or manipulating Samantha's behavior through social work counseling, might have relocated Samantha from fear to safety, although not as immediately and potently as proximal chemical environmental manipulation. The initial route to move Samantha is mapped by one's values and chosen environmental theoretical frame of reference.

THINKING POINT

Explore your values regarding chemical control of behavior. Think about the indications and the prohibitions. What are the ethical dilemmas that you face as you look into your own values?

To summarize so far, we have identified the values common to environmental theories. We have seen that healthy environments are desirable, but what constitutes them is not agreed upon. Moreover, because of the potential to manipulate environmental conditions through diverse strategies, the debate about healthy environments is heated and the subject of important ethical discourse. Similar to value debates about the legitimacy of developmental theory for social work, the concept of homogenization is at the root of much of the disagreement about who defines healthy environments, and then who determines what means are ethical and sound to produce them. Now, let us turn to a more focused discussion of legitimacy of distal environments to continue our analysis.

Because environmental theories are complex and consider interaction among a wide variety of conditions, the values that constitute healthy distal environments are critical to understanding and applying these theories. But, it is not so easy to identify a set of common values that are prescriptive of the meaning of *healthy*. Actually, what constitutes a healthy distal environment varies according to specific theory, and theories often are in heightened conflict with one another.

Consider health clubs. For some, health clubs are environments that produce desirable cardiovascular, musculoskeletal, and social health outcomes. Yet, others assert that these environments exist because necessary movement is removed from daily distal work environments, and thus, the replacement of activity through paid membership is contrived and unhealthy (Schnall, Dobson, & Rosskam, 2009).

THINKING POINT

Identify examples similar to the one preceding in which environmental theories are at odds in defining what is desirable.

As discussed, many environmental theories distal to the corpus posit the conditions that are desirable for human behavior and its production. Applied behavior theory, shaping, and enriched learning environments are all contained under this rubric and are captured by social workers to guide the development of valued conditions that produce health.

Environmental Theory Legitimacy of Ideas

First, we visit the derivation of environmental theories to understand what is valued as their evidentiary basis. As noted in Chapters 6 through 8, the epistemology of environmental theories is varied. Nomothetic designs, those based on finding commonalities within groups and distinguishing them from other groups, are primary to many proximal and distal behavioral theories. Biological researchers who attempt to isolate the phenomenon under investigation in order to determine its causes and consequences, particularly in the arena of clinical trials, are a good example.

In pharmacological research, the preferred method of inquiry is experimental clinical trial, in which a sample of participants is randomly selected from a larger group, called a population. *In research parlance, population does not refer to citizens in general but rather to a group whose characteristics are known, specified, and can be represented proportionately in a smaller subgroup or sample. So, the term* random, *dissimilar to popular usage, does not refer to haphazard and nonorderly. Rather,* random selection *refers to a systematic procedure designed to eliminate the potential for the sample selection process to influence the outcome of the research. In this procedure, with probability theory as its driver, each element of a population has an equivalent chance of being selected for the sample, and thus of being exposed to any extraneous conditions that could effect outcome.*

Theoretically, the bias of purposive selection and contamination is neutralized through random sampling and assignment procedures. Once a sample is selected, it is randomly divided into two or more groups, one receiving the drug (the experimental group) and one not receiving the drug (the control group). The term placebo *may be familiar, a treatment given to the control group that has no pharmacological value but aimed at disguising the knowledge of participants regarding which group they have joined. Both groups are then tested for the desired outcome, and if the drug is successful, the experimental group shows the benefit. This research design provides the only legitimate evidence within the medical industry that a drug produces its desired outcome.*

Similar methods are attempted in behavioral research. The only element that changes is the nature of the experimental condition. Instead of a drug, an environmental manipulation functions as the object of inquiry and the desired cause of change in the outcome.

In addition to the experimental-type tradition that provides evidence through clinical trials and true experimental approaches, inductive and abductive research methods have been increasingly accepted as legitimate strategies to generate knowledge about the range of proximal to distal environments. To review these logic structures, we refer you back to Chapter 1. Using inductive reasoning, researchers search for general rules or patterns by linking specific observations. There is no "truth" or general principle that is accepted *a priori* or before the study begins. This type of inquiry is most often used to elucidate environments when the knowledge sought is context bound, or existing theory is not accepted as satisfactory. Abductive approaches are used to find the most feasible fit of theory with data. This logic structure is most typically used when multiple frames of reference may be relevant, but the application of diverse thinking would meet varied purposes.

First, to illustrate induction, remember that Chapters 5 and 8 identified Kohlberg and Gilligan as two important theorists who examined moral reasoning. Kohlberg posited a developmental theory of moral maturation, which when applied to both boys and girls, observed and thus analyzed the girls as less morally sophisticated than the boys. Along came Gilligan, who questioned the fit of the theory to females, given that it was developed initially on observations of males. So, Gilligan set out inductively to characterize moral reasoning in women by conducting extensive open-ended data collection, in which she obtained reasoning decisions and patterns from women through posing a scenario and then listening to and interviewing women about the basis for their moral decision making. Gilligan then looked for repetitive themes in the data. Different from Kohlberg who located moral reasoning in development, with independent moral decision making as most advanced, Gilligan used inductive methods to theorize about moral reasoning. From her inductive research, she reached conclusions that greatly departed from Kohlberg's predeterministic theory, revealing that women's moral decision making is a distal social-environment process.

Now, consider abductive reasoning. From the preceding example, Kohlberg and Gilligan are well-supported theorists of moral reasoning. Suppose you were interested in creating a program to improve moral reasoning for teens with diverse sexual orientations. Which approach would you select? Through abductive logic, you would fit one or both theories to your needs-assessment findings to structure and examine the outcome of your environmental intervention.

As the examples relay, inductive, abductive, and deductive approaches to generating ideas and verifying them are important and legitimate in the range of environmental theories. The choice of method and evidence depends on the theory, the discipline, and the fit of the theory with one's observations, values, and beliefs. Moreover, as Gilligan's work illustrates, theories that we have located under rubrics other than environmental have frequently been indicted for inadequacy and then nullified on the basis of distal environmental influence. Inductive and abductive approaches to inquiry have the potential to move beyond monism and bring environmental theoretical investigation into the 21st century.

THINKING POINT

Can you think of some theories that have been challenged or revised through inductive methods of inquiry?

Now we move to the "idea world" of policy. Because this theoretical school of thought has such a wide girth of policy implications, we cannot cover them all. So, discussion focuses on health care reform policy, and we once again invite you into the extrapolation theater.

Think about health care reform. Is it distal or proximal to the corpus? How distal from human health is policy? When we think of *health care* and then its reform, perhaps we might be tempted to consider policy as most concerned with embodied health. As we read about the Patient Protection and Affordable Care Act (Deloitte Development, 2010), perhaps we might see the proposed expanded qualification for health services as beneficial to proximal embodied environments. Yet, in our examination of health care reform, the actual impact that this legislation will have on "health care," and thus health, is a ghost. Rather, this environmental policy projects itself distally to the financial universe of who will be eligible for health insurance, what will be covered, under what circumstances, and even more distally, the alleged substantive increase in the national deficit. To some extent, the policy is so distal to the health of individuals that the misnomer of *health care reform* is rarely the topic of discussion. The policy addresses the distal environment of dollar exchange among corporations within the health care arena, and more abstractly within the government deficit understood by so few, and only tangentially through that maze is the proximal organic body affected. How many dollars will be paid for catastrophic care, and what will the government role be in health care financing? To us, health care reform is nowhere to be found within the thicket of fiscal environmental conditions that are these distal policies masquerading as proximal to human health address. We use this exemplar of environmental policy and ideas not to propose a position on recent health care reform initiatives, but rather to illustrate the confluence of proximal and distal environments addressed throughout the book.

We did try to find a single policy proximal to embodied environmental conditions. However, given that policy is in itself distal and abstract, even those policies that directly address corporeal phenomena have a hard time being extracted from the distal ideas of ethics, values, and of course, resources.

THINKING POINT

Can you think of proximal environmental policies?

Now that the application of environmental theory to legitimacy decisions and actions regarding environments and ideas has been examined, let us consider the fit of these theories with social work values.

Fitting Environmental Legitimacy With the Value Base of Social Work

Table 17.2 illustrates the articulation of social work and environmental legitimacy values. It is interesting to note that, even within this table, the division between proximal and distal is vague.

Table 17.2   Social Work Values and Environmental Legitimacy

	Social Justice	Integrity	Respect for Individual Dignity and Worth
Proximal environmental legitimacy	Responsibilities and rights are linked to individual characteristics and personal responsibility.	Adherence to moral principles as the basis for decision making and behavior is explained as a proximal process.	Dignity and worth are determined by the extent to which proximal structures and processes are sound and within conceptualizations of what is acceptable for quality of human life.
Distal environmental legitimacy	Responsibilities and rights are defined by social, cultural, economic, and other contexts.	Adherence to moral principles as the basis for decision making and behavior is a socialization process.	Dignity and worth are determined by the extent to which individuals and groups are responsive to contextual expectations.

As depicted in Table 17.2, through the lens of environmental legitimacy, the proximal or distal gaze differentially interprets each of the central social work values. And of course, for us, these are not at all mutually exclusive nor are the boundaries between them well drawn.

Recently, in the New York Times *(Ornstein, 2010), a compelling article appeared about the extent to which logofying breast cancer (a distal environmental practice) ostensibly for the purpose of promoting awareness, health, and research support, has derailed the proximal health agenda. Trumping the improvement of research and health, distal social strategies such as slogans like "save the tatas" are sexualizing breast cancer and locating it as an offense to a sexy and desirable female body. Moreover, the huge profit agenda siphons resources from proximal suffering bodies to the corporate world of branding and consumption of "pink socially responsible purchases."*

The same issue of the New York Times *illuminated the difficulty in separating the distal practice of advertising from proximal neural response. In the new field of neuromarketing, brain responses to product advertising are measured with neurosensors and used as the basis for the*

design and sales of advertising campaigns, and thus maximization of the distal world of corporate profit. According to Singer (2010), preference surveys and those which ask direct questions are now inadequate to inform profit driven distal agendas in that they miss the nuances of neuro-logical responses that are not within the direct awareness of the unsuspecting consumer.

Finally, consider the issue of chemical alteration of the proximal environment to avoid change in distal conditions. We recently spoke to man who indicated that in order to tolerate the noxious work environment, he had to take antidepressant medications.

THINKING POINT

 Compare and contrast the distal and proximal environmental values and outcomes in the preceding examples.

We leave this part of the chapter with more questions than answers and refer you back to your values for guidance.

Environmental Social Work Legitimacy: A Case Illustration

Now let us turn to an example to illustrate the use of environmental theories for social work legitimacy in the domains. Because we have advanced the tenet of complexity and pluralism as desirable to inform social work practice, here we illustrate an integrated approach to environmental theory.

First, consider the application of environmental legitimacy to the proximal environmental social work practice domain. Terry, a 31-year-old woman, works in a grocery store as a checkout clerk. Although she had dabbled in drugs for several years, she did not become addicted to heroine until 10th grade, when she met a 22-year-old woman, Stacy, who was an addict. Terry dropped out of school and lived with Stacy in an intimate relationship until, at age 28, Terry almost died from a drug overdose. Terry was brought to the emergency room and then sent to an inpatient detox unit at the local hospital. While in the hospital, a social worker evaluated Terry to determine her legitimacy for long-term rehabilitation. The social worker looked through environmental perspectives to determine if Terry was a legitimate candidate for rehabilitation, and if so, what the legitimate social work response should be.

From the proximal environmental perspective, the social worker assessed Terry's internal motivation and readiness to change her behavior. While the social worker acknowledged the biological, physiological processes of addiction and withdrawal as important in understanding Terry's needs, he did not use this theoretical framework as the basis for her professional action, since these two domains were not within the purview of social work expertise and intervention. Rather, the social worker concentrated his effort on two environmental arenas: psychological readiness to change and proximal motivation. Also critical in informing the social worker's legitimate response to Terry was the distal element of social support giving the social worker the rationale for removing Terry from a social environment that supported illicit drug use, to the safe conditions of the residential drug rehabilitation unit.

Applied to the distal environmental domain of social work practice, the social worker involved Terry in the development and conduct of substance abuse prevention programs in high schools. Informed by environmental theories, the social work value on equality of access to information provided the legitimate rationale for educating youth about the consequences of addiction and setting the expectations that they will make efficacious behavioral and socially responsible decisions. Because the social worker does not consider himself a public health expert, he did not frame his responses at that distal environmental locus, but his plan to engage Terry's more immediate distal environmental conditions in this activity had a significant influence in arenas much more distal that the social worker had acknowledged.

Summary

This chapter discussed environmental legitimacy in social work practice. The inherent values of proximal to distal environmental theories were examined, exploring their fit with social work values and then applying environmental theories to a case example.

References

Conrad, P. (2007). *The medicalization of society: On the transformation of human conditions into treatable disorders*. Baltimore: Johns Hopkins University Press.

Deloitte Development. (2010). *Patient protection and Affordable Care Act*. Retrieved from http://www.deloitte.com/view/en_US/us/Industries/health-care-providers/center-for-health-solutions/health-care-reform/index.htm?id=USGoogle_hcreform_310&gclid=CML_l7mC8aUCFUdX2godYgy7YQ

Greenberg, G. (2010). *Manufacturing depression: The secret history of a modern disease*. New York: Simon & Schuster.

Ornstein, P. (2010, November 14). The way we live now: Think about pink. Retrieved from the New York Times: http://www.nytimes.com/2010/11/14/magazine/14FOB-wwln-t.html

Schnall, P. L., Dobson, M., & Rosskam, E. (2009). *Unhealthy work: Causes, consequences, cures*. Amityville, NY: Baywood.

Singer, N. (2010, November 14). Slipstream: Making ads that whisper to the brain. Retrieved from the New York Times: http://www.nytimes.com/2010/11/14/business/14stream.html

18

Application of Categorical Theory to Social Work

❖

Chapters 9 through 12 delved into categorical theories. This chapter looks at the "so what" of categories and tries to answer, within the framework of explanatory legitimacy, how the body of knowledge about human categories can be analyzed and used to make social work decisions and to inform professional action. Remember from Chapters 9 through 12 that we struggled with our carving techniques, trying to make sense of the large mass of theories that posit differences in humans on the basis of membership in preordained categories. In previous work, we had cleaved categories into interior and exterior but as our thinking has changed, this dualistic taxonomy did not serve us. Clearly, the discussions in the previous chapters demonstrated the arbitrary line between body and environment that also operates to make categorical distinctions opaque as well. So, this chapter, as in previous writing, addresses categories as proximal to distal and refers to the patina-depth continuum as well.

Common Categorical Theory Values

We tried with no success to find a common value set inherent in categorical theories. At first, we were puzzled by our failure, but then it became apparent that because of the purpose, derivation, and nature of categorical theories, there is no common value set. We were able to find common principles, however, listed in Table 18.1.

Table 18.1   Common Categorical Theory Principles

1. Categorical theories emerge within changing political, cultural, expressive, economic, demographic, geographic, religious, intellectual, and technological contexts.
2. Categorical theories are responsive to their contextual homes.
3. The principles inherent in categorical theories are relative to their specific contexts and thus they both represent and shape the diversity of values within those contexts.
4. Categorical theories, to a greater or lesser degree, aim to examine rights and needs as a function of category membership and thus have an action orientation, be it maintenance or change of the status quo.
5. Categorical theories wax and wane with regard to the desirability of homogenization and difference.
6. Categorical theories predict behavior, appearance, and experience in areas unrelated to the criterion for category membership.
7. Over the chronological history of categorical theories, there has been a shift from hierarchy of worth to the right to equality of members.
8. Only some groups are included in the discourses in categorical theory.
9. Categorical theory can both confer privilege and equality and curtail opportunity.
10. Coupling categorical theories with diversity limits diversity to predefined groups and human phenomena.

To understand the principles more fully, look back at the brief history of categorical theories presented in Chapter 9. Changes in the purposes, nature, and application of categorical theories were heavily influenced not only by population census data (Kertzer & Arel, 2002), contentious intergroup relations, war, and early 20th-century immigration (Heckman & Krueger, 2003; Painter, 2010), but also by the important intellectual and expressive shifts from monism to pluralism, the political economic context in which the theories were developed, and, to us, in large part by the advancement of technology (DePoy & Gilson, 2011).

Consider Delores and Amanda. They met and fell in love in 1968, when they were both undergraduates at the same university. At that time, due to the significant negative stigma and associated marginalization of same-sex couples, Delores and Amanda "neutralized" their home and their public behavior so that no one except for close friends, not even family, would know that they were a couple. Because of discrimination and stigma, Delores and Amanda remained skeptical about sharing their sexual orientation with work colleagues and family members until last year, when they announced their decision to marry.

Let us look at the changes in theory that have supported the differential behavior of Delores and Amanda with regard to their public assertion of being a committed couple. Remember that we indicated that before 1973, homosexuality was considered to be a mental illness. Thus, categorical theory of sexual orientation held heterosexuality, or the most typical publicly asserted and demonstrated orientation, as the only acceptable preference and all others as pathological. Had we been writing this book in 1970, we would have had to include gay theory under the rubric of proximal environmental conditions, as it was theorized at that time to be an intrinsic disease state. So, what factors provoked such a significant reconceptualization in theory? Certainly the descriptive behaviors of sexual orientation are no different than they were in 1970. Nor has any research supported a theoretical change.

According to Crompton (2006), the original location of homosexuality in the category of pathology had no basis in empirical inquiry at all. Embedded within a long history from normalcy and acceptance to discrimination, the diagnosis of homosexuality as pathological in the 20th century emerged from a panel of psychiatric providers on the basis of value judgments. Mental health professionals made these judgments about behaviors that they considered "sick." On the basis of what was typical and prescriptive for sexual preference, homosexuality was remanded to the stigmatized, undesirable category of mental illness. But, in the early 1970s, in a civil rights effort, gay mental health professionals challenged the diagnosis on the grounds that there was no evidence to suggest pathology. Their political action, not scientific narrative, was therefore responsible for eschewing homosexuality from the universe of pathology. So, peering into the underbelly of politicalization of pathology, we see the corporate, economic, and political posturing that explains behavior as pathological and place it in line for elimination until such time that the census or political winds shift in a favorable direction. If we look at LGBT and queer theories today, rather than ascribing the *p*-word (pathology), they explain group membership and experience as discrimination and curtailment of civil rights. Even outside professional contexts, a recent conversation with a friend about the notion of labeling transsexuality as pathology revealed that, according to her and echoing others' perspectives, pathological labeling is desirable for those with limited resources in order to receive reimbursed health services from public sources. On the other hand, those with resources prefer to eliminate the label and its stigma in light of their capacity to afford whatever services they desire. We take issue with both positions, suggesting that larger social change should move in the direction of replacing pejorative labeling with equality of access to resources. Let us now look at some of the reasons for our perspective.

First, within the current context of the politically correct labeling frenzy, those groups who are fortunate to be accepted as worthy of theoretical and naming attention are in large part in the same position as the LGBT group, at least rhetorically. As noted in Chapters 9 through 12, categorical theories have moved from characterizing selected, "politically correct" nondominant groups as inferior to the assertion that labeled groups have the right to equality of participation and opportunity. But do they? Let us look more closely.

Consider feminist theories, queer theories, ethnic and racial studies, and disability studies for examples. Categorical theories about women, sexuality, ethnic and racial minorities, and disabled groups have, to a greater or lesser degree, depending on the theory, attempted to provoke thinking away from what is deficient and devalued in each group to the position that violation of civil rights has truncated participation, equality, and access to goods and resources, and thus needs to be remediated by affirmative and other rights-based strategies.

THINKING POINT

Identify other groups who have been included in diversity discourse. How have they benefited from theory and legitimate response?

At this juncture, we want to raise an important point embodied in the meaning of Principle 9 in Table 18.1—one that may have become apparent about our thinking. While contemporary categorical theories historically were the strategy selected to ostensibly increase equality of opportunity and resources, and some affirmative strategies were successful in partially tackling disparity, we suggest that the aim must be separated from the method. The aim is essential but we assert that the strategies to achieve the goal of equality have not been sufficiently productive, and thus require major rethinking and revision. Do specialized strategies that create unique conditions for "inclusion" really equalize opportunity, or as Titchkosky (2007) and Badinter (2006) respectively illuminate, do these programs maintain segregation and sublimation, and thus the status quo? For us, the key to achieving equality of opportunity lies in changing methods to fit the context of the global economy, as discussed in Chapter 20. Simply doing more of the failed approaches is analogous to spreading a dollop of rancid peanut butter on more pieces of bread. Nothing is done to enhance the nutritive value of the peanut butter and it is spread more sparsely to groups, diluting human rights and maintaining the status quo while only providing a façade behind which conditions for disenfranchised groups remain dire.

Let us look at disability. As discussed in Chapter 12, disability at one time was viewed as a category in which one became a legitimate member only with a diagnostic condition that was determined by a medical authority to be disabling. As a result, disabled individuals were placed in a position of inferiority due to enduring pathology and their rights were significantly curtailed, even to the point of being institutionalized. However, due to disabling factors such as war, environmental pollution, and perhaps most important, the aging of the baby boomers in the United States, proximal explanations for disability have become more common among the population and theory has therefore shifted in response.

Moving from proximal medical-diagnostic deficit explanations to distal environmental discrimination and barriers, disability has moved into the discourse of discrimination and civil rights, with some legitimate responses rhetorically reflecting this notion. Looking at the Americans With Disabilities Act of 1990 (ADA) and the ADA amendments of 2009, these pieces of legislation, assumingly promulgated to mediate contemporary explanations of disability as constructed, ostensibly prohibit discrimination and set out affirmative conditions; these conditions must be met by architects, public agencies and organizations, employers, institutions of higher education, and virtual environments, among others. Some have used the term disability privilege *(Scotch, 2001; Stone, 2001) to refer to special affirmative responses such as hiring quotas, practices by national agencies such as the National Science Foundation that seek to admit disabled students into math and science higher education majors, and so forth.*

More recently, specialized higher education programs for students with intellectual impairments have hit the programmatic scene, providing alternative paths to and success criteria for higher education achievement (Institute for Community Inclusion at the University of Massachusetts Boston, 2010). The term privilege *implies that on the basis of legitimate category membership, one has advantage over others. And, while the ADA has created awareness of disability discrimination, danger remains in its long-term continuation on several fronts. First, if "special" status can be conferred from outside a group, it can also be removed. As evidence, the ongoing erosion of the ADA in court challenges decreased the scope of application of antidiscrimination legislation as we proceeded through the early 20th century. But more important, as long as affirmative action approaches are the means to assure rights for marginalized groups, they remain marginalized. That is to say, the groups who are supposed to benefit from affirmative action never become fully ensconced as citizens whose rights are protected under the legislation that protects all citizens (Titchkosky, 2007). And most critical, as long as aims are not parsed from inadequate rhetorical approaches to achieve them, the debate necessary for profound change does not occur.*

Reasonable accommodation is an excellent example here. An establishment only needs to address equality of access and resources if it is fiscally feasible. Finally, one has to qualify medically in order to be inadequately accommodated. Is the ADA better than no response at all? Would no response provoke deeper consideration of methods to achieve equality of access and opportunity? If so, who would suffer until such profound change takes place. We do not have answers other than to charge social workers with the challenge of clarity; to think of aims as distinct from methods; and to take the lead in meaningful debate, dialogue, and negotiation that move beyond inadequate strategies that derail our professional mission and ethics of equality.

Finally and most important with regard to the principles that inhere in categorical theories, as discussed in Chapter 9, we agree with progressive diversity theorists (Shiao, 2004) who suggest that the contemporary practice of equating categorical theories with diversity delimits diversity to embodied or contextual common characteristics—those we have named *bodies and backgrounds*. In our advanced technological world, where information and ideas can be shared without knowing the racial, ethnic, gender, diagnostic, or other category status of those who generate the ideas, we propose that uncoupling diversity from bodies and backgrounds characteristics will go far in promoting group symmetry.

Consider how design of virtual materials to meet diverse access styles and preferences would eliminate the need for special accommodations not only for those who are named in the ADA, but for others who are denied access without meeting ADA eligibility criteria.

THINKING POINT

Think of other groups who have been the objects of affirmative action and legislation. How has that legislation both benefited and disadvantaged the groups?

We now move to a discussion of the application of categorical theories to proximal to distal, and idea legitimacy.

Proximal to Distal Categorical Legitimacy

One of the most important elements of concern to social work decision making and response informed by categorical theories is eligibility for rights, resources, and services. Let's look at some examples to clarify.

First, we examine the right to marry. Within the past decade, the prohibition against nonheterosexual marriage has been challenged with the recent passage, in some states and countries, of legislation supporting the civil right of marriage for gay and lesbian couples. This civil rights legislation has been fraught with ambiguity and variation, however, fueled by disparate theory about explanations for sexual orientations other than heterosexuality. Moreover, as we look at the recent increase in genders described in proximal category theory in Chapter 11, the question of who is entitled to marry under affirmative legislation and who is not remains unanswered.

David and Joanna grew up in a small town in Mississippi and still live there. In 1984, they married, and then within the next 3 years had two children. However, they struggled in their marriage, particularly with their sexual relationship. One evening in May, 1990, David confessed a secret to Joanna that he had been holding inside since childhood: He identified himself as a woman in a man's body. The couple decided together that David would seek a sex change operation, which he did in 2008. He changed his name to Doris and both Doris and Joanna decided to remain married. However, in Mississippi, even in 2008, voters supported a ban on gay marriage. Where do Joanna and Doris now fit and what rights do they have with Doris's transsexual gender?

Now, to illustrate the role of categorical theory in resources and services, consider Mike, a 42-year-old male who is 5'6" and weighs 376 pounds. Until 7 days ago, he has been comfortably employed as a cashier in a large box store. However, last week, the management changed his job description. Previously, the majority of Mike's job as a cashier was spent ringing up purchases and accepting payment from customers. But as of last week, the management added stocking shelves to all cashier jobs, with the rationale that diversifying job duties would help cashiers know more about the inventory and its location. After 2 days of heavy lifting, Mike started experiencing chest and back pain. His physician placed him on short-term disability leave, having diagnosed him with severe back strain and at risk for a heart attack because of his weight. He was also advised to lose weight. Fearful of returning to work, Mike decided to apply for social security disability insurance and vocational rehabilitation. Informed by proximal categorical theory of motivation, the social worker who assessed Mike's legitimacy for benefits denied his claim, stating that obesity was his choice, and thus eliminated him from legitimate membership in the disability category and response.

Now consider an alternative scenario for Mike. Because of the denial of legitimate membership in the disability category, Mike sought assistance from the social worker at the state disability advocacy center. Different from the first social worker, the second social worker determined his legitimate membership in the disability category on the basis of his physician's report. And, rather than suggesting that Mike pursue safety net benefits, which would leave him unemployed and in poverty, he suggested that Mike return to his employer and ask for accommodation under the ADA.

Now, consider Ellie, a 21-year-old Puerto Rican woman. Ellie's brought her to the emergency room because she was hyperventilating and complaining of a severe headache. After taking vital signs and finding no pathology in her examination, the physician discharged Ellie with a diagnosis of anxiety. The next day, Ellie was back in the ER and this time, she was referred to a social worker for a mental health assessment. The physician's notes from the previous evening reflected the exam results and the physician's impression that because Ellie was a legitimate member of the categories of ethnic minority and female gender, that she was a likely candidate for high stress and anxiety. As the social worker interviewed Ellie and obtained a social history, she learned that Ellie's mother had died of brain cancer at a young age. The social worker thus determined that the proximal environment theory of medicine did not fit within the social work purview, and requested that Ellie be referred back to the medical field to rule out malignancy as the cause of her symptoms.

The preceding examples illustrate the vagueness of category assignment and response, and the dilemma that social workers face when encountering these factors in their practices.

THINKING POINT

Where do you stand on the right of Joanna and Doris to remain married? What explanatory categorical theory would you use to inform your opinion of a legitimate response to this couple?

In the example of Mike, the decision to admit him as a legitimate member of the disability category (or not) was critical in both determining his eligibility for social work services, and for shaping the nature of those services once the second social worker accepted him as a bona fide category member.

THINKING POINT

What theory would you use to explain Mike's descriptive needs and what legitimate response would be warranted?

The example of Ellie illustrates the difficulty of deciding when category membership, such as gender and ethnicity, are even relevant to the social work decision-making process. Had the social worker not asked about family history unrelated to bodies and backgrounds, the proximal environment theory of pathology might not have been applied, and could have resulted in serious consequences for Ellie, and even possibly death.

Before leaving the application of categorical theory to proximal conditions, we direct attention to one last question raised by the example of amniocentesis to screen for genetic disease.

THINKING POINT

Examine your own values about abortion and the criteria for legitimately sanctioned abortion. Who should be excluded and why?

As noted in the principles common to categorical theories, belonging to a category brings with it assumptions about many issues and experiences that may be unrelated to the membership criterion. Looking at abortion practices in the United States, we can infer the worth value of categories. Aborting a fetus with Down syndrome is a well-supported legal and medical practice; this reveals the assumption that membership in this category may be associated with such presumed heinous experiences that life is not warranted. We are not taking a position here, because we believe that application of categorical theory to decision making about the value of human life is complex and involves multifaceted thinking. Rather, we mention this issue to illustrate the ethical dilemmas that reasoning about category membership and worth present.

Categorical theories applied to distal environments, especially for social workers, are particularly important in informing social justice efforts.

> Consider once again Mike's situation. Mike returns to the social worker at the disability advocacy center to report that the management has decided to lay him off because he is no longer qualified for the cashier job. Applying categorical theory to decision making, the social worker assesses that the social environment of the store, through redefining the cashier's job, has created discriminatory conditions and has abridged Mike's civil rights. In collaboration with the human rights commission, the social worker engages the management in discussions and practices to provide accommodations to Mike so that he can do his work. The management, after much discussion, decides to train Mike to use a mechanical lift and to pair Mike with another cashier for assistance in reshelving heavy merchandise. We suggest that such strategies be made for all qualified workers, not just those who meet eligibility criteria for mandated response, and thus for whom the employer is obliged to respond.

As this example illustrates, the process through which Mike's employment was maintained was adversarial rather than cooperative.

Let us now take on the legitimacy of cultural competence. We devoted significant attention to this term and its vagueness in Chapter 10. Yet, cultural competence remains well-ensconced in the literature, narrative, and teaching in social work practice. As you may have surmised by now, we look at cultural competence as a field that raises awareness of difference but threatens to simplify and essentialize it. Embedding the complex construct of culture within a diversity depth perspective frames legitimate social work responses in which human variation and difference are not located in a single trait and then assumed to be experienced by all who possess it.

> Applying these principles to Ellie's case, the physician who made negative stereotypical assumptions on the basis of Ellie's dual membership in bodies and backgrounds categories would not

have made that decision from our envisioned practice perspective of cultural competence. Rather, Ellie would have been engaged in the dialog and decision making to collaborate in her care and to eliminate the potential health disparities that she may have encountered on the basis of category membership.

Once again, as Ellie's example illustrates, we challenge social work to take leadership in this progressive and essential trend.

THINKING POINT

Who should be involved in community negotiations and discussions, and how can social workers promote this important agenda?

To summarize so far, unlike other theoretical domains discussed in this book, we were unable to find a set of values common to all categorical theories. However, principles were articulated that inhere in the theories and guide their application. Categorical theory was then applied to proximal and distal environments, highlighting the importance of this theoretical body in informing practice aimed at reducing and eliminating discrimination, marginalization, and exclusion. We now turn to legitimacy of ideas to understand the epistemology, legitimate evidence, and application of categorical theories to abstracts.

Categorical Theory Legitimacy of Ideas

First, we visit the derivation of categorical theories to understand what is valued as their evidentiary basis. As noted in Chapter 9, categorical theories are primarily based on nomothetic concepts. They seek to look at commonalities within groups and distinguish differences among groups. However, because of the nature of these theories, traditional research methods that look for averages and apply these averages broadly without regard for categorical uniqueness are often seen as antithetical to the purposes and concepts that embody this class of theory. We are not suggesting that research in the experimental-type tradition is not used and useful in developing, testing, and applying categorical theories, but rather that numerous and progressive methods are considered sound for generating knowledge about the common as well as divergent experiences and nature of category members.

Let us consider some examples of each epistemic approach. It is not uncommon to see categorical differences examined through statistical methods in which the common differences between groups are examined.

Think of how many granting agencies require the inclusion of specific populations in health research studies. In pharmacological research, studies on the differential effects of drugs on the basis of category membership has been sought and supported by the National Institutes of

Health to redress historical exclusion of women, children, and other subpopulations. While this approach has increased the inclusion of specific populations, we assert that it is not universal to all people and may, through essentialism and exclusion of groups yet to be identified, counter its aim of equality.

Experimental-type research methods are used not only in health and medical research, but also in social science and educational research. For example, in order to enhance equality of opportunity for admission to rehabilitation programs for disabled students, Gitlow (2001) examined the social environment of faculty attitudes towards these students using survey design. She also separated faculty by category membership such as education and gender. Should she have tested categorical differences? If so on what basis, if not, what might have been lost in the generation of knowledge?

However, as illustrated by Gilligan's classic work on moral reasoning in women and by many other inquiries, inductive methods are often applied when existing theory is not credible or when the investigator wants to characterize the uniqueness of categories and category members. A look back at the work of Cramer, Gilson, and DePoy (2001) on domestic violence in women with disabilities will help illustrate.

Cramer et al. (2001) were concerned that women with physically disabling conditions were not experiencing equality of access to and response from domestic violence providers. They therefore set out to examine why. Building on previous work, they pursued an inductive inquiry to interview women with physical impairments who had been victimized by domestic violence in order to examine the fit of current theory with this categorically based experience. Through the interviews, they learned that domestic violence was perpetrated against this category of women in ways that would not be considered under typical theories and understandings of domestic violence. For example, a woman who had limited use of her hands was victimized by her husband who refused to help her open the bathroom door, resulting in her humiliation and serious negative health and hygiene consequences. Under the power and control taxonomy of harm from domestic violence, however, refusing to assist in opening a door would not be measured as violent behavior. The conduct of inductive methods of inquiry allowed this categorical knowledge to be revealed.

Many cultural and feminist research methods rely on inductive methods, based on the theoretical tenet that category membership produces different experiences from those characterized and investigated by experimental-type research (DePoy & Gitlin, 2011). Both inductive and deductive approaches to generating ideas and verifying them, then, are important and legitimate in categorical theories. The choice of method and evidence depends on the theory, the discipline, and the fit of the theory with one's observations. Moreover, once again, as Gilligan's work illustrates, theories that we have located under rubrics other than categorical have frequently been challenged on the basis of the unique experiences of category members, with inductive approaches supporting new conceptualizations. We also suggest that abductive approaches to inquiry are not only relevant but warranted in the complex theoretical world of the 21st century. Applying fuzzy set theory, introduced in Chapter 14 (Rangin, 2008), to categorical research is more logical, as it allows membership in a category to be viewed not as binary but rather as proximal to distal and dynamic. Suggesting differential meaning and importance of category membership changes the essentialist nature of bodies and backgrounds theory by introducing nuances along with graduated membership and meaning into the explanation of human description.

> *Think of Susan and Alice. Both are lesbians, but to Susan, her sexual orientation is a large part of her identity, and thus her membership in this category is proximal and compelling. For Alice, however, her sexual life is private and not self-defining. Rather, her work as a watchmaker and her excellence as a swimmer are her most proximal categories with sexual orientation being extremely distal. Assuming that both women experienced similarities on the basis of sexual orientation would be inaccurate. Any researcher locating them in a study distinguishing the politics of lesbian from heterosexual women would be well-advised to examine the meaning of sexual orientation as fuzzy and diverse.*

Moving to the idea world of policy, as revealed in the discussion of the ADA, legitimacy of categorical theories is a critical influence on another set of ideas, social justice, and distributive policy. As noted, categorical theories have been instrumental in informing many civil rights policy arenas. But in addition, the United States, unlike several other liberal democracies such as Canada and the United Kingdom, has used categorical theory to inform health care policy reform as well.

> *Canada has rationed health benefits by condition. That is, health insurance is universal for all citizens, but their national policy and financing only cover certain conditions. The United States, however, chose to ration health care coverage and thus limit access to services by population category (Light & Light, 2002; Weissert & Weissert, 2002). For example, eligibility criteria for publicly supported health benefits, such as Medicare, stipulate category membership in the group delimited by age 65 and older, not condition. Similarly, public Medicaid benefits are only available on the basis of membership in the category of poverty, with state variations in eligibility.*

THINKING POINT

 Can you identify other policy agendas that categorical theories inform? How do the theories shape legitimate policy responses?

Now let us look at the fit of categorical theories with social work values.

Fitting Categorical Legitimacy With the Value Base of Social Work

Because we were not able to ascertain value commonalities among categorical theories, we cannot look at the relationship between the total of all categorical theories and social work values. We have therefore selected feminist theories as the basis for value analysis and illustration in social work practice. So, of course, remember the extrapolation stage as you apply this knowledge to other domains.

In Chapter 11, we discussed diverse types of feminisms and used Thomas's (2001) work to examine five types of theories: (1) liberal feminism, (2) radical feminism, (3) multicultural feminism, (4) Marxist feminism, and (5) ecofeminism. Table 18.2 examines the fit of social work values with the central values of each of the five types of feminist theory.

Table 18.2 Social Work Values and Feminist Theories

	Social Justice	Integrity	Respect for Individual Dignity and Worth
Liberal feminism	Males and females should have equality of opportunity.	Contemporary understandings of gendered power imbalance and inequity should inform decisions.	Assumptions about individual capacities on the basis of maleness and femaleness should not be made.
Radical feminism	All genders and sexual orientations should have equality of opportunity.	Contemporary understandings of power imbalance and inequity on the basis of sexual orientation and gender should inform decisions.	Assumptions about individual capacities on the basis of gender and sexual orientation should not be made.
Multicultural feminism	All genders in all cultures should have equality of opportunity.	Contemporary understandings of gendered and culturally based power imbalance and inequity should inform decisions.	Acceptance of power differentials on the part of women is caused by enculturation and should be examined and eliminated.
Marxist feminism	All genders should have equality of economic and political opportunity.	Contemporary gendered power imbalance and inequity are a function of misogynist capitalist systems and this understanding should inform decisions.	Political and economic systems should provide the means and processes to value men and women equally.
Ecofeminism	All people are entitled to and responsible for healthy environments.	Decisions and actions should be based on promoting healthy environments, not on male models of exploiting environmental resources.	Worth is based on one's contribution to healthy environments, a predominately female model.

As depicted in Table 18.2, each feminist theory advances a similar but somewhat different view of what constitutes social justice, the basis for sound professional decisions, and values of dignity and worth. The similarities of intersecting values all lie in the legitimacy of equality of opportunity and resource distribution across genders, but what constitutes genders, the scope of the equality (power, resources, environments, economics, political opportunity, etc.), the targets of change, and the means to enact change differ.

Comparing and contrasting two legitimacy approaches through the frameworks of liberal feminism and Marxist feminism will illustrate.

> *Loretta is a 29-year-old mother of three young children. She stays at home to take care of the children and do housekeeping while her husband works as a civil engineer. On a regular basis, her husband, Matt, comes home drunk after going to the bar with his male work buddies. When he is intoxicated, Matt becomes violent, yelling at his wife and throwing objects around the house. On the evening that he first strikes Loretta, she bundles up the children and seeks help at the local battered woman's shelter.*

Liberal feminist theory would suggest the following principles and action:

1. Loretta is entitled to a safe and supportive environment.

2. Matt is beating Loretta because he has been socialized to be dominant.

3. When Matt is intoxicated, he exercises his dominance and thus violence.

4. With counseling and resocialization, Matt's behavior can and needs to change, or Loretta needs to take the children and leave him.

The Marxist feminist perspective would suggest the following principles and action:

1. Loretta is entitled to an environment in which she has and exercises equal resources and opportunity respectively.

2. Loretta's child and home care should be valued equally to Matt's work.

3. Matt is beating Loretta because of the misogynist capitalist system in which women's work, and thus women, are devalued.

4. Loretta and all women should seek the resources and power to which they are entitled.

As the operationalization of legitimacy illustrates, from both perspectives, the social work values of social justice, integrity, and human dignity assert the need to remediate inequality and provide sound, safe environments for women. However, the causes, consequences, and thus actions informed by each perspective differ, one espousing values that situate the obligation for change as a female response to male behavior and the other locating the target of change within a patriarchal system of production and male advantage.

THINKING POINT

 Use the preceding model to examine and operationalize the intersection of social work values and race theories to a social work issue.

Categorical Social Work Legitimacy: A Case Illustration

Now let us turn to an example to illustrate the use of liberal and Marxist feminist theories for social work legitimacy in the domains of environment and ideas.

First, consider the application of liberal feminist legitimacy to the proximal social work practice domain. Returning to Loretta and Matt, after assessing Loretta for legitimacy of services at the shelter, the social worker determines that Loretta and her children are eligible for residential protection at the shelter until legal action against Matt is taken and he enters a batterers counseling program.

From the Marxist feminist perspective, after assessing Loretta for legitimacy for shelter protection and services, the social worker works with Loretta to identify areas in which Loretta can work or be retrained to work remuneratively. Loretta remains at the shelter while she applies to community college to get her electrician's license and locate subsidized housing.

Applied to the distal environmental domain of social work practice, the social worker proceeding from a liberal feminist approach has decided to engage in junior high and high school programs aimed at educating girls about domestic violence, and enhancing their social worth and self-esteem, as the basis for preventing domestic violence. The social worker who uses a Marxist feminist perspective to inform her practice is participating on a grant project funded by the National Science Foundation to increase the number of women who enter science and technology careers.

At the idea domain of social work practice, both social workers are involved in policy advocacy. The liberal feminist social worker is involved in advocating for policy that provides additional funding for shelters and male batterers programs, while the Marxist feminist social worker lobbies for paid child care, and for higher education policy to support women's scholarships and affirmative action to enter what were traditionally seen as male careers.

Summary

This chapter examined categorical legitimacy in social work practice. Due to their diversity of ideas and scope, values common to all categorical theories were not advanced, but common principles were analyzed. After focusing the analysis of the intersection of feminist categorical theories and social work values, liberal and Marxist feminism served as exemplars through which to illustrate categorical legitimacy in social work practice.

References

Badinter, E. (2006). *Dead end feminism.* Malden, MA: Polity Press.

Cramer, E. P., Gilson, S., & DePoy, E. (2001). Disability and domestic violence: An expansion-limitation paradox. *AFFILIA, 16*(2), 220–236.

Crompton, L. (2006). *Homosexuality and civilization.* Cambridge, MA: Harvard University Press.

DePoy, E., & Gilson, S. (2011). *Studying disability.* Thousand Oaks, CA: Sage.

DePoy, E., & Gitlin, L. (2011). *Introduction to research.* St Louis, MO: Elsevier.

Gitlow, L. (2001). Occupational therapy faculty attitudes toward the inclusion of students with disabilities in their educational programs. *Occupational Therapy Journal of Research, 21*(2), 115–131.

Heckman, J. J., & Krueger, A. B. (2003). *Inequality in America: What role for human capital policies?* (J. P. Jacobsen, Ed.). Cambridge, MA: MIT Press.

Institute for Community Inclusion at the University of Massachusetts, Boston. (2010). *Think college.* Retrieved from Think College: http://www.thinkcollege.net/

Kertzer, D., & Arel, D. (2002). *Census and identity.* Cambridge, UK: Cambridge University Press.

Light, A., & Light, D. (Eds.). (2002). *Rationing: Constructed realities and professional practices.* Oxford, UK: Blackwell.

Painter, N. I. (2010). *The history of white people.* New York: W. W. Norton.

Rangin, C. (2008). *Redesigning social inquiry: Fuzzy sets and beyond.* Chicago: University of Chicago Press.

Scotch, R. (2001). American disability policy in the twentieth century. In P. Longmore & L. Umansky (Eds.). *The new disability history: American perspectives* (pp. 375–392). New York: NYU Press.

Shiao, J. L. (2004). *Identifying talent, institutionalizing diversity: Race and philanthropy in post-civil rights America.* Durham, NC: Duke University Press.

Stone, D. (2001). *Policy paradox: The art of political decision making* (3rd ed.). New York: W. W. Norton.

Thomas, R. M. (2001). *Recent theories of human development.* Thousand Oaks, CA: Sage.

Titchkosky, T. (2007)). *Reading & writing disability differently: The textured life of embodiment.* Toronto, Canada: University of Toronto Press.

Weissert, C., & Weissert, W. (2002). *Governing health: The politics of health policy.* Baltimore: Johns Hopkins University Press.

19

Application of Systems Theory to Social Work

❖

Chapter 13 discussed systems theories and indicated that these approaches to describing and explaining human phenomena proceed from the tenet of inter-relationships, communication, and feedback. That is to say, systems, no matter what size and how organized, are all comprised of smaller parts that interact with one another. Thus, the interaction between and among the parts and other influences inform our understanding of humans. As with all legitimacy chapters, this chapter looks at the "so what" and tries to answer, within the framework of explanatory legitimacy, how systems theories can be analyzed and used to make social work decisions and to inform professional action.

Always keep in mind that within the framework of explanatory legitimacy, eligibility and response decisions are value determinations based on explanations, not descriptions. From a systems perspective, legitimacy decisions may refer to all or part of a system if it can be known. So before we illustrate theory specific legitimacy, let us look at the values inherent in systems theories as a first step.

Common Systems Theory Values

Because systems theories are concerned with interaction, they are particularly relevant to explaining relationships, communication mechanisms and responses, and related change in proximal to distal environments and ideas.

Looking at family systems theories, we see that the focus can be on the family as a whole system acting within the larger social system; on the component parts of the families such as parents, children, and extended family members; and even on redefining and reconceptualizing family systems in response to cultural, population, economic, intellectual, religious, and expressive trends. If we see families as predictable, then we might characterize them as linear systems with subsystems nested within a larger hole. If, however, we dare to suggest that families are not predictable, complexity theory, chaos theory, or even fuzzy systems theories might be most useful as an explanatory tool.

Regardless of the degree of predictability theorized, the values common to systems theories shape our understanding of viable and worthy system parts, processes, and influences.

As discussed in Chapter 13, systems theories have a rich history back to ancient Greece, and thus are diverse in their scope and values. However, in looking at this bolus of theory, despite the significant shapes and activity contributed by diverse systems theories, we are able to ascertain the common values presented in Table 19.1.

Table 19.1   Common Systems Theory Values

1. Systems are purposive in that the parts all coalesce in trends or vectors.
2. Systems are dynamic or they cease to exist.
3. Positive change, regardless of nature and length of process, over the long term is desirable.
4. Feedback should produce change, preferably toward a unified goal, in system components and in systems.
5. In order to transmit feedback, sound and efficacious communication among system elements and influences is necessary.
6. Stabilized and dynamic systems are desirable even if they proceed through tumultuous periods.
7. Direct and indirect influences on systems should be identified as essential to understanding system operation and change.
8. Maintenance and preservation of systems are desirable.
9. Adaptation is a desirable system characteristic.
10. Because systems are comprised of parts, research methods must be able to identify, characterize, and ultimately predict the interaction among the parts.
11. Subsystem movement from proximal to distal membership in systems is typical and desirable.

Now, let us look more critically at these values. What is desirable in systems theory? Preservation, adaptation, growth, stabilizing change, and civility are all positive characteristics. And, even if the purpose of systems is only their own preservation, systems should advance a common purpose or goal. Undesirables in systems include mayhem; poor methods of providing, understanding, and responding to feedback; and limited consideration of the totality of influences on system performance and achievement of purpose. Even chaotic systems that proceed through periods of destabilization, while not linear, can be mapped as orderly over the longitude of time. Similarly, complex systems cannot necessarily be understood through linear methods of inquiry, but rather require contemporary modeling and mapping analyses in order to be captured as systematic, dynamic, and goal oriented. The application of fuzzy sets to systems is one approach that can put this map into action through tracing the membership intensity of subsystems within a larger entity.

> *Looking at a family system to illustrate, Abdul, his wife, Nora, and their two young children, age 9 months and 2 years, moved to New York in 1999. They emigrated from Saudi Arabia to the United States in order for Nora to study advanced civil engineering at a large urban university in the city. Abdul drove a taxi to earn money for his family and then enrolled in night school to work toward his master's degree in computer science. The young family enjoyed the safety and friendliness of their lower Manhattan neighborhood and Abdul was pleased that he was able to earn a good living in a flexible job. The communication within the family system was positive, and from feedback that all subsystems gave to one another, the family seemed stable and provided the foundation on which growth and positive change was occurring. Thus, from a family systems perspective, the family microsystem and the larger systems in which the family was embedded were stable, goal directed, dynamic in an orderly fashion, and desirable.*
>
> *But the morning of September 11, 2001, activated chaos, when the World Trade Center Towers collapsed. Over the next few weeks, previously stable systems such as neighborhoods, transportation systems, social systems, and economic systems spiraled out of control and then resettled as fractious. The university suspended classes, taxi travel was slowed, and the neighborhood looked with distrust and skepticism at Abdul, Nora, and the children. The family system was now in a state of destabilization, clearly an undesirable condition for a system. The influence from a single unpredictable event had an observable negative impact on the family system, revealed in the changing behavior of the children and the arguments between Abdul and Nora. Moreover, loyalties to nationality were questioned and rearranged, with Nora denouncing Saudi Arabia and Abdul magnetically drawn to defending his national origin.*

As the example illustrates, systems, especially those that are open and permeable, are subject to conditions that they cannot necessarily predict. And, the inherent values of order, growth, and purpose were no longer visible within the family system. Degree of membership dissipated in some systems and became fervent in others. Thus, through the lenses of systems theory, the system was unbalanced, destabilized, and in danger of dissolution.

THINKING POINT

How did Hurricane Katrina influence the Louisiana and Mississippi school systems in the fall of 2005?

These scenarios illustrate the important value points in diverse contemporary systems theory, as well as the application of linear family systems approaches to the nested microsystem of the nuclear family. The exemplar also illustrates the distinction between linear and nonlinear systems theories. If we were to characterize the family system as linear, erratic activity would be considered dysfunctional. Yet, through complex systems approaches, volatility is expected. "Slice in time" portals cannot do justice to complex systems, as these snapshots do not follow chronological change. Contemporary systems thinking visualizes systems as elastic. Calm is intertwined with havoc, with system elements tethered and shifting between repelling and rebounding, to bond in novel, flexible configurations.

> *Looking at Abdul and Nora once again, what if we only met them on September 15, 2001? Using traditional family systems theory, we might conclude that the family system was in disarray. But over a longer period of time, observing their process would have revealed that the family system was changing, intact, and able to make sense of and respond as a viable system to the unanticipated influence of 9/11.*

THINKING POINT

How might complex systems be applied to understanding patterns of health epidemics?

Proximal to Distal Systems Legitimacy

Although systems theory informs many areas of human behavior, one of the most important elements of concern to social work decision making and response to which systems theory applies is human communication and interaction. Different from developmental theories, which explain the maturation of communication as a proximal individual process, systems theory is similar to frameworks positing that communication and response are choreographed among system elements and influences. Thus, the value orientation of classical systems theory would suggest that a sound and stable system with clear communication, initially at the microsystem level but extending up through the macrosystem, is most desirable but perhaps not most attainable over chronology.

> *Robert is a 26-year-old construction contractor and Andrew, his partner of 4 years, is a librarian. They live together in a small house at the end of a cul-de-sac in suburban Richmond, Virginia. When they met, Robert was openly gay but Andrew was not. Andrew was raised in a Christian fundamentalist family, who disapproved of same-sex relationships. As a result, at the beginning of their relationship, Robert respected Andrew's wishes to keep the intimate nature of their relationship private. However, after 4 years, Robert is tiring of the secrecy and as gay marriage gains legal status in some states, Robert wants to marry Andrew. Now entered into the scene are the trends of legalizing gay marriage and the backlash from those who oppose the extension of marriage to this population.*

If we look at the family system from a traditional systems perspective, Robert and Andrew comprise the primary microsystem embedded within the larger microsystems of extended families. The values, communicated from Andrew's microsystem family of origin identifying same-sex intimacy as undesirable, although not directly emergent from the primary system, have an observable and important influence on Andrew and Robert, to the extent that they made a decision not to publicly display themselves as a family unit, despite their nonacceptance of the religious values in Andrew's family of origin. However, as time passes, numerous factors influence the small family unit comprised of Andrew and Robert, and thus the microsystem must change in response. Moreover, the interaction within the relationship has provided clear feedback to Andrew that their way of "doing business" so to speak, must change. Andrew has not communicated clearly with his family of origin, who begin to wonder about his health. As we see here, the valued conditions of stability and clear message transmission are sketchy in this family system, and thus, are beginning to unravel into a chaotic state that is uncomfortable but also opportunistic for change.

> *In efforts to preserve their family system, Andrew tells his family of origin that he plans to marry Robert and immediately he is asked to leave the house and never return. Over the next month, Andrew and Robert begin to argue, Andrew misses too many days of work, and each wonders how to proceed.*

Through the lens of linear systems theory, the intrusion of negative feedback from Andrew's family, along with the rejection of Andrew by his family system of origin, have clear effects on the family microsystem comprising Andrew and Robert, as well as on the mesosystem of Andrew's work, Robert's exosystem. Now clearly considered a destabilized system, the family system would be considered legitimate for family counseling and response to assist the individuals within the system to regain the desired state of function and stability.

Now, let us look more distally at systems theories. Recall that, in Chapter 9, *environment* was defined as a set of conditions, and thus, by looking at the intersection of this definition and theory, we can examine how systems theories characterize and prescribe desirable environmental conditions at multiple system levels, within varied system sizes, shapes, purposes, and characteristics.

THINKING POINT

How many environments can you identify in the Robert and Andrew scenario?

As part of the family system, the family environment (or the distal social environment) is comprised of all of the individuals who interact, including but not limited to Andrew, Robert, their families, friends, coworkers, neighbors, and so forth. The physical conditions of the environment in which the primary system operates are the home and community. And, with the exception of the social elements of Andrew's family of origin, from the scenario it appears that environmental conditions are supportive of the primary system of the couple. But now, we move distally to get a more complete as well as complex tapestry of conditions that interact in diverse ways. What if we look at the spiritual elements of Andrew's family system? Using Bronfenbrenner's levels, we could characterize it as an exosystem for Andrew and Robert. That is to say, they are not directly involved in it, but it has an influence on them, and in this case, an unsettling influence. If we then stray into the chronosystem, Andrew and Robert might have some good news as the legislative acceptance of same-sex marriages is being debated and advanced over time.

In a dynamic system, the distal environment is often a point of potential change. But in the example of Andrew and Robert, from a linear system approach, only some distal elements might be change targets, particularly if change is viewed as an incremental phenomenon as is the case in functional systems approaches. This point is very important for social work practice, in that systems theory not only provides the framework to identify and analyze system parts and interactions, but also provides the analytic lens through which to identify options for change as well as those that may be intractable, at least for the short run.

THINKING POINT

 What elements and systems in Andrew and Robert's lives cannot be changed by social work intervention? On what theoretical framework, in addition to systems theory, do you base your opinion?

However, contemporary systems theories, such as chaos, have an extended longitudinal concern and thus can visualize how intractables can be destabilized and reconstituted to desirables.

Andrew's parents have been friends with a family in which the son, Tom, close to Andrew's age, was gay. Similar to Andrew's parents, the family rejected Tom and the family system became estranged. After Tom was killed in a head-on collision, Andrew's parents contacted Andrew and Robert to kindle a new system connection. The unanticipated exosystem event, Tom's death, was an immediate agent that derailed the dispersion inertia within the system, promising new opportunity at least for Andrew, Robert, and Andrew's parents.

THINKING POINT

 What other system elements might you identify in Andrew and Robert's life as the locus for change? Why did you select those?

To summarize so far, we have identified the values about proximal and distal environments that are common to systems theories. We also looked at contemporary theories, which have relied on elongating time and broadening scope to observe and characterize the behavior of complex systems. The values and principles were then applied to examples to illustrate how each iteration of systems theory differentially sketches and activates systems.

We now draw attention to another important point that has been emerging in this chapter. As you might have noticed, systems theory provides a skeleton on which other theories can be muscled for explanation.

THINKING POINT

What theories other than systems theory did we invoke in order to provide direction for explanation and action? What theories did you invoke?

Now, we move to the application of systems theory to ideas.

Systems Theory Legitimacy of Ideas

Let us begin this section with an examination of the evidentiary basis of systems theory. Because of their multiple parts, even linear systems were initially investigated through the development and application of mathematical hypotheses and models.

For example, Von Bertalanffy, a biologist, observed what he saw as interrelated system components and then fit mathematical models to his observations. He subsequently tested the hypothetical models on similar systems to derive common principles for system behavior. If we look more closely at the evidence for the existence of systems, we see that for the most part, systems are depicted as maps. Early systems thinkers represented systems as two-dimensional maps that linked entities through a series of linear relationships and networks. This approach is reflected in graphics such as the genograms and organizational structural maps illustrated in Chapter 13, which show the points and direction of interaction and articulation within systems (Bowen, 1985). Current systems theorists rely on multidimensional computer-generated models to reveal patterns and represent them in graphic form (Gleick, 2008; Wolfram, 2010).

One method that has been very valuable in investigating and empirically characterizing the nature of systems is case study. The primary purpose of case study research is the description, explanation, or prediction of a single phenomenon in context (Yin, 2008). A single phenomenon may be composed of a single subject, a single part, or many subparts. Case study does not exclusively rely on strategies from either the experimental-type or naturalistic tradition. Rather, case studies are flexible in their methods and can use and even combine methods from either research tradition

(DePoy & Gitlin, 2011; Yin, 2008). Because of its purpose, methods, and capacity to capture complexity, case study approaches are ideal for investigating systems, their descriptions and explanations.

Suppose you selected Andrew and Robert's family system as your case in order to predict the system success in problem resolution and expanded networking to distal family. Using inductive methods of inquiry, you might begin to tease out the values that are important to each subsystem (Andrew and Robert, Andrew's parents). Finding value differences, you then might want to examine ways to facilitate their ultimate goal of reunion by observing their interaction and communication. So, at this juncture, you might look at a trajectory of recent family history from the point of disclosure to dissolution and then reconnection as influenced by an unexpected event. Depending on the purpose and consent procedures for your inquiry, you might even represent the system with a visual model.

From this case study, you could develop or verify theory of successful problem resolution in similar systems and test it in larger scale studies or other case approaches. Because case study approaches look to characterize complexity, they lend themselves to explaining systems through multiple theories.

THINKING POINT

 What theories within the systems framework might you engage to further inform system rebalancing?

Systems legitimacy of ideas is an important influence on policy, with a particular focus on the interaction among ideas and entities. As discussed in Chapter 13, traditional systems theory is valuable in approaching policy legitimacy from a rational perspective (Jansson, 2005) and complexity theory informs policy legitimacy from a nonrational model (Gilson & DePoy, 2008).

Consider the legitimacy of policy supporting gay marriage. From a rational model of policy analysis, we might look at the linear relationship among the following system elements: the numbers of gay couples who would marry, the economics, the supporters of gay marriage, and the opponents of gay marriage. The relative benefits and disadvantages on social systems, political systems, and economic systems of proceeding or not with policy to support gay marriage would weigh in on the legitimacy of the policy and how it should be shaped.

From a nonrational perspective, the analysis would consider the causative factors that brought this issue to the forefront at this point in chronological history, including but not limited to unanticipated factors that coalesced, unusual events such as a court case which brought gay marriage into the headlines in Massachusetts, the decisions by some county clerks to issue marriage licenses to gay couples, partner benefits, and so forth.

Each approach provides a differential evidentiary basis for the legitimacy of policy decisions. Rational models based on traditional systems theory would provide support for a linear approach for lobbying and other actions necessary to obtain public sanction and experience success in policy implementation. From a nonrational perspective, policy passage would capitalize on serendipity and nonlinear events.

> *Using a rational approach, gun control policy was minimally successful. Yet, several unplanned events—such as the shooting of Ronald Regan in which James Brady was shot with a handgun; the shootings at Columbine; and attacks on university campuses, public schools, and in workplaces around the United States—coalesced to highlight the danger of weapons and provoke success of gun control legislation.*

> *Conversely, there are many who would claim that the vast majority of policy gets passed on the evidentiary foundation of rational analysis. For example, deinstitutionalization of inpatients in state psychiatric hospitals was anchored on an analysis of the economic benefit of community-based treatment over the high cost of institutional treatment models (Advameg, 2010).*

Now that we have examined and analyzed the application of systems theories to legitimacy decisions and actions, let us consider the fit of systems theory with social work values.

Fitting Systems Theory Legitimacy With the Value Base of Social Work

Table 19.2 illustrates the articulation of social work and systems theory legitimacy values.

Table 19.2 Social Work Values and Systems Theory Legitimacy

	Social Justice	Integrity	Respect for Individual Dignity and Worth
Systems	System elements should have equal opportunity for participation, contribution, growth, change, feedback, and response within the purposive framework of the system.	It is incumbent on professionals to understand the full scope of systems; their purposes; aims; processes, known and unanticipated; influences on the processes; and the influence of the system on other systems. Sufficient time should be devoted to knowing and working within systems. To work within a system, its values and perimeters should be respected. Change within systems is a systemwide concern.	Dignity and worth should be equally distributed throughout system elements. All elements should have equal access to feedback and equal opportunity for response. Negative influences on dignity and worth should be eschewed.

As depicted in Table 19.2, through the lens of systems legitimacy, each of the central social work values is delimited within the boundaries of the system processes and values. That is not to say that change does not occur within systems. As defined, systems are dynamic and must change. However, in order to participate in systems change, a social worker must understand the system, respect its components and processes, and work collaboratively with system elements and influences to promote productive feedback and response.

Systems Social Work Legitimacy: A Case Illustration

Now let us turn to an example to illustrate the use of systems theories for social work legitimacy.

Revisiting with Robert and Andrew, we first look at Robert and Andrew as the proximal microsystem embedded within the diverse mesosystems, exosystems, macrosystems, and chronosystems that influence them. The social worker proceeding from a linear systems perspective could provide counseling and guidance to the microsystem of Andrew and Robert by assisting them with interaction and communication between themselves, and with methods to identify and address more distal influences. Practicing from a distal perspective, the social worker might look to policy and educational macrosystems and exosystems, respectively, to collaborate on social change that would decrease discrimination and increase access to the institution of marriage for same sex couples. The social worker who proceeded through a nonlinear systems perspective might also see Robert and Andrew in a clinical venue, but may bring awareness of seemingly unrelated events and phenomena into the relationship that could help both men identify patterns and unanticipated consequences of diverse actions within the relationship, as well as outside of the immediate microsystem. For example, the movement of Andrew's parents from the anteroom into the center of the couple's lives may introduce unintended and unexpected stressors that arise from the back and forth movement from fuzzy to embedded membership.

At the level of ideas, this social worker working from the nonlinear perspective has decided to study historical events and turnings that have made immediate policy change as the basis for becoming involved in human rights efforts.

Summary

This chapter engaged with systems legitimacy. It began with examining and illustrating the values inherent in linear and complex systems and then looked at the application of systems to domains of social work practice. The interaction of systems theory with social work values was then identified, and the use of systems approaches was illustrated, integrating other theoretical frameworks through a case study.

References

Advameg. (2010). *Deinstitutionalization.* Retrieved from Encyclopedia of Mental Disorders: http://www.minddisorders.com/Br-Del/Deinstitutionalization.html

Bowen, M. (1985). *Family therapy in clinical practice.* Lanham, MD: Jason Aronson.

DePoy, E., & Gitlin, L. (2011). *Introduction to research.* St Louis, MO: Elsevier.

Gilson, S., & DePoy, E. (2008). Explanatory legitimacy: A model for disability policy development and analysis. In I. Colby (Ed.), *Comprehensive handbook of social work and social welfare* (Vol. 4, pp. 203–217). Hoboken, NJ: John Wiley & Sons.

Gleick, J. (2008). *Chaos: Making a new science.* New York: Penguin.

Jansson, B. S. (2005). *The reluctant welfare state: American social welfare policies, past, present, and future.* Belmont, CA: Brooks/Cole.

Wolfram, S. (2010, April). *Stephen Wolfram: Computing a theory of everything.* Retrieved from TED: http://www.ted.com/talks/stephen_wolfram_computing_a_theory_of_everything.html

Yin, R. (2008). *Case study research: Design and methods* (4th ed.). Thousand Oaks, CA: Sage.

20

Application of New and Emerging Theories to Social Work

hapter 14 discussed the range of new and emerging theories. While many contemporary theories have been and continue to be developed, we delimited our discussion by including only theories that illustrate a postmodern or post-postmodern perspective, or those which espouse uncertainty, pluralism, interdisciplinarity, or complexity relevant to the emergent technological global economy of the 21st century. New iterations of classical theories that build on more traditional ontologies and epistemologies are not included in this chapter, but rather addressed in other chapters under whose rubrics we see a better fit. For example, new theories that build on Freud's theory of psychosexual development are not included here because they espouse monism, and to a greater or lesser extent, predeterminism (Lemma & Patrick, 2010).

Remember that explanatory legitimacy fits under this category due to its place at the pluralism table and its extension of invitations to diverse disciplinary conversations. In a sense, we are looking through the theory's own lens to examine its structure, function, and tolerance for hard work. This type of examination is characteristic of many contemporary theories that subject themselves to the same scrutiny that they apply to other texts and narratives. Especially because of the acknowledgment about the importance of context, the tenet that eligibility and response decisions are value-based determinations is explicit in all of the theories that huddle together under the umbrella of new and emerging theories. Thus, in order to apply them to legitimacy determinations and responses in social work, being able to understand and articulate theory as value is essential. But remember, in this genre of theories, the values can be elusive and complex.

So, now let us look at the value texts that lexically unite contemporary and emerging theories. Note that we use the term *value text* to highlight the focus on language and symbol, rather than on absolutes in new and emerging theories.

Common New and Emerging Theory Value Texts

Because new and emerging theories are concerned with contextually enshrined inter-disciplinarity, pluralism, and to some extent, symbolism, they are particularly relevant to explaining diversity depth. Therefore, what is common in the value texts of new and emerging theories is the view that values are not universal, but rather are narratives, images, representations, or reconfigurations encased in contextual boundaries.

> *Consider the following value statement: People should live within their financial means. Through the opaque window of postmodernist thinking, this statement would be considered as a text or narrative, or even to some, a grand narrative, as discussed in Chapter 14. The grand narrative, in essence, masquerades as a universal statement that all people ostensibly understand in the same way. Yet, does this value statement mean the same to the credit banker as it means to the young adult who has no credit card? The banker might interpret this statement as "people should spend only what they can afford to pay back to their lenders." To the young adult, it might mean that "people should only spend what they earn at work." The post-postmodernist might look at the juxtaposition of disparate disciplines to understand meaning.*

THINKING POINT

Can you think of other interpretations of the text "people should live within their means"?

As you read the subsequent value texts, then, keep in mind that our text, under this theoretical rubric, is a set of symbols that can provide an exegetical foundation for multiple disciplines and points of view.

Table 20.1 lists the value texts that we have inferred as common within new and emerging theories.

What do these textual value statements mean, at least to us? To a greater or lesser degree, depending on the theoretical perspective and the context in which they are interpreted, new and emerging theories do not impose a single truth as legitimate, and thus, a single set of values is not legitimate either. Grand value narratives, or those that are put forth as absolute value truths, are seen as purposive in agendas such as derailing equality or disguising uncertainty. Rather, pluralism of texts and their interpretations are of value. *Local*, which refers to a circumscribed context, and multiple refractions that yield different meanings are valued as the basis for understanding and assertion of legitimacy decisions and actions. Finally, unraveling traditional ontologies

Table 20.1 Common New and Emerging Theory Value Texts

1. Purpose should shape knowledge and action.
2. To understand symbols, we need to look at how meanings are constructed within interdisciplinary and diverse fields.
3. Pluralism is good.
4. Monism is a myth.
5. Diversity should be celebrated.
6. Monism stifles diversity.
7. Grand narratives are myths designed to derail equality.
8. Local is valued.
9. Complexity is to be celebrated.
10. Destabilization of traditional knowledge is good.

and epistemologies is considered desirable and warranted in itself by the postmodernists, and for the post-postmodernists, this thinking exercise provides opportunity for restructuring knowledge and its application.

> *In his inaugural address on January 20, 1961, President John F. Kennedy said "My fellow Americans, ask not what your country can do for you: Ask what you can do for your country." That text became immediately famous, but why? What did he mean? Could you possibly know? In Kennedy's address, the sentence that followed the famous quotation asked this of all people: "My fellow citizens of the world: Ask not what America will do for you, but what together we can do for the freedom of man."*

If we examine JFK's most famous quotation in the context of the text and the times, or what is referred to in new and emerging theories as *local*, we might guess that the new president could have been imploring U.S. citizens to give service to advance democracy throughout the world. However, as noted in Chapter 14, looking through postmodern lenses, democracy could be considered to be a grand narrative that disguises inequity and derails social action. Or, peering through a post-postmodern lens, combining multiple theories from diverse disciplines such as new political theory and marketing might reframe our interpretation such that we see this statement as a branded political entity designed for name recognition.

THINKING POINT

 What else could this famous quotation have meant, and in today's context, list some alternative meanings that might be applied to the narrative.

Now, see if any of your ideas are reflected in Table 20.2, which presents diverse 21st-century interpretations of JFK's famous text.

As Table 20.2 illustrates, the interpretations are vastly different. The first interpretation by Wharton (2005) equates JFK's maxim with contribution to the U.S. economy through purchasing a car. We heard similar text after the World Trade Center disaster on September 11, 2001, in which Americans were urged to spend money to counter terrorism and contribute to rebuilding the economy. The second interpretation expands patriotism and citizen contribution to a variety of self-improvement and civic activities. In the third analysis, Ward (2003), a veteran of war, dissects the quotation to reveal what he considers to be its internal organs, those of major power differentials between people in high government positions who remand those with no power to give the ultimate sacrifice of their lives for their countries. He challenges the notion of government as a grand narrative, replacing it with his analysis of government as a collection of privileged and powerful individuals who hide behind the abstract of democracy. The final interpretation, a blog post, proposes the ludicrousness of the oration illuminating the nation as a needy freeloader.

Table 20.2   Interpretations of JFK's Famous Quote

Interpretation	Source
Buy American cars.	Wharton, 2005
Many can call themselves good citizens just because they work, pay taxes, and obey law. But is it enough? Not for everyone. Good citizens do not serve their own interest but rather understand that their deeds affect the world around them. They serve their families, friends, and others in need without prejudice and selfishness. They care about the condition of their community, country, and the world. For me, actions of a good citizen include protection of the country, education, and community service . . . A swallow may not make a summer; however, individual citizens, joining efforts—whether in a recycling center, a kitchen, a mathematics lab, or a primary classroom—can build a strong community and country.	Zlociutki, 2000
It is far more likely that these quotations from our illustrious leaders refer to the idea that our fellow citizens should not be asking what manner of welfare and free rides their country can provide for them, but what they can provide for their government. Ask not what the elite and powerful can do for you— ask what you can do for the elite and powerful.	Ward, 2003
But the most arresting phrase, and the most infuriating, is his call for Americans not to ask what their country can do for them, but what they can do for their country. The state behaves, at its most basic level, as a parasite.	Half-A-Man, 2009

In a recent election, a bond was floated that asked the citizens to support additional funding for the statewide university system. As Stan and Gloria were talking the next day, Gloria asked Stan how he voted. He did not support the bond because he said that capital expenses for building construction should not be a spending priority in a state that needed jobs and economic development. For Stan, the bond meant that scarce money would be siphoned off from other areas of need, such as job development, to educate the elite who could attend higher education. Gloria voted for the bond. Stan was puzzled, since he knew that Gloria did not go to the university. But for Gloria, who uses a wheelchair for mobility, the bond meant that she might be able to get the education that she has wanted but has been denied on the basis of wheelchair inaccessibility. Gloria has been excluded from attending the university to pursue a degree in computer science because she cannot access classrooms and computer labs.

The example illustrates the diverse value-based interpretations that individuals attribute to the same text. While Stan sees his vote as a legitimate action to advance needed economic development, Gloria views the bond as an affirmation of future opportunity for her and others like her who have been excluded from participation in education and the economy.

New and Emerging Environmental Legitimacy

At this point, you may be wondering how a body of theory suggesting that the decay of reality can be relevant in informing any thinking at all about proximal to distal conditions. We assert that this body of theory not only can inform social work thinking and decisions, but can do so in a way that is essential to diversity efforts and profound social change within our contemporary context. In the previous example, applying new and emerging theories that reveal the pluralism of language helps us see why Stan and Gloria attribute different meanings to the same text. From a postmodern gaze, we might stop at that understanding and ask them to agree to disagree, but as the post-postmodern thinkers emerge, the theoretical vacuum attracts and ingests new and vital ideas that provide energy to put a new body of knowledge to hard work.

Now apply these ideas to Dawn and Harold, who have just gotten married. At their wedding, Dawn became furious with Harold's mother, Louise, because Louise supported Lila's, her daughter and Harold's sister, decision not to come to the wedding because Lila had the flu. Dawn saw this action as an affront to both her and Harold, who have been loyal family members. But Louise and Harold viewed Louise's concern for her daughter as protective of her daughter's health.

Through the lens of explanatory legitimacy, Louise's behavior is interpreted as a proximal environmental decision by Louise and Harold and as a distal environmental decision by Dawn. The proximal environmental approach saw Louise's behavior as motivated by maternal instinct, while the distal environment approach located Louise's behavior within the rubric of social sanction for her own offspring, thereby marginalizing her new daughter-in-law.

THINKING POINT

Can you think of a third alternative for Louise and Harold's position? If so, what theoretical perspective informs your thinking?

What if we applied post-postmodern thinking to problem resolution? Perhaps Louise might have thought of Lila attending the wedding on video, protecting both her daughter and the health of those at the wedding. Synthesizing tradition with new technologies is an example of the potency of emerging pluralism to be applied for significant social change in the contemporary context. New and emerging theories increasingly gift us with the freedom of pluralistic explanation. Equipped with the understanding that a description can have multiple meanings, explanations, and attributed values, analysis of legitimacy for a response can be informed from diverse perspectives, including traditional as well as more current theories, where the variables of context and subjectivity are explicitly included in one's thinking and action. Thus, contrary to limiting one's understanding by eschewing a single, correct reality, we suggest that new and emerging approaches expand understanding of individual human phenomena through creative and current pathways.

To illustrate the application of new and emerging perspectives to distal environments, we have chosen two examples, one from the virtual environment and one which combines film and political action.

First, to illuminate the intellectual vigor of postmodernist deconstruction, we call attention to an article that appeared in a recent volume of the *New York Times* Magazine Section (Walker, 2010).

> *So you're about to have surgery. You're probably nervous. But the medical staff seems calm and competent, and that's reassuring, because you're counting on them to make pretty serious decisions. You glance over at a nurse, and you notice the tag on her scrubs. "Grey's Anatomy," it says. (para. 1)*
>
> *Whether you're a fan of ABC's hit hospital drama or not, you might find this . . . notable. A reader who had precisely this experience dropped me a line about it not long ago. "I asked her about it, and she said they were the most comfortable scrubs and very popular," he wrote. "How odd is it that a profession that asks people to trust its members to take life-or-death actions would advertise a brand based on a TV show on the job?" I'd prefer my fantasy/reality to not collide when in the hospital. (para. 2)*
>
> *In this exemplar, the branding simulacra, a television drama with no trace of substantive medical knowledge, becomes the symbol in the garb of those whom the drama imitates. Postmodern thought would lay bare not only the burlesque nature of the phenomenon, but might indict profit seeking in the branding practice. The question of what is "real," or at least credible, is raised in a situation that locates its façade deep within its substance.*

THINKING POINT

Think of the disjunctures between advertising and your experience in health environments. What explains this phenomenon to you?

Now consider Target department stores. In these stores, they display mannequins seated in wheelchairs. We could attribute this action to a commitment to full inclusion of impaired people into the shopping market of Target until we test their virtual website for accessibility, and find that it is inaccessible to people who cannot see or navigate websites in typical manners.

Through the lens of new and emerging theories, the narrative created in Target's physical environment is one of welcoming diversity, but this narrative is short-lived and local when considering the barriers to so many shoppers in Target's virtual environment.

Now, consider the power of realigning fields and disciplines through post-postmodernism. Recently, we were listening to public radio and heard about the unusual synergy between Harry Potter aficionados and social activism.

About 100,000 Harry Potter fans have been mobilized by HPA (Harry Potter Alliance, 2010) for causes including marriage equality, genocide prevention, and literacy. They raised enough money to send five cargo planes to Haiti bearing medical supplies after the earthquake there, and they've bought thousands of books for libraries in Rwanda and the Mississippi Delta. "This is a powerful new model for getting young people involved in the political process," says Prof. Henry Jenkins. (Ulaby, 2010)

To summarize so far, we have identified the value texts about the range of proximal to distal environments that are common to new and emerging theories. Also noted was that the value texts are symbolic, not monistic, and assert the positive value of diverse meanings, subjectivity, and realignment of traditional disciplines. We now move to the application of new and emerging theory to ideas.

New and Emerging Theory Legitimacy of Ideas

Let us begin this section with an examination of the evidentiary basis of new and emerging theory. Because of its pluralism, multiple and diverse approaches to inquiry are valued as methods that produce viable and credible evidence (DePoy & Gitlin, 2011). But, even more important is the postmodern revelation that all types of research in themselves are narratives, and thus the symbols in the methods—the words that are used to measure, assess, collect data, and report—are objects and subjects of scrutiny as well as opportunity for purposive, creative reconfiguration (Rangin, 2008). If we look at a research report as a local narrative, rather than interpreting it through the grand narrative of "science as truth," we can see that the structure and content of any inquiry is based on valued ways of knowing, valued sources of knowing, and valued approaches to credibility of knowledge. As stated by Bohm (1988) in his classic work,

> If science is carried out with an amoral attitude, the world will ultimately respond to science in a destructive way. Postmodern science must therefore overcome the separation between truth and virtue, value and fact, ethics and practical necessity. (67–68)

Although many would suggest that narrative inductive methods are the preferred epistemology of postmodern theorists, we challenge that notion. Because of its value on pluralism and the careful scrutiny of text as meaning rather than truth, all methods of systematic inquiry are relevant to new and emerging theories (DePoy & Gitlin, 2011). Moreover, because of its interdisciplinarity, post-postmodernism harvests and uses the most purposive medley of systematic methods to do its ontological work. DePoy and Gitlin remind us that knowledge is crafted by the nature of the research questions asked, the theoretical support for inquiries, and the way in which questions are answered. If you understand this point, you will no longer be puzzled when research on the same topic is contradictory. Let us look at this classic example from 1999 to illustrate.

> *Derek Freeman (1999) became famous for his public challenge of Margaret Mead's classic research on Samoan life. Mead (2001), through conducting inductive anthropological ethnography in 1926 and 1927 on the island of Samoa, characterized Samoan life as a paradise where free love reigned. From that study, Mead refuted the interior biological deterministic theory that asserted that adolescence had to be a tumultuous time in order for further maturation to occur. Her reasoning was based on her observations and conclusions that culture shaped behavior.*

> *Because girls in Samoa were not in crisis, she reasoned that culture produced the behavior. However, in the 1990s, through differential theoretical approaches, Freeman attempted to falsify Mead's observations and conclusions and through his analysis of her data set and then face-to-face interviews with some of Mead's original informants, asserted that these girls and women were subjected to misogyny, domination, and experienced crisis.*

THINKING POINT

Who is correct, Mead, Freeman, both, neither? Why?

Through the lens of explanatory legitimacy, we can say both or neither. Each entered the research endeavor at a different historical time, each looked at the narrative data of Mead's field notes with a different theoretical perspective, and each came away with a different conclusion. If you apply this analysis to all research methods, the credibility, and thus use of the research for professional legitimacy and response, are not based on the truth value of a study, but rather on understanding that research is a narrative to be examined and scrutinized for its inherent values and assumptions, as well as its creative and purposive structure and processes.

THINKING POINT

Identify two contradictory studies on the same topic that you have recently read. How do their methods and literature support differ?

As noted in Chapter 19, although there are numerous approaches to policy analysis, two primary frameworks are rational and nonrational analysis.

THINKING POINT

Can you identify which approach to policy analysis is best informed by new and emerging theories? Why?

If you said that both are relevant, you have understood the nature of new and emerging legitimacy. Logical, linear models as well as complex chaotic models are both considered narratives that yield different viewpoints and conclusions. The models themselves are set within a value perimeter and they can be sutured together in post-postmodern thought to produce policies that are consistent with the construct of diversity depth.

Let us look at a major policy debate to illustrate, physician assisted suicide.

Physician assisted suicide policy is at the center of contentious debate. Some disability advocates, Not Dead Yet (Stephen Drake, n.d.), for example, claim that specifying a category of people who are expendable and thus can be assisted to die on the basis of assumptions that they have low quality of life is no more than genocide masquerading in altruistic clothes. However, others do not even locate physician assisted suicide in the human value realm, but rather see it as a right of all people to make decisions about their own health and death with dignity. Those who see the policy as a value statement about who is worthy of life base their conclusion on a rational model of analysis in which the inherent worth of categorical groups is compared within the policy statement. From a nonrational model, the advent of technology to prolong life is the turning point, not the systematic weight of population categories. If both rational and nonrational arguments were framed within a purposive context, we might arrive at a new pier that floats in between the two anchored perspectives.

We propose that careful dissection of physician assisted suicide alongside technological body enhancement, educational—and even human rights policies—would begin to unravel the monistic skeins of a single model. It would also braid them into a multicolored understanding of the nature and limits of humanness. Such fundamental excavations could form the foundation for exposing complex but foundational values and thus a revisioning of human rights policies.

As you can see, the narratives of all perspectives differ, each encased in contextual, value perimeters about the nature of thought. Each approach provides not only a differential evidentiary basis for the legitimacy of policy decisions but diverse interpretations of the logical and methodological narratives.

Now that we have examined and analyzed the application of new and emerging theories to legitimacy decisions and actions, let us consider the fit of this genre of theory with social work values.

Fitting New and Emerging Theory Legitimacy With the Value Base of Social Work

Table 20.3 illustrates the articulation of social work and new and emerging theoretical legitimacy values.

Table 20.3   Social Work Values and New and Emerging Legitimacy

	Social Justice	**Integrity**	**Respect for Individual Dignity and Worth**
New and emerging	Social justice is a grand narrative that has diverse meanings according to context. Social justice equates with pluralism and respect for diversity depth.	It is incumbent on professionals to understand the pluralistic lenses that diverse groups and individuals attribute to meaning making and knowledge production.	Dignity and worth are grand narratives that are interpreted in diverse ways within their local contexts. Through the attraction and conjoining disciplines into new collages, dignity, and worth can become meaningful within local contexts.

As depicted in Table 20.3, through the lens of new and emerging theory, each of the central social work values is considered to be text that can be expanded to different meanings depending on the context, values, and time. As you can see by our inclusion of our own frame of reference, explanatory legitimacy, in this rubric of theory, we suggest that pluralism, meaning, and broad and synthetic consumption of knowledge are the most viable approaches to operationalizing social work values.

New and Emerging Social Work Legitimacy: A Case Illustration

Now let us turn to an example to illustrate the use of new and emerging theories for social work legitimacy.

> *Consider Ron and Sadie, a retired Jewish couple who live in an assisted living facility. Ron consults a clinical social worker because as he grows older, he becomes more despondent about the world. Ron and Sadie stopped attending synagogue 3 years ago because of their disagreement with their reform rabbi, who urged his congregation to examine the world from diverse perspectives.*

> *Is Ron a legitimate candidate for clinical social work? Susan, the social worker, conducted an in-depth set of interviews and standardized assessments with Ron, expecting that he would fit the DSM criteria for clinical depression. But when he did not, Susan discharged him as not legitimate for services. Ron continued to feel despondent, and so he and his wife joined a Jewish book group in their assisted living facility to find camaraderie, but as yet, have not found solace.*

THINKING POINT

Did the social worker make a sound decision? Why or why not?

Through a medical lens, the answer is yes. Perhaps, however, a social worker who applied explanatory legitimacy, and through that lens, looked for other perspectives might have been able to assist Ron to find some comfort. For example, Susan might have thought about the context in which Ron and Sadie matured and lived for much of their adulthood. From that perspective, Susan may have realized a historical explanation for Ron's mood. That is to say, it might be that Ron's own personal history in which he derived his esteem and positive outlook from his work was not present in his retirement. Or, Susan might have looked at the current distal social environmental elements of the assisted living facility as a possible explanation for Ron's mood that might have been expressed through his narrative about the world.

Expanding our gaze to Ron and Sadie's history and distal environment, consider how social work could apply new and emerging theory to determine a legitimate role for social work in facilitating a productive life role for Ron and in advancing the positive aspects of the assisted living facility distal environment. As noted, applying explanatory legitimacy to

Ron's descriptive picture may have led the social worker to consider Ron's history and distal social environment.

Had the social worker used a pluralistic explanatory approach, she might have even learned that because of the built environment, Ron could not navigate outside of his apartment without assistance, and thus could not even engage in volunteer work. The role of improving the assisted living social and built environment could have been legitimate for direct practice, community organizing, and policy practice as well.

Applied to policy, the social worker, informed through explanatory legitimacy, might advocate for access legislation broader in scope than the Americans With Disabilities Act to improve the distal built and natural environment for all citizens who found navigation barriers. Even more distal and yet extremely relevant, the social worker could have explored and invoked policies to provide support for the construction of virtual environmental elements that could reduce environmental barriers and improve interaction and productivity for residents.

Summary

This chapter examined new and emerging theories that fit within the boundaries of postmodern and post-postmodern theoretical approaches. Different from other categories of theory, it was noted that this genre has value texts, not values, in that the term *value text* reminds us that there are multiple interpretations to words and narratives that form value statements. Multiple meanings were then examined and illustrated that could be attributed to the value texts, followed by the application of new and emerging theories to social work. Locating explanatory legitimacy under this rubric, the use of this framework to create the intersecting dimensions of social work values and contemporary and emerging value texts was advanced and illustrated through a case study.

References

Bohm, D. (1988). Postmodern science and a postmodern world. In D. R. Griffin (Ed.), *The reenchantment of science: Postmodern proposals* (pp. 57–68). Albany: SUNY Press.

DePoy, E., & Gitlin, L. (2011). *Introduction to research.* St Louis, MO: Elsevier.

Drake, Stephen. (n.d.). *Bad cripple—Assisted suicide: No assistance wanted.* Retrieved from Not Dead Yet Blogspot: http://notdeadyetnewscommentary.blogspot.com/

Freeman, D. (1999). *The fateful hoaxing of Margaret Mead: A historical analysis of her Samoan research.* Boulder, CO: Westview Press.

Half-A-Man. (2009, April 1). *Ask not what your country can do for you.* Retrieved from Phased and Bemused: http://phasedandbemused.blogspot.com/2009/04/ask-not-what-your-country-can-do-for.html

Harry Potter Alliance. (2010). *Harry Potter alliance.* Retrieved from http://thehpalliance.org/

Lemma, A., & Patrick, M. (2010). *Off the couch: Contemporary psychoanalytic applications.* New York: Routledge.

Mead, M. (2001). *Coming of age in Samoa: A psychological study of primitive youth for Western civilisation.* New York: HarperCollins.

Rangin, C. (2008). *Redesigning social inquiry: Fuzzy sets and beyond.* Chicago: University of Chicago Press.

Ulaby, N. (2010, Nov). *Harry Potter, boy wizard and real world activist.* (NPR) Retrieved from Monkey See: http://www.npr.org/blogs/monkeysee/2010/11/17/131395444/harry-potter-boy-wizard-and-real-world-activist

Walker, R. (2010, Oct 1). *Branding operation.* Retrieved from New York Times: http://www.nytimes.com/2010/10/03/magazine/03fob-consumed-t.html

Ward, D. S. (2003). *Ask not what your country can do for you .* Retrieved from Library of Halexandria: http://www.halexandria.orgf dward821.htm

Wharton, W. (2005, November 9). *Letter was right—It's past time to start buying American.* Retrieved from Free Lance-Star: http://fredericksburg.com/ News/FLS/2005/112005/11092005/142982

Zlociutki. (2000). *"Ask not what your country can do for you, ask what you can do for your country": Good citizenship values.* Retrieved from http://prace.sciaga.plj4829.html

21

Putting Theory to Work

❖

W e now approach the end of our voyage through the universe of theory within the geographies of social work thinking and action, and are ready to settle down at home to resume work equipped with theory as a guide. This chapter elucidates only one of an infinite set of paths to integrate the propositions advanced in this book about the principles, values, and analytic thinking processes of explanatory legitimacy. And then, relying on case residents, we follow the logical twists and turns of the path.

Principles of Explanatory Legitimacy

Let's head into principles, values, and thinking possessions that you now hold as permanent tools in your social work repertoire, beginning with a recap of the central tenets of explanatory legitimacy theory in Table 21.1.

Throughout the book, we met and shook hands with explanatory legitimacy. Section I introduced the basic tenets and then applied them to organize the discussion and analysis of theory and its use to describe, explain, and respond to human phenomena, as noted in Principle 1. This first part of the book also illuminated the critical role of values in theory selection and use, and suggested that contrary to Enlightenment thinking and its contemporary successors, values are the foundation not only of decisions, but also of how we approach and generate knowledge, determine its credibility, and then put it to work. As such, values are not only part and parcel of explanatory legitimacy, but in our view, of all knowledge and emergent action.

Our intimacy with explanatory legitimacy materialized as the five theoretical genres were discussed and analyzed, emphasizing that theory is not truth, but rather a value-based descriptive or explanatory template or map, which has been generated and verified to varying degrees. Further, we did not prescribe the nature of evidence necessary to support or falsify a theory. Consistent with the fashion of the 21st century,

Table 21.1 Explanatory Legitimacy Principles
1. Explanatory legitimacy distinguishes among description, explanation, and legitimacy of judgment and response.
2. Values are inherent in all three areas of explanatory legitimacy.
3. Values are inherent in inquiry, theory selection, theory content, and application of theoretical knowledge to professional action.
4. Theory cannot provide explanatory truth.
5. Pluralism captures the complexity of human phenomena.
6. Diversity is owned by every human.
7. Professional attention is captured by description.
8. Legitimacy as a recipient of professional response is based on value judgments about explanations.
9. What social work responses are legitimate are determined by the theory selected as explanatory, as well as the values inherent in these chosen theoretical principles.

we preferred to accept diverse forms of evidence, provided that they meet and are massaged by one of three logic structures (deduction, induction, and abduction) to yield a coherent and defensible set of claims.

As discussed throughout the book but more fully in Chapters 13 and 20, where we "fessed up" about the post-postmodern nature of explanatory legitimacy theory, Principle 5 highlights the centrality of pluralism in our framework. That is to say, foundational to explanatory legitimacy theory, is the assertion that multiple explanations can be attributed to a single descriptive phenomenon and all, some, or none may be accurate.

Principle 6 speaks to pluralism by reminding us that diversity is a human quality, not just the province of marginalized groups. Two types of diversity were identified, patina and depth, each with their own strengths, limitations, and uses. Diversity patina applies to what we referred to as bodies and backgrounds group-specific membership criteria, while all individuals own diversity depth. Thus, patina is the visible or ascertainable variable or label upon which other assumptions about commonalities of category members are made, and through which groups and categories are differentiated from one another. Diversity depth refers to the unique views, beliefs, and experiences of each individual, which may be a function of patina or not.

Finally, explanatory legitimacy is a theory to actualize what Badiou (2005) tells us. "The point is not to interpret the world, but to change it" (p. xvii). Remember that we noted that through the typical/ atypical axis, social work professional attention is captured. Once captured, explanatory legitimacy sets out directional vectors for our for thinking and action. That is to say, we seek explanations for the descriptive bauble that catches our professional eye and on the basis of professional, social, and personal values, determine legitimate eligibility for social work action and the nature of our professional response.

Explanatory Legitimacy Theory Values

Because of the centrality of values to explanatory legitimacy, we look at the values that inhere in the theory itself in Table 21.2.

Table 21.2 Explanatory Legitimacy Theory Values
1. Clarity is desirable. 2. Verification of theory and practice approach is a professional social work obligation. 3. Clarifying values is a social and professional obligation. 4. Binary explanations are limiting. 5. Celebration of diversity should expand. (Flatten the curve.)

The first value speaks to positive value on clarity. First, the framework reminds us to qualify the nature of theory as descriptive or explanatory. This distinction is critical in order to make decisions and act at the level of why and how we think we know about something. If we only know the "what," then we cannot act on the "why." And, if we think we know the "why," we must be sure that we first know what we are explaining. This point calls for an example.

Consider Mabel, an 85-year-old nursing home resident who has always greeted you at the door when you arrive. When you come to the nursing home to see your clients at 1 pm, you see her in bed on three consecutive days and you begin to wonder what is happening. So, you document in Mabel's medical records that you are concerned that Mabel is sleeping during the day because she might be depressed, and therefore may be in need of social work counseling. In this case, you failed not only to clarify "what" but also "why." Later, you find out that Mabel is resting each afternoon so that she can be awake to get her grandson's telephone call each night from his military camp, where he is stationed as a soldier in Afghanistan.

Now, let us consider an example of what could happen if we do not distinguish description from explanation and verify our hunches, as advanced in Value 2.

After a serious car accident and the loss of her limb, Lisa has just received her new prosthetic leg. Phillip, Lisa's social worker, has been supporting Lisa to slowly adjust to the prosthesis and to regularly attend out-patient physical therapy. But, Lisa is not attending physical therapy and Phillip documents noncompliance. On that basis, Lisa's insurance company discontinues payment for rehabilitation. What Phillip failed to do was to make the distinction between the descriptor (not attending physical therapy) and the explanation (noncompliance), and then to verify his rationale for Lisa's behavior. In hopes of returning to her career as a dancer, Lisa has been getting therapy at home from her partner, who is a physical therapist for the ballet company with which Lisa dances. When Lisa requested reimbursement for equipment and was denied by her insurance company, she learned that the social worker had given an incorrect explanation for Lisa's behavior.

We already know through professional socialization that the code of ethics and social work values circumscribe our professional scope and action. Because explanatory legitimacy holds values as a central tenet, a major theoretical obligation lies in understanding, clarifying, and articulating the values that shape knowledge credibility and use.

The last two values in Table 21.2 have been advanced and discussed throughout the book. They are emphasized in this chapter because of their critical application to social work's commitment to diversity and social justice. But what do we mean by "flatten the curve"? Remember that we directed significant attention to the normal curve, which created the backdrop for binary thinking. To quickly review, the concepts of normal and not normal are anchored on the bell-shaped curve in which the most frequent occurrences are considered to be normal and those at the highest and lowest margins of the curve considered to be in the not normal range. The curves in Figures 21.1 and 21.2 illustrate. To demonstrate the concept of flattening the curve, let us think of these curves as denoting two groups of scores on an IQ test. By definition, approximately 66% of the area under every normal curve falls between the two lines designated by the double-sided arrow, and thus depicts the defined normal range in each. Note that Figure 21.1, the taller curve, has a smaller normal range than the normal range in the flatter curve, 21.2. A flatter curve has a larger distribution of scores, and thus a larger range of normal scores.

Now, apply that thinking to diversity of any type. If we expand the range of normal, we include many more people within it. If we flatten a curve altogether, it becomes a line as depicted in Figure 21.3 and the binary of normal and not normal disappears.

New and emerging thinking and action informed by these theoretical frames of reference promise the guidance for flattening the curve. They remind us that theory, knowledge, and science are purposive, value-based, and can be used to guide profound and meaningful social change. Second, these theories foreground intellectual tools and

Figure 21.1 Bell Shaped Curve 1

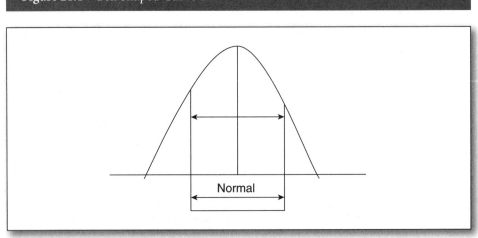

Normal

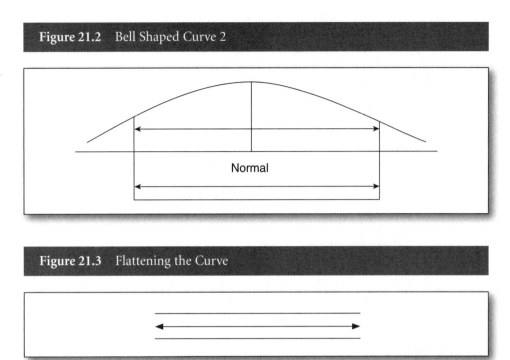

Figure 21.2   Bell Shaped Curve 2

Normal

Figure 21.3   Flattening the Curve

strategies through which to rethink diversity and respect for its depth. And third, contemporary thought locates informed action within a technological, complex world in which binaries—the research narratives—that reify them and their influence on social action are seen as value-laden and malleable, perhaps unearthed by chaos only to be reconfigured with interdisciplinary marriages that were not even imagined when "normal" and "not normal" were constructed. Because of its progressive history and commitment to social justice, we see social work as the field that can and should lead in the effort to flatten the curve. Explanatory legitimacy has the "ruby slippers" to organize theory and its use.

Thinking Possessions

We suggest that explanatory legitimacy provides what we call *thinking possessions*. Beyond tools or skills, we use the term *possessions* to suggest that you can own and shape the theory to fit your personal and professional style, and perhaps to advance flattening the curve. Table 21.3 lists the specific possessions that you can take with you and own.

We have illustrated our use of these thinking possessions throughout the book. As you read, you examined the three descriptive axes: typical-atypical, observable-reportable, diversity patina-diversity depth. Theories were illustrated and discussed in five content categories, followed by a demonstration of how the values that we hold personally and professionally have shaped our legitimacy judgments and responses.

Table 21.3 Thinking Possessions

Map of three domains

    Description – Three descriptive axes

    Explanation – Five categories of theory to provide directional signals

    Legitimacy – Scaffold for value judgment and informed response

Evidentiary Guidance to seek the basis for scope of description and foundations of explanation

Abductive Guidance to verify the accuracy and/or feasibility of the explanation.

Substantive Guidance to provide direction for professional action and identification of desirables

Evidentiary, abductive, and substantive guidance were provided and demonstrated through our narrative and case exemplars. You now have the thinking tools to use, build, and share.

A Final Exemplar

Yuri, a 39-year-old mechanic was born in Canada. Because of war, his parents were forced out of their country and immigrated from the Baltic states several years before Yuri was born. Then, right after Yuri's birth, the family moved to a suburb near Detroit. Yuri's father, who was well-educated in his home country, but who spoke minimal English when he immigrated to the United States, secured a job on an automobile assembly line. Yuri's mother, who was born into high society in her country, worked as a domestic, because she was not qualified for any particular skilled or professional work. Yuri and his older brother, Jan, both went to Catholic school and Yuri had aspirations to become a professor. However, similar to his father, he drank too much alcohol, and thus was not able to concentrate on his studies. He got married, had two children, and has just moved back to his parents' home because his wife threw him out when he was arrested for driving under the influence.

Social Work Practice in the Proximal Domain

Yuri was sent to a clinical social worker for substance abuse counseling. So, now let's put explanatory legitimacy to work. The descriptive atypical behavior that caught professional attention is alcohol abuse.

Table 21.4 illustrates the social worker's thinking about comparative explanations for Yuri's substance abuse and response options.

We selected six theoretical or categories or subcategories for illustration. As depicted, each theoretical explanation, with the exception of cultural normalcy, would be positively valued for social work intervention at the level of direct practice. Cultural normalcy as a rationale for alcohol abuse outside of the justice system would not be a likely candidate for legitimate sanction and social work response, because it is an undesirable and unlawful circumstance. But, all other explanations would be eligible and feasible.

Table 21.4 Social Work Practice in the Proximal Domain

Theoretical Category	Explanation	Judgment	Clinical Response
Developmental	Immature oral behavior	Eligible for clinical social work	Long-term psychotherapy
Proximal corporeal environment	Pathology	Eligible for medication	Referral and follow-up counseling
Distal environment	Learned behavior	Eligible for family and individual clinical work	Behavioral intervention
Categorical	Cultural normalcy	Not eligible for social work	Justice system response
Linear systems	Family dysfunction	Eligible for social work	Family therapy
New and emerging	Alienation	Eligible for social work	Narrative therapy

Using explanatory legitimacy, the social worker would seek evidence to make the most reasonable decision and then proceed with guidance from the scholarship. Note that multiple theories might be of use, but for instructional purposes, we have indicated the possible response guided by each individual genre. Also, note that responses vary according to the theory selected in each genre. For example, we allude to the selection of psychoanalysis as the developmental explanation. Remember that there are many other developmental theories, including but not limited to those discussed in Chapters 3 through 5. Had we selected a theory of moral development, rather than an intrapsychic one, Yuri might not be eligible for social work services, depending on the particular theoretical frame of reference that we chose.

Social Work Practice in the Distal Environmental Domain

Table 21.5 shows explanatory legitimacy at work in distal environmental practice domains of alcohol abuse.

Table 21.5 illustrates how distal environmental social work practice could be informed by differential application of theory. As we see in this domain, the social worker has selected four theory genres for potential explanations for alcohol abuse, each judging the distal environment as eligible for legitimate social work intervention. Different from the proximal domain, in which cultural explanations were not determined to be a legitimate for social work practice, the distal categorical explanation of cultural normalcy in this arena of social work practice would qualify for social work intervention at the community level. Also note the enlarged environmental scope, including the virtual world and contemporary strategies, such as social networking. Consistent with the principles of explanatory legitimacy presented in Table 21.1, verification of the accuracy of explanations would be systematically endorsed and accomplished before any action response would occur.

Table 21.5   Social Work Practice in the Distal Environmental Domain

Theoretical Category	Explanation	Judgment	Environmental Response
Distal environmental	Learned behavior	School and workplace eligibility	On-site and virtual alcohol abuse prevention programs
Categorical	Cultural normalcy	Community eligibility	Community organization focusing on educational and attitudinal interventions
Systems	Community and work system dysfunction	Eligible for social work	Community organization focusing on feedback and change
New and emerging	Social and other media narratives in support of alcohol consumption for profit despite its harmful effect on proximal and distal conditions	Eligible for social work	Social media, networking, marketing, and educational programs

Social Work Practice in the Domain of Ideas

Table 21.6 allows a comparison of how each theory genre mingles and works with explanatory legitimacy to address and mediate against the undesirable of alcohol abuse in the realm of ideas. Remember that we delimited this domain to abstracts such as inquiry and policy that are important elements of social work concern.

Table 21.6   Social Work in the Domain of Ideas

Theoretical Category	Explanation	Judgment	Environmental Response
Developmental	Immaturity	Inquiry eligibility	Systematic tests for the efficacy and outcome of intrapsychic interventions in contributing to maturation and sobriety
Proximal environmental	Pathology	Policy eligibility	Advocation for workplace policy to support proximal environmental prevention programs, to reduce violating suspension of driving license through policy supporting public transportation

Theoretical Category	Explanation	Judgment	Environmental Response
Distal environmental	Learned behavior	Inquiry and policy eligibility	Examination of the efficacy of on-site and virtual alcohol abuse prevention programs, advocation for prevention and treatment policy
Categorical	Multiple group-related associations and causes	Inquiry eligibility	Investigation of group commonalities and differences in alcohol use, responses to differential prevention and intervention, and advocation for policy to implement prevention and intervention on the basis of findings
Systems	Community and work system destabilization	Eligible for policy	Policy analysis and change to promote new policies and meaningful integration of prevention and intervention services in diverse systems, capitalization on public events to elicit immediate and profound change
New and emerging	Media messages, capitalism, and marketing in support of alcohol consumption	Eligible for SW inquiry and policy	Inductive, deductive, and abductive inquiry to investigate the explicit and tacit effect of images, narrative, and branded messages and marketing on alcohol consumption and policy to support progressive profitable prevention

As illustrated in Table 21.6, the idea domain can encompass all theory genres through inquiry and informed policy. Each theory genre directs the social work investigation of ideas to a specific slice of knowledge, and informed application to policy.

Your Turn

Now it is your turn. Take your possessions, own them, explore them, work with them, and capture the world of theory to bring to your professional thinking and action.

Reference

Badiou, A. (2005). *Metapolitics*. (J. Barker, Trans.). London: Verso.

Index

About the Authors

Elizabeth DePoy is professor of social work and interdisciplinary disability studies and also holds an appointment as Senior Research Fellow. Ono Academic College, Research Institute for Health and Medical Professions. Kiryat Ono, Israel. Dr. DePoy is a nationally and internationally recognized scholar in research and evaluation methods and original theory in the fields of disability, diversity, and design. Co-authored with Stephen Gilson, DePoy developed Explanatory Legitimacy Theory which analyzes how population group membership is assigned, is based on political purpose, and is met with formal responses that serve both intentionally and unintentionally to perpetuate segregation, economic status quo, and inter-group tension. Dr. DePoy has applied legitimacy theory to the analysis of diversity and human rights. Along with Gilson, DePoy has implemented her vision of socially just policy and praxis based on principles of full participation and access through the creation of a web portal that renders existing illness prevention information accessible to individuals across diversity category boundaries.

DePoy's most research interests and publications have focused epistemology and research methodology, disability as designed, human rights, and advancement of equality of access to environments and resources. Dr. DePoy is currently working on her 10th book, has contributed many chapters to edited collections, and has over 100 articles published in peer reviewed journals. She has earned over 7 million dollars in extramural research grants at the University of Maine. Dr. DePoy presents her work locally, regionally, nationally and internationally and has collaborative relationships with international scholars. In the service arena, Dr. DePoy provides evaluation, research and grant writing consultation to agencies and organizations.

Dr. DePoy's awards for scholarship include:

- Senior Scholar Award, Society for Disability Studies, June 2009.
- Elected to The Honor Society of Phi Kappa Phi, University of Maine, April 2009.
- Distinguished Lifetime Achievement Award, American Public Health Association, October 2008.
- Faculty Fellowship Summer Institute in Israel, Society for Peace in the Middle East, Summer, 2008.
- Sponsored by Bar-Ilan University,Hebrew University of Jerusalem, Ben Gurion University, Tel Aviv University, Haifa University, Technion – Israel Institute ofTechnology, Jewish National Fund, Media Watch International, Scholarsfor Peace in the Middle East University of Maine, Presidential Research and Creative Achievement Award, May 2007.
- Outstanding Achievement Award, Association of University Centers on Disability, November 2006.

- Allan Meyers Award for Scholarship in Disability, American Public Health Association, September 2005.
- Fulbright Senior Specialist Scholar, Grant awarded to Assuit University, Assuit, Egypt, March, 2003.
- Feminist Scholarship Award-Council on Social Work Education, March 2000.

Stephen French Gilson is professor of social work and interdisciplinary disability studies and also holds an appointment as Senior Research Fellow. Ono Academic College, Research Institute for Health and Medical Professions. Kiryat Ono, Israel. He is a theorist and policy analyst who is best known for his work in disability, diversity, and health policy through the lens of legitimacy theory. Co-authored with Elizabeth DePoy, Gilson developed Explanatory Legitimacy Theory which analyzes how population group membership is assigned, is based on political purpose, and is met with formal responses that serve both intentionally and unintentionally to perpetuate segregation, economic status quo, and inter-group tension.

His research interests and publications have focused disability identity, experiences of domestic violence and women with disabilities, disability theory, disability as diversity, social justice, and health and disability policy and advocacy. Dr. Gilson is currently working on his 9th book, has contributed many chapters to edited collections, and has over 60 articles published in peer reviewed journals. He is currently pursuing a collaborative research agenda to develop and test software that will provide full access to web and electronic information. Dr. Gilson presents his work locally, regionally, nationally and internationally and has collaborative relationships with international scholars. In the service arena, Dr. Gilson is extremely active on university, local, national and international committees, organizations, and concerns. His commitment to universal ideology as a means to promote social justice and equal opportunity guides his service work.

His awards for scholarship include:

- Society for Disability Studies (SDS), Senior Scholar Award, 2009.
- University of Maine, Department of Psychology, Stanley Sue Distinguished Lecture Series, Diversity Lecture - "Now guess who is coming to the diversity dinner: Disability and beyond bodies and backgrounds" 2009.
- Association of University Centers on Disabilities (AUCD), Multicultural Council Award for Leadership in Diversity, 2008.
- Faculty Fellowship Summer Institute in Israel, Society for Peace in the Middle East, Summer, 2008.
- Allan Meyers Award for Scholarship in Disability, American Public Health Association, September, 2005.
- CSWE Commission on the Role and Status of Women "Feminist Scholarship Award for 2000." E. P. Cramer, S. F. Gilson, and E. DePoy – "Experiences of Abuse and Service Needs of Abused Women with Disabilities."

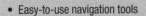